BEYOND MONOGAMY

BEYOND MONOGAMY
recent studies of sexual alternatives in marriage

Edited and with an Introductory Essay by
James R. Smith and Lynn G. Smith

The Johns Hopkins University Press
Baltimore and London

The Johns Hopkins University Press, Baltimore, Maryland 21218
The Johns Hopkins University Press Ltd., London

Library of Congress Catalog Card Number 73-19345
ISBN 0-8018-1577-0 (clothbound edition)
ISBN 0-8018-1578-9 (paperbound edition)

Originally published, 1974
Second printing (cloth), 1974
Library of Congress Cataloging in Publication data
will be found on the last printed page of this book.

Whatever marriage is, it is always and everywhere more than sexual intercourse. However divergent the directions may be in which marriage transcends sexual intercourse, the fact that it transcends it at all makes marriage what it is. Here is, sociologically speaking, an almost unique phenomenon: the very point that all marriage forms have in common is the one which they have to *transcend in order to result in marriage.*

Georg Simmel,
Sociology (1908)

. . . the couples who mutually agree that adultery is all right are a strange and interesting phenomenon in American life to-day. And what I have so far observed leads me to believe that such agreements are far more common than even students of these matters have any idea of. There is no means of telling to what extent the thing is happening, of course, because such agreements, when they exist, are sedulously secret. In many cases I have no doubt there is no candid agreement, but simply a tacit ignoring of the facts. In other cases, where the couple no longer care for each other, there may be some such agreement, with no further sex relations in their own marriage. But when couples that love each other enter on such an apparently anomalous course, that is surely indicative that something extraordinary is happening to one of the most firmly established of our customs.

Judge Ben Lindsey,
The Companionate Marriage (1927)

. . . how far marriage in any given case can admit of wider affectionate relationships must ever be a difficult and fascinating problem, to evoke the finest developments of discipline and of art.

Havelock Ellis,
The Future of Marriage (1928)

I think that where a marriage is fruitful and both parties to it are reasonable and decent the expectation ought to be that it will be lifelong, but not that it will exclude other sex relations.

Bertrand Russell,
Marriage and Morals (1929)

Contents

A Note to the Reader

This is a book about sex and marriage. It exists because in recent years a series of social issues pertaining to the complex relationships between human sexual behavior and the institution of marriage have been raised and joined which are not amenable to resolution by appeals to myth, opinion, ideology, or the pronouncements of religion. This volume is the collective product of investigation and reflection undertaken by a score of researchers and counselors who found themselves faced with questions they were unable to answer. This necessitated asking further questions of others whose experience and perspective provided the raw material, that putatively cold, hard, incorrigible stuff scientists refer to as data, upon which the following studies are based. Many of the questions remain unanswered; some remain yet to be formulated.

If, in the course of reading this volume, you find that certain questions are not answered to your satisfaction, or if you find other questions occurring to you which do not admit of ready or simple answers, there is a way your questions and the curiosity which motivates them can meet with our inquiry to produce a unique and mutually enlightening dialogue.

Marital and sexual research is based upon a very special kind of trust and a highly sensitive type of communication. Research into unconventional, deviant, or socially disapproved practices is especially sensitive because even confidential disclosure of such information involves a personal risk that is proportional to the perceived threat of possible exposure and potential recrimination, sometimes of the self-inflicted variety. For this reason, perhaps more than any other, research into such practices has been stymied and remains subject to severe limitations; it is thus indirectly one of the reasons for your curiosity and ours, and no amount of well-intentioned speculation or rumination will dissipate it.

Accordingly, we, and you, are at an impasse. The awareness of threat begets withdrawal; withdrawal, by a complex chain of events which conceals sexual information and hampers communication and the flow of ideas, intensifies the fear of exposure. The unfortunate result is that our collective capacities for reasoned discussion and informed decisions are extremely limited.

We would like to take steps to break this vicious circle by making a direct appeal to you as a potential reader of this volume. The American philosopher Charles S. Peirce, formulating a philosophical maxim for all science, said: "Do not block the way of inquiry." He might have added: Help clear it! If you find the path to and from knowledge of marriage and sexuality cluttered by prejudice, superstition, and pretense, you can aid us in our attempt to remove some of the emotionally charged debris which previous generations have left strewn about the social landscape.

We have organized a series of integrated and sustained research projects designed to investigate a cross-section of both monogamous and nonmonogamous practices in addition to the broader interpersonal dynamics of marital and sexual behavior. To succeed, these projects will require a large pool of volunteer subjects of every persuasion, circumstance, and marital status, including unmarried persons and cohabiting couples, and they will require a generous measure of rapport between the investigators and members of the research population.

We are led, then, to issue the conventional plea for volunteer research subjects in this somewhat unconventional format. Persons who, on the basis of assured confidentiality, would be willing to participate in any of these upcoming projects by granting interviews, filling out questionnaires, or providing other pertinent information are urged to contact us at the address provided below. Persons who wish to volunteer personal accounts or documents on an anonymous basis are also welcome to do so. Only by this direct appeal on a grass-roots level can a sufficiently large and varied bank of information be gathered that is adequate for real understanding.

All responses and subsequent communication will be held in strictest confidence, with access limited to the project directors and their immediate staff. No information gathered in the course of the project will be used for commercial purposes, except as data and documentation for books, reports, monographs, or other publications written or authorized by the project directors. Furthermore, we will not contact anyone, except to verify the responses, until the projects are actually set in motion. At the time of inquiry, additional guarantees of confidentiality will be set forth.

We would like to express in advance our gratitude for any information and cooperation that might be forthcoming and express our wish that in the long run our curiosity and yours may be a source of knowledge and freedom for persons unknown and perhaps yet unborn.

James R. Smith and Lynn G. Smith
Codirectors

Self-Actualization Laboratory
Research Division
Box 7135
Berkeley, California 94707

Summer Headquarters:
Lake Titus, Malone, New York 12953

Introduction

The motivation for collecting and editing the studies contained in this volume can be no better stated than by reaching back a generation to a book which, in an indirect and historical way, was responsible for arousing interest in behavior that is linked to the subject of the following studies. Judge Ben Lindsey wrote of his book *The Companionate Marriage* in 1927 that

the reason for this book is this: if some persons have the courage to try to think out their own private conduct for themselves and run the risk of the social swats which our semi-barbarous civilization visits on such independence, then it is up to somebody to tell about it and discuss it with an open mind, and, if necessary, take the swats that may be expected to result from that.[1]

It is difficult to improve on Lindsey's formulation. Our reason for presenting the essays and research reports which follow is precisely the same as his.

Our orientation, which we hope is not so defensive as Lindsey's at first appears to be, leads us to emulate both his critical perspective and his enlightened sense of values. Lindsey's message is that, somewhere in our collective moral space, some persons, because of their professional calling and normative commitments, are obliged to approach the realm

[1] B. B. Lindsey and W. Evans, *The Companionate Marriage* (New York: Boni and Liveright, 1927), p. 60.

of sociosexual change in the spirit of a humanist with the tools of contemporary science and philosophy. This obligation is neither a fool's errand nor a rank crusade, as the current presence of a degenerate journalistic mentality on this topic might attest, but leads by many twists and turns to a number of the most fundamental questions of psycho- and biosocial life.

This collection is not meant to justify or condemn what is misleadingly and often prejudicially referred to as *extra*marital sexual activity but to take a first step, by presenting the work of several independent theorists, researchers, and counselors, toward a social scientific understanding of several highly controversial patterns of sexual behavior that may eventually lead to more enlightened and humane action. Despite a generation of movement toward sexual liberalism and individualized sexual expression, the climate of opinion for such discussion is little better today, and in some ways worse, than it was in 1927 when Judge Lindsey made the statement above. The need for research and discussion, however, not only remains, but with the concurrent debacle of traditional marriage and the proliferation of a wide range of marital forms and sexual styles in and around the basic heterosexual, monogamic, nuclear, dyadic pattern, it has reached critical proportions.

These articles were selected with one eye on recent shifts and developments in the sexual freedom movement and the other on the interplay and tension between traditional marriage and family patterns and the mutations and variations which have sought to revitalize and restructure marriage as a truly private and moral, as distinct from a public and legal, institution. We assume at the outset that sexual liberation and the experimental movements to redefine marriage are not only closely interrelated but that they are integral aspects of the same basic social process. A corollary assumption is that, although the liberation of women is clearly a condition of the liberation of marriage, the liberation of sexual impulses and energies (specifically, nonprocreative sexuality) is somewhat less clearly a condition of the emancipation of both women and marriage.

Sexual liberation in the form of realistic individual autonomy in a viable dyadic relationship is at least as relevant and necessary for personal and interpersonal fulfillment in marriage as liberation from socioeconomic dependency and procreative (and anti-nonprocreative) institutions which serve the continuance of traditional family structures. That is to say, in practical terms, all the ranting and hoopla over open, free, or otherwise permissive marriage must be tempered by a recognition of the fact that for most couples, the most difficult part of achieving such a relationship is liberation from sexual possessiveness and all that it feeds and thrives on in the self and the environment. This is the damnable consequence of a process of repressive primary sexual socialization which, in fostering the cultural ideology of monogamy and perpetuating the procreative sex ethic as the indispensable dual standards of sexual relationships and sexual expression, eventuates in feelings of sexual jealousy and renders many persons emotionally lame and even physiologically impotent in the adult years. Their sexuality is stifled, truncated, and subject to a myriad of minor handicaps and self-negating blind spots. This, then, is the cultural and psychological point of departure for an overwhelming number of marital relationships and the partial cause of failure for a substantial portion.

If the coming generation bears any resemblance to the past one in this respect, the need for research will only increase as the social conditions become more and more a challenge to civilized social life. If the myriad pressures upon marriage increase in even arithmetic proportion during the next decade or two, the results, judged in terms of institutionalized subsistence requirements (e.g., permanency, sexual monopoly, general welfare, and protracted cohabitation), will be that over half of the legally consummated alliances must be deemed prima facie failures. If one proceeds to examine more deeply the interpersonal dynamics and the existential and eupsychian potential of marriage in its current state of evolution, it is a fair guess that perhaps a maximum of one in ten marriages would be estimated at something more than satisfactory or tolerable under the circumstances. The calls for alternative and experimental patterns will become, if they are not already, desperate cries for help.

The potential ramifications of a science, a genuine and humanistically committed science, of the relationships among marriage, sexuality, and social structure might carry us far in our understanding of human behavior in a variety of other contexts and ostensibly nonsexual settings. Such relationships, compelling in their own right, are commonly maligned and easily misunderstood aspects of human behavior.

The research and analyses, as presented in this volume, may be viewed as attempts to illuminate some of the darker corners and less accessible aspects of contemporary marital behavior. At first glance, these articles may be conceived as dealing with understudied and recently recognized types of sexual deviance. More deeply considered, their purpose may be taken as an attempt to make more rational a set of alternative behavior patterns which, when viewed together with the more easily identifiable and more widely received conventional sexual institutions and codes, often seem altogether radical, perverse, and/or immoral.

Such perspectives are easily blurred by counterpressures and countervailing tendencies implicit in the contemporary social framework. There is a grave danger that mass faddishness, overt commercialization, and Yankee pandering may reduce these behaviors and research into them to convenient localized clichés without ever allowing social consciousness to come to terms with the dynamic social implications that such behaviors suggest and that such research reveals. Such undermining and exploitive trends are discernible not only in the more grotesque swinging motifs in recent plays, films, and literature, including prime-time television, but also in many products whose promotion is based on appeals to the swinging life and swinging values. (Polaroid's Swinger camera and the Dodge Swinger come to mind, as do swinging health spas, swinging vacations, and swinging bars.) Such commercial treachery is no accident. It betrays anyone who takes nontraditional life-styles at all seriously. It threatens to generate packaged versions of the swinging world, imbued with and characterized by artifice, pretense, and sham values.[2] These versions traffic upon and exploit fantasy associations; and those who indulge in them unaware and intemperately are the prey of those who do the packaging and promoting. The briefest review of the media treatment and subsequent economic and social co-option of the beatnik and hippie movements illustrates this quite convincingly. Such packaging and promoting are not limited to the gimmicks, gadgets, and novelties that serve as accouterments for swinging life-styles. Sex clubs and swinging parties are themselves attempts to package sexual liberation and dish it up as needed, as though sexual freedom were on a par with items available in cafeterias, mail-order catalogs, and service stations. A similar fate has befallen many elements of the human potential and growth movements.

An apt illustration of this occurred in our field studies in the Los Angeles area when, in 1969 and 1970, we attended dinners and parties at a facility known as Sandstone. The surroundings were elegant, the food delicious, the pool truly Olympian, and the party large and active by most standards. But it was commercial fare from invitation to exit, available only to those able to pay for such lavish surroundings. It combined the imagery and equipage of the Playboy world with overt

---

[2] It is unfortunate, we think, that the free and easy use of the terms "swinger" and "swinging," as employed in some of the articles, may serve to promote and even embellish such clichés. The vocabulary of swinging, often tendentious in the first place, can degenerate into rhetorical generalizations and is subject to prejudicial reaction and misinterpretation.

group nudity, group sex, and a lively cocktail party atmosphere. We noted strong elements of emulation, sexual and otherwise, and a tendency to attract and encourage persons with a desire to be "where it's at." "Losers" were screened out and effectively, if not directly, asked to leave; "beautiful couples" were eagerly recruited.

Female attire was chic and provocative, definitely "mod," with many stylish coiffures and much jewelry, suggesting both the conspicuous leisure necessary for such primping and preening and the expenditures of wealth necessary to produce a conspicuous display of material artifice. The men played characteristic sex roles, initiating contacts, encouraging female participation, manipulating female-female contacts, and competing for access to the more desirable women.

The surroundings exuded a distinctly and deliberately sought country club or resort aura, and the staff was accomplished in the art of catering and party-giving. It impressed us as the Disneyland of organized swinging. Among all the places we visited, Sandstone seemed to us the one most "on the make." The emphasis was on what a "groovy scene" it all was, an emphasis reiterated in the brochures and newsletters soliciting new members. While advertising values (in travel-brochure format) of "openness," "honesty, sharing, and freedom from the artificial," they also offered a 50% discount on the then current one-hundred-dollar-per-year membership fee for "single girls." Our conversations with the member-guests at Sandstone led us to conclude that in many instances they were acting as if they wanted to impress the others present with the fact that they were good enough to be there. Nonetheless, the semistructured environment served as an effective vehicle for deviant subcultural contact and integration and provided an atmosphere of relative safety and acceptance for sexual experimentation.[3]

Present indications are that institutionalization through commercialization of the putative swinging movement is well under way. Whether swinging is a social movement and whether the prepackaged versions really are viable and realistic models for contemporary marriage are difficult questions, given the dearth of information now available. But in the light of recent studies, many included in this volume, one becomes more acutely aware of the stereotyping and oversimplifications that have prevailed in many treatments of the topic heretofore.

[3] For a more sanguine view based on a more recent and more thorough assessment, see Dr. Ralph Yaney, organizer of the Sandstone Experiment, whose preliminary report, entitled "Comments and Observations on Our Culture with Emphasis on the Sandstone Experiment of Open Sexuality and Therapeutic Implications," was delivered to the Southern California Medical Association in March 1973.

These studies contain far more than mere statements of fact or significant correlations of otherwise insignificant variables and can be approached in a variety of ways by a variety of readers. While none of them is either definitive or conclusive, many have ramifications for a wide range of medical, moral, and social problems. They bear critically upon those institutionally confined and culturally regulated behavior patterns that function to maintain and propagate the social status quo. Collectively, they frame a profound social issue—the present and future status of an array of marital arrangements, experiments, and proposals that are in sometimes banal, sometimes stark, contrast to that putatively normal but virtually fictitious entity known as the traditional monogamous marriage of virginal mates.

There is therapeutic potential here as well. Those attentive to the mass media and its mesmerizing influence are aware that currently there is much ado about sexual therapy. It is, to be sure, a great achievement in medical science. But this recently begun form of social engineering is still in its infancy, both in its scope and feasibility of application and in its methodology and level of refinement. Although it has been integrated with (or perhaps compromised by) many elements and techniques of standard psychotherapy, most of it as currently practiced—the best practitioners will be the first to agree—is at what is sometimes referred to as the "broken plumbing" level of treatment, though the diagnoses may now and then run beyond that point. As currently received, it is but a propaedeutic to the appreciation and integration of sexual experience into a personal style and outlook. It is programed fundamentally for deficiency and dysfunction and not for creative change and interpersonal transcendence. This is evidenced by the fact not that communication skills and interpersonal variables are ignored but that treatment ceases when orgasm or regular orgasm occurs. The idea of varying, intensifying, or improving the quality of sexual experience and the contexts in which it occurs is not, or at least not often, a therapeutic goal.

Sexual growth and sensitivity neither begin nor end with the capacity to have regular orgasms with one person designated "spouse" or "mate." And while every knowledgeable person agrees that *some* form of early sexual education would be the best preventative for sexual inadequacy in most cases, extensive adult sexual reeducation and experimentation (and in its course, sexual resocialization) is spoken of as another matter altogether, if it is spoken of at all. Few have yet countenanced the need for and desirability of a therapy-which-is-not-a-therapy designed to alter radically the ground, structure, and purpose of marriage itself to free it from some of its conventional fetters and limitations.

Might it not be possible to develop a eupsychian sexual philosophy for personal and interpersonal growth which conscientiously identifies and integrates metagoals that might radically extend and expand one's sexual horizon? Might it not be possible to develop a rational format for promoting *sexual eufunction* with just as much care and consideration as that which has generated the current therapies of *sexual dysfunction*?[4] Might we not fairly and without distortion of the idea of sexual therapy then contend that the person who is sexually possessive to the point of enforced exclusivity or sexually exploitive to the point of bartering his or her mate is sexually inadequate as well? It will, of course, depend on how one defines the concepts and applies the standards of sexual adequacy, health, and maturity. But in any case, the fact that adequacy consists of orgasmic capacity for some persons while for others it is a bare beginning of the experience and appreciation of sexuality suggests that the interpersonal and social possibilities for sexual therapy need to be critically reexamined and further developed.[5] Sexual function is more than sexual subsistence. This is implicit in much of the research presented.

---

[4] Recently, some attention and energy are being directed to that end. A report on a "sexual dysfunction" clinic, established under the auspices of Elysium Institute in Topanga Canyon, California, included the following statement: ". . . it is expected that the diagnostic clinic will attract fully functioning people who want more knowledge, such as . . . 'I want to learn how to improve an already good sex life'" (Elysium Institute, "The Sexual Dysfunction Diagnostic Clinic," *New Living*, no. 22, p. 8). The presumption that a good sex life cannot be better or that a good sex life requires no "therapeutic" attention will, we suspect, be eroded by the proliferation of such institutionalized and normalized options as suggested above. The fact that much of this "therapy" is permission-giving and reinforces preestablished goals takes nothing from its significance as a factor in sexual health or eufunction. One might even look forward to the day when both swinging clubs and sex-therapy programs are integrated into institutionalized adult sex play and interpersonal intimacy centers, wherein eufunction, including interpersonal communication and total bodily awareness, is the primary goal. A cautious look at the motivation patterns which lead some persons into either a swinging group or a sexual-therapy program might render this notion a little less wild than at first appears. The legitimization and normalization of intimacy and *all* forms of consensual sexual contact might carry our entire civilization beyond the prevailing mode of both diagnosis and treatment of sexual dysfunction.

[5] Based in part on this research, the Self-Actualization Laboratory is developing a radical therapy program for dealing with an extended range of problematic and sensitive areas of sexual relatedness, including interpersonal exclusivity, boundary definition and transformation, the dynamics of intimacy and jealousy, sex role relationships, and fantasy exploration.

The combined effect of these articles and reports should give members of the counseling professions cause for thought concerning their roles in the construction of social reality, in addition to some fresh insights into what constitutes a "normal" or "healthy" marital relationship. Judges, legislators, and those concerned with the legal aspects of marriage and sexuality should find something of interest as well, though the requisite conceptual bridges linking the two concerns, scientific and legal, have yet to be built. Furthermore, and of more importance, those potential actors who are convinced that marriage is or might be a largely private relationship, capable of independent definition arising out of the interaction and interpersonal negotiations of two (or more) persons, will find a trail being blazed here which may provide useful markers for critical decisions pertaining to many otherwise problematic intra-, extra-, and/or co-marital sexual possibilities. Finally, those who are involved, directly or indirectly, by word or by deed, may find in some generalization or other, in this observation or that, confirmation of an experience or a possible structure for thoughts that had previously lain fallow and unappreciated.

Despite the significance and potential of the research and analyses for raising relevant questions and providing preliminary answers regarding co-marital and related forms of sexual activity, a few words of caution are necessary about their scope, methodology, and reliability. Any interpretation must bear in mind the shortcomings inherent in the opening of any new line of social inquiry, especially one so fraught with controversy, prejudice, and downright painful ignorance. Those shortcomings cannot be overcome with the publication of a single volume or the undertaking of a single, however massive, research project. Nor can they be met by reliance on shibboleths and unquestioned, not to say unanswered, truisms inherited from the past. The issues are too weighty, the behavior too complex, the future too uncertain. Diligent, sustained inquiry, carefully interpreted and thoughtfully applied to the problems as they present themselves, is the way to reduce the anxieties, fears, and misgivings that permeate the sexual consciousness of every thinking creature. At its best, such research will be future-oriented and will anticipate the problems before they arise. A truly predictive science of marital and transmarital sexual behavior, the principles of which could also be turned to preventive ends to cope with otherwise unanticipated interpersonal mishaps and hardships, will require a much deeper and more thorough understanding of the social and cultural dynamics of sexuality than we now have. In the meantime, a few modest steps toward clarification and penetration are possible on the basis of currently available information.

On the positive side, the essays and reports all appear to pose or to begin from the same basic questions: What is marriage, what is its future, and more specifically, what are the reasons for and effects of deviating from or redefining the sexual norms which are presumed to govern its workings? This is a continuous theme that threads its way throughout virtually every paper. Marriage has always and everywhere been a commitment to some combination of socioeconomic and sexual roles with (in varying degrees) identifiable limits. Both the roles and their limits are, by dint of historical circumstance and intellectual curiosity, being subjected to serious examination by variously equipped inquirers throughout this volume. They may be seen as analyzing either a form of sociosexual pathology or the further growth and evolution of a currently threatened social institution. That there is a serious challenge to conventional or institutional marriage is manifest. Whether or not the responses to it constitute a breakdown or a build-up, or more likely, a complex amalgam of both, is yet uncertain.

These studies stand in the ambiguous interstices of those responses and seek understanding of relatively new patterns and styles which stand out against the background of the old frames of reference and social codes. The consequence is a complex set of contrasts which may be viewed summarily as a shift from *traditional* to *companionate* forms of marriage.[6] In the former, instrumental, material, and pragmatic con-

---

[6] Mary W. Hicks and Marilyn Platt, "Marital Happiness and Stability: A Review of Research in the Sixties," *J. Marriage Fam.* 32 (November 1970): 555. "Family sociologists have postulated for many years that at least two basic marital types co-exist in the United States: the institutional and the companionship. The assumption has been that the institutional is the older, more firmly established type, but that, for a variety of social and personal reasons, there is a shift toward the companionship marriage." Cf. Marvin B. Sussman and Betty E. Cogswell, "The Meaning of Variant and Experimental Marriage Styles and Family Forms in the 1970's," *Fam. Coordinator*, October 1972, p. 375. There, the distinction, couched in terms of a contrast between companionate and traditional orientations, is taken for granted as a point of departure. The precise wording is largely a matter of choice. We prefer the traditional-companionate distinction over the institutional-companionate formulation because we believe the companionate variations, although still latent, are in the process of progressive integration into the institutional structure of the entire society. Such divergent occurrences as the recognition of the "rights of consortium" in law, the ritualization of homosexual marriage, the various attempts to legislate equal rights for both sexes, and the mass media preoccupations with extra- and trans-marital sexuality are indicators that the companionate ideology is being "institutionalized" in American society as a viable way of life. On the other hand, one could argue that companionate marriage will create its own "tradition" and therefore confuse the linguistic distinction sought above.

siderations are uppermost; in the latter, affectionate, creative, and expressive relationships assume greater significance. A companionate marriage appeals to and is composed with regard to the "higher" needs.[7] It is more synergistic, less symbiotic, more developmental and dynamic, and less regimented around the needs for subsistence, safety, and security. It is, one might say with Abraham Maslow, a complex system and process of mutually negotiated and "dyonomous" interaction which is, at least in part, metamotivated.[8] Needs and wants are synthesized and coordinated so that, to an appreciable extent, the satisfaction of one person's needs tends toward the satisfaction of the other's. In its more eupsychian manifestations, it has built-in risk-taking, reality-testing, and conflict-resolution features.

The two types are not wholly disparate or discrete, and may only reflect differing value orientations and material conditions in the society at large. As such, they are outgrowths of and are continuous with the social structures and value cultures which partly support and partly inhibit each of them. Many other issues and problems are dealt with in the course of these studies, but the bulk of them examine tendencies toward and variations in the companionate form of marriage, which is

[7] It has been shown that, as instrumental and pragmatic needs are satisfied in a marital relationship, other needs emerge and assume greater importance. Levinger, for example, studied the sources of marital dissatisfaction among applicants for divorce and found that "spouses in middle class marriages were more concerned with psychological and emotional interaction; while the lower class partners saw as more salient in their lives financial problems and unstable physical actions of their partners" (George Levinger, "Sources of Marital Dissatisfaction among Applicants for Divorce," *Amer. J. Orthopsych.* 36 [1966]: 803–7). This has been interpreted to mean that, unless and until instrumental needs are met in marriage, the partners are unable to fully address themselves to the psychological and emotional levels of interaction (Hicks and Platt, "Marital Happiness and Stability").

[8] "Dyonomy" is a condition of dyadic autonomy (i.e., personal autonomy within a dyadic relationship which expands the resource potential of each person *because of the nature of the relationship itself*). It is intended to complement the concept of synergy, which contains no guarantee of self-governance or self-regulation. Dyonomy is the optimization of synergistic potential through an appropriate distribution of individual freedom within a dyad. The term "interonomy," which expresses a similar principle, could be usefully reserved for group or interpersonal autonomy. Thus, the vocabulary, relentlessly obscure but useful in many contexts, could be expanded by the use of such terms as "trionomy," "octonomy," "multonomy," etc., referring to the peculiar characteristics of interactionally magnified autonomy of individuals in groups of almost any size or composition. In almost any marriage the levels of synergy and dyonomy are always problematic, and the relationship between the two is generally positive and highly variable.

itself a complex response to new historical and social pressures on institutionalized sexual experience and traditional married life.

It may be argued further that consensual extramarital sex as an extension of marriage is incompatible with the traditional type of marriage but, in many respects, is continuous with the development of the companionate orientation, into which new norms and strategies are imported in an attempt to open or expand the interpersonal, emotional, and sexual dimensions of marriage.[9] This statement is not to be interpreted too literally. What might be added is the observation that, when consensual sexuality is practiced within a traditional marital framework, there is a strain generated in either the partners or the marriage itself. Strictly speaking, however, a tradition-based and -oriented marriage cannot genuinely incorporate *consensual* extra- or co-marital sexual relations easily, since one of the defining characteristics of such a relationship is alleged sexual monopoly with an emphasis on intradyadic dependence. Hence, with the appropriate qualifications, one can say that consensual adultery in any of its forms is incompatible with traditional arrangements. It is, to carry the argument a step further, a companionate relationship within a tradition-bound institutional framework that produces what appear as pathological conditions, patterns of conflict, and disintegrative interaction. Many of these effects are appropriately viewed as dysfunctional consequences of the *traditional pattern of marriage* but are at the same time highly functional when gauged in terms of *companionate* or *eupsychian* standards.[10]

---

[9] This appears to be the implicit and largely unspoken strategy of *Open Marriage* by Nena and George O'Neill. The theoretic norm of synergy becomes a guiding principle from which other techniques and tactics of interpersonal success in marriage are derived. An open marriage is not necessarily a promiscuous or even a sexually permissive one. But it is surely one in which the issue of recreational and transmarital sexual potential has been examined and explored and resolved in a synergistic manner. An optimally open marriage might even be regarded as the end point or goal of a primary companionate relationship, as the next stage perhaps in the evolution of contemporary marriage. Note, however, that this kind of relationship, if it succeeds in realizing its synergistic potential, is the product of highly rationalized and deliberately adopted ideas and techniques for transforming the interpersonal space and dynamics of a given dyad. If it is evolution, it is evolution which has become collectively, or at least dyadically, conscious of itself and directed itself to a designated greater good. Such a process of voluntary interconscious change might be better termed "eupsychian evolution" or "euvolution," for short.

[10] A more fully elaborated theoretical rationale of this topic will appear in a book by James R. Smith and Lynn G. Smith to be entitled *Eupsychian Marriage: A Humanist Marriage Manual for the Twenty-first Century*. This work will take as its point of departure Abraham Maslow's posthumously published questions,

If one accepts this general line of reasoning, it is clear that many companionate and communal possibilities are emerging as practical alternatives to the traditional pattern. The results of theoretical and empirical inquiry suggest that they are nascent social realities but that the current legal system and moral codes, in their current state and circumstances, are incapable of recognizing and integrating them. Throughout the studies included, there is a focus upon the increasingly diverse range of sexual alternatives and options available to married persons, options which are made possible and manageable by the companionate form of marriage.[11]

Part 1 contains a series of critical and analytic essays which raise issues central to an evaluation and assessment of the various contemporary alternatives to sexual monogamy. Historical, speculative, and theoretical in nature, they attempt to synthesize various trends and findings into an explanatory picture. Most of them are searching for the relevant questions, the historical antecedents, and the edifying perspectives from which reliable theories may be drawn and around which future research may be shaped. There is an effort to appreciate, in the full sense of that term, some aspect of transmarital sex or consensual adultery and to provide a viable framework for further discussion of the cultural redefinition of the dynamics of sex and marriage. There is also an attempt to generate a vocabulary, to identify patterns, and to clarify issues.

Part 2 consists exclusively of empirically based research reports and interpretations. They are for the most part independent of one another, and many of the researchers did not know of the other projects until we began organizing the material for this volume in the summer months of 1970. The material in both parts is, as the section titles imply, preliminary. It is also tentative, rudimentary, and therefore inconclusive. It represents the first theoretical and empirical steps into a hitherto unex-

---

the answers to which are only schematically anticipated in his work: "What would a Eupsychian marriage be like, i.e., between the self-actualizing male and the self-actualizing female? What kinds of functions, duties, what kinds of work would the females do in Eupsychia? How would sex life change? How would femininity and masculinity be defined?" (Abraham Maslow, *The Farther Reaches of Human Nature* [New York: Viking], p. 220).

[11] This does not mean that no swingers are parties to traditional relationships or that all swingers are companions, but rather that many of the variations in *extra*marital sexuality, when successfully integrated as a part of the marriage relationship, may be viewed largely as an outgrowth of a companionate orientation and ideology which transforms and transcends the interpersonal limitations (e.g., mutual sexual possessiveness) of the traditional institutionalized pattern.

plored realm of deviant but possibly liberating and civilizing behavior speculated on and anticipated by John Stuart Mill, Havelock Ellis, and Bertrand Russell. This realm is now countenanced by a growing number of contemporary writers and counselors who are willing to look beyond monogamy for a more viable and fulfilling sexual life. A small but no less significant group has demonstrated a willingness to look not only beyond monogamy but also beyond swinging and swapping for the ways and means to transcend the now arbitrary and often pointless strictures of monogamic exclusivity.

It cannot be said, at this point, with any degree of assurance whether the similarities and differences in the findings are a result of sampling and recruitment procedures, methodological orientations and research techniques, data interpretation and analysis, or actually different patterns of behavior. However, it is worth emphasizing that the authors were for the most part unknown to each other at the inception of their projects.[12]

There is a definite advantage in the lack of contact among the authors. When more than one independent researcher achieves similar results, there is obviously greater plausibility. For this reason, we have chosen not to eliminate the overlap and duplication which the reader will find at some points. The remarkable fact is the relative lack of disparity. The disagreements in interpretation and differences in subject populations are real enough. But not only are many of the writers asking the same fundamental questions; in some cases they are exposing the same fundamental patterns and sequences of fact.

The articles which follow not only bring a variety of alternative marriage arrangements and experiments into clearer focus, they examine, usually in a scientifically cursory or exploratory fashion, the behavior that may constitute a further step in the evolution of interpersonal relations. Sex clubs, swinging parties, and contemporary orgies may seem to belie such a contention or to indicate that the evolution is limited to the most casual forms of physical contact. But culturally and scientifically, we have yet to dig far enough beneath the swinging and swapping to reveal the diversity of motivational patterns, the linkage between social environment and sexual experimentation, and in particular, the complex relationships among sexual history, sexual values, and current behavior—in short, the dynamics of sexual socialization and

---

[12] See, e.g., Gilbert Bartell, who remarks that "for the first two years of our research we were unaware that other social scientists were also investigating swinging" (Gilbert Bartell, *Group Sex: A Scientist's Eyewitness Report on the American Way of Swinging* [New York: Peter H. Wyden, 1971], p. 21).

resocialization. In any case, it is not yet clear that even casual sexual contacts are so damaging and demoralizing as often contended. It may be that in some contexts casual sexuality is all that is expected, required, or appropriate and it may, upon reexamination, turn out to be a healthy form of physical and interpersonal exercise in and of itself.

Further, and perhaps of greater importance from a critical point of view, would be an answer to the question: What is the nature and structure of a social system which generates and seemingly promotes exploitive sexual attitudes and superficial forms of sexual behavior, especially when so much more seems both possible and desirable? If the recreational sex of certain persons or even classes of persons is limited to the swinging variety—i.e., sexual activity by both members of a given heterosexual dyad at the same time and at the same place with relative strangers and preestablished and prescribed limits for emotional attachment—we must presume to inquire more thoroughly into the institutional framework which surrounds and vitiates this sexual style, and also into the actual social and personal dynamics which cause such behavior patterns.[13]

Simple appeals to anachronistic religious norms or psychoanalytic clichés will not suffice to explain the complexity of motivational patterns, the changes in institutional structure, and the manifold reactions to new opportunities for sexual expression afforded by a pseudopermissive society. As social scientists we should not be too quick to judge, morally or even clinically, the propriety of such private desires.[14] But

---

[13] See, e.g., Bartell, *Group Sex*, p. 291: "In a society of alienated human beings, sex, after all, serves a socially integrating function. Among swingers sex all too often replaces authentic intimacy." Bartell also tells us that ". . . their human relationships outside the dyad are not good" (p. 292). This leads us to note a possible confusion here: in a "society of alienated human beings" presumably no one's human relationships are very good. Thus, it is difficult to say, without substantial evidence, whether the relationships of swingers are better or worse than the average or typical case. The average swinger is probably no better or worse than the average person on that score, and both are fictions in any case.

[14] John F. Cuber remarks that in the study of adultery the ". . . concern has been more moralistic than empirical, more hortatory than analytic." In spite of pronouncements and avowals of objectivity ". . . there is still, even among the more scientific, a clear tendency to concentrate on negative aspects and to present them more vividly." Further, most analysts tend to ". . . overlook the enormous variations in adulterous experience with respect to its function in the lives of the participants, its relationship to marriage, and its impact on the mental health of the participants. . . . The effects on the marriage of the adulterous spouse have been presumed always to be destructive, and the effects on the mental health of all participants have been assumed to be deleterious" (Gerhard Neubeck, ed., *Extramarital Relations* [Englewood Cliffs, N.J.: Prentice-Hall, 1969], p. 190).

we should be both quick and ready in the effort to study them fairly and impartially, insofar as social need requires and scientific capability allows.

If the "new morality" requires that "myriad sexual decisions are in the hands of the individual moral agent,"[15] no one should be surprised if some treat it as play and some treat it as sport. In formal terms, the "new morality" appears to make room for such behavior at the periphery of sexual normality by recognizing altered boundaries between public and private behavior and allowing greater latitude and scope for self-regulated and self-determined action.[16] However, it does not provide adequate answers to a range of highly perplexing questions regarding the consequences of such behavior for social and marital life, nor does it render us wiser concerning the psychosocial nature of the moral agent in question and the manner in which private sexual decisions and policies are made. The currently emerging model for sexual morality, summarily referred to as the sexual interaction of consenting adults, assumes and obscures the very point it should render clear, i.e., the problematic status of consent, understood as a function of (presumed) individual autonomy in a (presumed) favorable environment. The nature of individual and collective sexual consent remains ambiguous at the very time sexual agency is unambiguously couched in terms of it.[17] We are still left with a host of questions regarding the interconnections between sexual consent, moral agency, and the subsequent happiness, growth, health, and freedom of the individual. The "new morality" has not yet found its scientific complement in the field of sexual behavior, though efforts at integration are not altogether wanting.

Maslow has provided initial clues to our understanding of the dynamics of consensual sexuality by conceptualizing healthy sexual

[15] Frederick C. Wood, Jr., *Sex and the New Morality* (New York: Association Press, 1968), p. 150.

[16] ". . . The so-called new morality involves a shift from the morality of significant acts to the morality of personal competence. Sexuality gives the individual at least the sense of making moral decisions. . . . The movement of the sexual out of the domain of the publicly significant and moral into the domain of the privately moral and individual begins to shift radically the relationship between sex and the law . . . As the morality of sexuality tends to move from the public to the private arena (following the consenting behavior between adults model) then the laws themselves seem less important and less necessary" (John H. Gagnon and William Simon, eds., *The Sexual Scene* [Chicago: Aldine, 1969], pp. 17–18).

[17] Cf. Germaine Greer, "Seduction is a Four Letter Word," *Playboy*, January 1973.

expression in terms of "spontaneous sportiveness." Nearly twenty years ago he wrote that

it is not the welfare of the species, or the task of reproduction, or the future development of mankind that attracts people to each other. The love and sex life of healthy people, in spite of the fact that it frequently reaches great peaks of ecstasy, is nevertheless also easily compared to the games of children and puppies. It is cheerful, humorous, and playful.[18]

In the course of our own study we observed such qualities in the sexual interaction of small groups on a number of occasions where there was prior exposure, a modest but significant level of trust, and an ongoing relationship among relatively secure and uninhibited persons.

Again, while not all persons who are involved in swinging or who are parties to a sexually permissive marriage could be described as high-dominance types, Maslow's study of dominance and sexual expression provides a useful perspective for the study of transmarital sexuality. Among high-dominance persons he found that

every aspect of [sex] is eagerly, enthusiastically accepted and warmly thought of (where ego-insecurity is not too great), experiments of all kinds are made, all sexual acts are thought of as "fun," rather than as a serious business. Very frequently, in a marriage between high-dominance people, it is found that there has been experience, if only a single experiment, with practically every form of sexual behavior known to the psychopathologist as well as the sexologist, many involved and curious positions or combinations of positions in the sexual act, sodomy, homosexuality, cunnilingus, fellatio, sadism-masochism, exhibitionism, and even coprophilia, sexuality in a larger group, etc. These acts have no pathological tinge nor are they pathogenic in any way. It would appear that no single sexual act can *per se* be called abnormal or perverted. It is only abnormal or perverted individuals who can commit abnormal or perverted acts. That is, the dynamic meaning of the act is far more important than the act itself.[19]

Such descriptions by no means characterize all, or even most, of the sex-oriented parties we attended or the couples or groups we studied.

[18] Abraham Maslow, *Motivation and Personality* (New York: Harper, 1954), p. 195.

[19] Maslow, "Self-Esteem (Dominance-Feeling) and Sexuality in Women," in M. F. DeMartino, ed., *Sexual Behavior and Personality Characteristics* (New York: Grove Press, 1966), pp. 103 and 105. High-dominance persons were characterized by Maslow as ". . . uninhibited or unrepressed, as people whose fundamental impulses, animal or otherwise, are apt to come out freely in behavior, without limits set by the society."

Some gatherings and some couples were unquestionably conservative with very ordinary and uninspired sexual expression whose only striking feature was coital contact across marital lines. Some groups were grim and dreary; others were noticeably stiff and competitive. Yet others were joyful, playful, and intimate. Either way, depending on the relative absence of a critical level of inhibition (on the part of at least a few) needed to generate initial sexual activity, there was a substantial amount of sexual experimentation, sometimes random, sometimes structured, and the commonly sought end, one not always achieved, was indeed fun.

The differences in orientation among these groups generally could be traced, without rigor to be sure, to any number of circumstances and variable conditions, but the quality of the experiences and the relationships seemed to vary with general levels of personal and interpersonal security, relative levels of individual maturity and candor, frequency and nature of prior exposure to the persons involved, and the degree of commitment and felt involvement in the context of an ongoing relationship.[20]

While many couples are sometimes clumsy and naïve in their sexual experimentation, it is apparent that, even though not everyone is capable of it, (1) such experimentation is not limited to the marital dyad, and (2) the experimentation itself is both normal and healthy. Although errors in judgment and failures to perceive are not uncommon and can lead to serious rifts in a marital relationship, it is through such experimentation that these couples learn about and more consciously establish their own proclivities and limits for sexual interaction. It is a form of reality-testing just as much as a form of acting-out behavior. The testing and acting, in the form of concrete situational experimentation, can be superficial or profound.

In the course of extensive involvement, experimentation often includes a further definition of sexual identity, establishment of higher levels of tested self-esteem and sexual function, and a reexamination of the commitment to and stability of the primary relationship. In many cases, and this accounts for the apparently high divorce and separation rate among the experimenters, they are testing some basic aspects of

---

[20] It is of interest to note that on some occasions it appeared that the lack of inhibition and the willingness to experiment freely were directed and positively related to (1) the degree of anonymity and (2) the lack of threat of exposure. On rare occasions, a high degree of conviviality prevailed among those who had no or little prior exposure to each other but found each other momentarily in the same mood and space.

marriage itself.[21] Sometimes, the results of the tests are negative, and the penchant for viewing marriage as a presumptively stable, healthy, and socially desirable state is thereby subject to serious challenge. Dissolution is not merely and always disintegration and deterioration; it can be the spark of growth as well. What Jung said of marriage is true also of divorce: "There is no birth of consciousness without pain."[22]

Whether the individual tests or acts out, the fact is that he or she has moved. In the process, depending on the level of involvement and nature of the motivation, the participants are, in various ways and in varying degrees, sexually resocialized. This process of resocialization takes place over a period of usually not less than six months, and it may continue for as long as two to five years. There are wide individual and interpersonal variations in this process, depending on level of security, self-esteem, capacity for communication, opportunity for involvement, and suitable supportive social environment and/or peer group. By this process—complex, subtle, and far-reaching—individual sexual consciousness and all that is related to and influenced by it are definitely, in most cases irreversibly, and in nearly all cases observably changed. The process of adult resocialization is made necessary by repressive initial socialization in childhood and adolescence, which is inadequate preparation for expanded adult options.

In no instance that we know of did any member of our research population retain the same sexual values and schedule of priorities, including taboos and restrictions, that characterized his or her childhood, adolescence, and initial participation. And very few couples began or initiated their relationship in an open mode, sexual or otherwise. Rather, by dint of their enculturation, education, and socialization in sexual matters, they frequently regarded themselves as initially disadvantaged and thereby forced to achieve such a relationship if they were to have one at all. This process of resocialization certainly does not always result in intramarital stability, personal maturity, or total liberation, but it does tend to demystify and desanctify many sexual activities and render them amenable to experimentation and discussion on a more rational and humane basis.

---

[21] Figures on divorce and separation rates among co-marital participants are not yet known. They will only become available through longitudinal or large-scale survey studies. The editors have initiated a longitudinal study and propose to expand it in an attempt to ascertain such data.

[22] Carl Jung, "Marriage as a Psychological Relationship," in *The Portable Jung*, ed. Joseph Campbell (New York: Viking Press, 1971), p. 167.

The fact that some extramarital behavior, collective or otherwise, appears on examination to be childish, rebellious, and immature is due more to the type of culture in which it occurs than to some unenviable fixed trait or disposition in the personality tending toward what some view as pathological deviance. Whether or not it is pathological is a matter for further analysis and investigation. Preliminary findings suggest it is not so, or at least not necessarily or even predominantly so, among the populations studied to date. And while transmarital permissiveness may be deviant from some perspectives, James Ramey's paper wisely suggests that at least some of these persons transcend the rubric of deviance and are, in fact, innovative in their behavior.

The consequences for marriage are significant and dramatic. By eliminating or at least reducing the deceit associated with conventional adulterous behavior and by transcending the intramarital demands of sexual exclusivity, and at the same time achieving new levels of candor and freedom about sexuality, the conjugal relationship can be transformed into something very different which may be more trying and challenging but also more rewarding and fulfilling. By studying the behavior of those who adopt such a strategy, the presumed relationships between sexual deviance and marital pathology and health can be reconceptualized by means of a theoretical inversion and subsequent reinterpretation of the entire issue. From this perspective, those couples whose transmarital potential remains a threatening and unapproachable "problem," often not even perceived as such because of evasion, dishonesty, and lack of communication, can be viewed as suffering from a condition of insecurity and dyadic pathos, which may well become, and very often is, pathogenic with respect to the marital relationship. In short, they can be seen as suffering from what might be called an adultery-evasion complex or a trust-deficiency syndrome, obscure names for altogether common maladies.

Such an understanding of the matter takes the sting, not to mention the presumptive validity, out of the judgments of pathology so glibly dished up to explain highly liberalized sexual practices and stimulates a demand that traditional theories of sexual socialization and psychosexual development be either refurbished or discarded. What is presumptively perceived as pathology can be alternately viewed as the consequence of a complex social learning situation in which there is little, if any, preparation (other than a range of more or less conventional premarital practices) and few, if any, reliable guides. Clearly some marriages deteriorate, and some persons encounter unanticipated difficulties in the course of, and sometimes because of, transmarital involvement, but the message is equally clear that there are many healthy persons who approach sexuality in a more or less self-experimental way and operate within different frames of reference with apparent success.

Transmarital sex can be better and more consistently understood in the historical, social, and normative contexts in which it occurs than from some external vantage point having little relevance and no bearing on the issue. Furthermore, not only are those more general environmental contexts important, but the psychosocial expectations and perspectives of the individual actors are what determine, more than any historical or environmental variables, just what the specific effects of transmarital activity will be. In Maslow's terminology the "dynamic meaning," not the behavior itself, is the critical feature in determining individual outcomes.

The theoretical recognition of differential dynamic meaning as perceived and expressed by sexual actors has been sporadic and retarded among behavioral scientists. Nonetheless, there is what one might call a vague but tenacious tradition which attempts to analyze the significance and consequences of what is broadly and somewhat misleadingly referred to as "nonprocreative sex."[23] The terms *non*procreative and *non*reproductive, like the terms *pre-* and *extra*-marital, suggest the traditional value orientation which generated them and thus reveal the historical and biological bias implicit in the very formulation of the concepts. A similar bias is hidden in the concept of adultery, which is misleading in the same manner. This altogether common and notorious linguistic usage betrays the presence and influence of the cultural ideology of monogamous sexuality, restricted to and governed by, somewhat imperfectly to be sure, the boundaries of marriage itself. It suggests an intellectual prejudgment that is carried into the most abstract realms of talking and thinking about human sexuality.

The problem is that the terminology and basic conceptual categories make it appear that sexuality is presumably procreative in all times and in all places but that in the contemporary world, some alien and contrary element intervened. Phlyogenetically, there may be some point to this remark. But as it affects the motivation of individuals and groups of individuals in the contemporary social world, this is a presumption which smacks of insidious moralism. To rectify

---

[23] For a witty tour de force in that tradition, see James Collier, "The Procreation Myth," *The Sensuous Society* (Chicago: Playboy Press, 1973). Cf. George Gilder, *Sexual Suicide* (New York: Quadrangle, 1973) for an opposing point of view.

this bias, we have selected the term "transmarital" to convey a generally positive or at least sympathetic meaning to much of the nonprocreative behavior that constitutes the focus of the studies included in this volume.[24] Transmarital sexuality refers to any sexual activity, interaction, relationship, or ideological scheme which aids and abets the transformation of the institutional superstructure and/or the interpersonal infrastructure of traditional marriage in a way which allows greater relative interpersonal autonomy and independence and fosters a greater capacity for intimacy and sociability. It includes at least the following categories of interpersonal arrangements:

1) Married persons who engage in direct and indirect sexual activity with a person other than their primary partner but with the knowledge and consent of their partner. (Hence, while the effects of conventional adultery upon a marital relationship are still a matter of controversy, the fact that deception is involved negates any transcendent potential for the primary relationship, though discovery and/or disclosure of deception produces a crisis situation that it can function as a catalyst for change.) This may include individual, cross-dyadic, co-marital, or group alliances and activities.

2) Couples who cohabit on a regular basis and who have established an ongoing relationship on the basis of mutually negotiated needs for intimacy, welfare, and the like, but who have not sought legal and/or religious certification of their arrangement.

3) Group marriages, communal living groups, and other nonconventional variations of transdyadic arrangements among adults.

This might be thought of as a preliminary typology of transmarital types, but the fundamental point concerns not classification but legitimization and acceptance of purpose. They all involve a redefinition of interpersonal boundaries and a rescheduling of value priorities and provide an intentional framework which promotes (but by

---

[24] Corollary terms, which could be defined and applied in a similar manner, are *transproductive* sexuality and *transfamilial* relationships. However, neither of these terms should be construed as distinctly incompatible with child-bearing or -rearing: rather, the social structures in which procreation takes place may be seen as manifest and intentional departures from traditional family norms and practices. For laudable efforts to produce a viable vocabulary of nonreproductive sexuality, see Saul Rosenzweig, "Human Sexual Autonomy as an Evolutionary Attainment, Anticipating Proceptive Sex Choice and Idiodynamic Bisexuality," in *Critical Issues in Contemporary Sexual Behavior*, ed. Joseph Zubin and John Money (Baltimore: The Johns Hopkins University Press, 1973).

no means guarantees) a recasting of the traditional relationships among sexuality, marriage, and social structure.

Some hypothetical questions and some tentative answers may be usefully proffered in the course of analyzing the structural readjustments and realignments among those social entities described above. In particular, the social status and function of nonprocreative sexual interaction remains obscure. No one is very clear or thorough in pursuing an answer to the question: What is the role, function, purpose, or value of sexual expression that is consciously and conscientiously aimed at something other than the begetting of children? Privately, everyone knows the answer, regardless of upbringing, level of repression, or religious orientation. It is, among other things, for personal and interpersonal pleasure, solitary if need be but preferably shared, which ideally is intimate, authentic, and mutually satisfying. Any person who has ever masturbated to orgasm and any couple who ever, consciously or unconsciously, mechanically, chemically, or rhythmically avoided a pregnancy during coitus can attest to this fundamental fact.

Many things are projected onto the pursuit of this pleasure and the frankly hedonistic orientation it implies, and there is much about contemporary liberal sexual behavior patterns which is compensatory and overdetermined.[25] Liberal sexuality, like liberal politics and liberal economics, rests on illusions of autonomous, self-sufficient, self-sustaining social monads (or dyads), each satisfactorily maintaining their own private status quo. As a widely vaunted sexual ideology it has a confused regard for historical conditions, environmental influence, sexual equality, and collective human potential and is anything but the last word in the process of sociosexual development. It assumes that a certain level of perceived personal freedom and presumed sophistication, once reached, is a summit from which one assays and understands everything sexual without further reflection or effort. Sexual liberals, like their ideological counterparts in politics and economics, rest content with doing what they want without asking why they want it or what consequences follow, individually and collectively, in the wake of the progressive satisfaction of those wants.

At the same time, it must be said that, where sexual pleasure is not accepted as a positive good or where acceptance is not integrated into the psychic and somatic life of the individual, there follows the

[25] See, e.g., Gagnon and Simon, "Perspectives on the Sexual Scene," in *The Sexual Scene*, ed. Gagnon and Simon; and Mary L. Walshok, "The Emergence of Middle-Class Deviant Subcultures: The Case of Swingers" (in this book, pp. 159–69).

inability and the unwillingness to feel pleasure and joy, even ecstasy, and the neurotic, deadening, and repressive tendencies which characterize sexual insecurity and sexual puritanism. In the pursuit of that pleasure, who knows a priori where to draw the line between experiencing it with one and experiencing it with many? Who knows where the psychological ax will fall between compulsive promiscuity and multiple person-oriented involvements in which sex is a significant part? And who knows just what is a joyous meeting of minds and bodies among swinging couples and what is a deadly compromise in the face of a sagging marriage?

The increase in frequency and visibility of nonprocreative sexual contacts and relationships, conceived as both human impulses and a social trend, forces a shift in consciousness that is only beginning to manifest itself in proportion to the probable extent and future status of the behavior itself.[26] Such behaviors, taken collectively, constitute a historical change of great moment and far-reaching consequences, requiring what Thomas Kuhn has called a paradigm shift in sexual theory and social philosophy.[27]

Sexual expression and marriage itself may no longer be taken for granted as for the sake of procreation or indeed for the sake of anything but themselves. The shadow of procreative values, which has traditionally dominated virtually all thought about sexuality and provided it with its traditional dynamic meaning, is being rolled back by the recognition, somewhat belabored and belated, in law, science, and philosophy, as well as in the consciousness of sexual actors, that under certain conditions the purpose of sex is fun.[28] In a recent

---

[26] See, e.g., Max Lerner, *Marriage: For and Against* (New York: Hart, 1972), p. 103: "If it is true that at the start of the 70's, several million Americans are taking part in group sex, my guess would be that double or triple that number will be taking part in it at the end of the decade. It will remain a minority form of marriage, but an increasing minority. In time, it may crowd the majority form—monogamous marriage after premarital co-habiting for a stretch, and with continuing extramarital infidelities and affairs, secret but recognized."

[27] Thomas Kuhn, *The Structure of Scientific Revolution* (Chicago: University of Chicago Press, 1962).

[28] Albert Ellis put the matter as bluntly as possible: "Sex is fun" (*Sex without Guilt* [New York: Lyle Stuart and Grove Press, 1965]). It would not be out of the way to make reference to the lexical definition and synonyms of the term "fun" inasmuch as they reveal an entire syndrome of meaning and value which underscores the notion that recreational sexuality is aimed at no end or goal other than its own spontaneous expression. "Fun" is defined as "sport; merriment; playful action or speech"; and its synonyms include jest, sport, game, and play. "Play" is "an exercise or action intended for amusement or diversion; amuse-

panel discussion Phyllis Kronhausen, referring to group sex and sex parties, came to the point in linking practice with principle: "It's fun. You go there just to have a good time. If we could get just one message across to the young . . . it would be that sex should be for recreation, not procreation."[29]

There are many associated reasons and motives for engaging in transmarital sexuality, not the least of which is some sexual deficiency or dysfunction within marriage. However, this shift in perspective does reinterpret the dynamic meaning attached to sexual experience in a way which makes it not only consistent with much transmarital behavior but both rational and comprehensible. Besides, the deficiency and dysfunction in question might be only a felt lack of sexual

---

ment; sport; frolic" (*Webster's New International Dictionary*, second edition). Recreational sex has no purpose outside, above, or external to its own enjoyment, which some will regard as a way of saying that it has no purpose at all. Like leisure, which is a condition of recreation, sex is psychologically attractive, on the one hand, but, being of no immediate utility and having no justifying standard external to itself, is experienced internally as vaguely discomforting and perceived externally as a wasteful (hence immoral) activity. Language traffics on this confusion. Here again our sexual vocabulary and syntax fail us, and their inadequacies lead straightaway into a linguistic (hence ethical) trap. This can be avoided by keeping in mind the simple fact that sex need not be "for the sake of" anything but itself. Rhetorically, its point is that it is pointless, but that does not mean it has no meaning or is devoid of psychic significance for those experiencing it. Failures to make distinctions of this kind plague attempts to analyze play in general. See, e.g., Josef Pieper, "Play—A Non-Meaningful Act," in *Sport and the Body: A Philosophical Symposium*, ed. Ellen W. Gerber. But for an alternative perspective of the problem compare Kenneth L. Schmitz, "Sport and Play: Suspension of the Ordinary," *Ibid.* Cf. also, Alex Comfort, *Joy of Sex* (New York: Crown, 1972); and Herbert A. Otto and Roberta Otto, *Total Sex* (New York: Peter H. Wyden, 1972), chapter 19. "*Adult play is defined as spontaneous, free-flowing, creative, joyous, or pleasurable activity. Relatively devoid of structure and without the element of competition, it is essentially a leisure activity with directions emerging from within the person . . .*" (Otto and Otto, *Total Sex*, p. 299, italics in original.) One anomaly that might be noted with respect to the Otto volume is that, in the extensive list of sex games in Chapter 19, there is no mention of sex play in groups. The index is devoid of all reference to group or transmarital phenomena, a curious omission for a book entitled *Total Sex* and professing a holistic philosophy of human sexuality. One wonders if there is not a pragmatic contradiction involved in recommending and promulgating play as a standard of sexual behavior while ignoring completely the transdyadic potential implicit in adopting such a standard. But cf. pp. 274–75 for comments on sex fantasies about group involvement.

[29] Phyllis Kronhausen, "New Sexual Life Styles," *Playboy*, September 1973, p. 84.

playfulness and spirited, but nonproductive and nonreproductive, interaction capable of generating a truly recreative mood.

This purpose and this mood, far from making us mere animals, is precisely what is most human about sexual expression, i.e., its inherent tendency to become civilized adult play.[30] Implicit in the full articulation of such a thesis and its corollaries is the suggestion that, since play is at its best and fun is most fulfilling (or at least heightened and intensified) when shared, sex pursued in the same ideological and/or interpersonal frame of reference will include activity in peer groups and among intimate networks. This is not to be misinterpreted as an argument for group sex in which the principle of the-more-the-merrier is thought uniquely appropriate. Neither is it to disparage or diminish the significance of one-to-one, face-to-face relationships. Rather, it is to recognize that if sex is fun, play, or sport, it is so partly because it is a social activity, restricted to legally certified dyads only by invoking what might be called the "procreative fallacy."

The procreative fallacy is committed by all those who assume that sexual reproduction is the universal or primary norm which governs all rightly ordered socio-sexual structures and the behavior of all properly socialized persons.[31] The persistent commission of this

---

[30] In his well-known and highly regarded study (*Homo Ludens: A Study of the Play Element in Culture* [Boston: Beacon, 1955], chapter 1, pp. 43–45), John Huizinga objects to conceiving sex as play. While he concedes that elements of "wooing and flirting" may be viewed as play behavior, he contends that "copulation" itself is not an act of play (p. 43). In this we think he is in error and suggest that the source of the error lies in an inadequate conceptualization of nonprocreative sexuality. Huizinga may be correct in saying that under some circumstances copulation itself is not play, though we suspect that given the wide range of both copulatory and precopulatory behaviors many of the characteristics of play, as he conceives and defines them, are incorporated in its expression and serve as tacit goals of those behaviors. In the course of an otherwise remarkably original and insightful analysis of the cultural significance of play, his treatment is flawed by a very subtle form of the procreative fallacy, one which arises not from authoritative and universalistic pronouncements concerning the genital aim or the primacy of offspring but from a mere matter of emphasis on biological functions and biosocial conceptions as the appropriate context for assessing the parallels and overlaps between sexual expression and play behavior in man. But cf. Alex Comfort, *Sex in Society* (New York: Citadel, 1966), who maintains that ". . . numerically at least the chief biosocial function of coition in man is play" (p. 26).

[31] Wilhelm Reich (*The Sexual Revolution: Toward a Self-Governing Character Structure*, 4th ed. [New York: Noonday, 1962]) wrote that, "according to conventional sex morality, *the sexual act is not supposed to be an act of sexual*

fallacy has extensive ramifications for a wide range of social issues including abortion, population control, sexual deviance, the social role of marriage, and the institutional and cultural regulation of reproduction. The fallacy consists in the attribution of a single and overriding purpose to human sexual interaction which is commonly presumed to be incompatible with other ends and values. It erroneously assumes that sex is predominantly and/or exclusively directed toward reproduction.[32] It is a subtle form of intellectual and moral totalitarianism which tacitly assumes that what is right for some, in particular the propagators of the reproductive norm, is not only right but actually binding upon all. In short, sex is valued for its species-survival capacity. Its significance as an interpersonal art form, a spontaneous expression of feeling, or a type of social play ideally

---

pleasure and gratification apart from reproduction. Official sanctioning of the sexual act apart from reproduction would mean throwing overboard all officially accepted secular and ecclesiastical concepts of sexuality. Thus, for example, writes Max Marcuse in his compendium *Die Ehe* (in the chapter on 'Contraception in Marriage'): 'Should it become possible to sterilize women temporarily at will by internal medication, the most urgent task would be that of working out a method of distribution of these drugs which would make them available where indicated for reasons of hygiene and at the same time safeguard against the enormous danger presented by them to sexual order and morality, more, to life and culture in general.' What one should add, of course, is the danger to *authoritarian* life and culture" (pp. 37–38). Reich's reference to the passage from Max Marcuse shows, with unusual clarity, both the commission of the procreative fallacy and the nonsensical corollaries which were (and are) derived from it. "What is really meant by this 'enormous danger,'" adds Reich, "is the danger of separating sexuality and procreation" (p. 38).

[32] It is a matter of some philosophical significance that even Bertrand Russell comes dangerously close to committing this fallacy in *Marriage and Morals* (New York: Bantam Books, 1966). At one point he writes, ". . . I regard marriage primarily as a sexual partnership, but above all as an undertaking to cooperate in the procreation and rearing of children" (p. 151). Again, as a sort of salutatory assumption at the outset of the chapter on "Population," he writes, "The main purpose of marriage is to replenish the human population of the globe" (p. 162). But cf. his comments on the effects of contraception at p. 156 and elsewhere. ". . . Contraceptives have made it far more possible than it formerly was to distinguish sexual intercourse as such from marriage as a procreative partnership. On this ground it is now possible to attach much less importance to adultery than is attached to it in the conventional code" (p. 156). Events of the past half century have made it clear that reliable contraception renders the hypothetical distinction between procreative and nonprocreative relationships an existential choice among alternative sexual patterns. And it removes one of the chief dangers to any form of extra- and/or trans-marital sexuality, namely, unwanted pregnancy and its aftermath of unwanted offspring of uncertain paternity. In short, contraception both reveals and nullifies the effect of the procreative fallacy.

transcending the need for game structure is not only underplayed or denied, but also depreciated as a form of evil that might be incompatible with the demands of procreativity. In a society where unchecked reproduction threatens to produce a structurally dysfunctional and possibly even disastrous condition, that logic can and must be reversed. In such a society there is no room to eulogize reproductive sexuality at the expense of its recreational, relational, and sensual counterparts. Procreative and nonprocreative sexuality must coexist in a balance relative to both individual (or dyadic) wants and needs and the long-range requirements of survival and evolution. This issue is summarily argued by Alex Comfort in "Sexuality in a Zero Growth Society," chosen as the lead article in Part 1.[33]

Few have worked their way through the metaphysical thicket of procreative values and institutional requisites so that the issue of nonprocreative sexuality can be raised without obfuscation. When one does so the entire gamut of sexual customs and rule systems may be seen from an entirely different perspective and with an inverted order of sexual priorities and purposes. The parameters of biosocial interaction may then be reviewed in somewhat different terms with the sociologically interesting result that, once procreation is transcended or suitably regulated, the social restrictions and legal prohibitions on all consensual sexual activities and outlets must be suspended or repealed for lack of a justifying principle.

In pointing out the procreative fallacy and following up some of its many ramifications, we are, in effect, anticipating a comprehensive formulation of a *ludenic* theory of human sexuality as an explanation of much contemporary sexual behavior.[34] Such a theory would recognize the relevance of the pleasure principle but would transcend the old hedonic theories by recognizing that sexual play requires elements of variety, spontaneity, and creativity that the subjective experience of pleasure itself does not. It rests on a humanized pleasure-seeking in which the "higher" and "lower" needs are integrated into an appropriately functioning whole. Various aspects of politics, communication, art, sport, consumer behavior, and all manner of leisure pursuits and expenditures would also come under the

---

[33] Rudiments of this point of view can be found in "The Future of Marriage," *Sex and Marriage*, ed. Havelock Ellis (New York: Pyramid, 1957).

[34] See William Stephenson, *The Play Theory of Mass Communication* (Chicago: University of Chicago Press, 1967), p. 47. We borrow and emulate William Stephenson's pardonable travesty on Latin grammar because it sounds nice in English and avoids the bombastic charge of superficiality that the use of the terms "play" and "fun" invite.

heading of such a theory and could suitably be understood in its terms.

Contemporary sexuality in particular awaits a theory constructed from the ludenic perspective as a way of rationalizing a wide range of otherwise perverse and immoral-appearing behaviors whose incidence and appeal are increasing at an undetermined rate. From the ludenic perspective, group sexuality and other contemporary variations on a theme of nonprocreativity are conceived not as hotbeds of neuroticism but as forms of noncommittal, nonobligatory intimacy which thrive upon the values of leisure, play, and relaxation. Sex parties are, after all, parties, and while parties serve a multiplicity of psychic and social ends, their ostensible and projected purpose (their end-in-view, so to speak) is to relax and have fun. In serving such a function they are on a sociological and psychological par with holidays, vacations, festivals, folk humor, hobbies, avocations, religious rituals, and other presumptively acceptable distractions from the exigencies and earnestness of the work-a-day world.

The nonreproductive orientation, which, as a matter of interpretation, is displayed in all manner of recreational and transmarital sex behavior, provides sexuality with a dynamic meaning that clashes with all those institutions, myths, codes, and theories formulated under the cultural weight of procreative sexuality. Play in particular provides sexuality with a dynamic meaning which has fundamental consequences for assessing marital and transmarital sexual behavior.

In a revealing and virtually prophetic article entitled "Sex as Play," Nelson Foote (1953) contends that ". . . play—any kind of play—generates its own morality and values."[35] If sexual activity is regarded as a form of play, resulting in a drive for recreation and gratification, it should be expected to generate its own culture or subcultures, its own complex of symbolic associations and expression, and its own myths in a manner not altogether unlike the sexual ideology and mythology of romanticism, puritanism, asceticism, communism, or any other ism which professes a particular set of relationships among sex, love, marriage, and reproduction. Play presents its own demand for suitable equipage and a supportive environment. It is not without significance that the bedroom is jokingly regarded as the metaphorical playground of marriage. From this viewpoint which steps lightly from nonprocreative to recreational sex, fun is not the absence of a sexual standard but the presence of a counter-

---

[35] N. Foote, "Sex as Play," *Sexual Behavior in American Society*, ed. J. Himelhoch and S. Fava (New York: W. W. Norton & Co., 1955), p. 240.

cultural one subject to gross misconstruals and prejudicial interpretations.[36] This perspective allows one to see more clearly that sexual
contact is not merely the instinctual life-line to collective survival
but is, as Alex Comfort maintains, ". . . the healthiest and most
important human sport. . . ."[37]

This is apparent in Wardell Pomeroy's account of a sexually permissive group of married couples, proffered at a seminar on adulterous sexual behavior. His comments are among the most enlightening
on the subject anywhere and are worth quoting at length.

A few years ago I knew a person who was involved in a wife swapping
club. I told him I was interested in the whole phenomenon and I had the
privilege of meeting with a group of wife swappers at a natural wife
swapping occasion. I felt very privileged that they would let me come in

---

[36] This use of the term "recreational" is not to be confused with Carolyn
Symonds's use of the term in drawing a distinction between "recreational" and
"utopian" swingers. Her distinction, which attempts to isolate an important
difference in motivational patterns among participants in co-marital sex misses
the fact that both recreational and utopian swingers pursue sex concretely as a
form of interpersonal play and social recreation but differ in their sexual value
orientations and priorities, subcultural expectations, and degree of integration
of their deviant style. Our use in the present context turns on a basic contrast
between *procreative* and *recreative* sexuality, conceived broadly as biosocial orientations, and not a distinction between recreational and utopian swingers, a topic
we have addressed ourselves to elsewhere in this volume (Lynn G. Smith and
James R. Smith, "Co-Marital Sex: The Incorporation of Extra-Marital Sex into
the Marriage Relationship"). As a matter of speculation, one might venture to
say that those persons to whom Symonds was referring as utopian swingers are
far more profoundly recreative than the often inhibited and unintegrated "recreation" of their deviant counterparts. In other words, Symonds's "utopians"
are, from our perspective, more likely to be recreational (i.e., more playful) than
the "recreational swingers." (Carolyn Symonds, Pilot Study of the Peripheral
Behavior of Sexual Mate Swappers, Master's thesis, University of California,
Riverside, 1968, pp. 4–5; "Sexual Mate-Swapping: Violation of Norms and Rec-
onciliation of Guilt," in *Studies in the Sociology of Sex*, ed. James M. Henslin
[New York: Appleton-Century-Crofts, 1971], pp. 81–112.

[37] Comfort, *Sex in Society*, p. 26. "Probably the main function of the frequent
coition found in man is social, like much bird display—it serves primarily to
keep the couple together as a breeding and mutually supporting unit. But it also
seems reasonable to regard sexual intercourse as an important recreation which
is biologically very well adapted to release residual anxieties of all kinds, and
which has a physiological means of abreaction—the orgasm—'built in.' It is, in
other words, the healthiest and most important human sport; and the need to
consider it in other, medical or sociological, contexts, should never be allowed to
obscure the fact." See also Comfort, *The Joy of Sex*, p. 85. ". . . Sex is the most
important sort of adult play. . . . The rules are only those of childplay. . . ."

and do this. There were six couples: one college professor, two high school teachers, one truant officer and his wife, and an engineer and his wife, and another couple. Upper-class group. They met in a very nice home about 8:00. All came in and immediately disrobed. The whole group took off their clothes. They sat around in the living room, and I was free to talk to them singly or in groups. The conversation was not ribald at all; it was calm conversation, essentially nonsexual conversation. One of the men would say to the lady next to him, 'Would you care to come in the other room?' She would accept. They would retire to the other room and would stay, I timed anywhere from twenty minutes to maybe as long as forty-five minutes, but usually about half an hour. No comments were made as they left. No comments as they returned. They would return to the group, and a little while later, would leave with another partner. So in the course of the evening each man would tend to see five other women; never his wife— that could be done at some other time. Then they would put on their clothes and go home and that was the evening. In talking with these people, and I interviewed all of them individually as well as getting this group flavor, they were reporting consistently a happy marriage. Almost all of them had children; they ranged in age from about thirty to forty-five. They had responsible jobs and expressed concern that their children not learn of this. The children didn't know of this activity. The couples involved would usually do it once a week or once every two weeks, and they wanted to sort of separate out this sexual activity from their marriage. . . . Affairs in terms of seeing these people outside of this relationship was taboo. There was absolutely no sexual activity going on in the living room with the other people there. In this sense, this was all private. They all felt that this was something beneficial to their marriage. They were happy they were doing it. They certainly reported no feelings of guilt on a conscious level. They appeared certainly not to have them. One couple said they only joined the group two months ago, and prior to that both of them were having a great deal of extramarital intercourse, with recriminations, with fights over the activity of the spouse, until they joined the group. When they were able to do this openly with each other, all recriminations seemed to stop. They thought it was a very healthy thing in their marriage to do it. These people obviously had a totally different idea of what a commitment was or what part sex had in marriage, but I was sort of struck by the fact that they seemed to be making this type of adjustment seemingly comfortably. I couldn't get any other pathologies, if you want to call this pathology. . . .

The reason I was bringing it up was to try to show an example of a group of people who did look on sex pretty much like tennis. It was sort of a bridge game, and it was fun, too. All I'm trying to point out is that I think we can do this in a different way. I'm not trying to say what is right or wrong, but as far as I could determine, these people, from other criteria, had a good marriage, in the sense of responsibility, raising children, having good jobs, being happy, and so on.

. . . In my way of looking at these people, it seemed to me that they were handling it, although in a totally different way, not necessarily a "wrong" way or a destructive way, or in a way that was interfering with their lives. It was just different. And what I was hoping the group would accept was that people can be different in many different ways.[38]

Clearly, a principle of tolerance is relevant at both the theoretical and the normative levels of appreciation. While the members of this particular group manifest a relatively high need for structure (as evidenced by the apparent rotation procedure) and for dyadic privacy (as evidenced by their almost systematic withdrawals and reentries), they individually see themselves and sexuality from a different point of view. Whether or not that point of view constitutes a mere rationalization, in the pejorative sense in which that term is colloquially used, or a rationalization in the sense of a structuring or unifying orientation in experientially ambiguous and indeterminate situations, their viewpoint must be reckoned with, methodologically by the scientist and normatively by the moralist, as a factor which colors every feature of the case. Their "set," and therefore their reasons and motives, is different and must be appreciated as such.

This is borne out in various studies wherein fundamental differences in attitude structure were found among couples with co-marital experience. Sex was dissociated from romantic love interests to a marked degree and contrasted clearly with the attitude structure displayed in both control groups and, so far as can be determined, the general population. Our own findings also support this contention and suggest that some aspects of current and future sexual behavior may be increasingly differentiated in purpose not only from procreation but also from the romantic mythology of love.[39]

If swingers indulge in their activities solely from sexual bore-

[38] Neubeck, *Extra-Marital Relations*, pp. 31–38.

[39] For a more complete discussion of this and related issues, see James R. Smith and Lynn G. Smith, *Consenting Adults: An Exploratory Study of the Sexual Freedom Movement* (in preparation); Brian Gilmartin, "Sexual Deviance and Social Networks: A Study of Social, Family, and Marital Interaction Patterns Among Co-Marital Sex Participants," (in this book, pp. 291–323), whose study of one hundred "swinging" couples and one hundred matched control couples provides striking evidence in this direction, and Cherie E. Schupp, "An Analysis of Some Social-Psychological Factors Which Operate in the Functioning Relationship of Married Couples Who Exchange Mates for the Purpose of Sexual Experience" (Ph.D. dissertation, United States International University, June 1970), who found a similar difference in attitude structure between control and experimental groups.

dom, a common but often perniciously articulated and easily misunderstood hypothesis, then it would seem that sexual play and sexual variety, pursued in a sensitive, mature, and integrated manner, might be a perfect tonic, so long as the tonic is not also toxic, a fact that must be empirically and scientifically, as well as individually, determined. One could then rely on the normative maxim—fun is a good thing as long as it spoils nothing better—as a justification for even the most limited and superficial types of sexual interaction, if that maxim were genuinely applied.[40] The really difficult, and yet most important, issue for actor and observer alike, is whether the superficial contacts impede one's capacity for serious and sustained involvements on a deeper plane. Furthermore, one might inquire whether the demands of primary sexual attachments and primary emotional allegiances within a given dyad are necessarily incompatible with secondary sexual relationships and whether the former must always be significant in a way that, so it is presumed, the latter cannot or should not be. To resolve that question, the critical tools and techniques of social science and philosophy must be brought to bear on those persons attempting to expand their sexual alternatives.

In addition, the obverse question can be raised, though as yet no clear answer is forthcoming. What, we should want to know just as fervently, are the effects of *not* expanding one's sexual life? What are the effects of monogamy, both as a state-sanctioned institution which places a limit of one on the number of (concurrent) conjugal mates and as a psychosexual value syndrome which, formally at least, also restricts each person to one sexual partner?[41] What are the consequences of involuntary monogamy, monogamy which is in fact one-sided, monogamy sustained by threat and intimidation, and monogamy already gone sour but not legally and morally terminated? What are the effects of the conflict between cultural requirements and individual desires? Does sexual jealousy impede the progress of civilization? What might sexual life be like without it?

---

[40] This contention rests on the assumption that sexual play is a value of considerable social and psychic import and should be treated as such. That is to say, sex, taken as a species of recreation or amusement, is a pursuit in which moral decisions are made, resources allocated, and energy expended in the course of nonutility bearing or nonproductive activity which must be justified intrinsically if it is to be justified at all. For an examination of this topic, see Smith and Smith, "Sex as Play: The Ludenic Theory of Human Sexuality," draft available from The Self-Actualization Laboratory.

[41] Cultures which place formal prohibitions on multiple mateships and premarital and extramarital liaisons are exceedingly rare (C. S. Ford and F. A. Beach, *Patterns of Sexual Behavior* [New York: Ace, 1959], pp. 115 and 119).

Approaching these questions seriously, we remain more impressed with the way in which monogamous heterosexuality denies the multiplicity and latitude of sexual and interpersonal experiences that are available to healthy and mature persons than with the dire warnings that sexual freedom will always and everywhere be twisted into sexual license and unchecked promiscuity.[42] From an interpersonal point of view, living in a monogamous relationship is not unlike having sex with one's clothing on: it diminishes sensitivity and restricts movement.

From a radical perspective, strict monogamy is seen as fetishistic, for it makes a sexual fetish (not to mention a virtual possession) of one person exclusively. Indeed, insofar as it guarantees and underwrites sexual access and sexual privilege to one person while denying it to all others, it makes a qualified possession of the genitals themselves. It gives one person control over the genital activity of another. Monogamy, understood as an institutionalized form of marital hygiene become cultural norm, makes a fetish of the very genitals it seeks to protect from the intrusion of and violation by others. It also, in its course, elevates the stimulus value and desirability of the "private parts" of others by placing a taboo on them. A more psychically and interpersonally self-defeating plan can hardly be conceived.

Capitalism, Marx contended, makes a fetish of commodities by obscuring their origin in human labor and gives them status as the sole source and standard of economic value. By a similar dynamic process, monogamy, a form of marriage uniquely suited to a capitalist society, makes a fetish of persons and their bodies. A monogamic culture does this by (1) obscuring the origin of sexual attraction in spontaneous human feeling and expression and then (2) legitimating a given person's status as the sole obligatory source and standard of emotional intimacy and sexual satisfaction for another person. It places a duty in the path of a feeling. And Kantians to the contrary notwithstanding, if one performs sexual acts out of duty alone, or if one's sexual feelings are tainted by dutiful expectations in which the emotions are given a subordinate role, the result is moral and interpersonal chaos.[43] In short, monogamy promotes dyadic monopoly

---

[42] See, e.g., P. Sorokin's gloomy forecast, based on historical data of operatic proportions, in *The American Sex Revolution* (Boston: Porter Sargent, 1956).

[43] The reason this has not been perceived clearly is that women have a "built-in" disadvantage and men a corresponding physiological advantage. Women can consistently "perform" (i.e., allow themselves to be penetrated as wives and/or prostitutes out of duty or for money). On the other hand, the man's "performance"

and supports interpersonal possessiveness. The implicit market mentality and subtle prostitution betrayed in this process is obfuscated
and then justified by the entire ideological and cultural context in
which the process occurs. The cultural ideology of monogamy rests
upon systematic illusions of voluntary selection and spontaneous response and is sustained by institutionalized inequality between the sexes.

This is testable at the extreme in that legalistic homily to monogamy which states that a man cannot rape his own wife and even
allows him grounds for divorce if sexual privileges are withheld or
denied. Surely this is *not* merely the sexual privilege as a means to
reproduction but is the privilege of sexual pleasure per se and as
such. From this viewpoint, monogamy, especially the double-standard variety so commonly practiced and so audaciously defended by
American males, can be seen as a condition of forced sexual privilege
and whorelike dependence that is interpersonally self-defeating. The
altogether too-common result is that such a relationship becomes
significantly depersonalizing for both parties. Along with those ami-
able sexual façades of virginity and premarital chastity, monogamy of
the sexually monopolistic variety may come to be viewed not as a
model of interpersonal relationships but rather as a form of emotional
and sexual malnutrition, a condition of sexual deprivation for both
male and female rather than of sexual privilege.

(as distinguished from his spontaneous or induced response pattern) demands an
erection suitable to the situation, which is somewhat beyond his voluntary control. Every sexually experienced woman alive knows the old lube-it-up-to-make-
him-happy-whether-I-am-ready-or-not routine, which is the all too-common
consequence in this culture. The female is always able, even during menstruation,
to physically *perform* her "duty" whether she is or is not inclined to *respond* to
it from within. The male is not always capable of spontaneous erection. (One
wonders what the consequences might be if the physiological capabilities were
somehow reversed, that is, if women were simply physically unable to perform
without sufficient arousal, rather than psychologically unwilling to respond, and
the male were provided with a switch-on dildo which women manipulated according to their own purpose and pleasure). The rise in reported male impotence, and certainly premature ejaculation, may be linked to this physical
difference, inasmuch as women are now making demands, e.g., for protracted
performance, which many males, in their current state of enculturation, education, and socialization, are simply unable to meet. "Prematurity," lest it be overlooked in this context, is a relative term, used fundamentally in reference not to
the male's internal timing but to the rapidity of the female's orgasmic response
as compared with the male's. Whether the male is unduly premature or whether
the female is simply late is an open and psychologically loaded question for any
given couple. Without much imagination, the proverbial "battle of the sexes"
can be construed in terms of this difference in sexual response patterns.

Monogamic marriage is, in its own macabre way, a legitimized and normalized form of emotional and erotic bondage, as evidenced by its obligatory character, intended as a matter of course to insure social and familial stability against the wild winds of sexual passion. Historical and social conditions, especially the current rate of divorce and the increasing frequency of extramarital sexual contacts, now suggest that this grand strategy may have backfired. The tie that binds under some conditions may be self-defeating and self-destructive under others. Resentment and frustration over the traditional restrictions placed on marriage and fear of the consequences of stepping outside its presumed boundaries, whether by mutual consent or unilateral decision, often emotionally outweigh the urges to change or transcend the restrictions. The monogamic code is so antisocial and contrary to human nature that an entire social ideology and an assortment of socially engineered pretenses and excuses have been devised to avoid and evade it. It is a curious fact that there are more, or at least as many, forms of adultery as there are of marriage. One might well argue that the latter is both the necessary and sufficient condition for the former, an overstatement that warrants some further analysis.[44] There is the aching feeling abroad that something is wrong, not with marriage per se, but with the monogamic system of institutionalized customs and habits that has its prime expression in contemporary western culture. There is a recognition that monogamy pushes as many persons apart as it brings together and that this forsaking-all-others and til-death-do-us-part business is neither realistic nor humane.

Similarly, the list of salvos for modifying monogamous sexuality is as long as the list of sanctions against doing so. From a critical viewpoint, monogamy in the form of sexual monopoly can be seen as a compromise between personal autonomy and interpersonal security which has survived in spite of itself, largely as a legal shell meant to contain the psychological reactions against it. In such a relationship, one presumes and intends to gain security and privilege in the form of a permanent and regular sexual partner but, outwardly at least, at the expense of spontaneous sexual feelings and a range of intimate relationships, both sexual and nonsexual. It seems reasonable to believe that, for many persons, the tension generated therefrom could be partially resolved and the attendant problems transcended if new forms of marriage were legitimized and integrated into the

[44] Reich, *The Sexual Revolution*, p. 35.

social system of which they are already a nascent and peripheral part.[45]

It might be that the rejection of the ideals of monogamy, the nuclear family, dyadic privacy and exclusivity, rigid sex roles, and traditional child-rearing and socialization practices signals a move away from a capitalist socioeconomic system. In view of the unsubstantiated fact that marriage is under fire and giving way to new sexual and social patterns, including swinging, in many urban areas of Europe, Japan, the Soviet Union, and even South Africa, it is more likely that this is another manifestation and revelation of the recent and more advanced phases of technologized industrialism. Such a system, as has commonly been observed, produces greater and more rapid interaction and, therefore, more sexual interaction—and, therefore, more opportunities for extramarital and indeed all manner of sexual experience. In this way industrialization, urbanization, and "mediafication" of the modern world are fragmenting the traditional family structure on a world-wide scale, more or less independently of national politics or social tradition. And with exponential increases in population and the dim public awareness of the eventual consequences, there is a variable reaction which views all manner of non-

[45] It has been suggested, employing a commonly cited political model, that America is a pluralist society ready to integrate all manner of marital styles and ideologies. Sussman and Cogswell maintain that recent trends in variant family structures give ". . . renewed supports for the ethos of pluralism. The society is demonstrating its great absorptive capacities by recognizing these alternatives or options for acceptable behavior and for finding one's place and self-fulfillment" (Sussman and Cogswell, "The Meaning of Variant and Experimental Marriage Styles and Family Forms in the 1970's," p. 376). It is true that, up to a point, such diversity is tolerated, even emulated, in some quarters. But that point is precisely the one at which such arrangements and beliefs become public and seek a substantial place in the economic, political, and legal scheme. When that point is reached, whether in the attempt to pass solid and effective reform legislation or in the effort to procure material social support for the substantial integration of group marriage or homosexual relationships, the situation is much the same as with virtually any minority-group interest. An interesting illustration of this lies in the public reaction and response of the athletic bureaucracy which rules the world of baseball to the exchange made by New York Yankee players Fritz Peterson and Mike Kekich and their wives. The players came in for considerable heckling from the fans and abuse from the press, and Commissioner Bowie Kuhn, with umpire-like finality, called the exchange "deplorable" (*Oakland Tribune*, March 19, 1973). Recognition and reception, regardless of the misdirected attention visited on such phenomena by learned academicians and clever journalists, is largely a combination of grudging tokenism and reactionary backlash. Pluralism as a matter of sexual ideology versus social reality is still the liberal's dream and the radical's nightmare.

procreative experience and relationships in a vaguely favorable light. Indeed, if we push the point far enough, in logic or in future time (assuming current growth rates), procreative sex may have to be morally, and perhaps legally, enjoined and recreative sex become the norm of sexual interaction.[46] If, as a culture, we have lost the childlike approach to and capacity for play, we may now with adult bodies, temperaments, and talents, be forced to recover it . . . on pain of boredom or loneliness.

If we are to settle these and related issues, we must have sound longitudinal and sophisticated comparative, or better still where possible experimental, data. This will require serious and sustained research that is undertaken from a positive but critical perspective.

Scientific inquiry into transmarital sex will likely unearth a number of confusing and surprising findings. It can tell us how far we are from a universal acceptance of dyadic heterosexual monogamy, and it can illuminate alternatives to that basic pattern. It can even yield answers to questions about the consequences of such behavior.

[46] The assumption of stable growth rates in American society is a tenuous one according to the most recent reports. However, we submit that the decline of birth rates in the past two years is not merely coincidental with the proliferation of co-marital and extramarital sexual outlets. The decline is most dramatic in the very areas in which recreational and swinging subcultures are most prominent and visible (e.g., Los Angeles, San Francisco, Chicago, and New York). Again, many persons, particularly among swinging populations, are turning to sterilization and various surgical procedures as permanent birth-control measures, thereby removing one basic sexual motivation and simultaneously providing an expanded range of sexual opportunities and potential partners without fear of pregnancy. And there seems to be an increase of cohabiting couples for whom offspring is neither an issue nor an expectation. These and similar trends all feed into and draw upon a recreational and transmarital ideology for sexual behavior which is not only consonant with what has been said above but provisionally confirms it. On the basis of such unstable trends one could hypothesize that there is a definite and positive correlation between the decline of birth rates and a retardation of population growth, on the one hand, and a rise in the number of nonprocreative relationships and recreative sex behavior, on the other; one could seek further evidence for such relationships and behavior by surveying specific regions and locales in which co-marital and transmarital subcultures were, or are, developing. The general theoretical lesson one might expect to learn as a result of such inquiry is that manifest and widespread changes in the social function of human sexuality are corollary with and integral to a solution of the population problem as currently conceived. As a matter of general policy, one could argue that, if population stabilization or decline is proposed as a social goal, then nonprocreative or "extraceptive" sexuality must be intelligently integrated and institutionalized as not only normal but laudable behavior.

What it cannot do, of course, is clear forever the ambiguities that surround emergent social trends. These are fired in the crucible of social history and distilled within the individual biographies of those who experiment with them. Despite clarification, we shall still be faced with the moral problem of whether such alternatives are desirable and how we are to decide, individually and collectively, what sexual behavior ought to be permitted, what ought to be proscribed, on what basis, and with what institutional and cultural means. The desirability of transmarital sex, as either individualized experiments or as a series of institutionalized alternatives, is as yet an open and compelling question which science alone cannot resolve.

As we have indicated, both the pragmatic relevance and moral desirability of marriage itself, especially in its traditional form, is also far from unequivocal and uncontroversial. If, as some have argued, traditional marriage is a form of serfdom or slavery, especially for women, we may be witnessing a series of social changes which, by comparison with the emancipation of serfs of medieval Europe and the slaves of early colonialism, are long overdue. The current and widespread preoccupation with "wife-swapping" (a revealing and entirely chauvinistic misnomer) may not seem to raise these issues in such a serious manner, but this is primarily the result of a lack of concern by professionals to look beneath the surface image created by a sensational press and an anxious populace who feeds upon it. The conquest of sexual jealousy, if achieved, could be the greatest advance in human relations since the advent of common law or the initiation of democratic processes. The increasing frequency and incidence of swinging and swapping (as forms of consensual adultery) could then be viewed not as evidence of the decline of western civilization or Christian morality through promiscuity and debauchery but as restless and untried attempts which presage a new era in sexual and interpersonal relationships.

One fundamental change in social thought and cultural ideology that will be necessary in such an era is a shift from considering sexuality in primarily ethical terms to construing it in an appropriate esthetic context. This is not to avoid dealing with normative requirements and ramifications of human sexuality but to recognize that, with the presence of contraception, affluence, leisure, mobility, a relatively educated middle class, and a host of minor influences upon sexual decision-making, the kind of consequences which follow from sexual interaction are more akin to a living art (which ideally engages all of the sensibilities as well as all the senses) than a moral problem. Once the ethical requisites are transcended or satisfied, the relevant test of propriety is whether or not a given sexual experience is pleasurable. At that point, there is no other court of appeal to rectify or confirm one's behavior. Personal taste is king, court, and code, just as in art, esthetic realists and sexual moralists to the contrary notwithstanding; and one must exercise and experiment with taste to know it without apprehension and diffidence.

The nominal rubric of sexual ethics may be retained as a matter of shorthand convenience, to be sure, but any future sexual philosophy which is to be both viable and relevant will have to recognize and integrate the esthetic dimensions of sexual experience and adequately define the relations between ethics and esthetics.[47]

This shift in perspective is justified if only because it has not often been taken seriously and because preliminary excursions indicate it to be viable, if lamentably unstructured and easily misunderstood. It is also justified because, and this is crucial, this is how *some* of the actors perceive and understand their own behavior, whether or not they consistently succeed in realizing the ideals of sexual freedom and whether or not their own sense of taste and style is well developed and sufficiently inner directed.

In addition to the above issue concerning the critical but limited capacity of science to contribute to and resolve moral issues, there are a number of more specific weaknesses and shortcomings present in this research which it would be well to point out in advance. They will be apparent to the critical reader, but an enumeration of them may provide some assistance for evaluating many of the articles from an appropriate viewpoint.

1) There is a gross problem concerning vocabulary. It is not simply that the epithet "swinger" is misleading but rather that many of the terms and definitions used vary from one article to the next, with only approximate agreement as to meaning, both denotative and connotative. This, by the way, reflects the actual situation of the vocabulary of the actors.

2) Integrally related to the first problem is that of conceptualization, which is currently inadequate for the purpose of research and

---

[47] George Santayana, *Sense of Beauty*, pp. 23 ff. Some appreciation of this distinction between sexual ethics and sexual esthetics may be gained by attention to Santayana's comments on esthetic versus moral judgments and his comments on the cultural significance of play. "By play we are designating, no longer what is done fruitlessly, but whatever is done spontaneously for its own sake, whether it have or not an ulterior utility. Play, in this sense, may be our most useful occupation" (p. 28). See also, Huizinga, *Homo Ludens*, and William Stephenson, *Play Theory*, chapters 4 and 15.

theory. The nontheoretical entities (classification schemes, ideal types, scales, and the like) are not always clearly articulated and those that are employed are in need of further refinement and elaboration.

3) There is the ever-present problem of sampling. There is no instance of reliable random sampling for the simple reason that there is no way of ascertaining the size and location of the relevant statistical universe. In Brian Gilmartin's research, an appropriate matched sample was employed to make some comparisons. All the rest were selected by the researcher or were composed of volunteers drawn from a variety of regions, strata, and groups. Since we do not know the size and extent of the subject population and since no sample was randomly drawn from any known group, we have no way of knowing with any degree of precision how representative the data are in any given study. However, as the number of subjects swells with each new study, there are increasing inductive grounds for the reliability of discrete findings.

4) As mentioned previously, in most cases the research design is by comparison primitive and does not lend itself to conclusive results. Most of the designs are exploratory, historical, or one-dimensional and therefore suffer from the limitations imposed by logic upon those designs.

5) As a consequence of the fourth weakness, there are few hypotheses directly tested, though a number of important ones are tendered as a result of exploration. There is a good deal of post-hoc hypothesizing on the basis of one-shot questionnaire and interview data. Current and proposed research should soon amend this situation.

6) There are many cases, therefore, in which conclusions hang in the air with only modest success in integrating findings into previously developed theories of sociosexual behavior.

7) There is only a modest amount of comparative research in which the work of one researcher has been employed as a soft test for the reliability of another.

8) There is no experimental research whatsoever, although the reasons for this are many and manifest.

9) There is no clear picture of the relationships between the facts discovered and the values which they might reinforce or undermine. The normative dimensions of transmarital sexuality remain largely a matter of speculation.

10) Finally, while the research is pregnant with implications, there has been no sustained attempt to draw out the therapeutic ramifications

of the data. The broader therapeutic, as well as the resocialization and educational potentials of various transmarital behavior patterns, have hardly been recognized, let alone understood.[48]

These, then, are what we consider to be the limitations of this research. Any fair assessment of it, either piecemeal or as a whole, must take them into account. Despite these limits, it is clear that the research raises possibilities, suggests new relationships, and paves the way for an appreciation of some of the contemporary sexual alternatives in marriage that have either not been heretofore available or available only in esoteric social scientific journals.

An essay of this kind would not be complete without the customary editorial plea for more research and more support to make it possible. It is by now a hackneyed point, the spate of "how to" and biographical revelations to the contrary notwithstanding, that there is neither enough research into sexual behavior nor sufficient financial support to sustain it. Sex research has always been a hazardous and controversial field of scientific inquiry. The fact that we are so much in need of it is a commentary on contemporary life. The rapid and not always well-anticipated changes that have taken place with respect to sexual behavior in the twentieth century, and especially since the end of World War II, leave many persons in a state of anxiety and confusion. At the same time, much of the security which remains is pseudosecurity, a kind of smug or cocksure confidence, based on presumptive judgments concerning facts that have never been researched. The gaps, which are filled only by presumption, may eventually be closed when science and ethics cooperate to yield a relevant and informed set of principles for sexual experience. In the meantime, American social consciousness is fraught with and caught between the pragmatic contradictions generated by combining a sexual morality taken from the past with a science of sexuality which could be realized in the future.

Social change is not, of course, generally and directly based on scientific inquiry. The usual pattern is the reverse. A change takes place which is then observed and recorded by scientists. The observations and records are later digested and theories are formulated upon which therapies, policies, or recommendations for further changes are often

---

[48] In the Yaney study of co-marital and group sex the consensus of the observers was that there was a significant measure of ad-hoc therapeutic effect on many of the participants and that marital relationships did improve for some couples (Yaney, "Sandstone Experiment").

based. In this way, science ideally contributes to freedom of action. But there are a number of instances where science itself is the key to the change, and the pattern tends to become more complex, even to reverse itself as we move into the future. Science provides not only solutions to problems and crisis situations; it also provides the rationale and reveals the means for changes that were always implicit in or possible for human action. It also, where it is wise, sets a limit to its contribution, not allowing itself to assume a predominant role but playing an appropriate part by revealing possibilities and providing facts, explanations, and accounts that may be integrated into personal behavior patterns and developing social structures in a useful and liberating manner. A comprehensive and established science of human sexuality could serve such a purpose, yielding a sound perspective for what is a natural internal inclination. In a word, it could help us understand ourselves better.

Harking further out, we might even say that it is here—in the realm of inquiry—that the most significant part of the putative sexual revolution is taking place. Sexuality has been a fact of life throughout all time and is a universal theme in the art and literature of every culture, however repressed and dogmatic its expression. But the systematic study of human sexual behavior is of relatively recent vintage. It is so recent that its social effect is viewed as disruptive and consistently disintegrative. No other science enjoys such widespread popular consumption. No other science affects the individual consciousness so thoroughly and completely. And no other science is subject to such controversy and resistance.

The social science of human sexuality is at an incursionary stage of development, exploding one myth and prejudice after another about a wide variety of sexual practices, styles, and customs. It must assume a posture of defensive offense for the most part to secure its aims. As a consequence, its agents and practitioners are often seen as provocateurs, not to say saboteurs, of the old moral order. The historical fact, if one may use the term and remain aware of its empirical prematurity, is that the old moral order is based on a series of misconceptions about the possible and desirable relationships among pleasure, sexuality, love, marriage, and social structure. It also miscasts the role of science as a protector of stability and severely limits its function as a progenitor of change.

This series of misconceptions, however, is still the ideological and moral base of nearly every institution which now touches on or significantly influences social and sexual life. The portrayal of science by the old order has by now been rendered historically irrelevant and morally suspect. There is, therefore, no denying that simply to do sex research, however innocuous and uncontroversial the behavior in question turns out to be, is to engage in a far-reaching and profound moral struggle for the promulgation and promotion of one set of sexual attitudes as opposed to another, one set based on rational analysis, controlled inquiry, and scientific methodology, and another based on religious myth, social prejudice, and any man's fancy for the truth. The decisive difference, if we may reiterate a lesson from C. S. Peirce, is not in the content of a given truth but in the method used to establish it. One is open, one is closed.

Closed minds produce closed methodologies which, in the contemporary world, are the cornerstones of closed philosophical and social systems, not to mention closed marriages. The implications of a highly developed social science of sexuality are ideologically threatening as a matter of course to individuals, groups, and even classes of persons who are shifting mental and emotional gears from one orientation and level of consciousness to another. New elements of ambiguity and uncertainty pervade one's private decision space. Where once there were warm presumptions and comforting, if inhibiting, legends validated by the presence of the Almighty and His pious earthly henchmen, one is now confronted with the empty existential space of personal choice. Where once there were answers, now there are many questions.

Some of these questions are addressed in the course of these articles, which represent but a bare beginning in the study of the sexual variations in contemporary marriage. It is a beginning, however, full of promise if the obstacles and impediments to such research can be transcended successfully and if the knowledge thus gained is distributed widely and received without undue prejudice and fear.

James R. Smith and Lynn G. Smith
Berkeley, California

Self-Actualization Laboratory
Research Division
Berkeley, California

References

Ackerman, N. et al. 1972. *Marriage: For and Against*. New York: Hart.

Bartell, G. D. 1971. *Group Sex: A Scientist's Eyewitness Report on the American Way of Swinging*. New York: Peter H. Wyden.

Becker, H. S. 1963. *Outsiders: Studies in the Sociology of Deviance*. New York: Free Press.

Campbell, J. (ed.). 1971. *The Portable Jung*. New York: Viking Press.

Comfort, A. 1966. *Sex in Society*. New York: Citadel.

Comfort, A. (ed.). 1972. *Joy of Sex*. New York: Crown.

DeMartino, M. F. (ed.). 1966. *Sexual Behavior and Personality Characteristics*. New York: Grove Press.

Ellis, A. 1965. *Sex without guilt*. New York: Lyle Stuart and Grove Press.

Ellis, H. 1957. The Future of Marriage. In *Sex and Marriage*, ed. H. Ellis. New York: Pyramid Books.

Ford, C. S., and Beach, F. A. 1951. *Patterns of Sexual Behavior*. New York: Ace.

Gagnon, J. H., and Simon, W. (eds.). 1969. *The Sexual Scene*. Chicago: Aldine.

Gerber, E. W. (ed.). 1972. *Sport and the Body: A Philosophical Symposium*. Philadelphia: Lea & Febiger.

Gilder, G. 1973. *Sexual Suicide*. New York: Quadrangle.

Greer, G. 1973. Seduction is a Four Letter Word. *Playboy*, January.

Henslin, J. M. (ed.). 1971. *Studies in the Sociology of Sex*. New York: Appleton-Century-Crofts.

Hicks, M. W., and Platt, M. 1970. Marital Happiness and Stability: A Review of the Research in the Sixties. *J. Marriage Fam.* 32:553–74.

Himelhoch, J., and Fava, S. (eds.). 1955. *Sexual Behavior in American Society*. New York: W. W. Norton & Company.

Huizinga, J. 1955. *Homo Ludens: A Study of the Play Element in Culture*. Boston: Beacon.

Kuhn, T. 1962. *The Structure of Scientific Revolutions*. Chicago: University of Chicago Press.

Levinger, G. 1966. Sources of Marital Dissatisfaction among Applicants for Divorce. *Amer. J. Orthopsych.* 36:803–7.

Lindsey, B. B., and Evans, W. 1927. *The Companionate Marriage*. New York: Boni and Liveright.

Maslow, A. H. 1954. *Motivation and Personality*. New York: Harper.

Maslow, A. H. 1971. *The Farther Reaches of Human Nature*. New York: Viking.

Neubeck, G. (ed.). 1969. *Extramarital Relations*. Englewood Cliffs, N.J.: Prentice-Hall.

O'Neill, G., and O'Neill, N. 1970. Patterns in Group Sexual Activity. *J. Sex Res.* 6, no. 2, pp. 101–12.

O'Neill, N., and O'Neill, G. 1972. *Open Marriage: A New Life Style for Couples.* New York: Evans.

Otto, H. A., and Otto, R. (eds.). 1972. *Total Sex.* New York: Peter H. Wyden.

Reich, W. 1962. *The Sexual Revolution: Toward a Self-Governing Character Structure.* 4th ed. New York: Noonday.

Russell, B. 1966. *Marriage and Morals.* New York: Bantam Books.

Santayana, G. 1961. *Sense of Beauty.* New York: Macmillan.

Schupp, C. E. 1970. An Analysis of Some Social-Psychological Factors Which Operate in the Functioning Relationship of Married Couples Who Exchange Mates for the Purpose of Sexual Experience. Ph. D. dissertation, United States International University.

Smith, J. R., and Smith, L. G. *Consenting Adults: An Exploratory Study of the Sexual Freedom Movement* (in preparation).

Sorokin, P. A. 1956. *The American Sex Revolution.* Boston: Porter Sargent.

Stephenson, W. 1967. *The Play Theory of Mass Communication.* Chicago: University of Chicago Press.

Sussman, M. B., and Cogswell, B. E. 1972. The Meaning of Variant and Experimental Marriage Styles and Family Forms in the 1970's. *Fam. Coordinator.* (October 1972): 375–81.

Symonds, C. 1968. Pilot Study of the Peripheral Behavior of Sexual Mate Swappers. Master's thesis, University of California, Riverside.

Wood, F. C., Jr. 1968. *Sex and the New Morality.* New York: Association Press.

Zubin, J., and Money, J. (eds.). 1973. *Contemporary Sexual Behavior: Critical Issues in the 1970's.* Baltimore: The Johns Hopkins University Press.

part one

Preliminary Analysis:
Orientations
and Perspectives

Sexuality in a Zero Growth Society

Alex Comfort

We are on the verge, in developed countries, of a society in which zero population growth will be an overriding social objective. Few people will have more than two children, and many will have none. By the mid-2000s people will probably live and remain vigorous longer through the control of natural aging. It will be a new game with different rules. The concept of the family which will alter—and is already altering—is that which folklore still maintains as our ideal expectation —the exclusive, totally self-sufficient couple relationship, involving the ideal surrender of identity and of personal selfhood, which excluded kin and only grudgingly included children. The expectation, implied in so many novels and films, was in fact only rarely fulfilled. Unlike the older pattern, where there were other and supporting satisfactions besides each other's company, it was often a neurotic expectation. Young people today see this and, without diminishing their capacity for love, shy away from the idea of total self-surrender: "I am I and you are you, and neither of us is in this world to live up to the other's expectations. . . . I love you, but in forty years we may be different people." This view, if not romantic, is at least realistic in terms of human experience.

Reprinted, with permission, from the December 1972 issue of the *Center Report*, a publication of the Center for the Study of Democratic Institutions in Santa Barbara, California.

Yet another change is that contraception has for the first time wholly separated the three human uses of sex—sex as parenthood, sex as total intimacy between two people ("relational" sex), and sex as physical play ("recreational" sex). "Morals," in their usual and sexual meaning, reflect in rules the culture's image of what the family should be. Religion, which in our culture traditionally rejects pleasure as a motive, has tried hard to fence in the use of recreational sex. Until lately it did this by asserting that reproduction was the only legitimate use of sexuality. With the growth of the image of the ideal couple, it changed its ground, rather behind the event, so that today, together with many of its later successors in psychiatry and counseling, it asserts that worthy sex can only be relational. There has been no time in human history when either of these valuations was wholly true, though they have served in their time to reinforce the uses which that time made of the family. Even in the most strongly kin-based cultures, gaps were left for sexual activity which was not an expression either of a wish for children or of an all-embracing personal relationship. Such gaps concerned chiefly the male, who was often the legislator and who claimed the right to experience sexual relations in a nonrelational way, while excluding women from doing so, either by moral codes, or by the indoctrination of girls with the idea that relational sex is the sole kind of which women, as opposed to men, are capable.

The Pill has altered that. Secure from unwanted pregnancy, an increasing number of women have discovered that their capacity to experience sex at all three levels, either together or on different occasions and in different contexts, is as great as a man's, if not greater. The adult of today has all three options—sex as parenthood, sex as total relationship, and sex as physical pleasure accompanied by no more than affection. Older people looking at the young today realize increasingly how much the confusion between these modes, which they could not foresee or even choose voluntarily between, has often complicated their lives: when play between girl and boy resulted in pregnancy and a forced marriage between mere acquaintances, when one partner misread the other's degree of involvement or falsified his own selfishly to overcome reluctance.

Greater choice can bring greater problems and greater opportunities. It will bring problems in any event, and these can only be reduced by recognizing how great the range of situations is in which sex relations now take place and by learning to handle them to meet our own and our partner's needs. If we can do this, then the new freedom, though it now seems to be generating confusion, could reshape our living to meet the needs which were once met by the traditional human family pattern. We have dispensed with kin—to support us in life and look after us in old age. Consequently, we are lonely, and we go to "sensitivity groups" to relearn how to treat people as people. The fantasy-concept of total one-to-one sufficiency has let us down. Since sex is now divorced from parenthood, there are many more relationships into which it can enter if we choose.

All that can be certainly predicted for the future is that the variety of patterns will increase as individuals find the norm that suits them. For some, parenthood will still be the central satisfaction, carrying with it the obligation of giving the children the stability they require. For others, sexuality will express total involvement with one person. For others, one or more primary relationships will be central but will not exclude others in which the recreational role of sex will act as a source of bonding to supply the range of relationships formerly met by kin —an old human pattern in which sexual contacts were permitted between a woman and all her husband's clan brothers or a man and all his wife's titular sisters.

In the zero-population-growth world we are all "clan brothers" and will have to find ways of expressing the hippy ideal of universal kinship. For many of the young today, a wider range of permitted sexual relationships seems to express this ideal, and even the rather compulsive wife-swapping of middle-aged couples in urban America seems to be reaching toward the same solution. What is clear is that we cannot reimpose the old rigidities. In going forward to newer and more varied patterns, our sense of responsibility and our awareness of others is going to be severely tested if we are not to become still more confused and unhappy. If we pass the test, we may evolve into a universal human family in which all three types of sex have their places, in which we are all genuinely kin, and in which all but the most unrealistic inner needs can be met in one form or another.

Conventional morals are probably correct in asserting that all satisfactory sex is in some degree inherently relational—if it is satisfactory, and mutually so, a relation subsists. Only the wholly insensitive mate mechanically, even under the conditions of permitted nondiscrimination which characterize a ritualized orgy. A society like ours, which has traditionally feared and rejected close personal contact, has also generated a mythology of all-or-none involvement which profoundly influences us to our hurt. Unable to exclude the recreational and the partly relational modes of sex, it has set about rejecting or falsifying them. Once rid of this ideology, it might find that the relation present in purely recreational or social sex is a uniquely effective tool in breaking down personal separateness—of which the proprietary notion of love is an offshoot—so that, for us as for many primitives, social sex comes to express and cement the equivalent of kinship through a general intimacy and nondefensiveness, reinforced by the very strong reward of realizing suppressed needs for variety and for acceptance.

Our society has moved illogically in this direction by virtually institutionalizing adultery: a growing number of spouses permit each other complete sexual liberty on the conditions that there shall be no "involvement" and that the extracurricular relations are not brought to their attention. It is beginning to institutionalize ritual spouse exchange. This is more honest, and a better bet anthropologically; noninvolvement is, as it were, written in, the exchange is nonsecret, and the partners, instead of excluding each other, share in the arrangement. How far conventional middle-class "swingers" profit emotionally in openness from their swinging is arguable—most studies suggest that they keep it in a watertight compartment and ritualize it as a sort of charismatic hobby or secret society, which embodies all current prejudices and does little to create any universal openness. At least, however, it marks the end, or the beginning of the end, of proprietary sexual attitudes. In part it has spread to the middle-aged from the young; older couples want to imitate their freedom without abandoning present attitudes. Unless the result disturbs children and leads to a backlash generation, the genuine insight present in "swinging" by the bored and the unrealized could expand into something far more like institutionalized sociosexual openness.

This process, so far as it has gone, would have been impossible without a gradual change in attitudes toward, and anxiety about, bisexuality. Mate-sharing, both psychoanalytically and in primate ethology, reveals a surrogate sexual relation between males—expressed covertly so far in the gang night out and the attraction of the prostitute or "shared" woman, acceptable substitutes for overt male-male contacts because they are covert. The potential for more open bisexual contacts is greatly increased by two-couple activity. Men tend still to be disturbed by this, but women, who are in general less anxious about their bisexual potential, often embrace the opportunity with male encouragement. In fact, judging from primates, the state of sharing with another male, which reinforces individual dominance, could well help rather than hinder the heterosexuality of anxious people—dominance anxiety plays a large part in the suppression of heterosexual drives in most persons who regard themselves as constitutionally homosexual. Besides reinstating the kinship of men and women, a wider and opener use of sexuality is quite likely to reinstate, and reinforce, the kinship between men and men, which we now studiously avoid erotizing or expressing. In a fully erotized society, bisexuality, expressed or not, could cease to be a problem simply because social attitudes have changed.

Another important casualty of this process is likely to be sexual jealousy. Much argument has been devoted to discussing how far jealousy is a normal emotion, the counterpart of love, and how far it is a product of indoctrination. It would probably be true to say that, in the traditional family, jealousy was based on reproduction (knowing that my children are mine) and ideas of property, while in the romantic couple situation it is a product of the fear of rejection implicit in a surrender so alarmingly total. Modern attempts to transcend jealousy through wife-exchange or greater tolerance of affairs are often uncertain and anxious, but they have positive features—acceptance of a more realistic view of the needs of couples and individuals for variety, and recognition that the meeting of needs rather than their frustration is a gift which expresses love rather than devalues it and strengthens the primary bond. (One need not be like the mischievous lovers of "*Les Liaisons Dangereuses*" to recognize this.) Such a recognition is important as marking the end of the mutual proprietorship, physical or emotional, which has so often characterized human sexual relationships in the past and which modern woman, as well as modern man, rightly rejects as neurotic and immature. To our grandchildren, nineteenth-century opera may be emotionally unintelligible.

Some will feel that the use of wider sex as a substitute for kinship devalues love and will leave us emotionally shallow. Others will see it as the defusing of a dangerous fantasy concerning the total nature of human love, which no society has enacted in fact or found satisfactory in the enactment but which the folklore of the postkinship family has wished on us to our hurt. The relationships of the zero growth society will have to be relationships between whole, adult people, dependent on their own resources, not using kin, family, and children as boltholes or one another as climbingposts; but if this kind of adulthood can be attained at all widely (it will never be practicable for all), it could lead to relations far more supportive in a truly human sense than any we have so far known. Certainly none of the past fictions embodied in our stereotypes of male and female sex roles, of totally exclusive love, or even of central parenthood can readily persist unaltered.

We are not here talking about change which we can further or prevent, simply about changes which are now taking place. If we approach them on the basis of anxiety, past expectation, and folklore, they will only generate more of the anomie which we have now. The alternative is to see whether we can approach them with insight and compassion for one another.

Extension of survival into old age has already led to the concept of "two lifespans," with a second, adolescence-like identity crisis around the age of 40, when realized and unrealized goals are reassessed: the crisis may end in a resumption of established relationships, illness or depression, or a total recasting of relationships. The crisis is more prominent in men—their societal opportunity for a "new start," occupationally and sexually, is the greater—and it often leads to the starting of a second family with a younger partner. Women's opportunities are more cruelly circumscribed at this age—they tend to find themselves deserted, having "run out of" family and an established role. Any further extension of vigorous life through interference with aging might put them on a more equal footing with men; it will certainly increase the tendency for life-styles, and families, to be serial, so that each individual has the option of continuing in one pattern or of entering a wholly different one at the age when in the traditional family one was preparing for dependent senescence. The decline of the kinship family has borne excessively hard on the old—dependency is rejected, and they become increasingly isolated in a forced "independence" which is worsened by the shortage of kin. Perhaps more than anyone they would benefit from a "spreading" of the couple-preoccupied family into something more like a tribe of friends.

I would expect accordingly to see a society in which pair relationships are still central, but initially less permanent, in which childbearing is seen as a special responsibility involving a special life-style, and in which settled couples engage openly in a wide range of sexual relations with friends, with other couples, and with third parties as an expression of social intimacy, without prejudice to the primacy of their own relationship and with no more, and probably less, permanent interchange than we see in the society of serial polygamy with adultery that now exists. Such a pattern is coming into existence in America and is beginning to become explicit. Whether it will devalue relationships or only deprive them of neurotic compulsion will depend on the persons involved, the amount of support they receive from the social ethic, and the accuracy of the expectations with which they enter maturity. If these expectations become realistic, it will be the first time that a modern generation has been reared with confidence but without illusions.

The political implications of universalized kinship are interesting. Marcuse, in discussing the "erotization of relationships" as a political force, was once challenged to "go erotize the state of Kansas." My suggestion is that this may in fact be happening. The family is in fact the microcosm of politics with a one- to two-generation timelag. Institutional politics today reflects combative paternalism, which had its family counterpart in the 1850s, and liberal politics, the social expression of the ideal of individualist romantic love. It is possible to overstate the inherently revolutionary potential of "universal kinship," but if, as I suggest, it is explicitly erotized, it will find a counterpart socially in an anarchic community action. How far it produces such action, and how far the nonpossessive individual and the antiauthoritarian society are products of the same change in social requirement, is hard to say. The acceptance of sensuality, and the widening of its focus to include not one but many others, would seem in itself to be an emotional technology capable of fitting well into the less compulsive and more gentle world view of the twenty-first as against the nineteenth and twentieth centuries. Marcuse is probably right in seeing justice, nonpossession, nonexploitation, ecology, and the wider erotization of relationships as possible correlates. We may have a rough few years ahead before this pattern emerges, but when and if it does, one could wish to live in those times.

Open Marriage:
The Conceptual Framework

Nena O'Neill and George O'Neill

In the wake of increasing dissatisfaction with the prevailing pattern of traditional monogamous marriage and the vague but general discontent with our impersonal and fragmented existence, a number of alternative marriage styles have begun to emerge. These experimentations vary from those involving more than three persons in the basic pattern—including group marriage, communal life-styles, and polygamous patterns (more often triadic and more often polygynous than polyandrous)—to modifications in the basic one-to-one monogamous configuration. The latter group may be divided into those which are nonmarriage relationships (still monogamous but extralegal) and those which represent innovations, changes, deletions, and additions to the standard expectations for those legally married. These modifications may include such items as separate domiciles, extramarital sexual relations in group or partner-exchange contexts, and reversal of traditional role patterns (i.e., woman provides, man housekeeps). None of these patterns is particularly new in transcultural contexts since all have occurred elsewhere in other societies at one time or another. However, their proliferation and the motives which have impelled men and women in our society increasingly to seek innovations in our marriage style deserve closer scrutiny.

An abbreviated version of this paper appears in *Fam. Coordinator* 21 (October 1972): 403–10.

It is not enough to say that we live in a pluralistic society and that these alternate patterns for marriage have appeared in response to the changes in our society and the development of different life-styles. Even though one can foresee a future in which there will be a range of marriage patterns to choose from, the questions still remain: Why have so many experimental forms appeared? And more important, what are the personal motivations for seeking these innovative styles? Compendiums of sociological explanations have seemed somehow to pass over the personal dimensions involved. Yet these questions are exceedingly important for the future, especially since that future will affect our styles of child-rearing and thus the perpetuation of those values we deem most humanistic and worthy of saving. Even if experimental family forms are excluded, Sussman (1971) has pointed out that some children already live in variant forms of the traditional nuclear family during their formative stages. Under these conditions some changes in our value system are to be expected. The questions are, Which values and how many changes?

With the above questions in mind we began to explore contemporary marriage in 1967. During the four years of our research we interviewed approximately four hundred persons. Our informant-respondents were seventeen to seventy-five years of age and urban and suburban middle class in orientation and occupation; approximately 75% were married or had been married. Thirty interviews, both formal and informal, with professional therapists and marriage counselors supplemented these data. The interviews included individual and couple in-depth sessions and short mini-interviews in a variety of social settings. While some topical and background questions were used (i.e., "What is your age, occupation, marital status, etc.?" and "What do you think the ingredients of a good marriage are?"), the interviews were primarily open-ended and exploratory in nature, focusing on eliciting information through face-to-face encounters about values, feelings, and attitudes toward marriage and what changes were perceived as necessary for improvement.

Our interviews began first with those who were involved in experimental structures and in the greatest variations from the norm in traditional marriage. We felt that these innovators would have greater insight because they had already opted for change and would perhaps be more articulate and perceptive about why they had chosen change. We then moved on to the divorced, the nonmarrieds,[1] the singles, the

---

[1] The term "nonmarrieds" applies to those relationships which involve some commitment but which are not legalized. They can range in time from a few

young, and both those who were disillusioned and those who were
contented with traditional monogamous marriage. As research was
carried out in a primarily middle-class settting, Cuber and Harroff's
(1965) delineations of types of marriage relationships (i.e., conflict-
habituated, devitalized, passive-congenial, the vital, and the total)
gained increasing validity. During our research in the anthropological
literature we found that little attention had been given to the interpersonal dimensions of marriage or to the interrelation of the intrapsychic
and ideological aspects of marriage. However, we did feel that the
anthropological perspective gave a holistic approach to the problems of
contemporary marriage that we considered valuable. In fact, one of
the major causes of confusion for many married couples was the per-
sistence of traditional cultural ideologies and prescriptions for marriage behavior in the face of changing needs, changing value orientations, and changing behavior in marriage.

The Problem

As our exploratory insights to the problems evolved, we became
increasingly convinced that the central problem in contemporary marriage was relationship. The attempt to solve the problem by moving
into group and communal situations did not seem to mitigate the problems we discovered in interpersonal relationship. With the breakdown
of many external supports for traditional marriage, the pressures on the
interpersonal husband-and-wife relationship became intensified. There
was an increasing need for that relationship to provide more fulfillment
and benefits on both a personal and interpersonal level. Problems in

---

months to a lifetime. The participants can be never-marrieds, formerly-marrieds,
those still married but separated, or any combination thereof. The difficulties in
comprehensive terminology for emerging relationships of varying degrees of
commitment are apparent. "Premarital" is an accurate term for only a portion of
these relationships since some never intend to marry the nonmarriage partner
or the relationship is frequently considered only a temporary plateau before each
has the sustaining personal resources to move on to another level (possibly marriage) or another relationship. The word "cohabitation" is also misleading as a
coverall term for these relationships. Since cohabitation implies both a shared
domicile and sex without legal marriage, it did not apply to some relationships
encountered, e.g., a couple who did not share a domicile but did form a cohesive unit insofar as they shared all their spare time, vacations, and sex and
presented themselves as a couple in social situations. Therefore, the term "nonmarrieds" is suggested.

marriage were manifested by the inability of the majority of individuals to find in the marital relationship both intimacy and opportunity for developing their personal potential. Our understanding of the problem concluded in addition that

1) marital partners and those contemplating marriage expressed a need for intimacy and growth in a relationship where they could actualize their individual potential without destroying the relationship.

2) most people did not have the skills in relating and in communicating which would allow for growth in a noncritical atmosphere. The typical dyadic marital role relationships had already been precut for them, locking them into a negative involuted feedback system. This was their perception of their situation as well, although not with the same terminology.

3) many of the innovations and experimental forms, although not all of them, nor all of the people involved in them, were a reflection and indication of this lack of skills in interpersonal relations.

4) other important impediments to growth were the unrealistic expectations and myths stemming from the traditional marriage format of the past, overriding emotional dependencies, and possessive jealousy.

As observers and researchers we had two options available to us: (1) reporting the alternate marriage and relationship styles with their attendant disillusionments and problems or (2) choosing a less orthodox path in utilizing our research. The presentation and analysis of data may benefit policy makers, academicians, and the counseling professions, but such analysis offers little to the individual in the way of ameliorating the problems he faces. Despite the fact that some have already opted for change on an individual basis or in group contexts, the bulk of the population remains, along with the innovators, unaware of the problem in its larger cultural and anthropological framework. Therefore, we chose to utilize our research in another manner.

The Action Model

The concept of open marriage, which is outlined elsewhere in detail (O'Neill and O'Neill 1972), is primarily based on the expression of desires for change and the perceived routes to change drawn from our interviews conducted over a period of four years and upon our observations of actual changes taking place in many relationships. The research we conducted was utilized to create a model for change. In so doing we have stepped beyond the role of objective researcher reporting data and findings into the realm of what can be termed "action anthropology." By this we mean delineating a model for change that places the problem areas in their present and past cultural contexts and presents various available options for change in marital behavior and attitudes. An attempt has been made to present the traditional marital configuration in its societal setting and to delineate the cultural imperatives and values implicit in these imperatives for examination by those involved in marriage relationships. The first purpose, then, was to make it possible for individuals to become aware of the idealized precepts of the institution of marriage and the forces influencing their attitude toward and their behavior in marriage. Without an awareness of former expectations and present conditions, they cannot perceive the pathways to change. It is to be fully understood that some will choose to remain within traditional marriage, where the perimeters and dimensions are defined for them by the norms. But for those who feel a need for change, awareness and insight are necessary first steps to determining or discovering what pathways are available. The second objective was to outline those options for change in marital interaction which we had found in our research.

Action anthropology, defined elsewhere in traditional anthropological contexts by Peattie (1970) and Piddington (1970), is a variation on the theme of action research. In the past, action research (Festinger and Katz 1953; Selltiz et al. 1963) has been directed toward finding solutions to organizational or social problems. The flow has been from the institutional level down to the individual in effecting change. More recently it has been recognized that individuals can initiate measures for change and thus reverse the flow to effect change on the institutional level. Weinberg (1970) has noted that we are a problem-solving, action-oriented society; he continues:

On this action level, society and the person are both symbolic systems with varying capacities for solving problems. Both society and the person can respond to problems in terms of their knowledge and their capacity for decision making and executive knowledge. Both can communicate, plan, and implement programs to solve problems. . . . The individual deliberates about alternatives before selecting a problem-solving response.

Today, the orientation toward methods of change must begin with the individual. The need for a measure of self-determination is paramount. Yet the individual is frequently overlooked as a primary force for change, and the assumption is made that his behavior is shaped by impinging social forces in the environment and that he neither has sufficient knowledge and perspective to perceive these forces nor is adequately equipped to institute directive and self-motivated change. This attitude underestimates the individual. Our sample encompassed a broad range of middle-class informant-respondents. The majority expressed a desire for some feeling of self-determination and autonomy in their lives and marriage behavior. Many had already instituted it. Furthermore, most had a knowledge of what the problem areas were in marriage. We offer one quote from an interview with a twenty-three-year-old single woman, who was at that time in a nonmarriage relationship with a young man and seriously contemplating marriage:

I don't want to say yes, yes we are going to be in love forever. It's like saying, yes, yes you know the ocean—and the next wave is going to look like this one, but I *can* say it is worth the risk *if* I feel I can do something about it. I want to be understanding, and start out with the attitude of well, it ain't going to be bliss but if I do my homework I stand a very good chance, and knowing what the chances are and stepping into it with your eyes open, you got a chance of making your marriage work . . . and there is a lot more homework to do today because people have to make decisions they never had to make before in marriage, but those marriages will be better for it. . . . It's not I'm doing this because I've got to do it, it's doing this because I *chose* to do it, and that's what it is, man is a thinking animal, therefore I am. Once you get down to this kind of foundation and you can build, you know, "well begun is half done."

While our model is directed to the individual, we are well aware that many structural and institutional changes must of necessity also occur.

The Open Marriage Model

Open marriage is presented as a model with a twofold purpose:
1) to provide insights for individuals concerning the past patterns of traditional marriage, which we have termed *closed marriage*. As a closed systems model, traditional marriage was perceived as presenting few options for choice or change.
2) to provide guidelines, based on an open systems model, for developing an intimate marital relationship that provides for growth for both partners in the context of a one-to-one relationship. This does imply some degree of mutuality. It does not imply that growth will always be bilateral but rather that there will be supportive assistance and tolerance during unilateral growth. Shos-

trom and Kavanaugh (1971) have delineated a rhythmic relationship which exemplifies this pattern.

The guidelines have been designed in answer to the needs expressed by the majority of our informant-respondents for a relationship which could offer them more dimensions for growth together than either could attain singly. The principle through which this mutually augmenting growth occurs is *synergy*. Many couples found that this synergistic self-actualizing mode of relating became possible only through the revision and deletion of some of the unrealistic expectations of closed marriage.

Open marriage thus can be defined as a relationship in which the partners are committed to their own and to each other's growth. It is an honest and open relationship of intimacy and self-disclosure based on the equal freedom and identity of both partners. Supportive caring and increasing security in individual identities make possible the sharing of self-growth with a meaningful other who encourages and anticipates his own and his mate's growth. It is a relationship that is flexible enough to allow for change and that is constantly being renegotiated in the light of changing needs, consensus in decision-making, acceptance and encouragement of individual growth, and openness to new possibilities *for* growth. Obviously, following this model often involves a departure, sometimes radical, from rigid conformity to the established husband-wife roles and is not easy to effect.

In brief, the guidelines are: living for now, realistic expectations, privacy, role flexibility, open and honest communication, open companionship, equality, identity, and trust. The first step requires each partner to reassess the actual or prospective marital relationship in order to clarify and determine both individual and mutual expectations. Couples in today's society are not educated for marriage or in the requisites of a good human relationship, nor are they aware of the psychological and myriad other commitments that the typical marriage contract implies. The expectations of closed marriage—the major one being that one partner will be able to fulfill all of the other's needs (emotional, social, sexual, economic, intellectual, and otherwise)—present obstacles to growth and attitudes that foster conflict between partners. Awareness of these expectations and a realignment more in accord with a realistic appraisal of their capabilities are fundamental to instituting change and to solving their problems in relationship.

Living for now involves relating to the present rather than to the past or to future goals which are frequently materialistic and concrete rather than emotional and intellectual in nature. The granting of time off, or *privacy*, can be used for examination of the self and for psychic regeneration. A way out of what many marital partners conceive of as the role-bind involves working toward a greater *role flexibility* by exchanging roles and role-associated tasks either on a temporary or part-time basis and utilizing role reversal as a device for understanding the self and the position of the other partner. *Open and honest communication* is perhaps the most important element in an open relationship. The lack of communication skills creates a formidable barrier between husband and wife; yet these skills are the most important in sustaining a vital relationship, promoting understanding, and increasing knowledge of self. *Open companionship* involves relating to others, including the opposite sex, outside the primary unit of husband and wife, as an auxiliary avenue for growth. *Equality* involves relating to the mate as a peer in terms of ways to achieve stature rather than in terms of the status attached to the traditional husband and wife roles. *Identity* involves the development of the individual through interaction with his mate and others, through actualizing his own potentials and through building toward autonomy and personal responsibility. *Trust*, growing through the utilization of these other guidelines and based on mutuality and respect for each other's integrity, creates the climate for growth. Liking, sexual intimacy, and love grow through the exercise of these elements.

The system of guidelines for open marriage can be seen as an expanding spiral of evolving steps in complexity and depth in the marital relationship. The model begins with the self and the premise that internal communication is necessary to attain disclosure of inner feelings to one's self and subsequently to one's mate. Once open and honest communication is established with the mate, in addition to feedback from the mate, the partner's relationship can evolve through the guidelines with multilevel feedback reinforcing each phase. The system operates through the principle of synergy, a concept drawn from medicine and chemistry and first utilized by Benedict (Maslow and Honigmann 1970) in cultural, and later by Maslow (1965, 1968) in interpersonal, contexts. In open marriage, the concept of *synergic build-up* is defined as a mutually augmenting growth system. Synergy means that two partners in marriage can accomplish more personal *and* interpersonal growth together than they could separately and without the loss of their individual identities. Synergic build-up is the positive augmenting feedback that can enhance mutual growth and dynamism in the man-woman relationship.

While only a limited few may be able to utilize all these guidelines in their totality and simultaneously, open marriage can best be considered a *resource mosaic* from which couples can draw according to their needs and their readiness for change in any one area.

The majority of our sample had already explored the possibilities for change in some of the areas covered by the guidelines. Many of them required only a change in attitude, while they acknowledged behavioral changes as difficult. The two areas of greatest difficulty were the conflicts arising from changing man-woman and husband-wife roles and the problems encountered in self-development.

The question of marital and extramarital sexual behavior, while ever present, did not seem to be the central problem with which they were coping. While marital sex sometimes posed problems, many felt the emphasis on sexual adjustment, as presented in published manuals and in the media, was exaggerated. Although many felt that they could not cope with sexual jealousy in terms of extramarital sex, they were on the verge of deciding that sex per se was not the central problem in their marriage. Numerous couples had already effected some degree of sexual latitude in their own relationships. Some had done so with tacit knowledge but without verbalized agreement. Others had done so in various types of consensual arrangements, including individual contexts, group sex, and partner exchange. While some benefits were noted for those involved in extramarital relationships which included sex, it was observed that by and large these experiences did not occur in a context where the marital partners were developing their primary marriage relationship sufficiently for this activity to count as a growth experience. Frequently this involvement became an avenue of escape, intensified conflicts, and actually obscured problems in the primary relationship. For some, however, it did become a means of revealing other problem areas in the marriage and for achieving greater understanding.

Underlying the marital couple's explorations into any area of nonconformity, whether it was extramarital sex or the equally important area of changes in typical role behavior (i.e., male-female, man-woman, husband-wife), was the central problem of relationship.[2] That is, How can the marital partners relate in terms of their

[2] Concerning these two areas of change, the authors are least optimistic about the movement into group marriage and communal living situations which involve

changing needs and those of society in a mutually beneficial fashion? Open marriage presents some of the elements in interpersonal relationships that allow for change, for increasing responsibility for the self and for others, and for increased understanding between husband and wife.

Most people enter marriage without preparation for this long-term intimacy and without preparation to meet changes in themselves and in society. Education for the marriage relationship in all its ramifications, from the relational and sexual aspects, through child-rearing, and on to the mature years when the children are grown, is notably absent. Skills for communication,[3] self-discovery, problem-solving, and relating in intimacy can be learned. Such skills do not demand therapy or deep introspection, for knowledge of self will evolve in progression if the skills are learned and if motivation for change follows the insights gained.

The open marriage model offers insights and learning guides for developing more intimate and understanding marital relationships. An open relationship in marriage, as well as in any interpersonal matrix, involves becoming a more open person. Since the open-minded personality is one which can perceive options and alternatives and make decisions about the paths to change (Rokeach 1960), efforts to help the marital couple in perception and skills should increase their ability to solve many problems in marriage. However, it will not be easy for most couples. Emotional maturity, and the

---

random or structured sexual intimacy among many. No true group marriage, as it is being explored in our society with an equal valence of roles and sexual sharing among all partners, has existed, according to the anthropological literature. Among all societies where larger family structures exist, they are maintained by elaborate kinship ties and other supportive structures interwoven with the institutional framework of the society; thus, goals are integrated for the group or extended family. Certainly, communal or community situations where the goals are banding together to share economic, child care or recreational activities have many advantages and, it is hoped, will increase. But when couples and individuals in groups are pressed into situations of total intimacy—including the sexual dimension—for which they have not been prepared emotionally either by training or by conditioning, the strain of the multistranded relationships tends to fragment the group. The goals of cooperation and support are difficult to maintain under the pressure of emotional conflicts which are intensified by prescriptions for sexual intimacy.

[3] An excellent example of a program in which these skills are taught is the four-session format developed by the Minnesota Couples Communications Program.

development of responsibility and confident identity, cannot emerge overnight. But standing still or merely exploring experimental *structural* forms without attention to the interpersonal factors seems to increase the number of problems in marriage and decrease the benefits to be gained from it. Open marriage is not intended to solve marital problems, but by using the open marriage model, the couple will at least be substituting problems which promote growth and learning for problems which are currently insoluble.

Implications

It is in the arena of interpersonal relations that marriage and the family will have to find new meaning and gain greater strength, no matter what the configuration of the sociocultural framework may be. Children cannot be taught the value of supportive love and caring, responsibility, problem-solving, or decision-making skills unless the parents have first developed these qualities in their own relationship. The inadequacy of our organized institutions to instill these values and skills is only too apparent. Therefore, intimate, long-term relationships such as those of marriage and the family must provide them, and to do this, they must be more rewarding and fulfilling for their members and there must be feedback and caring for each other's welfare.

Focusing on the methods for achieving a rewarding one-to-one relationship provides something that individuals can deal with and work with on a self-determining level. By encouraging personal responsibility, self-growth, and bonding through the synergic relationship, the basic unit of husband and wife should become more rewarding and offer more avenues for fulfillment.

Building from within strengthens the individual, the couple, and then the family unit, and thus the entire social structure, since the fundamental unit of society is the family. Whatever form the family unit may take, its strength will still depend on the rewards gained from interpersonal relationships. It is in this sense that the individual, and the married couple, can become not only a fulcrum for change but also a key factor leading to the strengthening of the social structure. Thus both family and society can be better equipped to cope with accelerating technological and cultural change. It is hoped that open families can evolve to an open society and eventually to an open world.

References

Cuber, J. F., and Harroff, P. B. 1965. *Sex and the Significant Americans.* Baltimore, Md.: Penguin Books.

Festinger, L., and Katz, D. 1953. *Research Methods in the Behavioral Sciences.* New York: Holt, Rinehart and Winston.

Maslow, A. H. 1965. *Eupsychian Management.* Homewood, Ill.: Richard D. Irwin, Inc.

————. 1968. Human Potentialities and the Healthy Society. In *Human Potentialities,* ed. Herbert A. Otto. St. Louis, Mo.: Warren H. Green, Inc.

————, and Honigmann, J. J., eds. Synergy: Some Notes of Ruth Benedict, *Amer. Anthropol.* 72 (April 1970): 320–25.

O'Neill, N., and O'Neill, G. 1972. *Open Marriage: A New Life Style for Couples.* New York: M. Evans & Company, Inc.

Peattie, L. R. 1970. The Failure of the Means-End Scheme in Anthropology. In *Applied Anthropology,* ed. James A. Clifton. Boston: Houghton Mifflin.

Piddington, R. 1970. Action Anthropology. In *Applied Anthropology,* ed. James A. Clifton. Boston: Houghton Mifflin.

Rokeach, M. 1960. *The Open and Closed Mind.* New York: Basic Books, Inc.

Selltiz, C.; Jahoda, M.; Deutsch, M.; and Cook, S. W. 1963. *Research Methods in Social Relations.* New York: Holt, Rinehart and Winston.

Shostrom, E., and Kavanaugh, J. 1971. *Between Man and Woman.* Los Angeles: Nash Publishing.

Sussman, M. B. Family Systems in the 1970's: Analysis, Politics, and Programs. *Ann. Amer. Acad. Pol. Soc. Sci.* 396 (July 1971).

Thomlinson, R. 1965. *Sociological Concepts and Research.* New York: Random House.

Weinberg, S. K. 1970. *Social Problems in Modern Urban Society.* Englewood Cliffs, N.J.: Prentice-Hall, Inc.

The Sociology of Mate Swapping: Or the Family that Swings Together Clings Together

Duane Denfeld and Michael Gordon

In the early decades of this century, and to a certain extent still today, social scientists equated deviant behavior with disease and set about to find the cures. The tone of this early perspective is nicely illustrated by the following excerpt:

> The study of social pathology is undertaken not to breed pessimism but to furnish a rational ground for faith in the future of the world. The diseases of society, like the diseases of the human body, are to be studied so that remedies may be found for them where they exist, but most of all, that by a larger wisdom the number of diseases may be reduced to the lowest terms and we may set ourselves to social tasks with the ideal of conquering them altogether (Smith 1911).

So firm a commitment to the extirpation of "social pathology" obviously precluded consideration of any contributions its phenomena might make to the social order.

More recently there has been a reappraisal of the role of deviant behavior in society. Albert Cohen (1959), for one, has admonished his colleagues for equating deviance with social disorganization, and

Reprinted, by permission of the publisher, from *J. Sex Res.* 6, no. 2. The authors would like to thank the scholars who made their work available to us on unusually short notice. The theoretical section of this paper benefited greatly from the comments of Professor Albert K. Cohen.

other sociologists have begun to focus their attention on deviance as a societal process rather than as a social disease. Howard Becker, a leading proponent of this new position, has argued:

We ought not to view it [deviant behavior] as something special, as depraved or in some magical way better than other kinds of behavior. We ought to see it simply as a kind of behavior some disapprove of and others value, studying the processes by which either or both perspectives are built up and maintained (Becker 1963).

Perhaps of greater significance for the viewpoint of this paper are the opinions of the students of deviance who claim that deviance may support, not undermine, social order; among the most eloquent of these is Kai Erikson:

. . . Deviant behavior is not a simple kind of leakage which occurs when the machinery of society is in poor working order, but may be, in controlled quantities, an important condition for preserving the stability of social life. Deviant forms of behavior, by marking the outer edges of group life, give the inner structure its special character and thus supply the framework within which the people of the group develop an orderly sense of their own cultural identity (Erikson 1966).

We shall maintain that only from the perspectives found in the writings of Becker, Erikson, and their associates can the social scientist understand mate swapping and the role it plays in American society.

In this country there has been a tradition of great ideological commitment to the importance of confining sexual behavior in general, but sexual intercourse in particular, to the sanctity of the marital bed. Concomitantly, there has also been a rich history of institutionalized nonmarital sex. One of the foremost historians of colonial family life has noted that "the cases of premarital fornication [in colonial New England] by husband and wife were evidently numerous" (Calhoun 1960). Further, prostitution never appears to have been completely absent from these shores. However, it was not until the second half of the nineteenth century that sexual morality and prostitution especially became a national concern. David Pivar in his history of the Social Purity Movement in the United States claims that

during the nineteenth century many social evils existed, but *the* Social Evil was prostitution.

Prostitution, its development and spread, constituted the primary element in the moral crisis that shook Western civilization in the latter decades of the nineteenth century. A premonition that traditional morality was failing permeated the fabric of American life, and reformers increasingly expressed alarm over a general decay in morality. Religionists and moralists found decay manifestly evident in official life, but most strikingly in the man-woman relationship (Pivar 1965).

Attention to the destructive effects of prostitution did not cease with the coming of the new century, or even with the moral revolutions supposedly wrought by World War I; in a very much milder form it is present still.

Nevertheless, in 1937 Kingsley Davis published a paper that was to cause many social scientists, at least, to reappraise this great "Social Evil." He advanced what has since come to be known as the "safety-valve" model of deviance, developing with great insight and much cogency the idea that

. . . the attempt of society to control sexual expression, to tie it to social requirements, especially the attempt to tie it to the durable relation of marriage and the rearing of children, or to attach men to a celibate order, or to base sexual expression on love, creates the opportunity for prostitution. It is analogous to the black market, which is the illegal but inevitable response to an attempt to fully control the economy. The craving for sexual variety, for perverse satisfaction, for novel and provocative surroundings, for ready and cheap release, for intercourse free from entangling cares and civilized pretense—all can be demanded from the women whose interest lies solely in price (Davis 1966).

A further point implicit in Davis's argument is that since the prostitute by "virtue" of her profession is, for the most part, excluded from the ranks of potential spouses, the risk of romantic involvement which may threaten a man's marriage is greatly reduced.

Let us stop at this point to look more closely at the underlying assumption of this safety-valve model of deviance: a society may provide certain institutionalized outlets for forms of behavior which are condemned by the prevailing legal and/or moral system. This is not to say that in every society all deviants will find some structured way of satisfying their proclivities with minimal danger of running afoul of the law. A good case in point here would be pedophilia. With the virtual disappearance of child brothels, the pedophile must, if he wishes to gratify his need, engage in acts which almost certainly will result in a confrontation with the police; in contrast is the man who frequents houses of prostitution for some unusual form of sexual activity. Therefore, the safety-valve model does not assume that *all* forms of deviant behavior will be provided with outlets but rather that *some* of those forms for which "frustration and discontent may lead to an attack on the rules themselves and on the social institutions they support" (Cohen 1966) will be provided with outlets. So, then, in the case of prostitution (or any other form of deviance), the safety-valve model does not explain why it exists but why it is tolerated: presumably it is supportive of monogamous marriage. It should be emphasized that this idea is best thought of as a hypothesis, not as a law. Interestingly enough, one of the few other convincing applications of the safety-valve model also applies to sexual behavior.

Ned Polsky recently applied Davis's ideas concerning prostitution to pornography and claimed that the latter was a functional alternative to the former:

> In saying that prostitution and pornography are, at least in modern societies, functional alternatives, I mean that they are different roads to the same desired social ends. Both provide for the discharge of what the society labels antisocial sex, i.e., impersonal, nonmarital sex: prostitution provides this via real intercourse with a real sex object, and pornography provides it via masturbatory, imagined intercourse with a fantasy object (Polsky 1967).

He places particular emphasis on a point which Davis mentions but does not elaborate, viz., that prostitution and pornography cater to a considerable amount of what, in the parlance of the prostitute, is known as "kinky" sex—oral, anal, masochistic, fetishistic, etc. To this extent, pornography, more than prostitution, provides a safety valve for those sexual inclinations for which no institutionalized behavioral outlets exist, e.g., pedophilia, which we have already mentioned.

In both the Davis and Polsky papers the focus is almost exclusively, if not exclusively, on male nonmarital sex. Males prostituting themselves for females has never been common, perhaps merely because, apart from their economic positions, males are constitutionally less suited for frequent and prolonged intercourse. Drawing largely on the Kinsey studies, Polsky argues that pornography is largely produced for, and consumed by, males. Kinsey found that relatively few women are aroused by pornography and even fewer use it as grist for the masturbatory fantasy mill (Kinsey et al. 1953). While no reliable systematic data are available, there is some indication that at least one form of pornography, the "stag" film, is migrating from the fraternity house and VFW lodges—though not abandoning them altogether—to the suburban home, i.e., it is now being viewed by heterosexual audiences (Knight and Alpert 1967). A replication now of the section of the Kinsey study dealing with female response to pornography might yield some surprising results.

If, in fact, pornography is now becoming more of a heterosexual item—and we must emphasize again that this is by no means documented—it provides support for the main argument of this paper: mate swapping (we will use the terms "mate swapping" and "swinging" synonymously) is an outgrowth of the dramatic changes that have taken place in this century in the position of women in American society and, more crucially, changes that have taken place in the conceptions of female sexuality and female sexual rights. While the contention that women are now seeing and enjoying pornography more than was so previously cannot be proved, there is no lack of documentation for the larger changes noted above. Evidence can be found both in the realm of sexual ideology and behavior.

One of the most vivid indicators of the degree to which American women have come into their own sexually since 1900 is the marriage manual. Michael Gordon (1972) has recently completed an extensive study of American marital education literature for the period 1830 to 1940. Perhaps the most striking finding to emerge from his work is that the transformation in the prevailing conception of female sexuality, and marital sex in general, took place in the first four decades of this century. The following passage is based on the Gordon article.

Throughout most of the nineteenth century the commonly held attitude toward sexual intercourse was that it was, unhappily, required for the perpetuation of the species. Not only was it an unfortunate necessity, but a dangerous one at that. Frequent indulgence by the male in the pleasures of the flesh could lead to an enervating loss of the "vital fluids" contained in the sperm; for the female it could result in nervous and constitutional disorders. In short, sex was a seriously debilitating business. As the century drew to a close we begin to get rumblings of acceptance of marital sex as something which, apart from its procreative function, was beneficial to the marriage, but such views are very much in the minority even in the 1890s.

With the first decade of the twentieth century, however, and reaching—if the reader will pardon the expression—its climax in the 1930s, there is a growing belief not only in the fact that women experience sexual desire (which in its own way is held to be as strong as that of men) but also that this desire should be satisfied, most appropriately in intercourse resulting in simultaneous orgasm. What we observe in these decades, then, is sex moving, ideologically, from an act whose prime purpose is procreation to one whose prime purpose is recreation, a shift which has been commented on by others (Foote 1948; Sprey 1969). Because this development has been extensively documented in the article by Gordon, there is no need to explore it further. Let it suffice to say that by 1930 the concern with marital sex, its "artistry" and technique, has reached such proportions as to allow characterization of the authors of marriage manuals of the time as proponents of a "cult of mutual orgasm."

The increasing acceptance of the pleasures of marital sex seems to have had an impact on a number of areas relevant to the theme of this paper; possibly the most important of these is prostitution. To the best of our knowledge there are no data available which support the contention that since 1900 prostitution has been a declining profession. However, it has been claimed (Kinsie 1967) that there has been a reduction in the number of brothels in American cities; furthermore, there is good evidence on which to base the opinion that premarital intercourse with prostitutes is declining:

The frequencies of premarital sexual relations with prostitutes are more or less constantly lower in the younger generations of all educational levels. . . . In most cases the average frequencies of intercourse with prostitutes are down to two-thirds or even one-half of what they were in the generation that was most active 22 years ago (Kinsey et al. 1948).

This, it could be reasoned, may well be related to a finding reported in the second Kinsey volume:

Among the females in the sample who were born before 1900, less than half as many had had the pre-marital coitus as among the females born in any subsequent decade. . . . For instance, among those who were still unmarried by age twenty-five, 14 per cent of the older generation had had coitus, and 36 per cent of those born in the next decade. This increase in the incidence of premarital coitus, and the similar increase in the incidence of premarital petting, constitute the greatest changes which we have found between the patterns of sexual behavior in the older and younger generations of American females (Kinsey et al. 1953).

It should be noted by way of qualification that Kinsey also found that most women who did have premarital intercourse had it exclusively with the men they eventually married. These two phenomena

—the decreasing amount of premarital contact with prostitutes for males and the increasing amount of premarital sex for women—give credence to our argument that the acceptance of female sexuality and the pleasures of marital sex has grown in this century. It is unusual now to find a man saying he has intercourse with prostitutes because his idealized wife-mother image of his spouse prevents him from carrying out the act with her (Winick 1962). Furthermore, there are also attitudinal data on the breakdown of the double standard in this country (Reiss 1967).

It is implicit in our thesis that shifts in attitudes toward female sexuality, premarital sex, and especially, marital sex, which we have been discussing, are crucial to the understanding of mate swapping as an institutionalized form of extramarital sex. Another factor which has undoubtedly also made a contribution to the development of mate swapping, or at least has facilitated its growth, is the revolution in contraceptive techniques that has occurred in the past decade. A study done in 1960, based on a national probability sample, found the following order of frequency for contraceptive techniques: condom, 50%; diaphragm, 38%; rhythm, 35%; douche, 24%; withdrawal, 17%; and others in small percentages. (The total exceeds 100% because many couples used more than one method [Whelpton, Campbell, and Patterson 1966].) Similar studies are yet to be made for the last years of the 1960s, but some comparative data are available. Tietze (1968) estimated that as of mid-1967 there were six and one-half million women in this country on the pill and somewhere between one and two million using the IUD. A recent Gallup poll estimated that eight and one-half million American women were on the pill (*Newsweek*, February 9, 1970). Figures such as these allow us to estimate that about 10% of the fecund American women take the pill and another 1% use the IUD.

The emergence of chemical and intrauterine birth control methods is of significance on several counts. First, they are considerably more reliable than the previously available techniques and thus, one would assume, dramatically reduce anxiety over unwanted pregnancy. Second, and the importance of this cannot be minimized, they separate the act of prevention from the act of sex. While the new methods insure against pregnancy resulting from failure to take contraceptive measures in the heat of spontaneous passion, they also improve what could be termed the aesthetics of sex, i.e., there need be no hasty retreat to insert a diaphragm or roll on a "safe" (to use an antiquated but charming term). All in all, then, the new contraceptives allow sex to be indulged in with less apprehension and more pleasure.

We shall now try to summarize and more explicitly state the argument contained in what we have written up to this point. The current conception of female sexuality as legitimate and gratifying coupled with enlarged opportunities for women to pursue sex without unwanted pregnancies is likely to have greatly increased the incentive for women to seek—as men have always done—sexual variety outside marriage. Among the available ways for both husbands *and* wives to find such variety, mate swapping is the least threatening and the one most compatible with monogamy.

Of the alternatives to mate swapping, the one which comes to mind immediately is what might be called "bilateral prostitution" (a term suggested to us by Albert Cohen). We have already pointed out that constitutionally males seem less suited than females for prostitution, although there may be some homosexual hustlers who can turn "tricks" at a surprising rate but nothing that compares with that of their female counterparts. There are, however, economic problems associated with bilateral prostitution. It might place a greater drain on the family's financial resources than swinging and, more significantly, create conflict over budgeting for the extramarital sexual expression of the husband and wife; i.e., how is the decision on allotment of funds to be made? It is perhaps of greater concern that it would separate the husband and wife for recreation at a time when a great deal of emphasis is placed on "familistic" activity, especially of the recreational variety, e.g., couples play bridge together, bowl together, boat together, and so on. That is to say, bilateral prostitution would enlarge their private worlds at the expense of their common world.

Given such considerations, the advantages of mate swapping as a solution to the problem of marital sexual monotony become obvious, though in all fairness we must note that many of the points we are going to make cannot be fully appreciated until the reader has completed our description of mate swapping himself. To begin with, the cost is probably less than that of bilateral prostitution and is much more easily integrated into the normal recreational or entertainment budget. Second, it keeps the couple together, or at least in the same house. But further, it is an activity which involves common planning and preparation and provides subject matter for conversation before and after, and thus it could further consolidate the marriage. Finally, the sexual activity that takes place is, to a greater or lesser extent, under the surveillance of each; this means that each exercises control over the extramarital activity of the other, and the danger that the sexual relationship will become a romantic relationship is minimized. This, of course, is also facilitated by the brief and segmented nature of the relationship.

In summary, then, for the couple committed to the marital relationship and for whom it still performs important functions for which no other relationship exists, mate swapping may relieve sexual monotony without undermining the marriage.

The Study of Swinging

Swinging, or mate swapping, has been a subject that sells "adult reading" paperbacks, but few social scientists have analyzed it. Fortunately, there are a handful of serious studies of the swinging scene. This is not to maintain that we know all we need to know; the analyses available must be viewed as tentative. The findings of the research are problematic because designs have not been employed which allow generalization. Furthermore, some crucial aspects of the phenomenon have been neglected; e.g., what are the characteristics of those who drop out of swinging? We say this not by way of criticism of the research of our colleagues; they are pioneering in an area that involves great technical as well as ethical problems. Our statements are merely intended to qualify what we have to say in the rest of the paper.

Despite the problems cited above, there are studies which provide excellent descriptive data based on participant observation and interviewing (Bartell 1969; Breedlove and Breedlove 1964; Smith and Smith 1969; Symonds 1968). We will use these ground-breaking papers to test the model presented earlier. It is hoped that the important contributions of Symonds, Bartell, the Smiths, and the Breedloves will encourage further research in this area. Before evaluating our model it is necessary to specify the term "swinging," to discuss the emergence and extent of swinging, and to describe the swingers themselves.

Swinging

One definition of swinging is "having sexual relations (as a couple) with at least one other individual" (Bartell 1969). Another definition, and more appropriate for our purposes, is that swinging is a husband

and wife's "willingness to swap sexual partners with a couple with whom they are not acquainted and/or to go to a swinging party and be willing for both he and his mate to have sexual intercourse with strangers" (Symonds 1968). The latter definition directs our attention to swinging as a husband-wife activity. The accepted term among mate-sharing couples is "swinging"; the term "wife swapping" is objectionable, as it implies sexual inequality, i.e., that wives are the property of husbands.

Swingers, according to Symonds, are not of one mold; she distinguishes "recreational" from "utopian" swingers. The recreational swinger is someone "who uses swinging as a form of recreation"; he does not want to change the social order or to fight the establishment. He is, in Merton's typology of deviance, an "aberrant." The recreational swinger violates norms but accepts them as legitimate. The utopian swinger is "nonconformist," publicizing his opposition to societal norms.

He also tries to change them. He is generally acknowledged by the general society to be doing this for a cause rather than for personal gain (Merton 1966).

Swinging, for the utopian, is part of a new life style that emphasizes communal living. The proportion of utopians within the swinging scene has not been determined. Symonds feels that their number is small. She found the utopians more interesting

because of their more deviant and encompassing view concerning the life that they desire to live if it ever becomes possible. In some respects, they fall close to the philosophy of some hippies in that they would like to retreat from the society at large and live in a community of their own kind (Symonds 1968).

In societal terms, the recreational swinger is a defender of the status quo; the utopian swinger is one who wants to build a new order.

We are most interested in the recreational swingers, because their deviation is limited to the sharing of partners; in other areas they adhere to societal norms. Couples who engage in recreational swinging say they do so in order to support or improve their marriage. They favor monogamy and want to maintain it.

The Swinger

The swingers who advertise and attend swinging parties do not conform to the stereotypical image of the deviant. They have higher levels of education than the general population; 80% of one study had attended college, 50% were graduates, and 12% were still students. They are disproportionately found in professional and white-collar occupations (Smith and Smith, 1969). They tend to be conservative and very straight.

They do not represent a high order of deviance. In fact, this is the single area of deviation from the norms of contemporary society. The mores, the fears, that plague our generation are evidenced as strongly in swingers as in any random sampling from suburbia (Bartell 1969).

Every study we looked at emphasized the overall normality, conventionality, and respectability of recreational swingers.

Extent of Swinging

The number of couples engaged in swinging can at best be roughly estimated. The Breedloves developed, on the basis of their research, an estimate of eight million couples. Their figure was based on a sample of 407 couples. They found that less than 4% of them placed or replied to advertisements in swinging publications, and in the year prior to publication (1962–63) of their study "almost 70,000 couples either replied to, or placed ads as swinging couples" (Breedlove and Breedlove 1964). With this figure as a base they arrived at their estimate of the number of couples who have at one time or another sexually exchanged partners. They further concluded that, conservatively, two and one-half million couples exchange partners on a somewhat *regular* basis (three or more times a year).

Getting Together

The "swap," or swingers', club is an institutionalized route to other swingers, but it is not the only method of locating potential partners. Bartell suggests four ways: (1) swingers' bars, (2) personal reference, (3) personal recruitment, and (4) advertisement (Bartell 1970). The last method deserves special attention.

Advertisements are placed in underground papers and more frequently in swingers' magazines. The swingers' publications, it has been claimed, emerged following an article in *MR.* magazine in 1956.

Everett Meyers, the editor of *MR.*, later claimed that it was this article which touched off a flood of similar articles on wife-swapping, or mate-swapping. In any event, *MR.* followed up its original article with a regular monthly correspondence column filled with alleged letters from readers reporting their own mate-swapping accounts (Brecher 1969).

Publications began to appear with advertisements from "modern marrieds" or swingers who wished to meet other swingers. *La Plume*, established about 1955, has boasted in print that it was the first swingers' magazine. A recent issue of *Select*, probably the largest swingers' publication, had 3,500 advertisements, over 40% from married couples. *Select* and *Kindred Spirits* cosponsored "Super Bash '70'" on April 11, 1970. It was advertised to be "the BIGGEST SWINGDING yet," and featured dancing, buffet dinner, go go girls, and a luxurious intimate ballroom. Clubs such as Select, Kindred Spirits, Mixers, and Swingers Life have moved beyond the swingers' party to hayrides and vacation trips.

There are at least a couple of hundred organizations like Select throughout the country. Many of them are very small, some with only a few members, and many of them are fly-by-night rackets run by schlock guys less interested in providing a service than in making a quick buck. Most, however, are legitimate and, as such, very successful. They have been a major factor influencing the acceleration of the swapping scene (Fonzi and Riggio 1969).

Our review of the swinging club and magazine market located approximately fifty nationally sold publications. The "couple of hundred" figure reported above may include some lonely hearts, nudist directories, homosexual, and transvestite organizations, some of which serve the same purpose as swingers' publications. They bring together persons with the same sociosexual interests.

A person's first attendance at a swingers' party can be a difficult situation. He must learn the ideologies, rationalizations, and rules of swinging. These rules place swinging in a context that enables it to support the institution of the family. We turn to these rules in the next section.

Rules of the Game

Our model views swinging as a strategy to revitalize marriage, to bolster a sagging partnership. This strategy can be seen in the following findings of the empirical research. Evidence to support the model is divided into four parts: (1) the perception of limitation of sex to the marital bond, (2) paternity, (3) discretion, and (4) marital supportive rules.

1. "Consensual adultery": the perception that sex is limited to the marital bond.—Swingers have developed rules that serve to define the sexual relationship of marriage as one of love, of emotion. Some of the Smiths' respondents would answer "no" to questions pertaining to "extramarital sexual experience" but would answer "yes" to questions pertaining to "mate-sharing or co-marital relations" (Smith and Smith, 1969). Sharing, for the swingers, means that the marriage partners are not "cheating." Swingers believe that the damaging aspects in extramarital sex are the lying and cheating and that if these are removed extramarital sex is beneficial to the marital bond. In other words, "those who swing together stay together" (Brecher 1969). Swingers establish rules such as not allowing one of a couple to attend a group meeting without the other. Unmarried couples are kept out of some groups, because they "have less regard for the marital responsibilities" (Breedlove and Breedlove 1964). Guests who fail to conform to rules are asked "to leave a party when their behavior is not appropriate."

For one group of recreational swingers, it is important that there be no telephone contact with the opposite sex between functions. Another group of recreational swingers always has telephone contact with people they swing with, although they have no sexual contact between functions (Symonds 1968).

2. Swinging and children.—"Recreational swingers are occasionally known to drop out of swinging, at least temporarily, while the wife gets pregnant" (Symonds 1968). By not swinging, the couple can be assured that the husband is the father of the child; unknown or other parentage is considered taboo. This reflects a traditional, middle-class view about the conception and rearing of children.

Swinging couples consider themselves to be sexually avant-garde, but many retain their puritan attitudes with respect to sex socialization. They hide their swinging publications from their children. Swingers lock their children's bedrooms during parties or send them to relatives.

3. Discretion.—A common word in the swingers' vocabulary is "discretion." Swingers desire to keep their sexual play a secret from their nonswinging or "square" friends. They want to protect their position in the community, and an effort is made to limit participation to couples of similar status or "respectability."

Parties in suburbia are restricted or limited to couples only. In the area of our research, singles—male or female—were discriminated against. Blacks were universally excluded. If the party was closed, there were rules, very definitely established and generally reinforced by the organizer as well as other swingers . . . stag films were generally not shown. Music is low-key fox trot, not infrequently Glenn Miller, and lighting was definitely not psychedelic. (Usually nothing more than a few red or blue lightbulbs.) Marijuana and speed were not permitted (Bartell 1969).

The swinging suburban party differs, then, from the conventional cocktail party only in that it revolves around the sexual exchange of mates.

   4. Swingers' rules.—We suggest that the above rules on sex and paternity are strategies to make swinging an adjunct to marriage rather than an alternative. Another set of rules or strategies that is relevant is that dealing with jealousy. Swingers recognize the potentially disruptive consequences of jealousy and are surprisingly successful in minimizing it. The Smiths found that only 34% of the females and 27% of the males reported feelings of jealousy. Some of the controls on jealousy are (1) that the marriage command paramount loyalty, (2) that there be physical but not emotional interest in other partners, (3) that single persons be avoided, and (4) that there be no concealment of sexual activities. The sharing couples

reassure one another on this score by means of verbal statements and by actively demonstrating in large ways and small that the marriage still does command their paramount loyalty. Willingness to forego an attractive swinging opportunity because the spouse or lover is uninterested or opposed is one example of such a demonstration (Brecher 1969).

Developing a set of rules to control potential jealousies demonstrates the swingers' commitment to marriage.

Conclusion

In this paper we have attempted to account for a new form of extramarital sexual behavior in terms of a sociological model of deviance.

We have contended that swinging may support rather than disrupt monogamous marriage as it exists in this society. A review of the volumes of the *Reader's Guide to Periodical Literature* and *The New York Times Index* failed to reveal any articles dealing with this phenomenon in the United States. This would suggest that swinging has not as yet been defined as a social problem in the traditional sense of the word. Thus swinging, like prostitution, despite its violation of the social and, in many cases, legal norms is permitted a degree of tolerance, which would appear to demonstrate the appropriateness of our model.

Finally, it should be said that we make no pretense to having touched upon all the changes that have played a role in the emergence of swinging. Restrictions of space prevented our looking at the larger societal trends that may have been at work here, e.g., feminism, the changing occupational position of women, suburbanization, and so on. Nevertheless, we do feel that we have delineated those issues which are most directly related to it. The validity of our model will be tested by time.

References

Bartell, G. D. 1970. Group Sex among the Mid-Americans. *J. Sex Res.*, 6, no. 2, pp. 113–30. [In this book, pp. 185–201.]

Becker, H. S. 1963. *Outsiders*. Glencoe, Ill.: The Free Press.

Brecher, E. M. 1969. *The Sex Researchers*. Boston: Little, Brown & Co.

Breedlove, W., and Breedlove, J. 1964. *Swap Clubs*. Los Angeles: Sherbourne Press.

Calhoun, A. W. 1960. *A Social History of the American Family*, vol. 1. New York: Barnes and Noble.

Cohen, A. K. 1959. The Study of Social Organization and Deviant Behavior. In *Sociology Today*, ed. R. K. Merton et al. New York: Basic Books.

———. 1966. *Deviance and Control*. Englewood Cliffs, N.J.: Prentice-Hall, Inc.

Davis, K. 1966. Sexual Behavior. In *Contemporary Social Problems*, ed. R. K. Merton and R. A. Nisbet. New York: Harcourt, Brace and World.

Erikson, K. T. 1966. *Wayward Puritans*. New York: John Wiley.

Farber, B. 1964. *Family: Organization and Interaction*. San Francisco: Chandler Publishing.

Fonzi, G., and Riggio, J. 1969. Modern Couple Seeks Like-Minded Couples. Utmost Discretion. *Philadelphia*, 60, no. 9, pp. 76–89.

Foote, N. N. 1948. Sex as Play. In *Mass Leisure*, ed. E. Larabee and R. Neyersohn. Glencoe, Ill.: The Free Press.

Gordon, M. 1972. From a Functional Necessity to a Cult of Mutual Orgasm: Sex in American Marital Education Literature, 1830–1940. In *The Sociology of Sex*. New York: Appleton-Century-Crofts.

Kinsey, A. C., Pomeroy, W. B., and Martin, C. E. 1948. *Sexual Behavior in the Human Male*. Philadelphia: W. B. Saunders Company.

———, and Gebhard, P. H. 1953. *Sexual Behavior in the Human Female*. Philadelphia: W. B. Saunders Company.

Kinsie, P. 1967. Her Honor Pushes Legalized Prostitution. *Soc. Health News*, February 1967.

Knight, A., and Alpert, H. 1967. The History of Sex, Part 17: The Stag Film. *Playboy*, November 1967.

Merton, R. K. 1966. Social Problems and Sociological Theory. In *Contemporary Social Problems*, ed. R. K. Merton and R. A. Nisbet. New York: Harcourt, Brace and World.

Pivar, D. J. 1965. The New Abolitionism: The Quest for Social Purity. Ph.D. dissertation, University of Pennsylvania.

Polsky, N. 1967. *Hustlers, Beats and Others*. Chicago: Aldine.

Reiss, I. L. 1967. *The Social Context of Premarital Sexual Permissiveness*. New York: Holt, Rinehart and Winston.

Smith, J. R., and Smith, L. G. 1970. Co-Marital Sex and the Sexual Freedom Movement. *J. Sex Res.*, 6, no. 2, pp. 131–42. [In this book, pp. 202–13.]

Smith, S. G. 1911. *Social Pathology*. New York: Macmillan Company.

Sprey, J. 1969. On the Institutionalization of Sex. *J. Marriage Fam.* 31: 432–40.

Symonds, C. 1968. Pilot Study of the Peripheral Behavior of Sexual Mate Swappers. Master's thesis, University of California, Riverside.

Tietze, C. 1968. Oral and Intrauterine Contraception: Effectiveness and Safety. *Internat. J. Fertil.* 13: 377–84.

Whelpton, P. K., Campbell, A. A., and Patterson, J. E. 1966. *Fertility and Family Planning in the United States*. Princeton: Princeton University Press.

Winick, C. 1962. Prostitutes' Clients' Perception of the Prostitutes and of Themselves. *Internat. J. Soc. Psychiat.* 8: 289–97.

Co-Marital Sex:
The Incorporation of Extramarital Sex
into the Marriage Relationship

Lynn G. Smith and James R. Smith

Many of our social institutions are facing the challenge of change, and the institution of marriage is no exception. Predictions for the future of marriage include a continuation of the trend toward serial monogamy or serial polygamy, as it is alternately designated, as the primary pattern plus an emergent secondary pattern of experimentation with innovations and alternate models of the marriage relationship (Farson et al. 1969). Many of these innovations and alternate models involve a rejection of the monogamic ideal and an incorporation of extramarital sex into the marriage relationship (Otto 1970).

Recently, some couples have moved into the public and scientific spotlight who are exploring and practicing a substantial inclusion of extramarital sex into their marriages. These are couples who participate in mate sharing or co-marital sex and who have popularly been labeled "swingers." This practice has been the subject of our research for the past four years, and it is the purpose of this paper to present some of our findings and to provide a conceptual framework for understanding this type of marital arrangement.

This paper is based on an exploratory field study undertaken in 1966 in the San Francisco Bay area. After gaining access to the sexual

Reprinted, by permission of the publisher, from *Critical Issues in Contemporary Sexual Behavior*, ed. J. Money and J. Zubin (Baltimore: Johns Hopkins Press, 1973).

freedom or swinging subculture through its member groups, the project involved (1) taped in-depth interviews with group leaders, (2) behavioral observations at over one hundred fifty "sexually liberal" gatherings, (3) informal interviews with over two hundred participants, and (4) 503 completed questionnaires. A full report of the study is in preparation entitled *Consenting Adults: An Exploratory Study of the Sexual Freedom Movement*.

Initially, we may inquire into the fundamental social characteristics of the target population by asking: Who are these persons and what is the apparent magnitude and scope of their behavior? Virtually all studies, our own included, of those involved in co-marital sex have shown the majority to be middle- and upper-middle-class individuals, many of them rather highly educated, relatively affluent, and engaged in professional or semiprofessional occupations. Their religious commitment tends to be low, and politically they range from radical to ultraconservative (Smith and Smith 1970). They do not fit popular conceptions of deviant individuals and do not exhibit a high order of deviance. Presumptions of pathology and pathological motivation, so frequently espoused in psychoanalytic literature, have not been supported by any empirical studies to date. One recently completed study employing the Minnesota Multiphasic Personality Inventory (MMPI) found the profiles of participants to be what is sometimes called uninterestingly normal (Twichell 1974).

The extent of co-marital sexual involvement in our population is a question which must be approached with caution. Estimates have ranged from one to eight million couples (Bartell 1971; Breedlove and Breedlove 1964). It is always difficult to obtain reliable incidence figures on deviant forms of behavior, but tentative indicators are now becoming available which provide a more scientifically respectable basis for estimation. In a recent questionnaire survey of sexual attitudes and behavior, the question "Have you ever participated in wife swapping?" was included (Athanasiou 1970). In a national sample of twenty thousand respondents, 5% of the married respondents indicated that they had participated in "wife swapping" either once or twice or frequently. One-third of the married respondents indicated that they had not participated in the past but that they might in the future, perhaps if the opportunity arose. Findings from this survey are not presented as directly applicable to the country as a whole as the respondents were predominantly young (the majority were under thirty), well educated (the median level was college graduate), of relatively high socioeconomic status (almost two-thirds earned over ten thousand dollars), and their religious commitment was low (nearly one-third claimed to be atheists or agnostics). However, the authors suggested that their findings were descriptive of a well-educated, intelligent group that "just might be a wave of the future." Our sample (N=503) drawn from those participating in co-marital sex was found to exhibit very similar demographic characteristics (Smith and Smith 1970).

Studies of co-marital sex have indicated that it is more often the husband than the wife who instigates such involvement (Bartell 1970; Bell 1970; Schupp 1970; Smith and Smith 1970; Varni 1971). Similarly, Athanasiou found in his sample that twice as many of the husbands (41%) as of the wives (22%) were interested in "swapping." When only those married respondents in his sample who had a history of extramarital sex are considered, almost 10% had experienced it in its co-marital form. While still small, this is perhaps a surprisingly large percentage. Another recent study also sheds light on the question of the extent of co-marital participation. In a study of extramarital sex among a sample of middle-class, middle-aged, midwestern couples, a 5% level of co-marital experience was also found (Johnson 1971). These two studies constitute the best indicators of the extent of actual involvement at the present time. Thus, psychologists and counselors can no longer simply assume that when adultery occurs it is carried out in a furtive, clandestine, deceptive manner.[1] More and more when the topic of extramarital sex arises, whether it is on a questionnaire (Anthanasiou 1970), as the subject of a discussion among professionals (Neubeck 1969), or among individuals in everyday life, the question of knowledge and consent by the spouse is raised and mediates in the resultant responses.

Deception has previously been a characteristic feature of adultery; and the effects of adultery have turned more on the success or failure of the deception than on the omission or commission of the adulterous act itself. Adultery is often accepted when it is practiced with discretion and no one is the wiser, and yet it is the deception that provides a large part of the sting when it is discovered.

We are now witnessing among a seemingly growing minority of our population an acknowledgment of the desire for and occurrence of extramarital sex coupled with a rejection of the deception which has previously permeated its practice. The emphasis of the 1960s on com-

---

[1] For the purposes of this paper the term "adultery" is used synonymously with extramarital sex. In our culture the former is legally defined by the latter, but in other cultures, the illegitimacy of adultery is not attached to all occurrences of extramarital sex.

munication—honesty and openness—and the youth culture's rejection of hypocrisy undoubtedly have been in part responsible for both. And it would seem that participants in co-marital sex have taken the spousal and familial "togetherness" emphasized in the 1950s a step further than anticipated or intended. Since there are significant variations in the forms that the contemporary practice of adultery is assuming, some distinctions are in order.

Forms of Adultery

We wish to distinguish two basic forms of adultery: *conventional* adultery and *consensual* adultery. The former is characterized by the presence of deception and is unknown to the spouse or known only ex post facto. The latter is characterized by a lack of deception and by both the knowledge and consent of the spouse. Consensual adultery may or may not involve spousal encouragement and may be undertaken as either an individual or dyadic activity.

Three substantially different forms of consensual adultery have emerged:

Adultery toleration. This is the form of consensual adultery that is most similar to conventional adultery. Spouses simply extend to each other the freedom to engage in extramarital sex individually, usually according to a dyadically developed set of ground rules. This may or may not involve encouragement or acceptance beyond the degree of simple toleration. Such adultery toleration pacts were reported to exist some years ago by Hamilton (1929) and by Lindsey and Evans (1929). Recent acknowledgments of adultery toleration pacts among the affluent have been described by Cuber and Harroff (1965). Adultery toleration allows extramarital sex into the marriage relationship on very much the same basis as conventional adultery, except that the partners are relieved of their commitment to sexual exclusivity. As a result, the necessity and rationale for deception are removed. They may still practice extramarital sex in a clandestine fashion, but they have what is sometimes simply called an understanding or arrangement. Adultery toleration may or may not involve both partners, that is, it may be a unilateral or bilateral toleration agreement and, if bilateral, may or may not be actually practiced by both partners.

Co-marital relations. Another form of integration of extramarital sex, one which further incorporates it into the marital relationship, is what is commonly called mate sharing or "swinging." Both partners participate and they participate as a dyad. We prefer the term "co-marital relations" to refer to this form rather than the popular term "swinging" because the latter is vague, misleading, and objectionable to some participants and because the term "swinging" is becoming almost exclusively associated with a certain subtype of co-marital sex, a type characterized by a strictly recreational orientation which discourages emotional involvements.

Co-marital sex is practiced both on a couple-to-couple basis and on a group basis. In the former, it typically involves one couple meeting with another couple to exchange partners for sexual activity. Sometimes this acquaintance is made through classified advertisements; sometimes it arises and develops more or less spontaneously from previous friendship relations. The sexual activity may take place in the same room, in different rooms in the same house, or in different houses with each couple retiring to separate dwellings with the temporary partner.

In the case of co-marital sex on a group basis, a number of couples meet at the same time and sexual activity may occur among any of those present rather than being limited to a direct switching of partners. Couples report that group affiliation presents more options than the double-dyad situation since sexual participation in any given instance may be unilateral or bilateral according to the group norms and expectations. More often than not, there is no formally circumscribed group such as a "swap club," as they have been designated, but rather simply gatherings of friends and recent acquaintances who choose to party together. The spouses in these cases usually know and interact with the extramarital partners and may well be friends.

This is an important dimension of co-marital sexuality which has received only scant and fleeting attention but which bears directly on the *interpersonal quality* of the co-marital experience. The image of swinging rendered by many studies to date is of a slightly compulsive, highly ritualized, totally impersonal, inevitably degrading set of behaviors which no self-respecting person could possibly find acceptable or attractive. This image, we submit, is not so much false as incomplete and one sided. Most studies have drawn their samples from organized groups of one sort or another, missing the point, perhaps, that the groups serve the same functions for the couples as they do for the researchers, that is, providing access and entry points, a context for desensitization and reorientation, and a recurrent source of new contacts and information. In short, by a sort of methodological sleight of hand, the visible and accessible groups have been interpreted as more or less "containing" the individual behaviors constituting them and the social movement associated with them. Confusion results when the attributes of the visible groups are subsequently predicated on their members and their activities without qualification. In doing so, there is a failure to note or reveal the more esoteric and personalized involvements which sometimes precede and commonly follow participation in organized, commercially oriented sex groups. Our data, and moreover our field observations, support this contention. Among the over four hundred persons in our sample who had attended sex parties, approximately one-fourth had attended only publicly accessible parties on a pay-as-you-come basis, and another one-fourth had attended both public and private parties in varying proportions depending primarily on length and extent of involvement. However, and this is where our data appear to depart from the findings of other studies, about half of the party-goers in our study had never attended a public party, restricting their involvement to private gatherings only. Our field studies suggest that couples able to establish contact with noncommercial, nonorganized groups, perhaps in conjunction with the initial access provided by public groups, often succeed in establishing basic friendship relations which yield more enduring and more rewarding social networks than the highly transient followings of the clubs and bars.

Group marriage.   A third form of consensual adultery, though one whose incidence is far lower than either of the above-mentioned forms, is group marriage. This, of course, involves going beyond the conventional two-person marital relationship. It is the extreme expression of the incorporation of extramarital sex into marriage, involving a significantly altered form of marriage. In a strict sense, therefore, it does not constitute extramarital relations, for all the parties consider themselves married to each other. This, of course, is not legally recognized, and so it constitutes an ambiguous analytic category but one which should be sociologically recognized nonetheless. Group marriage is a large and amorphous category that will need to be further refined along several dimensions to accommodate in a theoretically useful way the large range of involvements and affiliations, from casual cohabitation and casual but steady group liaisons to intimate peer groups and companionate families with a high degree of integration.

These forms of consensual adultery are not necessarily mutually exclusive and cannot be considered to form a typology.[2] One couple may participate in any or all of the forms, while others limit themselves

---

[2] There is no specific ordering variable that could be taken as reliable at this point.

to one form or another. Our research has been concerned primarily with the co-marital form of consensual adultery and, more specifically, with co-marital sex on a group basis.

Definition and Preliminary
Conceptualization of Co-Marital Sexuality

Co-marital sexuality may be usefully defined as mutually consensual sexual interaction (correspondence, parties), relations (members of a club, erotic comrades, playmates, coital partners, friends), or intentions (fantasies, seductions) between, among, and/or across married (or significantly paired) dyads with the knowledge and consent but not necessarily the presence or participation of each member. This involves interdyadic sexual contact and proximate behavior directed to that end, including at least one member of one married (or significantly paired) dyad and at least one member of another such dyad with the general concurrence of their respective mates. More simply stated, co-marital sex is consensual sex between and among married couples or established dyads.

Co-marital sex is differentiated from the broader category of consensual adultery in that, in the former, the focus of analysis and observation is on married *couples* interacting with other married couples rather than married *individuals* interacting with other married individuals. And it is differentiated from the more technical category of intermarital sex, i.e., sexual contact between married persons not married to each other, which may be either consensual or nonconsensual, but which stresses the significance of the relative independence of each participant. In the latter case, for example, it is possible to have both members of one dyad interacting sexually with both members of another dyad, but independently and in ignorance of the action of the other two members. This is, of course, sex across marital lines but is neither consensual adultery nor *co*-marital sex. It could be awkwardly labeled nonconsensual intermarital sex, a rare but nonvacuous species that has likely led to more than a few marital and even co-marital readjustments.

The knowledge-of-and-consent-to conditions are critical features; they are mitigating factors of considerable import for an adequate understanding of "consensual adultery." From a psychodynamic perspective, these factors are of greater significance and have wider ramifications than such commonly emphasized factors as sociophysical propinquity and actual mutual involvement. Couples with long histories of involvement and considerable experience in such matters seem to reveal this especially well, since (1) they are more apt to promote and allow a wider range of social and sexual options, including individual dates, unilateral relationships, separate liaisons, and meetings under special conditions (e.g., vacations), but (2) they are just as grieved and hurt when deceived. (More so, perhaps, because when there is protracted or extensive involvement there is also more trust at stake to undermine or destroy.)

From the conventional viewpoint, all co-marital sex is both extra- and intermarital sex since it "adulterates" the marital relationship by crossing marital boundary lines. However, co-marital partners, as opposed to intermarital partners, are assumed to have consciously and intentionally redefined those boundaries or at least have attempted to do so.

With respect to the extramarital category, it is important to note that the "extra" can no longer be presumed always to retain the conventional connotation, though it may retain the same denotation. This is because the "extra" has been more or less integrated into the marital relationship in the course of dyadic experimentation, exploration, or adventure with co-marital activity. The extramarital category is by this time so vague, elusive, and anachronistic that it is somewhat worse than useless. Like an elastic blanket it becomes less substantial the more it is stretched to cover diverse cases. As a nondiscriminatory and non-pejorative reference term, extramarital sex denotes any sexual contact or relationship with anyone other than one's legally defined marriage partner and is coterminous with the legal category of adulterous sexual behavior, whether of the conventional or consensual variety. It does not refer to the quality of the experience, the context in which it occurs, or the motives and intentions of the involved parties. It is, on this account, ambiguous to the point of incomprehensibility, since it overlooks essential differences in a vast range of sexual and interpersonal experience, and perceived results. From a contemporary viewpoint— whether it is welcomed or regretted, pathological or healthy, benign or detrimental, joyous or tragic—co-marital sexuality must be seen as an internal part of the marriage rather than as something external to it. It is a matter of internal concurrence and negotiation rather than external collusion and deception. Hence, "extra" is, strictly speaking, a misnomer.

From a viewpoint outside any given marital dyad, such sexual activity may well appear as something extra. But from a viewpoint internal to the dyad itself, where it may be said to count for something as it affects the principals, it may or may not be extra in the sense of a compensation or substitute but rather extra in the sense of an extension or expansion. These diverse meanings signal profound personal and interpersonal differences in both cognition and feeling by the participants. This suggests that there might be a discernible continuum running between the linguistically polar opposites of contramarital and pro-marital sexuality—that which deteriorates or undermines as opposed to that which promotes and supports—which radically traverses the extra- versus intramarital distinction.

The above definition of co-marital sex makes clear that the *dyad* is the actor, the unit of analysis, and a basic modal type of involvement in consensual adultery. Individuals constitute the dyad, to be sure, and the analysis would eventually be reduced in scope to individual actors and actions and to intrapsychic and intrasomatic process variables. But all methodological individualism is context dependent, and the level of analysis must always be relevant to the desired focus and scope of inference. For present purposes, co-marital sexuality is a mode of action or variable pattern (of sexual behavior) within a recognizably larger and superimposed mode of action or pattern (marriage), which is further embedded in the larger context of American social history and current social structures and cultural norms. It is a significant and defining part of an emerging marital form; it is a sub- and/or counter-cultural relationship between sexual actors; and it constitutes an institu-tional change, whose dynamics, energies, and nuances are the subject of much curiosity and little solid study.

This definition also recognizes the obvious social fact that one per-son can influence, indeed virtually determine, the behavior of another without actually being present. For example, a promise or agreement not to engage in a given sexual act or be intimate with a given potential partner is an effective variable in the analysis of a given episode or situation, even if that promise is broken in the absence of its probable enforcer. Ground rules and systems of tacit and/or informal agree-ments, so crucial to a psychodynamic analysis of co-marital sex, operate at a distance in both space and time, and their negotiation, definition, promulgation, application, and enforcement require, besides some vague internal condition of good will and a minimum of intelligence, much time and energy. Such meta-level interaction changes the course and colors the experience of co-marital sexuality in great measure. For this reason we disavow the necessity of requiring the actual physical presence and direct participation of all four persons in a double dyad during a specific episode in order to apply the label "co-marital sexual behavior." Indeed, what is crucial is whether mutual consent, knowl-edge, and approval are present among the participant dyads, not whether there are four (or more), as opposed to two or three, bodies present and accounted for.

Motivation Patterns

To date two main motivation patterns have emerged from studies of swingers, both exhibiting particular styles of expression, which have been labeled "recreational" and "utopian," and both transecting the co-marital forms mentioned above (Symonds 1967). These are best conceived as opposite ends of a continuum. Though they are only rudimentary descriptive categories, they are currently accepted as useful. A more recent attempt to establish descriptive categories, based on a participant observation study, yielded a five-part classification scheme: "hard-core," "egotistical," "recreational," "interpersonal," and "communal swingers" (Varni 1971).

If we utilize the currently employed recreational-utopian continuum, which may be reconceptualized as a continuum of isolated-integrated deviance, the "recreational swinger" at one end of the continuum is, as the term indicates, someone who "uses swinging as a form of recreation." These persons usually explicitly discourage emotional involvement with their extramarital partners. They are willing to participate sexually with relative strangers at parties and may do so on an anonymous basis. Address books are sometimes kept alphabetically by first names. Emotional attachment is considered threatening to the marriage, and co-marital relationships are thus kept on an allegedly "sex only" basis. Many curtail sexual involvements on an individual basis, such as individual dates or even unilateral involvement at a particular party, thereby attempting to guard against emotional involvement.

Recreational swingers are to a large degree conformists, deviating only in their sexual behavior. In fact, even in their sexual behavior, except that it does not take place on a totally monogamous basis, they are also conformists. They are more inclined to engage in sexual activity in relative privacy and less inclined toward group sexual experiences. They sometimes do not even engage in group nudity, but retire to a bedroom in private with a chosen sexual partner, disrobe, engage in sexual activity, and dress again before returning to the other couple or group.

The utopian swinger, at the other end of the continuum, is idealistic and sees swinging (if he employs the term at all) as a part of a new life-style that emphasizes communality and interpersonal depth. Persons of this type do not accept the norms of the conventional social order without question and are more likely to be social-action oriented, though not necessarily radical or militant. Emotional involvement with others is preferred. In this sense, they are not swingers, that is, couples who limit themselves to casual or anonymous sexual encounters and who discourage and severely restrict emotional attachments to others.

With reference to the utopian swinger in particular, it is important to draw a distinction between preference level and acceptance level. The two tend to coalesce in the recreational group, but for the utopians, despite the fact that the overt behavior may be similar, the structure of expectations is profoundly different. The utopian swinger prefers a total relationship but under varying circumstances will accept something less. There is another disparity between the two groups in that, as far as sexual involvements are concerned, the recreational type will accept his utopian counterpart but often feels threatened when invited into a more complex and committed relationship. The utopian will swing but is less likely to be fulfilled by that type of relationship. Their differing expectation and satisfaction levels are conducive to a pattern of conflict which promotes subgrouping along these differing motivational dimensions. Utopian swingers want to share more than sex. Their interpersonal goals include a measure of sociality and friendship. They speak of intimacy and self-development. They tend to show interest in alternate forms of social life, sometimes a willingness to share food, shelter, and other aspects of daily life.

There, in fact, appear to be two relatively distinct subcultures which may be suitably distinguished in terms of their value orientations. Subgrouping occurs along other dimensions as well, e.g., marital status, age, level of attractiveness, and type of drug use, but is most prominently exhibited in terms of this fundamental value orientation.

The utopian-recreational distinction to some degree parallels Reiss's distinction in a premarital context between "permissiveness with affection" and "permissiveness without affection" (1960). In the case of recreational swingers we find permissiveness without affection institutionalized. It is their way of reaffirming and securing their commitment to marriage; they remain emotionally monogamous while at the same time rejecting sexual monogamy. Recreational swinging is in this way a functional alternative to the declining practice of patronizing prostitutes, but on an ostensibly equilateral basis. It would appear that recreational swingers are less secure in their marriages than their utopian counterparts and thus jealously guard against emotional involvements with others as a protective precaution.

In between these two extremes are many who want more than sex from their extramarital or co-marital relationships but who do not anticipate communal living arrangements. They want to expand their interpersonal relationships to a more intimate level, sensing perhaps or reflecting a relationship between marital satisfaction and the number of close friends and relatives. A recent study (Renne 1970) found that people with few intimate associates were more likely to be dissatisfied with their marriages. This and other indicators suggest that the isolated nuclear family is experiencing an interpersonal intimacy impoverishment. Various forms of intimate networks are being proposed as therapeutic measures to relieve this condition (Farson et al. 1969; Stoller 1970). Utopian swinging fits such a pattern and may be considered a natural social experiment with as yet unknown results. Sexual intimacy, heretofore usually presumed to be purely dyadic, purely heterosexual, and purely private, is sought with a variety of persons as a means to establish such networks of intimacy. A developmental tendency is evident among some participants in co-marital sex. Initially adopting a recreational emphasis, they move, over time, toward a concern with interpersonal relationships. We are tempted to suggest that a maturation process occurs in which the key elements are increasingly straightforward communication, overt sexual experimentation, and a complex process of sexual resocialization.

Viewed from within the putative conventional structure of the social order, the above forms of adultery—conventional and consensual adultery and the three subforms of the latter—show a progression which may be mapped in terms of four separate but related continuums. These four continuums are (1) the relative frequency of occurrence in the general population, (2) the extent of incorporation of extramarital sex into the marriage relationship, (3) the degree of sociality of expression, and (4) the type of probable sanctions based upon the extremity and visibility of the deviant behavior. The underlying relationship between the degree of deviance from the conventional norms of monogamy and the degree of sociality and interpersonal intimacy appears to be a positive one. This, of course, suggests that, despite our theoretical prejudices and cultural biases, we live, at least sexually, in a basically antisocial environment and that Western Christian social life erects a barrier between group sentiment and sexual expression (Freud 1960). Recreational swingers maintain this barrier by allowing plural and group sex but restricting plural sentiment and group love.

Consensual adultery in its various forms thus involves an alteration of the marital ground rules in such a way as to incorporate extramarital sex. One result is that extramarital sex becomes subject to greater dyadic control. This appears to be one factor which attenuates a jealousy response. There is no a priori reason to believe that those couples who participate together in extramarital sex and those couples who extend sexual freedom to each other in the form of adultery toleration are any the less committed to their marriages or to the institution of marriage than those who participate in the conventional form of extramarital sex without their spouse's knowledge. In one sense, they are expressing a greater commitment to intimacy in their marriage by refusing to conceal their respective extramarital interests and proclivities. They are attempting to recognize and resolve a problem which has plagued monogamous marriage—the virtually universal sexual desire for persons other than one's spouse (Neubeck 1969)—by agreeing to a mutually acceptable outlet. In this sense they are creating their own marriage contract by defining it from within rather than simply conforming to preexisting institutional frameworks, though swinging already shows signs of becoming an institutionalized alternative.

Sampling inadequacies have prevented any conclusions to date about the relative success and failure rates of such ventures. Although there are and will be casualties from consensual adultery, the question remains whether there will be greater or fewer casualties proportionately than from conventional adultery. But that such alterations of marital ground rules can be successful is evident from isolated cases of couples who have happily maintained such arrangements for periods of twenty years and more. Whether consensual adultery is or will become a feasible alternative to conventional adultery for any sizable portion of the population is yet to be seen.

Premarital Ethics and Marital Sexuality

If we assume that the attitudes and value orientations which prevail prior to marriage tend to shape expectations for marriage itself, a relationship may be posited between premarital ethics and marital sexuality. We should like to offer a tentative hypothesis that the greater the frequency and degree of premarital permissiveness the greater the likelihood that married couples will display tendencies to engage in comarital relations or adultery toleration. A positive relationship between premarital and extramarital coital experience has previously been reported but has received little attention in recent years (Hamilton 1929; Kinsey et al. 1953; Landis et al. 1940; Terman 1938). A reexamination and refinement of the existence of such a relationship would appear to be warranted in the light of the recent proliferation of forms of adultery discussed above.

In the last century, the scientific study of and public concern with sexual activity independent of marriage has progressed from an emphasis on premarital to postmarital relations and only recently to extramarital relations. Attitudes toward premarital and postmarital relations have been modified in the direction of an increased tolerance and acceptance, and though it has long been debated and denied there appears to be an increase in the incidence level of premarital coitus as well, particularly among females (Christensen and Gregg 1970). It is likely that a similar shift is occurring with respect to extramarital relations (Farson et al. 1969; Pomeroy 1969). We can appreciate that extramarital relations are the last in this progression to be accorded tolerance and acceptance since, as a form of sexual relations independent of marital sanctions, they are generally considered the most threatening to marriage itself since they occur concurrently with the marital relationship and violate the notions that one cannot love and should not have sexual relations with more than one person at a time (Bowman 1949; Comfort 1966; Freud 1959a, 1959b).

There has been much controversy during the past few decades over the question of a sexual revolution. One of the confounding factors in such discussions has been the lack of a determination of what would constitute a revolutionary as opposed to an evolutionary change and of what particular expressions of sexuality one should look toward for evidence one way or another. The premarital realm is still the primary focus of the search for evidence of revolutionary change, though there is some evidence that, if there has been a revolutionary change in premarital sexuality, it occurred in the 1920s (Vandervoort 1970). We would do well to examine the effects of such premarital changes on other realms of sexuality, in particular, extramarital relations. Kinsey et al. (1953) found a higher incidence of extramarital sexual experience among females who had a history of premarital sex. Such an increase of premarital sex among females would suggest that we might expect a subsequent increase in the incidence of extramarital sex.

Whether or not we acknowledge a revolution in premarital sexuality, we can now see that an alternate premarital ethic of permissiveness has emerged and is competing with the nonpermissive premarital ethic. Both standards currently receive widespread social support. Employing Reiss's (1960) four-part distinction, "abstinence" and the "double standard" may be seen to constitute the traditional nonpermissive premarital ethical forms, while "permissiveness with affection" and "permissiveness without affection" may characterize the newer permissive ethical forms. Premarital nonpermissiveness has led rather naturally to the traditional nonpermissive "closed" form of marriage, defined as a permanent and sexually exclusive union. The move from the newer ethic of premarital permissiveness to the traditional nonpermissive marriage, however, may generate a cognitive and emotional strain. If that is the case, what we may be witnessing is the development of a corresponding alternate marital ethic, that of the more permissive "open marriage."[3] Adultery occurs in both marital forms, but the nonpermissive marriage would be expected to generate conventional adultery, whereas the permissive marriage would be expected to generate some form of consensual or mutually negotiated outcome.

Evidence supportive of a relationship between premarital and marital sexual ethics may be seen in the consistently high incidence of premarital coitus reported to date among participants in co-marital sex. In our study of co-marital participants, 93% of the married respondents ($N = 151$) reported a history of premarital coitus. Another recent study found that 91% of the experimental group of couples who had engaged in co-marital sex ($N = 60$) reported a history of premarital coitus, as opposed to 50% of the control group of married couples who had not engaged in co-marital sex (Schupp 1970). Preliminary examination of Athanasiou's data (1970) suggests the following relationships: (1) the greater the number of premarital partners the greater the likelihood of co-marital sex ($\chi^2 = 50$, $df = 21$, $p < .001$); (2) the further from marriage that first intercourse occurred and the lower the degree of commitment to the first coital partner the greater the likelihood of interest in co-marital sex ($\chi^2 = 56$, $df = 12$, $p < .001$); and (3) the greater the liberality of opinion about premarital sexual intercourse the greater the likelihood of co-marital sex ($\chi^2 = 107$, $df = 15$, $p < .001$). These data are currently being subjected to more stringent statistical examination, and so our conclusions must be viewed as tentative. Nonetheless, these data bear directly on the hypothesized relationship between the frequency and degree of premarital permissiveness and the tendency to engage in co-marital relations than do sheer incidence levels.

We do not suggest that premarital permissiveness by any means inevitably leads to a permissive marital ethic but only that it might be considered an important predisposing factor. Psychodynamically, what is involved is an acceptance by both partners of multilateral intimacy, whether previous or concurrent. The traditional fetish of virginity has been transcended by those persons accepting a single standard of permissiveness. Both male and female must accept the fact that their prospective mate will not likely be a virgin. A comparison of cross-cultural data gathered in 1958 and 1968 by Christensen and Gregg (1970) provides evidence of a decrease in preference for marrying a virgin on

---

[3] The term "open marriage" and a conceptual framework for this evolving mode have been developed by Nena O'Neill and George O'Neill and elaborated in *Open Marriage: A New Life Style for Couples* (New York: M. Evans, 1972).

the part of both male and female college students. This acceptance, if it is genuine, makes other such relationships both more likely and easier to cope with, as long as a basic trust is maintained. Such a trust is the basis for a new perspective on both adultery and infidelity.

The Concept of Infidelity

The development of permissive as well as nonpermissive marriages and the separation of adultery and deception necessitate a corresponding distinction between adultery and infidelity. For those persons involved in co-marital relations or any form of consensual adultery, adultery is not equated with infidelity. The concept of unfaithfulness for these persons is not wholly inapplicable to the act of adultery but is considered applicable only within a narrowed range, depending not on the simple occurrence of the act itself but on its surrounding circumstances.

From our study it is evident that the circumstances under which consensual adultery constitutes unfaithfulness or infidelity may generally be classified as those which involve (1) deception, (2) a breach of any specific agreement or rule of conduct as defined or accepted by the couple themselves, or (3) a violation of paramount loyalty. It is these same circumstances that generally constitute the basis for equating adultery with infidelity, in that at least one of these circumstances, and usually more, is present in the conventional adultery situation. This reconceptualization and reinterpretation of infidelity is simply, and quite importantly, a recognition that adultery or extramarital sex can take place without the simultaneous occurrence of any of these circumstances. Adultery does not necessarily involve deception, the breach of an agreement, or the violation of paramount loyalty—just as the realization of these three circumstances does not necessarily imply that the act of adultery has been committed. What constitutes fidelity has been reinterpreted by the actors themselves and is not presumed to be inextricably tied to the omission or commission of the act of adultery.

To a large degree, the effect of extramarital sex depends on the meaning assigned to it by the actors and on the ground rules they have established. When the meaning differs between the principals or the ground rules are not clear, conflict ensues. When one assumes that the occurrence of adultery implies preference for another or is symptomatic of the deterioration of the marriage, then extramarital sex tends to mean those things to those involved. Their responses will differ according to the system of agreements between spouses and their respective perceptions of the ways in which those agreements are upheld or violated. As Cuber (1969) has noted, the effect of extramarital sex on the marital relationship depends on several factors: "(1) whether the adultery is carried on furtively or is known by the spouse, (2) whether the marriage partners agree to the propriety or expediency of such behavior, (3) whether one or both participates, and (4) whether the condonement is genuine and based on principle or is simply the result of an ultimatum by one of the parties." A theory of extramarital sex which overlooks these factors is likely to produce faulty and misleading explanations of how and why it occurs in consensual contexts.

Conclusion

Consensual adultery in general and co-marital sex in particular need not be viewed as necessarily destructive of marriage but may well be an evolutionary development which will turn out to be supportive of marriage—simply one in a series of attempts to reform monogamous marriage (Beigel 1969). The reform in this case involves the sanctioning of extramarital relations. This incorporation of extramarital sex into the marriage relationship constitutes a redefinition of marital boundaries.

Whether such alternatives to and redefinitions of monogamic marriage will be viable in the long run remains to be seen. The study of consensual adultery and co-marital relations is a relatively new area of research. It is only beginning to emerge from the exploratory phase, as indeed are many of the participants themselves. Categorization of motivation patterns and types of involvement, even the vocabulary for analysis, are at this point rudimentary and tentative. To dismiss such behavior as a passing fad or neurotic obsession would be premature; to conclude that such behavior is inevitably detrimental or beneficial to marriage would be an oversimplification. Such judgments must be withheld until sufficient scientific information becomes available.

In virtually all other spheres of life, the existence of individual differences and the sanction of their expression is acknowledged and recognized. If we extend this realization to the marital and sexual sphere, then we must acknowledge that a proliferation of marital styles and frameworks may help the individual actor grow, develop, and meet his or her varying needs. From our perspective, the private actions of consenting adults are best left to the decisions of the individuals involved. At the same time, there is a manifest need for scientific understanding which would allow them to make those decisions in a more rational and humane environment.

References

Athanasiou, R. Shaver, P., and Tavris, C. 1970. Sex. *Psychol. Today* 4, no. 2, pp. 37–52.

Bartell, G. 1970. Group Sex among the Mid-Americans. *J. Sex Res.*, 6, no. 2, pp. 113–30. [In this book, pp. 185–201.]

Bartell, G. 1971. *Group Sex.* New York: Wyden.

Beigel, H. 1969. In Defense of Mate Swapping. *Rational Living* 4, no. 2, pp. 15–16.

Bell, R. R., and Silvan, L. 1971. "Swinging"—The Sexual Exchange of Marriage Partners. Paper presented at the meeting of the Society for the Study of Social Problems, August 1970, Washington, D.C.

Bowman, C. C. 1949. Cultural Ideology and Heterosexual Reality: A Preface to Sociological Research. *Amer. Soc. Rev.* 14: 624–33.

Breedlove, W., and Breedlove, J. 1964. *Swap Clubs.* Los Angeles: Sherbourne Press.

Christensen, H. T., and Gregg, C. F. 1970. Changing Sex Norms in America and Scandinavia. *J. Marriage Fam.*, 32: 616–27.

Comfort, A. 1963. *Sex in Society.* London: Duckworth. (Published in the United States by Citadel Press, 1966.)

Cuber, J. F. 1969. Adultery: Reality versus Stereotype. In *Extra-Marital Relations*, ed. G. Neubeck. Englewood Cliffs, N.J.: Prentice-Hall.

———, and Harroff, P. B. 1965. *Sex and the Significant Americans: A Study of Sexual Behavior among the Affluent.* Baltimore: Penguin Books.

Farson, R. E., Hauser, P. M., Stroup, H., and Weiner, A. J. 1969. *The Future of the Family.* New York: Family Service Association of America.

Freud, S. 1959A. Contributions to the Psychology of Love: The Most Prevalent Form of Degradation in Erotic Life. In *Collected Papers of Sigmund Freud* 4: 203–16. New York: Basic Books.

———. 1959B. Contributions to the Psychology of Love: The Taboo of Virginity. In *Collected Papers of Sigmund Freud* 4: 217–35. New York: Basic Books.

———. 1960. *Group Psychology and the Analysis of the Ego.* New York: Bantam.

Hamilton, G. V. 1929. *A Research in Marriage.* New York: Albert and Charles Boni.

Johnson, R. 1971. Personal communication, January 5, 1971.

Kinsey, A. C., Pomeroy, W. B., Martin, C. E., and Gebhard, P. H. 1953. *Sexual Behavior in the Human Female.* Philadelphia: W. B. Saunders.

Landis, C., et al. 1940. *Sex in Development.* New York: Paul B. Hoeber.

Lindsey, B. B., and Evans, W. 1929. *The Companionate Marriage.* New York: Garden City.

Neubeck, G., ed. 1969. *Extra-Marital Relations.* Englewood Cliffs, N.J.: Prentice-Hall.

O'Neill, G. C., and O'Neill, N. 1970. Patterns in Group Sexual Activity. *J. Sex Res.* 6, no. 2, pp. 101–12.

Otto, H. A., ed. 1970. *The Family in Search of a Future.* New York: Appleton-Century-Crofts.

Pomeroy, W. 1969. Two Clinicians and a Sociologist. In *Extra-Marital Relations*, ed. G. Neubeck. Englewood Cliffs, N.J.: Prentice-Hall.

Reiss, I. L. 1960. *Premarital Sexual Standards in America.* New York: Free Press.

Renne, K. 1970. Correlates of Dissatisfaction in Marriage. *J. Marriage Fam.* 32: 54–67.

Rudner, R. S. 1966. *Philosophy of Social Science.* Englewood Cliffs, N.J.: Prentice-Hall.

Schupp, C. 1970. An Analysis of Some Sociopsychological Factors Which Operate in the Functioning Relationship of Married Couples Who Exchange Mates for the Purpose of Sexual Experience. Ph.D. dissertation, United States International University.

Smith, J. R., and Smith, L. G. 1970. Co-marital Sex and the Sexual Freedom Movement. *J. Sex Res.* 6, no. 2, pp. 131–42. [In this book, pp. 202–13.]

————. *Consenting Adults: An Exploratory Study of the Sexual Freedom Movement*, in preparation.

————, eds. 1974. *Beyond Monogamy: Recent Studies of Sexual Alternatives in Marriage.* Baltimore: The Johns Hopkins University Press.

Stoller, F. H. 1970. The Intimate Network of Families As a New Structure. In *The Family in Search of a Future*, ed. H. A. Otto. New York: Appleton-Century-Crofts.

Symonds, C. 1968. Pilot Study of the Peripheral Behavior of Sexual Mate Swappers. Master's thesis, University of California, Riverside.

Terman, L. M. 1938. *Psychological Factors in Marital Happiness.* New York: McGraw-Hill.

Twichell, J. 1974. Sexual Liberality and Personality: A Pilot Study. [In this book, pp. 230–45.]

Vandervoort. 1970. Jake Gimball Lectures on the Psychology of Sex, November 1970, University of California Medical School, San Francisco.

Varni, C. 1971. A Participant Observer Study of Sexual Mate Exchange among Married Couples. Paper presented at the meeting of the Pacific Sociological Association, April 1971, Honolulu. [In this book, pp. 246–59.]

Emerging Patterns of Innovative Behavior in Marriage

James W. Ramey

The mass media are replete with sensational stories of free love, swinging, communes, and group marriages, usually implying ruptured standards, moral decay, and threats to the institution of marriage. Moralists point with alarm to one out of four marriages ending in divorce, freely circulating swinger-ad magazines, campus orgies, and flourishing communes. Here is their proof that the minions of hell are fast taking over. Fortunately, there is another, more positive, explanation. When we view these phenomena in the context of diffusion of innovation, we are witnessing the realignment of traditional marital-relationship patterns rather than deviations from the norm. As Beigel (1969) indicates, this is a supportive development aimed at reforming monogamous marriage.

Diffusion of innovation refers to the process of change and the generally accepted means of determining which of many possible changes is actually taking place. It has been found that no matter how long a particular practice has been accepted by small groups, such changes do not move into the mainstream of society until approximately 7%–10% of the population adopt them (Pemberton 1936). Once this level of saturation is reached, general acceptance rapidly follows so that within a few years the vast majority of people can be expected to accept ideas or activities that have been the

Reprinted, by permission of the publisher, from *Fam. Coordinator*, October 1972.

norm for a small percentage of the population for decades. As an example of this kind of change, some women were smoking more than a generation ago, but it was not until World War II that this activity was accepted generally as proper behavior. When acceptance did come, it happened almost overnight—in just less than a decade (Ramey 1963).

This paper presents a paradigm, or model, for research in the area of evolutionary sexual behavior in marriage. This model serves three purposes. First, it provides a basis for systematic classification of current research on alternative sexual life-styles for pair-bonded couples, particularly free love, swinging, communal living, and group marriage. Some of this research will be examined, and analysis of this material will be organized, in respect to the paradigm. A more critical look will be taken at current research findings, and gaps in present research knowledge will be identified. Second, the paradigm is designed to foster further inquiry and to suggest fruitful lines of endeavor for new research. It should not be conceived as a complete theory of evolutionary marital sexual behavior but is offered merely as a proposal that ultimately may lead to the development of a useful theory. Third, the model provides marriage partners with a cogent way of conceptualizing their relationship and hence affords them a guide for analyzing their pair-bond behavior and evaluating their own degree of commitment and effectiveness as partners in a union of equals.

Before introducing the definitions of the behaviors with which this paper is concerned, the scope of the inquiry, the point of view from which it is being undertaken, and the limits imposed upon it will be discussed. Initially, an attempt is being made to link together as part of a composite whole several types of marital behavior generally considered to be deviant. Reasons will be presented for the belief that these behaviors are, in fact, evolutionary, stemming from two basic changes in our society—the shift toward a temporary-systems society and the shift toward regarding women as people with equal rights, privileges, and responsibilities rather than as chattels. This is done as a means of clarifying the growing number of contradictory statements, many of which claim to be based on actual participant-observer experience, with regard to swinging, group marriage, and communes. It is hoped and believed that this approach will help to focus research in the field on the gaps and overlaps that would have the highest potential for increasing our understanding of what is happening. We do not propose to critique and/or relate all of the previous research in the field. It would seem much more important to sketch in the broad picture as we see it, leaving more detailed analysis to later efforts. We hope the sketch will prove sufficiently interesting to tempt others to do likewise.

It seems appropriate to begin with several definitions:

Free love is open-ended sexual seeking and consummating without legal or other commitment of any kind.

Swinging generally involves two or more pair-bonded couples who mutually decide to switch sexual partners or engage in group sex. Singles may be included either through temporary coupling with another individual specifically for the purpose of swinging or as a part of a triadic or larger group sexual experience.

Intimate friendship is an otherwise traditional friendship in which sexual intimacy is considered appropriate behavior.

When individuals agree to make life commitments as members of one particular group, rather than through many different groups, they may constitute a commune. The number of common commitments will vary from commune to commune, the critical number having been reached at the point at which the group sees itself as a commune rather than at some absolute number.

In a group marriage each of three or more participants is pair-bonded with at least two others.

The term "pair-bond" is used to reduce ambiguity. A pair-bond is a reciprocal primary relationship involving sexual intimacy. A pair-bonded couple see themselves as mates. This is not necessarily the case in a primary relationship, which can be one-sided and need not include sexual intimacy. The term "pair-bond" is preferred rather than "married couple" for another reason—not all pair-bonded couples are married.

The basic definitions deal with a range of behavior that is increasingly complex. They are interrelated and often sequential. They stem from the human propensity to become involved in ever more complex relationships, a propensity based on the fact that humans are problem-solving organisms. Today's world is increasingly inundated with evidence that this is so—that man seeks to increase the complexity of his interactions. Toffler (1970) adds a new word to our lexicon—future shock. Yet, one of the age-old institutions, marriage, has resisted this trend. Why should this be?

There appear to be two interrelated causes. First, there is the existence of male dominance in society, with all that it implies. Unequals tend not to form complex relationships. Second, in the past, and indeed in many subcultures and in much of the lower middle- and working-class levels of society today, two married persons in a stable and permanent social context need to seek little from each other. Psychological and interpersonal needs can be satisfied in a variety of ways through kin, neighbors, and friendship. Husband and wife literally live in two different worlds. As Bott (1957) points out:

Couples in close-knit relational networks maintained a rigid division of labor, were deeply involved in external bonds, and placed little emphasis on shared interests, joint recreation, or a satisfying sexual relationship. Couples in loose-knit networks, on the other hand, show little division of labor, emphasize marital togetherness, and are highly self-conscious about child-rearing techniques. The transition from working class to middle-class status and from urban villager to suburban environment tends to bring about a loosening of relational networks and is therefore usually associated with an increase in the intensity and intimacy of the marital bond, and a decrease in marital role differentiation.

Marriage did not change much over the ages until the pair-bond was composed of peers. As long as the woman was considered a chattel, the relationship was not one of equality. Such terms as "doing wifely duty," "marriage rights," and "exclusivity," literally meant, and for most people still mean, that the pair-bond is male dominated. There is little wonder, then, that marriage has so long resisted the universal human urge to intensify the complexity of relationships. Komarovsky (1962) and Babchuck and Bates (1963) strongly support the thesis that both husband and wife maintain close relationships with same-sex peers and that the marital relationship tends to be male dominated in both blue-collar (Komarovsky) and lower middle-class couples (Babchuck and Bates).

It is possible to point to attempts by some, at various times and places, to free marriage to some degree from the restraint of male domination, and by thus proclaiming equality of the sexes, to permit the emergence of alternatives to exclusivity in marriage. These efforts always failed or were tolerated only in certain special, small, restricted, and segregated groups because in the larger society women were not yet peers. Bird (1970) shows how, in a patriarchal society, conditions at a physical or economic frontier may, of necessity, produce equality of the sexes, but as soon as the period of consolidation and stability is reached, it becomes a mark of status to keep an idle woman. The emergence of free love in conjunction with revolutionary movements is noted time and again, only to be followed by the return of male-dominated pair-bond exclusivity as soon as the revolution succeeds or fails. Indeed, free love can be considered a revolutionary tool, for it quickly sets apart and isolates the in-group from family and friends, both symbolically and literally.

In this context it is important to understand that revolutionaries or dissidents can be political, social, religious, economic, cultural, or a combination of these. Often the combination is called utopian, hippie, or anarchistic without regard to the actual goals or beliefs involved. A few of these people are regarded as the lunatic fringe and are tolerated by the larger society because they are amusing and sometimes even productive, especially the cultural radicals such as musicians, artists, or theatrical types. Others have been less tolerated, typically driven out or underground, and often persecuted, no matter what the stripe of their dissident bent. The survival factor in such groups appears to be strong patriarchal and/or religious orientation and considerable structure. Almost invariably they have eased away from sexual experimentation in favor of exclusive male-dominated marriage bonds. This happens in spite of the fact that, in theory at least, any alternative to pair-bond exclusivity could be practiced in a closed group, provided the group was willing to accept joint child-rearing and nurturing responsibility.

Nevertheless, until the society as a whole began to accept the right of the female to be a peer, such excursions into marriage alternatives could only fail. A woman who is dependent on her husband must grant his requests, including the demand for sexual exclusivity, even though she may know that he is not practicing the same exclusivity. If she has no skills to sell, no viable means of support without him, she can hardly demur. An economically emancipated wife is in a much better position to insist on equality because she is self-sufficient, a factor that may also increase her social self-sufficiency. Thus, the stage is set for pair-bonding between equal partners, each able to sustain a life outside marriage, so that both enter into the relationship voluntarily on the assumption that the anticipated benefits will be greater than would be available in a non-pair-bonded state. Furthermore, survival of the marriage depends on each continuing to place a higher value on maintaining the pair-bond than on reverting to their previous state. In other words, a continuing relationship depends on each continuing to extend to the other the privileges of "open marriage" in the O'Neill (1972) sense. Osofsky and Osofsky (1972) characterize this as a form of parity or androgyny where each partner has an equal number of options for roles outside the marriage. Consensual sexual activity outside the pair-bond would be among these options but should not be construed as a determinant characteristic of a pair-bond. The final touch to this new equal status within the pair-bond is female control over conception for the first time in history. Pregnancy is no longer a viable threat to the female. The advent of the pill has removed the last major physical weapon in the male arsenal.

In the 1950s, trends toward increased geographic and career mobility and toward greater social and economic freedom for women began to come together for new life-styles in marriage. Academic, professional, and managerial people bceame increasingly mobile, leading William H. Whyte, Jr. (1956), to write *The Organization Man* and Russell Lynes (1953) to coin the term "upper bohemian" to describe these people. The United States Bureau of the Census pointed out that 20% of the population moved to a new location, outside the county in which they had been living, and much of this movement was accounted for by the aforementioned academic, professional, and managerial groups. Riesman, Glazer, and Denney (1955) pointed out that this is an other-directed society and identified these same types of individuals as typifying the new breed which must be capable of self-restraint while recognizing that groups vary in what they consider desirable and undesirable behavior. As Slater (1968) tells us, they saw the other-directed individual as one who must be acutely sensitive and responsive to group norms while recognizing the essential arbitrariness, particularity, and limited relevance of all moral imperatives. Pity the inner-directed conformist, therefore, the throwback who was programed from birth to display a limited range of responses in all situations, regardless of environmental variation, which, while possibly heroic, is excessively simple-minded.

As Slater develops the temporary-systems theme, following in the footsteps of Bott, Komarovsky, and others cited earlier, he says:

Spouses are now asked to be lovers, friends, mutual therapists, in a society which is forcing the marriage bond to become the closest, deepest, most important, and putatively most enduring relationship of one's life. Paradoxically, then, it is increasingly likely to fall short of the emotional demands placed upon it and be dissolved.

The end point of Slater's argument is that people can and must press toward the full exploitation of their talents, since in a truly temporary society everyone would have to be a generalist and be able to step into any role in the group to which he belongs at the moment. This is in marked contrast to the present situation in which the upper bohemians tend to specialize in certain roles (which is one of the reasons they are mobile) both on the job and in social situations. Consequently, each time they move to a new geographic location, they must search for groups that need their roles.

It is these several reasons that have caused some of the results in the sexual area of shifting from ritualistically determined marriages, based on rights, to self-determined ones, based on privilege. Highly mobile pair-bonds, who are here today and moved tomorrow, cannot depend on formal or ritual structure because they are perpetually in a time bind. They must turn to each other and evolve a much more complex relationship to replace the kin, neighbor, and friendship relational structure that is no longer available on a long-term basis. They must also develop means of getting informally plugged-in quickly whenever they move. When Lynes coined the upper-bohemian label, it was for the purpose of describing just such informal networks, although he did not describe their sexual overtones. It is interesting to find Farson (1969) and Stoller (1970) advocating various forms of intimate networks as a means of dealing with the interpersonal intimacy impoverishment of the isolated nuclear family. It is rather surprising that recognition of the existence of such systems has been so late in coming.

The temporary-systems strata is the group in which women are most likely to be treated as peers. This group is augmented by persons with sufficient education and exposure to ideas to be strongly influenced by current trends (Gagnon and Simon 1970; McLuhan and Leonard 1967; O'Neill and O'Neill 1970; Ramey 1972; and Smith and Smith 1970). Already, many of the college-age young people have the same attitudes toward peer relationships in the pair-bond as those that exist among some of the better-educated upper middle-class members of the depression generation. A surprising number of people in the general population seem to believe that, indeed, it is the young people who should be blamed for giving birth to the idea that men and women are equals!

The current forays into sexual alternatives to monogamy are seen as attempts to build a more complex network of intimate relationships that can absorb some of the impact of the new-found complexity of the pair-bond by short circuiting the process of developing ancillary relationships in the usual ritualistic manner. It is believed that this occurs for two reasons: (1) because there is not time to go through a long process of finding a group that needs the roles the couple can fill and (2) because using sexual intimacy as an entry role guarantees the couple that, other things being equal, they can fill the role. Particularly if such ties are to take up the slack of the unavailable kin-neighbor-friendship relational systems, as well as relieve some of the pressure on the newly complex pair-bond interaction, they must begin on a much deeper, more intimate basis than the ties they replace. Both time and emotional pressures will allow nothing short of this. The relationship must cut through the ritual layers quickly in order to be of any help, and indeed, as Brecher (1969) indicates, the entire courting sequence is often telescoped from several weeks or months to as little as an hour. What better way to insure that this will happen than to attempt to relate in a taboo area? Everyone has had the discouraging experience of pursuing a friendship for many months, only to discover suddenly an emotional block to further progress toward meaningful interaction, which was not apparent when the relationship first began. Usually there is no means of discovering what the other person's taboos will be until one comes up against them. While the assumption that those without sexual taboos will have a minimum of other taboos to intensive interaction on the gut level is not a valid one, it seems to hold up well for many people in many situations, perhaps because sexual inhibitions are among the deepest rooted.

Entry into free love or swinging relationships typically takes place from this set of circumstances. A less typical set will be described later. Entry into communes and group marriage sometimes takes place without going through either of these stages but, more typically, proceeds from them, especially among the thirty-and-over age group (Ramey 1972).

Given the societal conditions that have made it necessary for couples living in a temporary-systems world to find new ways to function as a couple that are more complex than have been necessary in the past, and given also that women are more likely to be peers at such a societal level than formerly, it does not follow that all couples in this situation will react by becoming involved in one of the alternative life-styles under discussion. But these conditions do foster such behavior on the part of some people, and for them it will be a more successful adaptation than for those whose pair-bond is not a relationship of peers. It is evident that this behavior is also emulated by others who are neither in the temporary-systems strata nor peers in the pair-bond as well as by a few who may be part of the working class (Bartell 1970; Ramey 1972; Smith and Smith 1970; Symonds 1970).

The Model

Much of the confusion in discussions of swinging, communes, and group marriage relates to the difference between committed and uncommitted relationships. For heuristic purposes, this embraces Kanter's (1968) three types of commitment: cathectic, or commitment to the individual; cognitive, which involves weighing the value of continuing in a group or leaving it; and evaluative, which involves belief in the perceived moral rightness of group ideology.

The following hypotheses are proposed:

1) Nonconsensual adultery and swinging are free-love activities which involve no commitment or minimal commitment.

2) Intimate friendship, evolutionary communes, and group marriage involve considerable individual commitment and, in the case of the communes and group marriage, commitment to the group as well.

3) Swinging may constitute a transitional step between minimal individual commitment and growth of such commitment between spouses.

4) Once husband and wife have begun to experience the joy and satisfaction of individual growth through joint dialogue and commitment, they may find their newly found responsiveness to one another so satisfying that they drop out of swinging.

5) As the marriage takes on more and more aspects of a peer relationship, the couple may consensually agree to increase the complexity of their relationship through the development of intimate friendships with other individuals or couples, through which the sense of commitment to the individual is extended to these significant others.

6) A significant portion, apparently about 50% (Ramey 1972) of the couples who become candidates for evolutionary communes or group marriage come from among those who have developed intimate friendships.

7) Group marriage, which combines commitment to the group with multiple pair-bonding among the members of the group, is the most complex form of marriage.

8) These various marriage alternatives can be placed on a continuum that ranges from dyadic marriage with minimal commitment (in which there may be nonconsensual adultery), to swinging, to peer marriage, to intimate friendship, to evolutionary commune, to group marriage.

In general, by commitment we mean a relationship involving dialogue, trust, and responsibility. Within the pair-bond, we accept Kanter's definition of cathectic commitment, i.e., willingness to accept unlimited liability for.

Neither of these profiles concerns intelligence, income level, or formal education, although it is unusual to find the committed person lacking money or education unless he has deliberately chosen to renounce them. Extreme pictures have been drawn in order to sharpen the contrast. Some people have insight in some areas and not in others, but it is nevertheless possible to clearly distinguish between those who seek to relate to others and those who do not find it possible to do so. This differentiation is necessary to comprehension of the diffusion process to be described, but it should be emphasized that these are normal, average people. Although their religious commitment tends to be low, they range politically from radical to conservative, are better educated than most of the population, and are of high socioeconomic status so that they hardly fit popular conceptions of deviant individuals (Smith and Smith, in preparation). In fact, one recently completed study employed the Minnesota Multiphasic Personality Inventory and found the subjects "uninterestingly normal" (Twichell 1974).

Figure 1 indicates the relationship between the degree of complexity of the commitment individuals are willing to make and the type of pair-bond relationship one is likely to find them enjoying. The figure reads in one direction only, i.e., not all individuals with deep and complex levels of commitment will necessarily join a group marriage, but individuals in a group marriage can be expected to

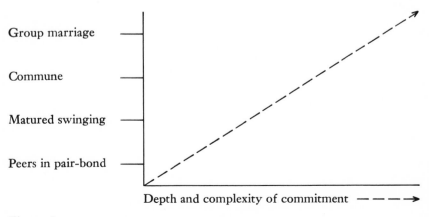

Figure 1

have such a commitment within their relationship. The pair-bond involving peers is deliberately indicated to be at a level above the zero point on this figure.

The first thing that is apparent from figure 2 is that free-love activities such as affairs, adultery, or swinging are treated differently from intimate friendship, evolutionary communes, or group marriage. Free love is an uncommitted activity (open-ended sexual seeking and consummating without legal or other commitment of any kind) that is widespread among both single and married indi-

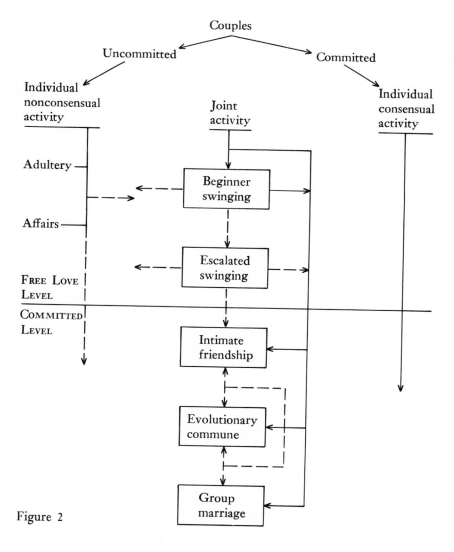

Figure 2

viduals. It may occur for both the marriage partners within some marriages and is the type of activity which Bell and Silvan (1970) refer to as "activity which usually involves guilt and dishonesty and often does not include any notion of fun and recreation." It is easy to understand that people caught up in the stereotype of high drama, jealousy, and tragic romance as part of their cultural expectation about a one-sided relationship outside the pair-bond not only would not have fun but would neither invest nor receive enough pleasure from the relationship to make it a joyous exchange rather than a contest-chase, tragic loss, or terrible trap.

There is a crossover between the free-love and committed levels through swinging. Most uncommitted couples never manage to get beyond the two stages of swinging, since their activity remains strictly on a free-love basis, even though it involves joint activity. Such a couple may decide to legitimize individual nonconsensual activity by becoming jointly involved in swinging. The reverse is also possible.

It is possible, though unlikely, that an uncommitted couple may become temporarily involved in intimate friendship, group marriage, or a commune. Intimate friendship, which will be more fully defined later, can be distinguished from free-love swinging in terms of Martin Buber's (1955) distinction between collectivity and community:

Collectivity is not a binding but a bundling together: individuals packed together, armed and equipped in common, with only as much life from person to person as will enflame the marching step. But community . . . is the being no longer side by side but with one another of a multitude of persons. And this multitude, though it also moves toward one goal, yet experiences everywhere a turning to, a dynamic facing of, the other, a flowing from I to thou. . . . Collectivity is based on an organized atrophy of personal existence, community on its increase and confirmation in life lived toward one another.

If such involvement results in the removal of blocks to the ability to develop and sustain complex relationships, it is well and good. In many instances, however, such attempts are indeed temporary and may be disastrous for the intimate-friendship group, commune, or group marriage involved. There is a great deal of evidence to support this contention (Kanter 1970; Nordhoff 1961). Many reports of communes and group marriages that have not succeeded indicate that the group was unable to deal with uncommitted people who had not been recognized as unable to deal with complex relationships before they were accepted into the group. It is usually easy for the intimate-friendship group to simply drop the couple (Breedlove and Breedlove 1964; Palson 1970).

Some uncommitted couples manage to grow sufficiently to graduate to either intimate friendship or consensual individual sexual activity that is based on more than simple sex. While this does not seem to be the case for most of the uncommitted, the potential is always present, and it is not unreasonable to conjecture that, if given time, greater numbers will move into the ranks of the committed. Considering the degree to which this has occurred over the past two decades, it may not take as long as expected. While most of these people continue to operate at the free-love level, many seem to be progressing from individual excursions outside the pair-bond to joint swinging. Even if they never move to a more complex relationship than this, they will have taken a significant and rewarding step toward ability to relate in their marriage, for the one spontaneous response interviewers frequently hear is the vast improvement experienced in their ability to talk to one another, not only about sexual matters, but in general (Brecher 1969; Denfeld and Gordon 1970; O'Neill and O'Neill 1970; Palson and Palson 1970; Smith and Smith 1970).

Turning to the committed side of figure 2, one finds that in a union of equals, both persons are free to explore on a consensual basis any and all forms of complex relationship that seem interesting. In the O'Neills' terms (1972), this activity can be termed "open marriage." Those who practice open marriage often develop intimate friendships. Some couples begin moving toward more complex experiences in this manner and progress to making multiple life commitments through the same group (generally identified as a commune) or to the most complex type of marital commitment—establishing more than one pair-bond simultaneously (group marriage). Other couples skip the intimate-friendship stage and move directly into the communal or group-marriage stage. How many will ultimately be satisfied to relate at which level is not known.

Since there are so many new recruits swelling the ranks of swingers, communalists, and group marriages, and there is also constant turnover of those who are interested but uncommitted and who find such activity too threatening once they have tried it, it is difficult to assess the degree of diffusion and the level of complexity at which most people ultimately establish relational-system homeostasis. One cannot guess how long the process will take for the average couple.

Sometimes, one or more group marriages can be found in a commune. Members of communes and group marriages almost always feel free to swing or engage in individual sexual activity outside the group with complete acceptance of such activity by the group. In addition, while many committed couples enter swinging activity at the intimate-friendship stage via personal introduction by friends who are already intimate, some go through the beginner stage first, especially if they live in a new neighborhood or a socially limiting situation that forces them to use surreptitious means (such as a blind ad in a swinging magazine) to gain entry into the swinging scene. A few of these people might pass through the escalated stage.

Swinging

Swinging was defined at the beginning of this paper as follows:

Swinging generally involves two or more pair-bonded couples who mutually decide to switch sexual partners or engage in group sex. Singles may be included either through temporary coupling with another individual specifically for the purpose of swinging or as part of a triadic or larger group sexual experience.

To say that swinging generally involves two or more pair-bonded couples may seem inexact. Actually, swinging may involve adding only one person of either sex to the pair-bond. Some couples find it easier to relate to one person than to two. Some find it easier to locate one person who is compatible with both than to find another couple in which both the male and the female are compatible with both husband and wife. Singles are thus involved in swinging directly. It is surprising that this point has been disputed by some reporters on the swinging scene (Breedlove and Breedlove 1964), especially since many acknowledge that it is the swinging singles who sometimes give the total swinging scene a bad name. Palson and Palson (1970) point out that

to singles, swinging looks more like a long time of sexual encounters with no attempt to form the "proper" kind of personal union, whereas married couples, secure in their own union, can experience friendly sex with others, knowing that they have achieved a permanence with one mate as morality ordains, and that sex with others can actually enhance this relationship.

Many researchers have interviewed threesomes (O'Neill and O'Neill 1970; Smith and Smith 1970), and it would appear that more stable threesome relationships exist than any other type. The author recently analyzed ads in four major swinger magazines and found that the second most-looked-for situation, whether the advertiser was a couple, a single male, or a single female, was "couples or single females desired." The third ranked desire was for "couples or singles, male or female." Bartell (1971) reports similar results.

The implied threat to the pair-bond of accepting a single into a sexual union, even temporarily, obviously is a problem for the committed couple. More couples swing with single women than with single men. In a male-dominated pair-bond, the male has little to gain from swinging with a single male, along with the threat of direct competition in the swinging situation with his wife, unless he happens to enjoy sexual contacts with other men. Even in the latter case, he would be unlikely to expose such inclinations to his wife. Such activity would be more likely to occur if the couple regarded themselves as equals, free to explore all kinds of multiple sexual relationships.

Some people, especially therapists, have characterized swinging as a male-dominated activity that serves largely to actualize male fantasies. The recent report of the President's Commission on Obscenity and Pornography (1970) suggests, as do Masters and Johnson (1966), that women are just as likely to have such fantasies. It has often been pointed out that men are most likely to suggest swinging, but it has been less-often remarked that men are also most likely to suggest getting out of swinging. This seems to occur because swinging is a great equalizer which appears to promote female independence as a result of markedly different capacity of the female for prolonged sexual involvement and the new found sense of self-worth. This is one of the reasons that many couples reevaluate their own pair-bonding relationship as a result of their involvement in swinging.

Our definition emphasized that swinging does not necessarily involve mate switching. It simply may involve participation in group sex, as defined by the O'Neills (1969). Some swingers who will not swing with a single are quite willing to involve singles in group sex, as at a party. Singles may also form temporary couples for the purpose of swinging with those couples who will not swing with a single alone or because the single is a married person whose mate refuses to swing.

Symonds's (1970) definition of swinging suggests that this is an activity involving strangers. Brecher (1969) points out, however, as others do, that the same sort of courtship occurs in swinging that occurs between two people on a conventional date but that this courtship is more likely to be truncated than it is among the unmarried.

Swinging has been separated into a beginner and escalated stage, both of which are uncommitted in nature and are linked to intimate friendship, to which many swingers graduate.

Couples become involved in swinging for many reasons. They want to make out, they seek an alternative to clandestine individual adventures outside the pair-bond, they see other people doing it, or one partner, usually the husband, forces the other into it, often to assuage guilt or to "save the marriage." They make an issue of swinging without any emotional involvement, at least at the beginning: "It is just a sex thing."

The committed couple, by contrast, becomes involved in intimate friendship because they wish to expand their already joyous relationship by joint investment in other people at the sociosexual level in responsive, responsible relationships. In either case, the societal pressures outlined earlier will have contributed greatly to developing the climate in which such activity can be expected to flourish.

Many committed couples grow into intimate friendship naturally with friends of long standing. Others are introduced into intimate friendships by mutual friends, where the person-to-person interaction is more important than the genital-to-genital interaction and the object is to form relationships that may include sexual involvement as one part of a much larger and more complex level of interaction. The complexity depends on the people involved. Some find that developing a close union with one or a few couples is sufficient to meet their needs. Others form looser bonds with a greater number of people. The nature of the involvement varies much the same way as the involvement between mates in a pair-bond.

How does one become a swinger? An essential ingredient is to see one's self as a swinger. Many people who switch partners occasionally do not consider themselves swingers, although others might say they are. Some, who do not actually swing, like to believe they are swingers, although they would not be so classified by others. Many would-be swingers try it once and decide it is not for them. Little is known about this group because they are hard to identify. No one can even say how large it is. While it may be relatively unimportant, there are those who are keenly interested because they are concerned about just how many swingers there are in the population. The percentage varies with the definition of swinger, not to mention the other difficulties with establishing it. In terms of the diffusion of innovation, however, it is of interest to know whether current saturation is nearing the critical 7%–10% level, at which one would look for rather rapid and overwhelming acceptance of swinging by the society.

Once the decision is made to try swinging, one must find the swingers. Many nonswingers think swinging is a made-up fantasy created by journalists and others with something to sell. Many swingers are convinced that the whole world swings! If the potential swinger does not have swingers that he knows about among his friends, he may attempt to seduce friends to try it. This can be risky business, especially for the neophyte, who may turn next to public entry points. Apparently only about 5% are forced to do this (Breedlove and Breedlove 1964), although Bartell claims it is the most-used method. A number of public swinging institutions have parallels in the singles world, such as swinging bars, socials, magazines, personal columns in underground papers, and the Sexual Freedom League. The uncommitted seem much more likely to use these public entry points than the committed, who find it much easier to relate to others in a meaningful way.

The second swinging stage, called "escalated swinging," is avoided by most swingers. Those who get there may do so because they made a poor decision. It may take some time for the uncommitted couple to arrive at this decision. She may begin to feel like a prostitute. He may become impotent. Having sex with people with whom one does not relate gets stale pretty quickly for most people.

Some people drop out at this point, deciding that swinging is not for them after all. Others realize that they must invest in people if swinging is to continue to have meaning for them. These people may graduate to intimate friendship. The sharing of intimacy not only has been working on them as a couple, it has also given them a bridge to other people. A few make the third choice—they escalate. They restore potency by upping the ante, experimenting with more and more "way-out" behavior. Ultimately, this path must form a closed loop, for such escalation cannot be continued indefinitely. Eventually they must drop out or begin to relate to people as people and not as sex objects.

Swingers do not appear to handle their swinging relationships on a different basis than other friendships. On the contrary, it would appear that most swinging couples simply add swinging to the list of criteria they use for selecting friends, just as the "sailing crowd" and the "mah jong" group choose most of their friends from among those who share these common interests. Reports that swingers compartmentalize swinging apart from otherwise ordinary lives appear to confuse the common tendency of some swingers to hide swinging from their business associates or others in "straight society" with having two "social worlds." Time constraints alone would argue against this. As Paul Goodman said in an interview (1971):

In the instances where I have been able to make a contact I have almost invariably found a friend and in many of these cases these friendship have gone on for 30 or 40 years. Even though they rapidly become non-sexual relationships. . . . St. Thomas Aquinas has pointed out the chief use of human sexuality, aside from procreation, is getting to know another person— in other words, you don't love somebody and then have sex with them. You have sex with them and then love them.

Many couples indicate that they were quite active when they began swinging but tapered off as soon as they found people with whom they shared the same norms and standards that they had previously used to select friends. The decision to confine their circle of friends to those people, they explain, is largely because relationships with these people are more honest and open on all levels and not just in relation to swinging. In a significant number of these relationships there is only occasional swinging, or no longer any swinging, and it is not unusual to find that these couples are no longer actively looking for new swinging partners.

No one knows, at this juncture, how many of the uncommitted get beyond the free-love levels we have been discussing. So many newcomers are joining the scene that the issue is quite confused. It may be some time before we can say with any assurance how many of the uncommitted are able ultimately to relate to others well enough to be graduated to the intimate-friendship classification.

Symonds (1970) classified swingers as either recreational or utopian, whereas Bartell (1969) claimed that the chief characteristic of all couples in his sample was their inherent normality. We believe Symonds may have failed to differentiate between those beginners who constitute the extremist fringe at the lower edge of the spectrum and those swingers who are in academic, professional, and managerial strata and tend to exhibit more of the attributes of her utopians than of her recreationals (Brecher 1969; Ramey 1972; O'Neill and O'Neill 1970). There is also the possibility that she failed to distinguish between this latter group and the beginners who are still overwhelmed with the idea of swinging and who are even more overwhelmed with relating to people on a more complex level. Most swingers exhibit *some* of the attributes she identifies with recreationals, while few, if any, exhibit all of her utopian attributes and none of the recreational. This may be especially important in California, where knowledge of swinging has permeated many layers of society that are not usually involved in complex pair-bond relationships.

An important distinguishing characteristic of the intimate friendship, commune, or group marriage is the open problem-solving and relating they favor. Carl Rogers said in 1951 that people resist experience which might force them to change through denial or distortion of symbolization. Thus, the uncommitted swinger must either drop out or ritualize the swinging experience. Recognizing this, those who wish to help the uncommitted bridge the gap must relax the situation and reduce the threat. As Rogers went on to say:

The structure and organization of self appears to become more rigid under threat; to relax its boundaries when completely free of threat. Experience which is perceived as inconsistent with the self can only be assimilated if the current organization of self is relaxed and expanded to include it.

The committed appear to recognize this.

This definition seems more restrictive than necessary. Huxley (1937) claimed that

all effective communities are founded upon the principle of unlimited liability. In small groups composed of members personally acquainted with one another, unlimited liability provides a liberal education in responsibility, loyalty, and consideration. . . . Individual members should possess nothing and everything—nothing as individuals and everything as joint owners of communally held property and communally produced income. Property and income should not be so large as to become ends in themselves, not so small that the entire energies of the community have to be directed to procuring tomorrow's dinner.

At all times and in all places communities have been formed for the purpose of making it possible for their members to live more nearly in accord with the currently accepted religious ideals than could be done "in the world." Such communities have devoted a considerable proportion of their time and energy to study, to the performance of ceremonial acts of devotion and, in some cases at any rate, to the practice of "spiritual exercises."

From . . . the salient characteristics of past communities we can see what future communities ought to be and do. We see that they should be composed of carefully selected individuals, united in a common belief and by fidelity to a shared ideal. We see that property and income should be held in common and that every member should assume unlimited liability for all other members. We see the disciplinary arrangements may be of various kinds, but that the most educative form of organization is the democratic. We see that it is advisable for communities to undertake practical work in addition to study, devotion and spiritual exercises; and that this practical work should be of a kind which other social agencies, public or private, are either unable or unwilling to perform.

Definitions of commune are difficult to find, but many of the elements are in this lengthy quote from Huxley. In order to encompass all of the groups that claim to be communes today, however, it is necessary to devise a less restrictive definition, such as the one at the beginning of this paper:

When individuals agree to make life commitments as members of one particular group rather than through many different groups, they may constitute a commune. The number of common commitments will vary from commune to commune, the critical number having been reached at the point at which the group sees itself as a commune rather than at some absolute number.

Although some communes do share dining and/or sleeping quarters and some espouse joint ownership, income, and function, this is not the case for all communes. Quite a few communes have separate quarters, either in a jointly owned apartment building or in separate houses, for example. The type and range of common commitments is such that being a commune is almost a state of mind. Some groups which have many more of the kinds of commitments in common usually associated with communes, call themselves "co-ops."

Which of the many life commitments are most commonly met through a commune? Creating goods and services, worshiping in a specific manner, merchandising, purchasing, owning and managing property, farming, traveling, educating and rearing children in a specific manner, studying, having friendships, and being involved in social or political action are some of the common attributes of communes. The world has always functioned through interest groups. The most common of these through the ages has been the tribe and its components, the families. One of the most frequently cited reasons for the current upsurge of interest in communes is the desire to return to an extended family or tribal grouping. Indeed, many communes refer to themselves not by name but simply as the family.

It is not by accident that the successful communes, i.e., those that have survived, have not been extended families but instead have been groups with a strong unifying and motivating drive and a strong leader. In many cases, this unifying factor has been religious. Currently, in addition to the religious drive, there is a substantial number of successful communes built around the desire to optimize coping capacity in a quasi-capitalistic society; i.e., to do better that which they as individuals are already doing well.

There are three major varieties of communes and one trial variety. They can be classified as the religious communes, which have existed in America since 1680, if not earlier; the utopian communes; and the new breed of evolutionary communes mentioned above. What distinguishes this last group is that they are not about to drop out of or attempt to change the existing society. They simply seek to increase their ability to work effectively within the system. The fourth type of commune is the student commune, which will be handled in a separate section because of its two unique characteristics—it is temporary, and it is a learning situation.

Religious communes have enjoyed the highest survival rate among all United States communes, probably because of their strong patriarchal, highly structured, and fervently goal-directed orientation. Although some have loosened up a bit over the years, others have survived with little change. The most successful group, the Hutterites, have grown from three original colonies in 1874 to over 170 colonies today, each averaging about 150 members. Most of these groups are in the provinces of Alberta, Saskatchewan, and Manitoba, Canada, but approximately fifty colonies are scattered through South Dakota and Montana. A religious group of more recent origin, the Brüderhof, came from Germany to the United States in the 1950s by way of England and Paraguay because of persecution that began in the 1930s. Already, the original settlement in Rifton, New York, has spawned two other groups, one in Connecticut and the other in Pennsylvania. Religious communes are not the concern of this paper, but for those who wish to pursue the subject, see Carden 1969; Hostetler 1968; Kanter 1970; Krippner and Fersh 1970; Nordhoff 1961; and Redekop 1969.

The utopian communes have suffered unreasonably at the hands of the press. Many are unjustifiably called "hippie communes," while others actually fit this designation. The most successful of these new drop-out groups are highly structured, centering around the leadership of strong charismatic individuals or deliberately submerging leadership in a consensual format that seeks to elevate all group members to the level of generalist. Some groups have strong political overtones, either in the revolutionary sense or in terms of complete withdrawal from society. These are the back-to-the-land, organic food, vegetarian, hand-labor groups who typically seek to become completely self-sustaining without recourse to the rest of society. Still other groups are "do your own thing—when the spirit moves you" groups. Some of these are heavily involved in the drug culture. Most utopian groups espouse the values of rural living, even though few of them are found in the country.

Just as the religious communes cluster at the highly structured end of the continuum, so do many of the utopian communes cluster at the unstructured end of the continuum, but the failure rate is extremely high among these groups. Other utopian groups can be found at points on the continuum, and many of them seem to be slowly migrating toward the more highly structured end. All of the utopian groups located in the country labor under the handicap of high visibility, which makes survival especially difficult in the light of sensational headlines in the mass media. A significant recent development among the utopians is the emergence of collectives of communes. There are at least a dozen of these collectives already, and more are being set up all the time. Free Vermont, for example, is a collective of sixteen communes, which sponsors a number of joint projects, such as a children's commune, a traveling medical test service, and a peak-load work-sharing system. The Powelton Village Association of Communes in Philadelphia, which includes thirty communes, operates a flourishing food purchasing co-op, a baby-sitting service, and a free garage for fixing communal automobiles at cost. They are now considering alternative ways of dealing with banks and insurance companies and setting up a car pool. As in the case of religious communes, the focus of this paper is elsewhere and the reader is directed for further information to Collier 1969; Hine 1953; Houriet 1969; Kanter 1970; Kriyanada 1969; *Modern Utopian*; and Spiro 1963.

UTOPIAN COMMUNE

Drop-out orientation
Do your own thing
Loosely organized
Usually subsidized
Youth oriented
Sometimes revolutionary
Usually short-lived

EVOLUTIONARY COMMUNE

High achievers
Highly mobile
Straight jobs
Upper middle class
Opinion leaders
Most over 30
Many post-children

RELIGIOUS COMMUNE

Highly structured
Authoritarian leader
Work ethic
Usually self-sustaining
Withdrawn from society
Family oriented

The new breed among communes, those the author calls "evolutionary communes," are the least known. They are springing up across metropolitan areas without fanfare, going out of their way to avoid publicity in most cases, realizing that if they attract attention they will be diverted from their goals. There is particular concern about evolutionary communes here because they appear to be the most attractive to those academic, professional, and managerial people who make up the temporary-systems strata, if they elect to continue working within the present society. Those who do not choose to do so can be expected to go in the direction of the utopian commune rather than the religious commune in almost every case. For this reason, many of the things said about evolutionary communes will also apply to some of the more highly structured utopian communes.

While there may be those who are enamored with the back-to-the-land movement, most evolutionary communalists have no intention of abandoning either their careers or their middle-class comforts. The basis for establishing such a commune is the desire of a group of committed people to cope with our present-day society in a more successful manner than they can manage as couples or individuals. This coping can take many forms, depending on the particular group. The desire to provide better schooling for their children; to pool resources for investment, shelter, and purchasing; and to provide access to luxuries otherwise unavailable are among the reasons for this movement. One group may be especially concerned about providing the buffer of group security against extended unemployment so that members can be free to stay in a particular geographic area without suffering career setbacks because they refuse to move physically in order to move up the career ladder. Few couples have sufficient resources of their own to take a chance on waiting, perhaps for several months, until an appropriate job can be found in the same city. A related concern in many groups is the desire to provide educational opportunities for group members or their children that are beyond the resources of a single couple.

The most basic reason for becoming involved in an evolutionary commune, however, is the desire to expand the complexity of interrelationships beyond the possibilities inherent in the pair-bond itself. In the widest sense, the key term is propinquity, for communal living makes possible a person-to-person intimacy on both sexual and nonsexual levels that goes far beyond even the most closely knit intimate-friendship group. It simply is not possible to sustain the same level of interaction among intimate friends that one has in the pair-bond, unless members of the group are in close proximity to one another much of the time. The level of interaction falls short of multiple pair-bonds (in most cases), however. While group marriages have been found in communes, most communalists are not yet ready to go so far as to consider themselves married to several people at once. The size of most communes argues against such intimacy, if the readiness state of the members does not, for evolutionary communes range in size from ten to 130 individuals.

As mentioned earlier, man is a problem-solving organism, happiest when he is solving problems of an ever-increasing degree of complexity. It is at the level of commune or group marriage that one most often hears couples speak about the joy of interrelating on a more complex basis. They speak with excitement and animation about personal growth in the shared context of a group larger than two, which seems to provide a different and more stimulating critical mass for personal development, often in directions the couple do not share in common and, therefore, cannot develop on their own.

An overriding external factor that may contribute to the predisposition of many people toward more complex interrelationships is the current swing of family life to its lowest common denominator—the barely viable nuclear family. When one leaves aside the political and economic forces that have promoted this move, the lack of viability remains sadly evident, since the norm of working father, housekeeping mother, and children actually exists in less than 50% of American families. The vast majority of Americans have had personal experience with the sense of aloneness that comes with growing up in or being a marriage partner in a nuclear family that must cope alone with the vicissitudes of life. Many know the burden of life in a nuclear family that proved not to be viable and became less than the norm—a single-parent family or a two-working-parent family. Childless couples or couples with grown children also experience great difficulty when problems threaten the viability of the family. The extended family is remembered as a less vulnerable life-style for the family because the larger size of the group made it more viable. Communes and group marriages are seen as a way of moving back toward that more viable group size and doing so, moreover, with *chosen* individuals.

Before we discuss evolutionary communes further, two important points about communes in general must be made: first, with respect to how they get established, and second, with regard to how they handle sexual intimacy.

Some communes are started with almost no preplanning or attention to the basic questions that should be answered in order to avoid almost certain failure. This is the case especially with so-called hippie communes, where the word of the day is "Action! Let it all hang loose and it will all come together." This kind of simple faith in miracles is pathetically common, and the communes that begin this way are almost certainly doomed to failure. Others engage in talk marathons that may go on for months, without ever discussing the basic questions that must be resolved or without resolving them. Again, the end result is usually failure. The religious-commune groups usually seem to avoid this problem because they are typically led by a strong man who makes all the decisions and will not brook dissension and because they are united in religious fervor, i.e., the strong leader is expressing God's will. The evolutionary communes are most likely to have approached the decision to establish a commune by establishing a consensual process for working through structure and process as the first step in moving from being talkers to becoming doers (Ramey 1967).

Five distinct types of sexual intimacy prevail in communes, some of which are so destructive that, everything else being equal, the commune is still very likely to fail because of the sexual structure. One of these patterns is celibacy. A commune that practices celibacy can last only one generation unless it is able to attract enough recruits to replace those who die. The Shakers were one such group that did not succeed. Exclusive monogamy is another sexual stance; in most religious communes exclusive monogamy is practiced with extreme prohibitions against the transgressor, who may even be expelled from the group. Free love is sometimes the sexual mode of the commune, but this is less often the case than is generally imagined. Free-love groups seem to be very short lived; probably a group that is uncommitted sexually is uncommitted in general and thus unable to sustain the level of cooperation necessary to the survival of a commune. A few communes claim to practice free love on a committed basis; i.e., the group consists of "brothers and sisters" who are all one family, and the family takes responsibility jointly for child-rearing and nurturing. Since they practice free love only within the group, albeit without pair-bonding, they are enjoying the best of two worlds. Their responsibility is to the group, not to the individual, but they are not a group marriage because no one is pair-bonded. The author knows of at least one such group that has survived for more than two years and appears to be getting stronger. It is too early to speculate about the long-range effects, however, even though one is strongly tempted to draw parallels with the early days of the kibbutzim, many of which began this way.

The most generally practiced intimacy pattern is intimate friendship, especially in the evolutionary commune but also in many utopian communes. Group marriages can sometimes be found in a commune, usually involving three to six individuals out of the total population. A commune that involves both group marriage and intimate friendship is not likely to break up over sexual problems. On the other hand, a commune that includes both exclusive monogamy and any kind of sex outside the pair-bond is a good candidate for trouble (*The Modern*

Utopian). Combinations of exclusive monogamy and free love, exclusive monogamy and group marriage, or celibacy and free love are very unlikely to occur. Swinging or group marriage and celibacy in the same group would seem an unlikely combination but not necessarily a fatal one, although such a combination would seem to lower the survival factor. The combination of either intimate friendship or group marriage with free love is unlikely, but if it did occur, survival of the group would probably depend either on weeding out the uncommitted or helping them work out their inability to relate to others on a responsible level. Examples of the problems discussed in this paragraph are most numerous in *The Modern Utopian* (vol. 1, nos. 1-6; vol. 2, nos. 1-6; vol. 3, nos. 1-3; and vol. 4, nos. 1-4), which contains many articles about the life and death of communes written by participants.

The evolutionary commune appears to be a comparatively recent development on the commune scene. It is clearly distinguishable from the utopian commune because its members are not reacting against the system. They come together out of the desire to do better that which they are already doing well. In an economic sense, the lesson of the co-op movement is not lost on these people. But in general, especially if they have already explored the possibilities inherent in intimate friendships, they are aware that there is a tremendous exhilaration in pushing the limits of interaction potential. They know that involvement at higher levels of complexity is more demanding on the individual than staying within the limits of the pair-bond. They are also aware that it is more rewarding, the degree of pleasure equaling the amount of investment in these relationships. As mentioned earlier, the committed pair-bond does not necessarily go through the transitional or experimental stage of intimate friendship along the route to the more complex communal or group marriage situation. Some couples develop friendships to a degree of interaction that transcends the usual taboos on gut-level dialogue and makes possible direct exploration of the possibilities inherent in communal sharing of life commitments. This paper has concentrated on the swinging stage of this development because, at this time, more people seem to be at this stage of growing into more complex interrelationships than are possible within the exclusive framework of the pair-bond.

Group Marriage

Group marriage involves an even greater degree of complexity of interaction than communal living. The Constantines (1971) have defined this type of union admirably. They state:

A multilateral marriage is one in which three or more people each consider themselves to have a primary relationship with at least two other individuals in the group.

The definition at the beginning of this paper is a restatement of the Constantines' definition that simplifies and clarifies the nature of the relationship:

In a group marriage each of the three or more participants is pair-bonded with at least two others.

The term "pair-bond" is more explicit than "primary relationship" for the reason stated earlier, i.e., pair-bonded individuals are mates.

Group marriage may involve a couple and a single, two couples, two couples and a single, three couples, or three couples and a single. As far as is known to the author, no group marriage consisting of more than seven individuals has been verified as existing, and the likelihood that such a group might exist is slight. The addition of one individual greatly increases the number of possible pair-bonds in the group. In a triad, each individual has twice as many pair-bonds as in a dyad. Six pair-bonds are possible in a group of four people, ten are possible in a group of five, fifteen are possible in a group of six, and twenty-one pair-bonds are possible in a group of seven people. The odds against developing all possible pair-bonds rises rapidly with additional group members, and yet a fully developed group marriage would presumably be one in which all possible pair-bonds did in fact exist. Thus, adding an eighth person would add seven more possible pair-bonds, for a total of twenty-eight. Triads and two-couple group marriages are the most popular types.

The suggestion was made that triads and pentads (Ramey 1972) should prove more stable than tetrads or hexads because they start out with odd numbers, and indeed, the Constantines have found more triads than any other size group, half of which involved two males and half involved two females. The argument is based on the somewhat negative assumption that couples may decide to form a group marriage on the basis of much less initial talking-through than would be likely with odd-size groups. This assumption is based on personal knowledge of several group marriages that were started on very short notice and lasted only a few weeks or months. In fact, one of these, involving three couples, began on the basis of three weeks of discussion among couples who were hitherto strangers! One would expect a great amount of soul-searching among three or five people before they entered into a group marriage. Of course, one would hope most couples would investigate thoroughly, but with the basic pair-bond relationship to fall back on, this might not occur.

Implicit in any serious discussion of group marriage is an examination of reactions to same-sex pair-bonds. Same-sex pair-bonds are most common among females in group marriages. The Constantines have found same-sex bonds between males both less frequent and much more critical to the success of the marriage. The author knows of other instances in which incipient development of a male-male relationship broke up the marriage. It would seem relatively safe to say that a group marriage in which everyone is ambisexual will have higher survival potential, all other things being equal, than one involving one or more monosexual individuals.

For some people the idea of being married to two or more individuals at once is overwhelming. But establishing a dyadic marriage involves a growing together, not a spontaneous happening. The same is true for a group marriage, which begins with a set of potentials that are developed fully only over time. To begin, all that is necessary is the assurance that everyone in the group can sustain multiple pair-bonding. This is why the definition specifies that each individual in the group have at least two pair-bonds before the group can be called a group marriage. Many groups that first appear to be group marriages do not meet this qualification, especially in the case of threesomes, in which two people are pair-bonded with the same person, usually of the opposite sex, but not with each other. There are many such relationships, and a number of people are led to believe that the number of group marriages is much greater than it really is because they assume these relationships to be group marriages. As a matter of fact, upon confirmation of such relationships, it would appear that there may be one hundred threesomes for each triad. Such a union might be considered an intermediate step between dyadic marriage and group marriage, but it is clearly two dyadic marriages with one common partner rather than a group marriage.

The complexity of interaction that must be faced upon establishing a commune or group marriage is greater than that faced upon moving from pair-bond exclusivity to intimate friendship. The situation is further complicated by the fact that each group must work out its own ground rules. Premarital courting at the dyadic level occurs within an understood structure that is already well defined by society. Each couple makes major and minor decisions in terms of already internalized givens and expectations about marriage, and what is appropriate and permissible within the framework of marriage. Since society has not proscribed norms, standards, and activities for group marriages or communes, a great deal more preplanning and exploration must be undertaken to work through expectations and structure behavior than is the case upon entering into dyadic marriage.

A representative list of the types of problems that must be dealt with will quickly indicate the magnitude of the task. The following list is not definitive, nor are the decision areas listed in order of importance, since there are matters that each group will have to decide for itself: decision-making procedures, group goals, ground rules, "no-no's," intra- and extra-group sexual relationships, privacy, division of labor, role relationships, careers, relationship with outsiders, degree of visibility, legal jeopardy, dissolution of the group, personal responsibilities outside the group (such as parent support), urban or rural setting, type of shelter, geographic location, children, child-rearing practices, taxes, pooling assets, income, legal structure, education, trial period, etc. Many decisions can be put off until after the group embarks upon their new adventure, but most of those listed above must be worked out in the planning stage.

Age appears to be a prominent earmark of success in both communes and group marriages. The complexities to be faced are such that personal hang-ups, pair-bond hang-ups, and career hang-ups should have been solved before a couple takes this step, since a tremendous investment of time, effort, and emotional energy will be required to achieve success in the new undertaking. It follows that one would expect to find people over thirty most often involved in a successful group, and indeed, this is the case. In fact, the Constantines have not found a group marriage with participants under this age level still extant, and there is knowledge of only one tetrad in which one individual is twenty-eight and another is twenty-five and the group is still extant.

The two areas of concern that are most frequently discussed in group marriage—money and the division of labor—are the least worrisome in actual practice. Developing a viable decision-making pattern is much more involved, because consensus takes an inordinate amount of time, and until the group develops the degree of trust necessary to be comfortable with differentiation of function and concomitant delegation of routine decision-making, there will necessarily be many hours spent in deciding as a group. Once sufficient trust has developed to assign functional responsibility, the group will only have to consider major or policy decisions, just as in a dyadic marriage or any other organization. Although a set of ground rules will probably be established initially, they will become less and less important as the marriage develops informal norms, standards, and activities. It has been suggested that a rough measure of the current stability of a group marriage is the degree to which they persist in clinging to the formal rules and contracts set up at the beginning of the marriage.

A trial period of some sort is essential to the success of dyadic marriage, in the eyes of many people. This is an even more important factor in working through the developmental stages of a group marriage and of a commune as well. This can become a problem if it is not handled on a reasonable basis. A recent advertisement in the *Village Voice*, placed by a group of would-be communalists, led the author to the interesting discovery, upon talking to the initiators, that they wished to start the commune with ten couples and that a prerequisite to beginning would be for all the individuals in the group to live with each other for one week in pairs first. A quick count reveals that 190 pairs are involved here, so that for nineteen weeks every individual would be separated from his own mate while living with all the others. Yet these people were surprised when the impracticality of this plan was pointed out to them. It had not occurred to them that they were talking about a nineteen-week project! Nevertheless, however it is arranged, some kind of physical sharing is an important step in the planning stage. Many people handle this trial stage by planning a joint vacation or renting a summer house together. Others may join one of the communal work brigades that are becoming an important part of the utopian rural commune scene. This mechanism not only provides the work brigade with a taste of working together as a communal group but also provides existing farm communes with essential seasonal labor.

It is important to remember that a group marriage is a hot-house situation, which generates intense pressure on all its members to grow. In such a situation, relaxation, quiet time, and personal privacy assume much greater importance than in the dyad. In addition, the group marriage should not lose sight of the need to have fun together. The old saw, "the group that plays together stays together" is not far wrong—remembering that pleasure and happiness are major goals of any kind of marriage.

Visibility is a special problem for both communes and group marriages, but particularly for the latter, since in most states, group marriage is not legal. Especially if there are children involved, the marriage is vulnerable to attack on the basis of contributing to the delinquency of minors, if not on the basis of fornication, adultery, immoral conduct, or operating a bawdy house. How will the group handle interaction with relatives, friends, neighbors, tradesmen, and the like? Will visitors or tourists be allowed and on what basis? Will the group maintain secrecy about its existence and how much secrecy? Location will affect the answers to these questions. Rural locations have high visibility, and so rural groups must be particularly careful to build bridges to the neighborhood. For example, Franklin Commune in Vermont was hassled by all kinds of official and unofficial groups for the first six months of its existence. They assumed that the work ethic of Vermont farmers was best for establishing peaceful coexistence with the community, and they devoted much of their energy to this end, which corresponded with their desire to make the farm self-sustaining. Soon these efforts began to pay off. In their second summer, they brought in 2,700 bales of hay plus 1,300 bales for their neighbors, which they did out of neighborliness and not for pay. This is only one example of their effort to be good neighbors. It is not surprising that they have earned the respect and admiration of their community, which is now willing to go to bat for *them* when the need arises.

Groups with children in public school have higher visibility than those with no children in school, but there seem to be no patterns of problems associated with this factor. Teachers and other children tend to see and hear what they expect to see and hear rather than the reality (Ramey 1968).

Perhaps the most deep-rooted difference that can develop in a group marriage regards child-rearing. Deciding about parentage is easy, and agreement on having children and on what to do about the children if the marriage breaks up can be settled beforehand. Groups that start with babies or no children find it much easier to work out a joint child-rearing agreement than those who come into the marriage with older children. Not only must the parents work out a mutually agreeable program that is also agreeable to the nonparents; there is also the problem of compatibility and adjustment among the children themselves. Finally, there is the incipient problem, which many swingers avoid, of deciding how developing children should fit into the sexual interrelationship of the marriage.

Uncommitted swingers almost universally hide their swinging activities from their children (how successfully is a matter of question), whereas many individuals involved in intimate friendships are as open with their children about their interfamily relationships as they are about all other aspects of life. Some of the successful communes (Oneida, for example) initiated the children into full sexual participation in the life of the commune at puberty. This is such a taboo area today that there are little or no data about current practices. Some swinging groups include unmarried teenagers and/or married children and their spouses. The author has heard of at least one group involving a three-generation swinging family. How widespread such practices are is unknown, since only very recently has it been discussed. The author has knowledge of one group marriage that consisted of a widow, her son and daughter, and their spouses. This group broke up over an incipient sexual relationship between the two males because one was unable to handle the possible implication that he would be deemed homosexual if he allowed the union to develop.

The types of problems we have raised as examples of issues facing a group marriage have had to do largely with the group maintenance aspects of marriage. There is also goal-directedness to be dealt with. Goals have not been discussed at length here because it is believed that those people who undertake to add a more complex dimension to marriage are not in basic conflict with the goals of marriage as generally espoused by today's society. Offered, therefore, is the following definition of the kinds of behavior desired of members of the intimate friendship group, evolutionary commune, or group marriage:

Desired behavior, as evidenced in intimate friendship, evolutionary commune, or group marriage, is behavior that permits and promotes the growth of the group in a shared direction. Growth of the member can be measured in terms of the degree and value of his active participation and demonstration of his capacity to cooperatively assist the group to successful achievement of its goals. Group achievement of goals must be measured by society.

Student communes were mentioned earlier in this paper but not discussed. Whether students call their shared living quarters a crash-pad, a co-op, a nest, a commune, or simply a shared apartment, all these loosely organized coed living arrangements have one thing in common. They are temporary. They afford students an opportunity to experiment with a number of living modes of varying complexity, with the tacit understanding that they are not making permanent commitments. Under these circumstances, free love, serial monogamy, and group sex can be fully explored without the pressure of value judgments with respect to success. Casual nudity, brother-sister–type nonsexual intimacy, and celibacy all find acceptance in such a setting. Changes in the personnel of the group often lead to dramatic shifts in sexual practices, and the pill makes all of this investigation safe, within a loving, sharing, nonjudgmental setting that permits much freer expression and exploration of relationship potentials than is easily possible in the more structured adult society.

Although this is almost always uncommitted behavior with respect to the individual, it is most decidedly committed behavior with respect to the group search for a satisfying life-style in terms of equality of the sexes and critical examination of accepted societal marriage standards. These young people can be counted on to form pair-bonds based on equality. With their trial experience in more complex relationships, they can be expected to swell the ranks of intimate friendships, evolutionary communes, and group marriages, if they decide to cast their lot with existing society and work within existing social structures. This, in turn, should have a major impact on restructuring marriage in the direction of societal sanction of intimate friendship, communes, and group marriage.

References

Babchuck, N., and Bates, A. P. 1963. The Primary Relations of Middle Class Couples: A Study in Male Dominance. *Amer. Soc. Rev.* 28: 377–84.

Bartell, G. D. 1969. Personal conversation reported by E. M. Brecher in *The Sex Researchers*. Boston: Little, Brown & Co.

———— 1970. Group Sex among the Mid-Americans. *J. Sex Res.* 6, no. 2, pp. 113–30. [In this book, pp. 185–201.]

————. 1971. *Group Sex.* New York: Wyden.

Beigel, H. 1969. In Defense of Mate Swapping. *Rational Living* 4, no. 1, 15–16.

Bell, R. R., and Silvan, L. 1970. Swinging: The Sexual Exchange of Marriage Partners. Mimeo. Read at annual meeting of the Society for the Study of Social Problems, August 1970, Washington, D.C.

Bird, C. 1970. *Born Female: The High Cost of Keeping Women Down.* New York: Pocket Books.

Bott, E. 1957. *Family and Social Network.* London: Tavistock.

Brecher, E. M. 1969. *The Sex Researchers.* Boston: Little, Brown & Co.

Breedlove, W., and Breedlove, J. 1964. *Swap Clubs.* Los Angeles: Sherbourne Press.

Buber, M. 1955. *Between Man and Man.* Boston: Beacon Press.

Carden, M. L. 1969. *Oneida: Utopian Community to Modern Corporation.* Baltimore: Johns Hopkins Press.

Collier, J. L. 1969. Communes: Togetherness Sixties Style. *True* (February).

Constantine, L. L., and Constantine, J. M. 1970a. Where Is Marriage Going? *Futurist* (Spring): 44–46.

————. 1970b. How to Make a Group Marriage. *Mod. Utopian* 4(Summer).

————. 1974. Sexual Aspects of Multilateral Relations. [In this book, pp. 268–90.]

Denfield, D., and Gordon, M. 1970. The Sociology of Mate Swapping: Or, the Family that Swings Together Clings Together. *J. Sex Res.* 6, no. 2, pp. 85–100. [In this book, pp. 68–83.]

Farson, R. E., Hauser, P. M., Stroup, H., and Weiner, A. J. 1969. *The Future of the Family.* New York: Family Service Association of America.

Gagnon, J. H., and Simon, W., eds. 1970. *The Sexual Scene.* Chicago: Aldine.

Goodman, P., 1971. Interview with Paul Goodman, *Psychol. Today* 5: 96.

Heinlein, R. 1967. *Stranger in a Strange Land.* New York: Avon.

Hine, R. V. 1953. *California's Utopian Colonies.* San Marino, Calif.: Huntington Library.

Hostetler, J. A. 1968. *Amish Society.* Baltimore: Johns Hopkins Press.

Houriet, R. 1969. Life and Death of a Commune Called Oz. *N. Y. Times Mag.* February 16, 1969.

Huxley, A. 1937. *Ends and Means.* Westport, Conn.: Greenwood.

Kanter, R. M. 1968. Commitment and Social Organization: A Study of Commitment Mechanisms in Utopian Communities. *Amer. Soc. Rev.* 33: 499–517.

———. 1970. Communes. *Psychol. Today* 4: 53–78.

Komarovsky, M. 1962. *Blue-Collar Marriage.* New York: Random House.

Krippner, S., and Fersh, D. 1970. Mystic Communes. *Mod. Utopian* 4(Spring): 4–9.

Kriyanada. 1969. *Cooperative Communities.* San Francisco: Ananda Publications.

Lewis, R. W. 1969. The Swingers. *Playboy* 16: 149–228.

Lynes, R. 1953. *A Surfeit of Honey.* New York: Harpers.

Marks, P. J. 1969. *A New Community.* San Diego: Youth Resources.

Masters, W. H., and Johnson, V. E. 1966. *Human Sexual Response.* Boston: Little, Brown & Co.

McLuhan, M., and Leonard, G. B. 1967. The Future of Sex. *Look* 31(July 25): 56–60.

Mod. Utopian 1 (1967), nos. 1–6; 2 (1968), nos. 1–6; 3 (1969), nos. 1–3; 4 (1970), nos. 1–4.

Nordhoff, C. 1961. *The Communistic Societies of the United States.* New York: Hillary House.

O'Neill, G. C., and O'Neill, N. 1969. Personal communication.

———. 1970. Patterns in Group Sexual Activity. *J. Sex Res.* 6, no. 2, pp. 101–12.

O'Neill, N., and O'Neill, G. C. 1972. *Open Marriage.* New York: M. Evans & Company, Inc.

Osofsky, H., and Osofsky, J. 1972. Androgyny as a Life Style. *Fam. Coordinator* 21: 411–18.

Palson, C., and Palson, R. M. 1970. *Swinging: The Minimizing of Jealousy.* Mimeo. Philadelphia, 20 pp.

Pemberton, H. E. 1936. The Curve of Culture. *Amer. Soc. Rev.* 1: 547–56.

President's Commission on Obscenity and Pornography. 1970. *The*

Illustrated Presidential Report of the Commission on Obscenity and Pornography. San Diego: Greenleaf Classics.

Ramey, J. W. 1958. The Relationship of Peer Group Rating to Certain Individual Perceptions of Personality. *J. Exper. Ed.* 27: 143–49.

———. 1963. Diffusion of a New Technological Innovation. *Health Serv. TV Bull.* (O.S.) 4: 2–3.

———. 1967. Conflict Resolution through Videotape Simulation. Paper presented at annual meeting of the American Psychiatric Association, Detroit, May 1967.

———. 1968. Teaching Medical Students by Videotape Simulation. *J. Med. Ed.* 48(January): 55–59.

———. 1972. Communes, Group Marriage, and the Upper Middle Class. *J. Marriage Fam.* 34: 647–55. [In this book, pp. 214–29.]

Redekop, C. W. 1969. *The Old Colony Mennonites.* Baltimore: Johns Hopkins Press.

Riesman, D., Glazer, N., and Denney, R. 1955. *The Lonely Crowd.* Garden City: Doubleday.

Rimmer, R. H. 1967. *The Harrad Experiment.* New York: Bantam.

———. 1968. *Proposition 31.* New York: Signet.

Rogers, C. 1951. *Client Centered Therapy.* New York: Houghton Mifflin.

Rossi, P. H., Groves, W. E., and Grafstein, D. 1971. *Life Styles and Campus Communities*, personal communication.

Scheflen, A. E. 1965. Quasi-Courtship Behavior in Psychotherapy. Monograph. William Alanson White Psychiatric Foundation 28.

Slater, P. E. 1968. Some Social Consequences of Temporary Systems. In *The Temporary Society*, ed. W. G. Bennis and P. E. Slater. New York: Harper and Row.

Smith, J. R., and Smith, L. G. 1970. Co-Marital Sex and the Sexual Freedom Movement. *J. Sex Res.* 6, no. 2, pp. 131–42. [In this book, pp. 202–13.]

———. (in preparation). Consenting Adults: An Exploratory Study of the Sexual Freedom Movement.

Spiro, M. 1963. *Kibbutz, Venture in Utopia.* New York: Schocken.

Stoller, F. H. 1970. The Intimate Network of Families as a New Structure. In *The Family in Search of a Future*, ed. H. Otto. New York: Appleton-Century-Crofts.

Symonds, C. 1970. The Utopian Aspects of Sexual Mate Swapping. Mimeo. Paper presented at the annual meeting of the Society for the Study of Social Problems, September 1970, Washington, D.C.

Toffler, A. 1970. *Future Shock.* New York: Random House.

Twichell, J. 1974. Sexual Liberality and Personality. [In this book, pp. 230–45.]

U.S. News and World Report. 1971. How the Four-Day Workweek Is Catching On. March 8, 1971.

Whyte, W. H., Jr. 1956. *The Organization Man.* New York: Simon and Schuster.

Infidelity: Some Moral and Social Issues

Jessie Bernard

Adultery versus Infidelity

Both exclusivity and permanence are required in marriage as institutionalized in our society. They may be incompatible with one another in the kind of world we now live in where men and women are, in Bernard Farber's words, "permanently available." Sapirstein (1948, p. 173) points out the difficulties:

> Monogamy began in societies which had strong religious injunctions against infidelity and used every possible device to limit the temptations. Contrast the Chinese peasant dress or the shaved head of the young Hebrew bride with the modern woman who, whether married or not, does all she can to heighten her charms.

It may be that we will have to choose between exclusivity and permanence. If we insist on permanence, exclusivity is harder to enforce; if we insist on exclusivity, permanence may be endangered. The trend, as we shall note presently, seems to be in the direction of exclusivity at the expense of permanence in the younger years but permanence at the expense of exclusivity in the later years.

Exclusivity is still buttressed and enforced by both religious and

Reprinted by permission of Grune & Stratton, Inc. and the author.

secular law; permanence, by personal promises and vows. Sexual relations with anyone other than one's spouse is forbidden by the seventh commandment and also by law. Adultery, though rarely prosecuted, is a crime in most states.[1] Society itself is the injured party.[2] Exclusivity is further buttressed by way of divorce legislation: adultery is universally accepted as a ground for divorce. The spouse is now the injured party. No marital partner has to tolerate it.

Infidelity, as distinguished from adultery, is the violation of a promise or a vow. Strangely enough, there is no universal, prescribed, or standard vow required of all those entering marriage. The officiating officer seems to have considerable latitude. Some denominations include both a promise and a vow, some only one or the other.[3] Some require

---

[1] "American law has tended toward the proscription of all extramarital sexual relationships; but in recognition of the realities of human nature, the penalties for adultery in most states are usually mild and the laws are only infrequently enforced. In five of the states the maximum penalty is a fine. There are three states which attach no criminal penalty at all to adultery, but civil penalties may be involved in these and in many other states. . . . The broadest definition of adultery and the heaviest penalties are concentrated in the northeastern section of the United States, all ten of those states being among the seventeen which may impose prison terms for a single act of extramarital coitus. In actual practice, such extramarital coitus is rarely prosecuted" (Kinsey et al. 1953, p. 429).

[2] However, the law is often used for quite different ends than the protection of society. In the summer of 1968, for example, a black minister in Irasburg, Vermont, was arrested on grounds of adultery by the state police. The governor of the state said the state police had "devoted their efforts to a persecution of the Rev. Mr. Johnson," and the whole episode was viewed as evidence of racism (Terry 1969). This incident illustrates the Kinsey statement (1953, p. 429) that "not infrequently the prosecutions represented attempts on the part of neighbors or relatives to work off grudges that had developed over other matters. In this, as in many other areas, the law is most often utilized by persons who have ulterior motives for causing difficulties for the non-conformant individuals. Not infrequently the prosecutions represent attempts by sheriffs, prosecutors, or other law enforcement officers to work off personal or political grudges. . . ."

[3] The Common Book of Prayer (1959) specifies the following promises: "Wilt thou love her, comfort her, honor her, cherish her, and keep her; and forsaking all others, cleave thee only unto her, so long as ye both shall live?" "Wilt thou love him, honor him, inspire him, cherish him, and keep him; and forsaking all others, cleave thee only unto him, so long as ye both shall live?" The Protestant Episcopal promise includes to have, to hold, to love, to cherish; the vow includes, for both partners, to have, live together, love, comfort, honor, keep, and forsake all others. The Lutheran promise: to take, plight troth; the vow, to love, have, comfort, honor, keep, and forsake all others. The Presbyterian promise: to promise and covenant to be loving and faithful; the vow, to have, love, honor, live with, cherish. The Baptist promise: to take, have, hold, love, cherish; the vow, to take, love, honor, cherish, and forsake all others. The Methodist promise: to have, hold,

a promise to cleave only to one another, some do not. Some require a forsaking of all others; a few do not mention this.[4] But almost every promise and/or vow incorporates permanence. This vow or promise is for keeps, till death parts them. Permanence, in brief, is more emphasized than exclusivity in the marital promises and vows.

The precise meaning of what is promised or vowed—to love, comfort, cherish, and so on—has been elaborated by one pair of commentators (Easton and Robbins 1938, p. 49). Love, they tell us, means that one will treat the spouse affectionately. Comfort means that one will impart strength, cheer, encourage, and gladden, as opposed to dispiriting, distressing, discouraging, saddening, or nagging. And the promise or vow to forsake all others includes more than other men or women as objects of attraction. It may include loving one's mother more than one's spouse, or children more than husband. It includes even imaginary clinging to old flames. Just thinking "If I had only married so-and-so instead of you!" constitutes a breach of this promise. And the fantasy of other sex partners does also. On the basis of this logic, a good case could also be made for including the man who prefers his work to his wife, a situation documented at least for some tycoons and no doubt characteristic of many ambitious professional men also.

Of special interest is the interpretation by Easton and Robbins (1938, p. 50) of the promise or vow to forsake all others as not demanding a too-rigid definition of exclusivity: "the right of husband or wife to the primary love of the other does not justify an insistence on exclusive possession nor condone jealousy of innocent friendships." Satiety and boredom should be avoided; external relationships should be encouraged. To be sure, these commentators are not advocating external *sexual* relationships; but it is interesting that innocent friendships—whatever that may mean—are not forbidden by the marital vows.

When we ask, therefore, what promises or vows are broken by marital infidelity, the answer is that they are promises to love, to honor, to cherish, and to comfort as well as to forsake all others and, in some cases, to cleave to one another. In a strict and narrow interpretation,

---

love, cherish. The Ian Maclaren Service vow: take, love, cherish, give loyalty; the wife vows to take, love, and honor. The Community Church Service vow: to take, live together, love, honor, trust, serve, be true and loyal. The scriptural service vow: to take, love, cherish, have, hold, forsake all others, cleave to one another (Leach 1959).

[4] Some include the forsaking in the promise, some in the vow, some in both, some in neither.

then, whenever one or both spouses ceased to love, honor, cherish, or comfort one another, they would be guilty of infidelity in the sense of reneging on a sacred promise. And, indeed, many men and women do in fact interpret infidelity in this way. But for our purposes here, the common conception of infidelity, though inadequate, is accepted.

To make a distinction between adultery and infidelity does not mean that there is an inconsistency involved. Any kind of extramarital sexual relations constitutes a violation of the law and hence, by definition, is adultery, a crime—an offense against the state. But they are not necessarily, or in all cases, as we shall note presently, viewed by the spouse as an offense against him (her) or as infidelity.

Infidelity and Deprivation

If there is no deprivation of a spouse—of promised love, honor, cherishing—has a promise been violated? If a husband's relations with another woman do deprive his wife so that she suffers a real loss—emotional, sexual, or financial—there can hardly be any question that he has violated a promise; he is unfaithful to her. He is, in the popular conception, "cheating on her." Even those who accept extramarital relationships would probably not condone such deprivation of a spouse. But suppose a husband still "cleaves to his wife," that is, continues to live with her, to support her, to assume all his responsibilities toward her, even to love her—perhaps more than ever[5]—so that there is no deprivation, can he still be accused of infidelity? And vice versa?

We do not know, of course, in what proportion of cases deprivation is present. On the assumption that, if infidelity causes no difficulty in a marriage, there is no deprivation present, we may find one clue in the Kinsey data (1953, p. 434), which show that so long as spouses did not know about extramarital relationships no damage was reported: "Extra-marital relationships had least often caused difficulty when the

---

[5] "There are some individuals . . . whose sexual adjustments in marriage have undoubtedly been helped by extramarital experience. . . . Some women . . . make better adjustments with their husbands. Extramarital intercourse has had the effect of convincing some males that the relationships with their wives were more satisfactory than they had realized" (Kinsey et al. 1948, p. 593). "Sometimes sexual adjustments with the spouse had improved as a result of the female's extramarital experience" (Kinsey et al. 1953, p. 433). These authors cite earlier studies also reporting improved marital relationships after extramarital experiences. Robert A. Harper (1961, pp. 384–91) arrives at the same conclusion. One young man, discussing wife-swapping clubs, rejected the idea that infidelity was involved; the practice, he said, often enhanced the marital bonds.

other spouse had not known of them. . . . Some of the extramarital relationships had been carried on for long periods of years without ill effects on the marital adjustment." Not deprivation to the spouse but knowledge of the relationship was the damaging factor: "The extramarital coitus had not appeared to do as much damage as the knowledge that it had occurred" (Kinsey et al. 1953, p. 434). Othello had taught us this long ago.[6]

But how often, one may legitimately ask, does the spouse know? Among marriages in which the wife had engaged in extramarital relations, the husband was not aware of the situation in about half (51%) of the cases; he knew in 40% and suspected in about 9%. But even among the 49% in which the husband knew or suspected, there was no difficulty reported—and presumably, therefore, no deprivation—in about two-fifths (42%) of the cases.[7] If, as estimated by Kinsey and his associates, 71% of the marriages in which extramarital relations of wives had occurred had not developed difficulties, the inference seems justified that deprivation was not involved. The wife's extramarital relationship did not deprive the husband[8]—at least not enough to create difficulties.

---

[6] I swear 'tis better to be much abus'd
Than but to know't a little. . . .
What sense had I of her stolen hours of lust?
I saw 't not, thought it not, it harm'd not me.
I slept the next night well, fed well, was free and merry;
I found not Cassio's kisses on her lips.
He that is robb'd, not wanting what is stolen,
Let him not know 't, and he's not robb'd at all. . . .
I had been happy, if the general camp,
Pioneers and all, had tasted her sweet body,
So I had nothing known. O, now, for ever
Farewell the tranquil mind! farewell content!
Farewell the plumed troop, and the big wars,
That makes ambition virtue; O, farewell! . . . (Shakespeare, *Othello*, act 3, scene 3)

[7] The proportion of cases in which there was serious difficulty when known by the husband was identical—42 per cent—to the proportion of cases in which there was no difficulty at all when known (Kinsey et al. 1953, p. 434).

[8] The proportion would probably be even higher in the reverse situation, that is, where it was the husband who engaged in the extramarital relations, for women were only half as likely as men to rate spouse's extramarital coitus as a major factor in divorce (27% and 51% respectively) (Kinsey et al. 1953, p. 438). If, however, the husband were diverting part of a modest family income to another woman, the wife might well feel that she was being deprived.

Forms of Infidelity

To speak, as we have done so far, as though extramarital relationships were all of a kind, simple and unidimensional, is of course misleading. They are of many kinds and assume different forms. It would be possible to draw up a complex systematic matrix inclusive of all combinations of duration, seriousness, and intensity of relationships and discuss each cell individually. Instead, discussion here is limited to only a few forms as they have been reported in the literature.

1. Of perhaps least moral and social significance is the kind of relationship which takes the form of coquetry and flirtation—"making love without meaning it"—commonly accepted in many social circles; no seriousness is attached to it by either party or by their spouses. Sapirstein (1948, p. 173) finds a functional use for it:

> The normal flirtatiousness and minor conquests which are part of every social gathering give ample opportunities for testing out the old desires. These can be shared and enjoyed together without the necessity of continually proving in the open market one's residual desirability in the romantic chase. While such a compromise is difficult in the framework of our monogamous culture . . . , it seems to be one of the few available compensations in this sensitive problem.

And this kind of relationship may be comprised in the "innocent friendship" which Easton and Robbins (1938, p. 49) believe is not required to be forsaken.

This form of relationship may even include physical embrace or petting. Kinsey et al. (1953, p. 426) found that "at dinner parties, cocktail parties, in automobiles, on picnics, and at dances, a considerable amount of public petting is allowed between married adults. At the time Kinsey and his associates were gathering their data, 16% of their women subjects had engaged in such extramarital petting. Kinsey was of the opinion that this kind of behavior was increasing, though he did not feel he could document such a conclusion from the data.

2. Conceivably more serious is the transient, even fly-by-night, sex-as-play form, a sometime thing that leaves little residue except as it may leave a precipitate of guilt. About 11% of the Kinsey female subjects (42% of the 26% who had engaged in extramarital relations) had limited their experiences to a period of one year or less. Roughly the same proportion had had only one partner. Rather than a regu-

larly spaced pattern, it was "more usual to find several nonmarital contacts occurring in the matter of a few days or in a single week when the spouse is away on a trip, or when the female is traveling and putting up at a hotel, or at a summer resort, or on an ocean voyage, or visiting at a friend's home" (Kinsey et al. 1953, p. 420).

3. Quite different is what Helen Gurley Brown (1965, Chapter 9) labels "the matinée." This is a purely playful relationship which arises between working men and women who use the lunch hour for their rendezvous at the woman's apartment. The basic rule for such a relationship is "Never become serious." The hazards, beyond that of being found out—for, of course, it must be secret—are that one partner or the other might become bored or fall in love and thus become serious. Either eventuality is fatal to the relationship. In fact, to forestall the likelihood that it may become serious, one of the conditions of success of the matinée is that one or both partners be happily married.

4. What might be called a quasi-matinée form of infidelity has been reported on by a team of sociologists, a form which Roebuck and Spray (1967) call the cocktail-lounge relationship. Its salient characteristics, so far as they are relevant here, are summarized (Bernard 1968a, pp. 69–70) as follows:

> The cocktail-lounge model is a semiserious, semicommitted relationship, semistable; that is, it is of more than transitory duration, definitely not a "pick-up" relationship in the usual sense. It tends to occur among fairly high-status individuals. Most of both men and women in the reported study had had at least some college education. The men were in business and professional occupations; most of the women were either college students (20 percent) or secretaries (33 percent). The employees of the cocktail lounge judged most (80 percent) of both the men and the women to be "stable." . . . The "natural history" of such relationships was one in which after a year or two the women marry (or remarry) and leave the system and are replaced by another cohort. The men do not drop out unless they have to leave town or, in some cases, become too old for these activities. In no case was the marriage of the man reported as disrupted.

The men tended to average in their late thirties, the women in their midtwenties, the medians being thirty-nine and twenty-four respectively.

5. There is, next, the long-lasting pseudomarital form of infidelity, a relationship which Cuber has found to be very similar to conventional marriage:

The dynamics of . . . [these] relationships . . . break with conventional stereotypes about them which generally run to assertions that such relationships typically follow a cycle which begins in infatuation, has a relatively short decline, ends in disillusionment, a new partner is found, and the cycle is repeated. We found examples fitting this model, to be sure, but typically the cases were otherwise. . . . In the prolonged . . . relationships there is often no more a "cycle" than there is to intrinsic marriage—the relationship is monogamous, continues "until death. . . ." Where there is a cycle in any real sense, it tends to be like the cycle in a goodly number of marriages. These relationships, like marriage, sometimes move from vitality and a strong erotic accent to a more matter-of-fact, comfortable kind of interaction. Surprisingly enough, some have settled into a kind of apathy which makes one wonder why they go on, since there are no institutional obligations involved. But perhaps sentiment and a quiescent kind of attachment may be stronger bonds than external social sanctions.

Cuber does not judge these relationships to be any more vulnerable than sanctioned unions. They appear to have powerful intrinsic supports which psychiatrists are in a better position to evaluate than laymen. Even to a layman, however, it is apparent that there must be overriding reasons why the partners in such relationships have not married. The relationship looks very much like polyandrous marriage. Kinsey et al. (1948, p. 593) reported similar unions among their male subjects. And among the 9% of their women subjects who had engaged in extramarital relationships for four or more years, there must have been some of the 11% who had had only one partner (Kinsey et al. 1953, p. 420).

6. Fantasied infidelity—relations with an imagined partner or imagined relations with a real person—is certainly far more common than acted-out infidelity but, according to St. Matthew (Matt. 5:28) no less real. "I say to you that every one who looks at a woman lustfully has already committed adultery with her in his heart." Just daydreaming. Even, presumably, looking at "Playmate of the Month." Or at any miniskirted girl on the street. From this point of view, it would be difficult for any man not to be judged guilty of adultery, however conformist his overt behavior might be. Or any woman, for that matter, who had been exposed to the seduction of an entertainment world personality. Or either husband or wife who fantasies another partner, real or imaginary, in the sex act.

This fantasy form of infidelity has been given some research attention by a team (Neubeck, unpublished report) who interviewed forty suburban couples in business-professional occupations, averaging about thirty years of age. The members of the team included items pertaining to sexual and emotional involvements as well as merely fantasy involvement and correlated their findings with measures of marital satisfaction and of "conscience."[9] They found, expectably enough, that "the less satisfied persons seek . . . satisfaction in fantasy" more than others do, but the same was not true with respect to the conscience variable. Those with high-conscience scores were as likely as those with low-conscience scores to have fantasy involvement.[10]

This lack of relationship between conscience score and fantasy involvement seems to contradict Sapirstein's conclusions (1948, pp. 173–74) based on his experience with patients:

> The inability to face the extramarital urge frequently has a disruptive effect on the marriage. When these feelings are repressed into the unconscious, they almost invariably are associated with hostility to the marital partner. The man may feel that his wife is playing a potentially punishing role toward him for his thoughts of infidelity, and he may begin to resent her. . . . He may be unable to accept this hostility, and live in constant preoccupation and terror about his sexual thoughts.

Perhaps the seeming conflict between Sapirstein and Neubeck is more apparent than real. The fantasy involvement may be present in almost everyone, but it may be a source of disturbance in only a few.

There seem to be no research reports on the relative frequency of the fantasy of the ideal surrogate lover we are told sometimes takes the place of the actual spouse in the coital act in order to render the experience more palatable.

7. There is a kind of noncoital, nonfantasy relationship which involves a profound sharing of the self with another, not a spouse, that is not adulterous in the legal sense though susceptible to the charge of infidelity. Such a situation was depicted in a recent London and Broadway play in which the wife is—justifiably—more fear-

---

[9] Marital satisfaction was measured on the basis of replies to fifteen statements such as "My spouse loves me, confides in me, shows me affection . . ." completely, fairly much, somewhat, little, or not at all. Conscience was measured on the Psychopathic Deviate scale of the Minnesota Multiphasic Personality Inventory, a score of sixty-one or more indicating low conscience and a score of sixty or less, high conscience.

[10] The low-conscience subjects were, however, more likely than high-conscience subjects to show sex involvement.

ful of the Platonic intimacy between her husband and another woman than she would have been of a coital relationship. The kind of relationship which can develop between men and women who work together as a team over a period of time sometimes assumes an emotional interdependence outweighing the marital bonds of either one without supplanting them. These may be among the innocent relationships which, according to Easton and Robbins, are not forbidden by the marital vows. It is an index of our relative concerns that little research attention has been devoted to this kind of relationship.[11]

Patterns by Sex, Age, and Class

By the age of forty, about twice as many of the Kinsey male subjects as of the female subjects had engaged in extramarital relations (50% and 26% respectively) (Kinsey et al. 1953, p. 437). In the Middle Ages when a man was to be away from his wife for any length of time he clamped her into a chastity belt to protect her, presumably, not only against trespassing males but also against her own carnality. Women reared in our society present—or have, until recently, presented—a somewhat different picture (*ibid.*, p. 409):

Most males can immediately understand why most males want extramarital coitus. . . . To most males the desire for variety in sexual activity seems as reasonable as the desire for variety in the books that one reads, the music that one hears, the recreations in which one engages, and the friends with whom one associates socially. On the other hand, many females find it difficult to understand why any male who is happily married should want to have coitus with any female other than his wife.

And their specific findings corroborated this conclusion; the patterns with respect to extramarital relationships differed considerably between the sexes.

Before age twenty-five, for example, there was no relation between years of education and active incidence of extramarital relations among women; among men, there was lower incidence among the more educated. After age twenty-five, however, education made little difference among the men, but among women the active inci-

---

[11] A considerable amount of attention is devoted to "innocent" relationships in one reference (Bernard 1968b).

dence was positively related to education, that is, higher among the better educated (*ibid.*, p. 437). The period of greatest incidence among women was during ages thirty-six to forty (17%); among men it was highest in the late teens (35%) and declined consistently thereafter. In general, the incidence among men tended to be more regularly spaced; among women, as noted earlier, more sporadic.

But far the most interesting finding was one with respect to frequency of coitus per week among those who engaged in extramarital relations. In the early years, it was four times greater among the men than among the women (0.4 and 0.1, respectively); in the early thirties, the frequencies were the same for both sexes (0.2). But in the early forties (41–45), it was twice as high among women as among men (0.4 and 0.2, respectively) (*ibid.*, p. 437). These data suggest that, although women were less disposed to engage in extramarital coitus, when they did, it was with greater frequency.

Infidelity Tolerance

A useful concept for thinking, researching, and hence ultimately, for counseling, might have to do with the relative tolerance of infidelity which spouses show. For such purposes, we might think in terms of a gradient. For example, a spouse might: (1) reject infidelity and divorce the partner, (2) reject the infidelity but not divorce the partner, (3) accept the infidelity grudgingly, under duress, (4) accept the infidelity willingly, or (5) urge or encourage infidelity. Both ends of this continuum have been documented in the literature (Kinsey et al., 1953, pp. 434–35). One's "infidelity tolerance" seems to be related to age, to sex, and to class. Women until now have tended to be more resigned to infidelity than men; about twice as many husbands (51%) as wives (27%) considered extramarital relations of their spouses as a factor in their divorces (*ibid.*, pp. 436, 438). The evidence with respect to age is not so clear-cut, but it appears that older men and women firmly anchored in a long-standing marriage tend to hesitate before breaking it up for infidelity. "In time," Kinsey notes, "[love, jealousy, and morality] seemed less important, and the middle-aged and older females had become more inclined to accept extramarital coitus and at least some of the husbands no longer objected if their wives engaged in such activities" (*ibid.*, p. 417). The wives of working-class men are often reared in an ethnic tradition which accepts infidelity in young men as a matter of course, as something to bear if not to grin about. In general, the cultural context in which the infidelity occurs seems to be as important as the specific situation itself, if not more so, in determining the level of "infidelity tolerance."

The Winds of Change

Despite the prevalence of the several forms of infidelity, the public, for the most part, still gives lip service to the standard of marital exclusivity.[12] But there are several straws in the wind which suggest that we are veering in a different direction—that attitudes, values, and behavior are changing with respect to this standard. Among these straws in the wind are (1) the increasing emphasis by researchers on the positive aspects of extramarital relationships; (2) the greater tolerance shown at least by some theologians or ethicists; (3) the position vis-à-vis adultery in current thinking about divorce legislation; and (4) the increase in extramarital relationships among younger women.

1. One of the most interesting indications of change now taking place is the apologia which is becoming fashionable among researchers in discussing extramarital relationships. It has now become the positive, functional aspects which are increasingly emphasized rather than, as in the past, the negative and dysfunctional aspects. Kinsey and his associates noted in 1948 that the research literature to date was almost uniformly unfavorable in its judgment. "Only an occasional writer suggests that there may be values in such experience which can be utilized for human needs" (p. 591). And in 1953 they pointed out that "certainly any scientific analysis must take into account the fact that there are both advantages and disadvantages to engaging in such activity" (p. 491).

Gerhard Neubeck (1962), on the basis of his research and counseling, has also concluded that there may be a positive function for extramarital relations in many marriages.

[12] On a television program broadcast January 23, 1966, 88% of a national sample said they believed that adultery was wrong for women and about the same number, 86%, said that it was wrong for men as well. These proportions of the sample were not very much higher than for premarital relations: 76% felt them wrong for women and 72% for men. More than half (57%) considered it wrong even for engaged couples. The conditions under which the questions were administered were not described, and so we have no way of knowing how much of an incentive there was for overstating a conforming attitude. With respect to extramarital relations, 26% of the sample—more men than women—would, it was reported, consider them acceptable under certain circumstances.

Marriage cannot serve to meet all of the needs of both spouses at all times. Many marriage partners define at least implicitly—certainly discreetly—what area of satisfaction they will leave to outsiders, and they are not only *not* disturbed that outsiders serve in this capacity but probably relieved that they themselves are not called upon to have to address themselves to each and every need or whim of their mates. In this sense the extramarital relationship becomes supplementary to the marriage relationship.

The current trend seems sometimes to be, in fact, not only in the direction of tolerance but even, in some cases, of advocacy. Some wives, Sapirstein notes (1948, p. 174) are relieved to find that the marriage is suffering from nothing more serious than infidelity. "If that's all that is bothering you, go ahead and get it out of your system, but please don't become emotionally involved."

2. This positive evaluation has also found acceptance in the so-called situational school of ethics among some theological thinkers. Thus Joseph Fletcher (1966), professor in the Episcopal Theological School of Cambridge, Massachusetts, writing in the Catholic *Commonweal* (83:431), has this to say:

There is nothing against extramarital sex as such, in this ethic, and in *some* cases it is good. . . . The *Christian* criteria for sex relations are positive: sex is a matter of certain ideals of relationship. These ideals are based upon a certain faith: about God, Christ, the Church, who man is, and his destiny. Therefore, if people do not embrace that faith (and most do not), there is no reason why they should live by it. And most do not. . . . If true chastity means a marital monopoly, then let those who believe in it recommend it by reason and example. Nothing is gained by condemning the unbeliever. Indeed, to condemn him is more unjust (immoral) than a sexual escapade.

In this emphasis on sincerity and emotional authenticity, Joseph Fletcher is articulating the creed professed and practiced by a certain segment of the younger population today. They too make a big thing about authentic emotion, about fidelity in the sense of being true to their own inner selves. They object to the games people play and to what they call "adult hypocrisy." The enormous emphasis on authentic emotion, on fidelity, on sincerity, tends to make the criterion for judging a relationship the way people feel rather than objective sanctions. One is reminded of George Sand's *obiter dictum* that the hours a woman spent with her lover were true and good; the nights she spent with an unloved husband were sinful and bad.

3. Another straw in the wind has to do with the trends in divorce legislation. I had occasion not long ago to review the grounds alleged for divorce over a period of time as an index or measure of our society's legal specifications for marriage. The permitted legal grounds have not changed very rapidly, but the grounds used have tended to change from a frequent use of adultery[13] to a more frequent use of cruelty. Now we are in process of arriving at the concept of the no-fault divorce. Under this new conception, all that is necessary is for a court to find that the marriage has broken down. The only proof needed will probably be a separation for a specified period of time. Until now—by universally accepting extramarital relations as grounds for divorce—we have demanded fidelity as a legal obligation of both spouses. With the introduction of the no-fault concept of divorce, such fidelity is no longer legally defined as part of marriage. That is, a person who engages in extramarital relationships but does not wish to have a divorce cannot necessarily be divorced for this reason alone. If the spouse wishes a divorce, he or she will have to separate him- or herself from the other and prove in this way that the marriage has in fact broken down. The separation, not the extramarital relations, is the proof the court will need to prove that the marriage has broken down. Unless someone wishes to prosecute a man or woman for the crime of adultery, it will disappear from the scene as a legal entity for all intents and purposes.

4. There is, finally, evidence of change in the actual behavior of women over time. Kinsey et al. (1953, pp. 422–24) reported among their subjects that by age forty, more than a fifth (22%) of the women born in the nineteenth century had engaged in extramarital coitus and almost a third (30%) of those born in the twentieth century. At age forty-five, the proportions were 21% and 40% respectively. By age 25, only 4% of the women born in the nineteenth century had engaged in such relations; twice as many (8%) of those born in the first decade of the twentieth century had; even more, 10%, of those born in the second decade had and 12% of those born in the 1920s.[14] It would be logical to assume that, for women born in

[13] We know that a considerable proportion of married men and women at some time or other engage in extramarital relations (about half of the men and a quarter of the women), but adultery is rarely alleged in actual divorce. A survey of 1,272 readers of the *Ladies' Home Journal* in 1968 indicated that 74% did not think a single act of adultery by either spouse should necessarily be a cause for divorce.

[14] The incidence was somewhat higher among educated women after age twenty-five than among less educated. Increasing education over time may therefore tend to accelerate the trend if the relationship between education and extramarital relations continues.

the 1930s and 1940s, now in their twenties and thirties, the proportion who have or will have engaged in extramarital relations by age twenty-five is or will be not less than, let us say, about 15%.[15]

Wave of the Future: Permanence or Exclusivity?

In the rapidly growing form of nonmarital relationship which young people are evolving today (Schein and Hale 1965), especially on university campuses, there are no vows of permanence. Nor are there any legal sanctions to buttress exclusivity. The emphasis seems to be on fidelity based on authentic emotion. One unpublished study of such relationships by Michael Johnson (1969) at the University of Iowa reports great emphasis on exclusivity, at least for the duration of the relationship. Among the findings with respect to twenty-eight couples are:

Does living together involve some conception of fidelity? The unmarried couples were asked two questions concerning their attitudes toward "adultery": "Under what conditions do you feel it would be all right for you to sleep with someone other than your partner?" and "Under what conditions do you feel it would be all right for your partner to sleep with someone other than you?" It is interesting to note that the respondents tend to put more restrictions on themselves than do their partners. Thus 48 per cent of the males as compared to 39 per cent of the females say that under no conditions would it be all right for the male partner to sleep with someone else. [But] 59 per cent of the females as opposed to 44 per cent of the males say that under no conditions would it be all right for the female partner to sleep with someone else. Less than a fifth of the respondents would accept such a relationship under any conditions at all. Once again we find the females more likely to be double-standard than the males. A somewhat extraordinary discovery is that 11 per cent of both males and females are double-standard in the direction of more freedom for the female. . . . As for sexual behavior, the females in our sample have more often encountered the opportunity to sleep with someone else, 78 per cent having had a chance as opposed to 64 percent of the males. However, when given the chance the male is more likely to take advantage of it.

---

[15] The increasing salience of "wife-swapping clubs" and other forms of extramarital relationships may accelerate this trend. I am indebted to Dr. Edward J. Rydman, executive director of the American Association of Marriage Counselors, for one such example, namely, Club Rebel "formed to serve the sophisticated new generation and . . . dedicated to those who have rebelled at outdated codes and morals . . ." (Personal letter, December 30, 1968).

The young men are theoretically more permissive with respect to women than to themselves but less "faithful" to their partners than the young women are in the presence of temptation.

But what seems more interesting is a rough comparison with the Kinsey findings of a generation ago. If we equate the Kinsey data (on the attitude that extramarital coitus justifies divorce) with the Johnson data (on the attitude that such relations on the part of one's partner are never justified)—admittedly not a completely legitimate equating of statements from a scientific point of view, but suggestive —we arrive at the data in table 1. The most interesting conclusions are that more young people in the Johnson sample seem to adhere to the standard of exclusivity than the subjects in the Kinsey sample. The one exception is the attitude of the men toward women's extramarital relations: here the Kinsey men seem to be more conservative. But a disparity of only seven percentage points in a comparison (in which one set of subjects numbers only twenty-eight cases) is not large enough to be unequivocally credited (cell A, table 1).

In the other cells, the disparities—especially in cell B and cell C —are large enough to be taken seriously even in so small a sample. The young women in the Johnson sample were far less tolerant of the extramarital relations of women than the women in the Kinsey sample were, 59% as contrasted with only 14% (cell B). They were also less tolerant of extramarital relations by men than the women in the Kinsey sample (cell D). The disparity was only a matter of twelve percentage points (thirty-nine as compared with 27%) and may therefore only hover on the brink of statistical significance. But

Table 1—Attitude toward infidelity by conventional spouses and by partners in nonmarital unions

Attitude toward Fidelity	Males in		Females in	
	Conventional Unions, %	Nonmarital Unions, %	Conventional Unions, %	Nonmarital Unions, %
Extramarital relations by wife or partner cause for divorce, or never justified	(A) 51	44	(B) 14	59
Extramarital relations by husband or partner cause for divorce, or never justified	(C) 18	48	(D) 27	39

Source: Johnson (1969) and Kinsey et al. (1953).

the disparity of thirty percentage points—48% and 18%—seems conclusive that the Johnson male subjects were more conservative with respect to the extramarital relations of men than were the Kinsey subjects (cell C).

I add all this up to mean that the women in the relationships which did not promise permanence were more conservative in their attitudes toward extramarital relations both for men and for women than were the women in the Kinsey sample and that the men in the Johnson sample were more conservative than the Kinsey men so far as exclusivity for men was concerned. Exclusivity seemed more important than permanence.

A *caveat* is in order. The factor of age may invalidate any reading of the accompanying table. The Kinsey data included more older subjects, and older spouses probably have more "infidelity tolerance" than younger people. Permanence far outweighs exclusivity on their scale of values, as we noted above in our discussion of infidelity tolerance. We may, therefore, be comparing young people with low infidelity tolerance, in a naturally conservative stage of the union, with older people in a less conservative stage with high infidelity tolerance. In any event, in these nonpromiscuous relationships, the relative emphasis seemed to be on exclusivity rather than on permanence.[16]

Jealousy and Anxiety

From a psychiatric standpoint, two facets of the problem of infidelity seem to warrant at least cursory mention: male jealousy and female security. Kinsey and his associates (1948, p. 411) made a considerable point of the mammalian origin of male jealousy. "While cultural traditions may account for some of the human male's behavior, his jealousies so closely parallel those of the lower species that one is forced to conclude that his mammalian heritage may be partly responsible for his attitudes." And Edward Westermarck (1922, chapter 9), the great historian of human marriage, was of the opinion that monogamy rested on male jealousy. But Kingsley Davis (1949, p. 184), a sociologist, argues the opposite point of view. Monogamy, by granting exclusivity to males, gives rise to jealousy. He sees jealousy as an institutional prop for monogamy. "Where exclusive

[16] There are other young people to whom neither permanence nor exclusivity is important. They believe in communal living in which everyone has access to everyone else, mutual attraction and affection being the only criteria of acceptability. It is doubtful if this pattern will find many adherents in the immediate future.

possession of an individual's entire love is customary, jealousy will demand that exclusiveness. Where love is divided it will be divided according to some scheme, and jealousy will reinforce the division."[17] I shall not go further into Davis's subtle and sophisticated analysis; this statement does not, obviously, do it justice. But I would like to suggest that jealousy used as a prop for monogamous relationships seems to be in a process of attrition. How many patients have any of you treated lately in which jealousy was an important element? How many plays has anyone seen which dealt with jealousy? How many movies? Television programs? Books?[18]

If male jealousy has been a major support for sexual exclusivity, anxiety and insecurity have served a similar function among women with respect to permanence. As recently as just a few years ago I was willing to say that extramarital relations had different significance for men and for women. I believed then that a woman could not be casual about such relations, that she was not likely to engage in them unless there was more than a touch-and-go depth to them, that she could not, like men, treat them incidentally. To her they implied a commitment. I am no longer convinced of this. It seems to me now that a new kind of woman is emerging—or, if you will, an old kind is reemerging[19]—on the scene. And one of the distinguishing characteristics of this woman is that she can be casual about sex, as few women could in the past. If women engaged in sexual relations outside of marriage, it was because they were involved; the relation meant a great deal to them. Husbands, therefore, were justified in their alarm when they learned of them. But for many women today this is apparently no longer true. They can accept the sex-as-fun point of view without conflict. Even a regular extramarital relation-

[17] Davis distinguishes jealousy as a reaction to illegitimate seizure of property from jealousy as the result of deprivation of a love object. From the point of view of competitive concerns, extramarital sexual relations are more threatening to men than premarital. If a girl who has had premarital relations marries a man, he can assume that, everything considered, he was the best sexual partner. At least he had something that compensated for whatever he may have lacked. But in extramarital sexual relations he has no such reassurance. He is competing with a partner or partners who, for all he knows, may be better performers than he. And further, a woman who has engaged in premarital sexual relations is more likely to engage also in extramarital relations than one who has not (Kinsey et al. 1953, pp. 427–28).

[18] Except, perhaps, in connection with homosexual or lesbian relationships where the total matrix is so different, where outside support is so equivocal, and where, therefore, normal social processes do not operate.

[19] Until fairly recently, it was taken for granted in many parts of the world that there would be sexual relations if almost any man and woman were alone together for any length of time.

ship does not faze them or, in fact, necessarily interfere with their marriages.[20]

I believe that the increasing economic independence of women has played a part in this change.[21] Much of the terror which gripped women whose husbands were unfaithful to them in the past stemmed from the threat that it posed to their economic security. What if the other woman won her husband away from her permanently? There is evidence in both Kinsey's statistical data and Sapirstein's clinical data that, when or if she was assured that this was not likely, tolerance of infidelity increased.[22] I am, however, far from believing that economic independence tells the whole story, for there are economically independent women who are as terrified of losing men as the most economically dependent. The prostitute-pimp relationship is only the most extreme example that can occur in any setting. Psychological dependency must certainly be included in any analysis of infidelity-tolerance.

Psychological Implications

Economic independence is a fairly simple phenomenon, merely a status, not intrinsic to the person who happens to occupy it. But psychological dependency is a personality trait and hence far more complex. Sapirstein (1948), in a book that has greatly influenced my own thinking, analyzed the nature of dependency needs in marriage,

[20] An undoubtedly exaggerated illustration of this trend was presented several years ago in Paris where economically successful wives were taking on young lovers. "All of my friends have young friends nowadays. The oldest . . . is 27. . . . There are so many handsome, eager, virile, appreciative young men in Paris, why should any of us ever again put up with men who are older and more tired?" (Leach 1959). The woman quoted was a fortyish manager of a beauty salon.

[21] "It's this way," Marianne said. "We are all making money nowadays. We have good jobs and we don't need what your musical comedies call sugar daddies. We can pick and choose and, after all, why not have someone who is young, easy, and amusing?" (Sheppard 1966).

[22] This is not to deny the anguish or the humiliation of knowing that they were less attractive sexually than the other woman. It is one of the hardest defeats in the world to take. It may be ineffable. Women learn to forgive if they have to, but rarely to forget. The wife quoted by Sapirstein who gave her consent to her husband's infidelity still did not want to know when it happened; it would be too hard to bear. "Don't let me know when you do it. I'll be hurt but I'll live through it." The same is true of men also, of course. Acceptance of this type of defeat has been almost impossible for men to swallow. The law has been lenient if he resorted to violence, even assault and murder. But even among men change has been rapid.

showing how normal they were in men and in women and how essential their fulfillment was. The basic function married partners performed for one another was, he showed, precisely that of satisfying the normal dependency needs that everyone experiences. The countless stresses, strains, and threats that life subjects us to find alleviation in the unfailing support which in a good marriage can be *depended* upon from a spouse. No matter how helpless we may feel, confronted by failure and disparagement in our nonmarital roles, we know that we can *depend* on our spouses to reassure us and build us up. He was writing in terms of threats from outside of the relationship—loss of job or difficulties with the children—which required reassurance from the spouse. But infidelity is a threat within the relationship itself, threatening the spouses with loss or diminution of the very support and reassurance marriage is supposed to supply. If we cannot *depend* on our spouses for such support, we may, Sapirstein notes, turn to others (*ibid.*, p. 170).

In connection with this analysis, I would like to raise a number of questions which psychiatrists are in a better position to deal with than sociologists.

1) Can you foresee any form of socialization which would obviate the dependency needs which Sapirstein finds so basic in people reared in our society today? If people could be reared in a way that such dependency needs do not exist, what would it do to the nature of the marital bond?

2) If infidelity tolerance in both men and women should increase, what can we expect this to do to the nature of the marital relationship itself? Will it mean marital relationships are so solid, so impregnable, and so secure that neither partner feels threatened by infidelity? Or so superficial, so trivial, so expendable, and with so little at stake that infidelity really does not matter? Will it mean that there is so little psychological dependency in the relationship that a threat of its loss is only a minor misfortune, not a major catastrophe?

3) The fact that in so many cases infidelity (if not known by the spouse) seemed to cause no deprivation in the spouse raises an old question: how many people can one love or be attached to at the same time? If one is "true"—in one's own fashion—to several persons at once, what is the quality of the relationships? Does anyone really have enough resources to supply the psychological dependency needs of several persons?[23]

23 In Mormon polygyny, there were strictly enforced institutionalized rules forbidding favoritism to any wife, which in themselves were doubtless supportive and reassuring. A man had, so to speak, to "ration" his need-fulfillment efforts.

4) If infidelity becomes an acceptable practice, will it be possible for spouses to *depend* on one another for the psychological support they need? Or will it deprive them of it? Do you accept the findings on deprivation presented above? *Can* a person supply reassurance to a spouse if involved with someone else?

I am sure a great many other questions have occurred to you; you may even have the answers.

References

Bernard, J. 1968a. Present Demographic Trends and Structural Outcomes in Family Life Today. In *Marriage and Family Counseling, Perspective and Prospect*, ed. J. A. Peterson. New York: Association Press.

Bernard, J. 1968b. *The Sex Game*. New York: Prentice-Hall.

Brown, H. G. 1965. *Sex and the Office*. New York: Pocket Books.

Common Book of Prayer. 1959. In *Cokesbury Marriage Manual*, ed. W. H. Leach.

Cuber, J. F. Adultery: Reality versus Stereotype. Unpublished paper, mimeographed.

Davis, K. 1949. *Human Society*. New York: Macmillan.

Easton, B. S., and Robbins, H. C. 1938. *The Bond of Honour, a Marriage Handbook*, New York: Macmillan.

Fletcher, J. 1966. Love is the Only Measure. *Commonweal* 83: 431.

Harper, R. A. 1961. Extramarital Sex Relations. In *Encyclopedia of Sexual Behavior*. New York: Hawthorn.

Johnson, M. P. 1969. Courtship and Commitment: A Study of Cohabitation on a University Campus. Master's thesis, University of Iowa.

Kinsey, A. C., Pomeroy, W. B., and Martin, C. E. 1948. *Sexual Behavior in the Human Male*. Philadelphia: W. B. Saunders Company.

————, and Gebhard, P. H. 1953. *Sexual Behavior in the Human Female*. Philadelphia: W. B. Saunders Company.

Leach, W. H., ed. 1959. *Cokesbury Marriage Manual*.

Neubeck, G., and Schletzer, V. M. 1962. A Study of Extramarital Relationships. *Marriage Fam. Liv.* 24: 279–81.

Roebuck, J., and Spray, S. L. 1967. The Cocktail Lounge: A Study of Heterosexual Relations in a Public Organization. *Amer. J. Sociol.* 72: 288–95.

Sapirstein, M. R. 1948. *Emotional Security*. New York: Crown Press.

Sheppard, E. 1966. Sugar Daddy's on the Shelf. *Washington Post*, February 9, 1966.

Terry, S. 1969. Harassing of Black Minister Brings Racism to Vermont. *Washington Post*, January 2, 1969.

Westermarck, E. 1922. *The History of Human Marriage*. New York: Allerton.

The Emergence of Middle-class Deviant Subcultures: The Case of Swingers

Mary Lindenstein Walshok

Introduction

Virtually all the discussions of what has variously been termed wife swapping, swinging, or co-marital sexual relations have been either highly polemical or only descriptive in content. Empirical studies of co-marital sexual relations have been largely participant observations (Breedlove and Breedlove 1964; Smith and Smith 1970). These factors, as well as our society's prevailing puritanism, have contributed to the marginal legitimacy of the systematic study of co-marital sexual behavior. Even if we use the term "systematic" loosely, there is virtually no systematic research on this topic. The theoretical aspects of this topic have also been neglected. The desire of observers to further or to indict the "cause" of particular sexual subcultures has all too often obscured their ability to contribute to a systematic and analytically insightful understanding of the relationship of these subcultures to the larger society and of their significance for a more general understanding of human behavior. Thus, this paper will attempt to deal theoretically with the emergence of the swinging subculture and its implications for contemporary American society, suggesting its relevance and legitimacy for sociological inquiry.

Reprinted, by permission of The Society for the Study of Social Problems, from *Social Problems*, 18, no. 4. I would like to acknowledge the assistance of George Hanson and William Sparks with whom research on this topic is currently in progress. I would also like to acknowledge Clarence Tygart and Joseph J. Hayes for their helpful editorial comments.

Co-Marital Relations Defined

The area of sexual experience discussed in this article needs to be defined explicitly. By "co-marital" I am referring to behavior which embodies two distinctive qualities. (These points will apply also to the term "swinging.") One is the agreement between husband and wife to have sexual relations with other people, but in contexts in which they *both* engage in such behavior at the same time and usually in the same place. Such sexual involvement may be either in a group situation, such as an orgy, or where couples go into separate rooms for coition in private. The second quality is that the pursuit of these relationships is primarily by means of some organized or institutionalized pattern, i.e., they are not spontaneous occurrences. Advertisements for interested couples in magazines or newspapers, membership in a club, institute, or bar scene, or attendance at social functions with explicit intention of sexual relations with other couples are common.

Such a pattern of sex relations outside the conventional context of marriage is quite different from extramarital relations, which are usually characterized by secrecy and spontaneity to the extent that they are relationships in the context of everyday life. They also are not uncommon occurrences in American culture. Kinsey et al. (1953) found approximately 50 percent of American males had had an extramarital sexual relationship by the age of forty; among women, approximately 26 percent reported such a relationship by the same age. There are no data on the extent of co-marital relationships in American society.

It is difficult to discover a clearly visible subculture in the service of extramarital relations, while the co-marital experience has fostered an elaborate subculture similar in form to the deviant subcultures associated with drugs and homosexuality. It is important to note, however, that participation in the swinging subculture rarely affects one's other role spheres to the extent that it does with other forms of deviance. It is this quality of co-marital sexuality as a deviant subculture that is of particular interest in this paper.

Finally, it is important to emphasize that couples living in communes or other forms of experimental communities are not included in this discussion, though mate sharing and group sex may be a dimension of their life together. What is distinctive about the organized nature of the social activities of the group under discussion is that it is primarily and admittedly for the sake of establishing sexual liaisons without disturbing the basic quality of other aspects of one's life. In Symonds's (1967) terms, this discussion focuses exclusively on "recreational swingers" rather than on the "utopian" ones, who apparently constitute only a very small minority of the total number of swingers.

Some Theoretical Perspectives on Co-Marital Relations

There are two theoretical approaches to the co-marital phenomenon, each of which places emphasis on distinct dimensions but both of which ultimately merge into a processual model of the development and maintenance of deviant commitments. The one is the functional argument which takes as its point of departure Davis's (1966) discussion of prostitution and, more recently, Polsky's (1967) discussion of pornography. The general applicability of what has come to be known as the "safety-valve" model of deviance has impressed other interpreters of the co-marital scene (Denfeld and Gordon 1970, pp. 86–87), though it has not been dealt with as extensively as here. This approach contributes less to our understanding of the etiology of this form of behavior than to an understanding of the maintenance and functional integration of a deviant commitment with a conventional life-style. Suggestive for an understanding of the etiology of co-marital commitments is the concept of marginality and its consequences for the development of unconventional or nonconformist behavioral and attitudinal orientations.

A Theoretical Perspective on the Etiology of Co-Marital Commitments

Group sex among married couples and exchange of partners among marital couples have been present throughout much of human history. Instances of such behavior can readily be found from Petronius's descriptions of ancient Rome to Gogol's portrayal of Russian peasants. However, as much as we can tell, instances of sexual deviance were generally limited to the aristocracy. Other classes most frequently indulged in deviant sexual practices in the context of festivals.

What makes contemporary co-marital behavior sociologically interesting is its preponderance among basically middle-class and essentially conventional people and its somewhat bureaucratized and decidedly *un*festival-like quality. But what kinds of social structure give rise to this subculture and what social psychological factors characterize individuals who are attracted to this subculture? These are the etiological questions to which I would like to offer a few suggestive leads.

Descriptive terms like "technological," "bureaucratized," "segmented," "transient," "affectively neutral," "mobile," and "anomic" all communicate a picture of urban and suburban life which is beginning to prevail in American society. The rapid decline of many traditional values, the development of instant communities in the suburbs, and the new-found affluence among many heretofore rural, uneducated populations characterize the ever increasing new middle class. It is within this group that the emerging pattern of co-marital relations is most widespread. In a very important sense, people new to the middle class occupy one of the most ambiguous statuses in American society.

The new suburban communities which have grown up around metropolitan centers in the last thirty years possess a number of qualities which suggest status ambiguity. They are characterized by a highly educated population, affluent standard of living, political conservatism, and an abundance of fundamentalist churches. The co-existence of these gross characteristics is surprising and deceptive; the qualitative nature of each factor needs to be specified. The residents of the new suburbs are predominantly upwardly mobile socially and economically, this by virtue of new and technical rather than traditional and general education and occupations. Many social scientists who refer to high levels of education focus more on quantity than quality of education. Four years in a technical college, or two years in a junior college, are qualitatively different than a major in literature at a state university or private school. The significance of this qualitative distinction for phenomena such as political attitudes has recently been noted (Holt and Tygart 1969).

Residents of the new suburbs are relatively new to metropolitan areas and are migrants primarily from more rural areas of the South and Midwest. The provincialism of many rural values is not lost with movement into the suburbs, and one finds, for example, a great deal of religious fundamentalism. The new suburban dweller's recent entry into the middle class also gives rise to stress and status anxiety, which some have suggested contributes to resistance to progressive social and economic legislation (Hofstadter 1964; Lipset 1964). People new to the middle class wish to maintain their status; any shifts in the environment might threaten their newly found status. Finally, the new suburbanites live entirely corporate lives. Most work for large companies, live in subdivisions, shop in shopping centers, and change jobs and neighborhoods relatively frequently.

The consequences of this corporate quality in all dimensions of life are far reaching, the most obvious being that the organization of personal lives and of small groups will, to some extent, reflect the more general predominating cultural and structural patterns in a society. Forms of organization and interaction are not simply a function of variations in size and goals but are routines or generalized forms to which people become accustomed and hence incorporate under most circumstances. Since large organizations predominate in society, one becomes habituated to affectively neutral, segmented, routinized, and bureaucratized forms of interrelating. Even when the situations do not necessitate such patterns, as with relations among friends, one may not have developed the behavioral or interpersonal skills necessary to establish relationships on a personal basis. It is easier to pursue relationships through some kind of predictable and organized structure which provides formats for interaction to which one has become accustomed. In this sense, suburban man lacks personal autonomy not only in work but in living and playing, which is another qualitative phenomenon that might prove fruitful in understanding the responsiveness to deviant subcultures, particularly if such subcultures provide an imagery of personal autonomy. Sexual subcultures certainly provide such imagery, for reasons to be mentioned below; and this increased sense of personal autonomy may enable people to cope more effectively with their lack of social autonomy in other spheres.

All these factors conspire to create situations of great ambiguity. In a very real sense, those individuals new to the middle class can be characterized as marginal people. They are no longer working class or rural dwellers, ensconced in a secure community of common values and sanctions; nor are they securely middle class in terms of general education, life style, job security, and community identity. People in marginal statuses are often forced to make innovative or adaptive responses to their ambiguous condition. By virtue of their marginality, they are more susceptible to pressures to make contact with others to share a common experience. Swinging provides one such opportunity. The plethora of other small group experiences such as nudism, sensitivity groups, courses and institutes on experimental living, and experimental sex among members of the middle class all suggest a general interest in new and intense forms of experience. Nonetheless, individuals involved in co-marital sexuality sustain highly conventional life styles in all other spheres except the sexual. Why is this the case? At this point a few comments on the "overdetermined" nature of the sexual experience in American society seem necessary.

As Gagnon and Simon (1970) have suggested, the overdetermined nature of the sexual experience in American society has led to its being a vehicle for the expression of many essentially nonsexual needs. For many it is a "test." For others, it is a "way station" in the pursuit of intense experience. For still others, it remains largely a realm of mystery, guilt, and anxiety (Gagnon and Simon, 1970, pp. 4-19). For virtually no one in American society is sex an experience or topic from which it is possible to separate one's more general social and psychological needs.

In the past, a person's virtue was tied to his capacity for sexual restraint at virtually every level of sexual expression in every context, including marriage. Today, we are witnessing a public eroticization of the environment which suggests that true happiness and self-affirmation are inextricably tied to one's competence in bed. Only in a society where sex was once seen as the consummate evil could it become construed as a consummate good. What is more important from a sociological standpoint than the goodness or badness of sex is its consummate value in our culture, such that human freedom and fulfillment become coterminous with sexual freedom and fulfillment. By affirming one's freedom from sexual restraint one obtains a feeling of personal freedom; this, in turn, sustains one in the routinized activities of day-to-day living.

It would seem that in one sense the development of sexually free subcultures which coincide so comfortably with conventional life-styles and commitments only reinforces the "one-dimensional" quality of human life. Participation in a subculture becomes but another piece in the complex, segmented puzzle of human life in mass society, but a far more important piece. Participation in the subculture is so important because of the saliency of sex for one's self-assessed competence and sense of freedom. Participation reinforces one's capacity to deal with conventional life rather than posing a fundamental threat to conventional living. Ellul (1964) has talked about the function of islands of diversity and contained diversity in a technological society as useful contexts in which people can act out their needs for freedom and variety without disrupting the smooth running of the well-oiled technological machine. The swinging subculture is an excellent example of Ellul's notion of contained diversity.

Those in our society for whom the sexual experience possesses such an overdetermined quality are individuals from more restrictive sexual backgrounds, which invest sexuality with excess meaning. This is also the case in the swinging subculture. Impressions from previous research and from research currently in progress suggest that co-marital couples in the swinging subculture have highly traditional religious backgrounds, have had little premarital experience, have married young, and did not initially have varied sex lives once married. The co-marital subculture provides the opportunity for both women and men from such backgrounds to discover adventure and sexuality while at the same time posing no basic threat to marriage or life-style. This is the dimension now to be elaborated.

The Functional Integration of
Deviant Sexual Commitments and Conventional Life-Styles

The one-dimensional quality of middle-class deviancy is merely a commentary on the one-dimensional quality of most aspects of middle-class life. In such a one-dimensional environment, the larger philosophical and political questions pertaining to the problems of meaning and choice in a routinized environment are rarely asked. Middle-class life instead fosters the desire for some kind of mini/max solution in which one can realize immediate psychic and recreational benefits with a minimum of personal risk and a minimum of change in the other spheres of one's life. However, from the perspective of the larger philosophical and political questions, this mini/max solution is a classic example of "bad faith" or "co-optation." What the institutionalized subculture provides is a functional alternative to a basic shift in social attitudes and institutions. For the reasons suggested earlier, it sustains and even augments the individual's commitment to prevailing values and institutions. In this sense it is similar to what Marcuse (1962) refers to as "repressive desublimation." One can conceive of the day, for example, when large corporations will throw massive swinging parties in order to improve employee morale and productivity.

Davis's (1966, p. 371) discussion of prostitution suggests that prostitution is tolerated because it allows impersonal sex outside of marriage while at the same time posing no basic threat to the availability of respectable women for marriage and family roles. Its basic causes are the institutional control of sex, the unequal scale of attractiveness, and the social and economic inequality between classes and between men and women. Davis suggests that, given the loosening institutional controls of sex and the greater emphasis on sexual pleasure for women in general, there has been somewhat of a decline in prostitution. Nonetheless, the continuation of inequalities in attractiveness, wealth, social advantage, and even in the desire for sex perpetuates a situation in which total sexual freedom and equality are very unlikely; so functional alternatives to the conventional outlets persist. The co-marital subculture is one such functional alternative.

Distinctive features of the co-marital subculture include a variety of symbols and mutual understandings which prohibit lasting emotional involvements between couples and perpetuate impersonal sex. This form of sexuality outside of marriage, like prostitution, does not constitute a significant threat to the more involving marital relationship and at the same time allows for sexual indulgence. But it is important to emphasize that the rewards of participation in this subculture very likely go beyond mere sexual gratification. The comments of many committed swingers suggest that co-marital sexuality has served to solidify their marriages, to expand their circle of friends, and to contribute to a more general sense of well-being. In this sense, participation in the sexual subculture may give a sense of competence and fulfillment which for many is lacking in their day-to-day work and living.

In addition to providing a functional sexual alternative and a functional alternative context for the realization of personal competence, the co-marital scene provides opportunities for indulgence in what Polsky (1967, p. 274) has referred to as "polymorphous perverse" sexuality. He discusses pornography as a functional alternative to conventional sexuality in the same sense in which Davis does and suggests that both provide for the discharge of what society labels as "antisocial" sex (Polsky, 1967, p. 271). He suggests that, additionally, pornography allows one, at least on the fantasy level, to expand upon the range of possible sexual behaviors and outlets. An often heard comment by swingers is that marital sex became more interesting, complex, and exciting as a result of co-marital encounters. The co-marital context provides an opportunity for sexual learning and experimentation in an affectively neutral setting. One can expand one's repertoire of behaviors, begin to feel comfortable with them, and then incorporate them into the emotionally involved marital relationship.

What adds credence to the functional alternative model are the characteristics of the swingers themselves. If they were perhaps primarily Symonds's (1967) "utopians" or members of groups existing on the fringe of society in other role spheres, such as communes, one might characterize swinging more as a social movement than as a functional alternative to conventional sexual norms. But descriptions of individuals involved in co-marital sexuality suggest hedonism more than commitment to social change. Only occasionally are swingers found at the forefront of movements for such things as abortion reform or changes in legislation pertaining to homosexuality. Swingers are rarely political or social reformers. In addition, given the conventionality of their behavior and relationships in other role spheres, the functional or safety-valve model seems to have some merit. Research has suggested that swingers are largely politically conservative, middle-income, middle-educated individuals in technical (I would suggest additionally, large organizational) occupations (Bartell 1970; Smith and Smith 1970; Symonds 1967). Many also marry early, appear to have limited premarital experience, and tend to have larger families. There are also some indications that many swingers have few outside interests and tend to be homebodies prior to swinging (Bartell 1970). Reliable data on swingers is unavailable; so much of this is speculation. However, it is consistent with the imagery of a highly mobile and transient population. In many ways they are the typical American couple, except for their deviant sexual interests.

General Summary

This paper has introduced three distinct points which, taken together, provide a general perspective on the emergence of a co-marital subculture among middle Americans. (1) The paper suggests that the centrality of sexual deviation within the middle class is a consequence of the high personal and social value placed on sexuality. (2) The emergence of this subculture in predominantly middle-class groups is suggested to be a consequence of the marginal status of individuals new to the middle class, which makes them more responsive to intense forms of experience. (3) Finally, the highly formalized and routinized quality of the swinging subculture is interpreted as essential for the maintainance of conventional commitments along with the deviant ones. This is particularly true among groups whose conventional life-style in general manifests elements of corporateness, standardization, and formalization.

The coexistence of conventional life-styles and deviant commitments, as manifested among middle-class swingers, is suggestive for more general theories of deviance. It suggests that the apparent contradiction between involvement in a deviant subculture and highly conventional commitments in other role spheres can best be understood with reference to (1) the saliency for personal identity of the cultural values from which the behavior deviates; (2) the initial social marginality of an individual which makes him more eager for identity confirmation or community membership; and (3) the organization of the deviant subculture, which has implications for the extent to which participation in the given subculture can be segmented from other roles. Participation in the deviant subculture thus becomes a functional alternative to potentially deviant commitments in other role spheres.

In the particular case of the co-marital subculture, it is likely that, given the overdetermined quality of sex in American society, forms of sexual deviance are particularly attractive to individuals who occupy marginal middle-class status positions and who come from more sexually restrictive social backgrounds. The combination of needs for relatedness and feelings of competence, which come with the marginality, and the image of sex as a means to such ends (as a consequence of its exaggerated—once negative, now positive—valences) gives rise to a responsiveness to deviant sexual commitments of a basically one-dimensional nature. The generalization of the rewards derived from the deviant behavior to other role spheres legitimizes its segmentation. Participation in the subculture provides the experience of impersonal and varied sex in a context which minimizes any threats to a conventional marriage and life-style. The organized, routinized paths to sexual encounters, be they clubs, ads, or cocktail parties, reinforce the impersonal quality of the sex and are consistent with the affectively neutral, segmented, and bureaucratized patterns of interaction to which technological man has become accustomed. In concert, these factors support what appears to be a growing pattern of sexual deviancy through organized groups.

References

Bartell, G. D. 1970. Group Sex among the Mid-Americans. *J. Sex Res.* 6, no. 2, pp. 113–30. [In this book, pp. 185–201.]

Breedlove, W., and Breedlove, J. 1964. *Swap Clubs*. Los Angeles: Sherbourne Press.

Davis, K. 1966. Sexual Behavior. In *Contemporary Social Problems*, ed. R. K. Merton and R. A. Nisbet. New York: Harcourt, Brace and World, Inc.

Denfield, D., and Gordon, M. 1970. The Sociology of Mate Swapping: Or, the Family That Swings Together Clings Together. *J. Sex Res.* 6, no. 2, pp. 85–100. [In this book, pp. 68–83.]

Ellul, J. 1964. *The Technological Society*. New York: Vintage Press.

Gagnon, J., and Simon, W. 1970. Introduction: Perspectives on the Sexual Scene. In *The Sexual Scene*, ed. J. Gagnon and W. Simon. Chicago: Aldine.

Hofstadter, R. 1964. The Pseudo-conservative Revolt. In *The Radical Right*, ed. Daniel Bell. New York: Anchor Books.

Holt, N., and Tygart, C. E. 1969. Political Tolerance and Higher Education. *Pac. Soc. Rev.* 12: 27–33.

Kinsey, A. C., Pomeroy, W. B., Martin, C. E., and Gebhard, P. H. 1953. *Sexual Behavior in the Human Female.* Philadelphia: W. B. Saunders Company.

Lipset, S. M. 1964. The Sources of the Radical Right. In *The Radical Right*, ed. Daniel Bell. New York: Anchor Books.

Marcuse, H. 1962. *Eros and Civilization.* New York: Vintage Books.

Polsky, N. 1967. *Hustlers, Beats, and Others.* Chicago: Aldine.

Smith, J. R., and Smith, L. G. 1970. Co-marital Sex and the Sexual Freedom Movement. *J. Sex Res.* 6, no. 2, pp. 131–42. [In this book, pp. 202–13.]

Symonds, C. 1967. Pilot Study of the Peripheral Behavior of Sexual Mate Swappers. Master's thesis, University of California, Riverside.

Group Marriage:
A Possible Alternative?

Albert Ellis

A type of marriage that seems to have always existed during the history of humanity is group marriage. In its strictest form, it consists of a relatively small number of adults—say, from four to fifteen—living together, sharing labor, goods, and services, raising their children in common, and engaging in promiscuous sex relations, so that every male in the group has intercourse, at one time or another, with every female in the group. In its looser form, it consists of communal or tribal marriage, where a larger group of adults—say, up to several hundred individuals—lives in a single co-operative community and all members have at least theoretical sexual access to all other members of the same community, although, in a year's time, an individual member of this sexual-economic cooperative may actually engage in intercourse and potentially procreate with only a few other members of the large group.

Small-scale group marriage has apparently been reasonably common throughout human history and definitely exists in various parts of the United States and the rest of the world today. Group marriages of this kind do not usually remain viable for any considerable period of time but break up for one reason or another, with some of the members, who are quite devoted to this kind of living, thereafter seeking and founding another small-scale group marriage arrangement in a different house or another community.

Large-scale or tribal forms of group marriage that have existed for even a few months at a time seem to have been rare in human annals. Many mythical ones have been reported over the years, but actual instances—such as that of the perfectionist Oneida Community in up-state New York, which lasted for thirty years during the middle of the nineteenth century (Noyes 1870)—have seldom been authenticated.

The anthropological and sociological literature of the late nine-teenth century was occupied—indeed, almost obsessed—with the question of whether primitive man generally lived in a state of group marriage. As Westermarck (1925, 1: 103) notes,

It is often said that the human race must have originally lived in a state of promiscuity, where individual marriage did not exist, where all the men in a horde or tribe had indiscriminate access to all the women, and where the children born of these unions belonged to the community at large. This opinion has been expressed by Bachofen, McLennan, Morgan, Lord Avebury, Giraud-Teulon, Lippert, Kohler, Post, Wilken, Kropotkin, Wilu-tzky, Bloch, and many others.

Among those cited by Westermarck, we may quote Lord Avebury (1912, p. 3), who strongly stated that

my position was that no such institution [as marriage] existed amongst our primitive ancestors, and that they lived in a state of what, for want of a better term, I propose to call "communal marriage." This has been admitted by some high authorities, but questioned by others, who do not seem, however, to be always consistent, and while denying it in some passages, appear to admit it in others.

Iwan Bloch (1908, p. 188) was, if anything, even stronger in his belief that monogamous or even polygamous marriage, as we know these forms of family relationships, did not exist among early man:

Whoever knows the nature of the sexual impulse, whoever has arrived at a clear understanding regarding the cares of human evolution, and finally, whoever has studied the conditions that even now prevail among primitive peoples and among modern civilized races in the matter of sexual relations, can have no doubt whatever that in the beginnings of human development a state of sexual promiscuity did actually prevail.

Sir James G. Frazer (1910, 4: 110-11, 137, 151), another great authority on primitive peoples, also strongly believed in the prevalence of group marriage in early times:

Exogamy . . . has everywhere been originally a system of group marriage devised for the sake of superseding a previous state of sexual promiscuity. . . . It appears to be a reasonable hypothesis that at least a large part of mankind has passed through the stage of group-marriage in its progress upward from a still lower stage of sexual promiscuity. . . . The age of sexual promiscuity belongs to a more or less distant past, but clear traces of it survive in the right of intercourse which in many Australian tribes the men exercise over un-married girls before these are handed over to their husbands. . . . Even these customs are by no means cases of absolutely unrestricted promiscuity, but taken together with the converging evidence of the series of exogamous classes they point decidedly to the former prevalence of far looser relations between sexes than are now to be found among any of the Australian aborigines.

On the other hand, many authorities have violently disputed the notion that group marriage was a general pattern early in human history. Arthur James Todd (1913, pp. 31-44) notes that

on the whole, the evidence is inconclusive for the former universality of group-marriage. I do not consider it necessary to assume that the race passed through this stage in the evolution of familial forms. Our own conclusion is that group-marriage has not yet been sufficiently established to build extensively upon. . . . We should be prepared to find in primitive society a varying condition of promiscuity and fixity in the marriage relation, which we might briefly term intermittent promiscuity.

William Graham Sumner (Sumner 1927, pp. 1547-49) opposed the theory of primitive promiscuity since he felt that any kind of marriage worthy of the name meant regulation and that regulation and pure promiscuity were incompatible:

The existence of the marriage institution means restriction upon the sex relation. If there ever was a time of no restriction, that was a time when marriage was absent. Since available evidence leads to the conclusion that there was less of regulation upon the earlier stages of institutional evolution than later, it is a logical inference that the slight restriction encountered under the most primitive of conditions was preceded by no regulation at all—none, that is to say, in the *mores*. . . . Evidence of this order is conclusive for a very slight degree of regulation, if not of utter promiscuity; however, cases of no regulation at all, that is, of the utter absence of marriage, are about as rare in ethnography as those of no religion. . . . What men did before the formation of society is a matter of considerable indifference to us, but we cannot see that any human society could have established itself or could have long endured without subjecting the sex relation to control. We prefer, therefore, to speak of minimal regulation or relative unregulation rather than of promiscuity.

The hypothesis that early man regularly and universally practiced tribal promiscuity or large-scale group marriage was thoroughly investigated and dealt what has been accepted as practically a death blow by Edward Westermarck (1925, 1: 336), who concluded in this connection,

It is not, of course, impossible that among some peoples the intercourse between the sexes may have been almost promiscuous. But the hypothesis according to which promiscuity has formed a general stage in the social history of mankind . . . is in my opinion one of the most unscientific ever set forth within the whole domain of sociological speculation.

As far as I can see, Westermarck was most probably right in this conclusion. It should be noted, however, that he merely stated that tribal promiscuity never seems to have been a *general* custom among primitive peoples. He does not say that it never existed at all, and he by no means rules out the occurrence, many times during history, of separate instances of small-scale group marriage. As Baber (1939, p. 59) notes,

The human family has not universally gone through a uniform series of stages in its evolution—there is every reason to believe that the development of the family was sometimes random and sometimes opportunistic, as has been the case in the evolution of many other phases of culture.

So, in all probability, group marriage has been with us from primitive times onward. Modern manifestations of this form of sex-love relationship are definite but hardly startling. Because I am one of the recognized leaders in the field of sexual liberalism and have written a good many articles and books espousing premarital sex relations and free love unions (Ellis 1965, 1966), many individuals and groups in the United States have been in touch with me during the past decade and have told me of their sex doings and problems. As a result of written and personal contact with these people, I have been apprised of the existence, from time to time, of about a dozen group marriage arrangements. Usually, these have been established by utopian-minded individuals who band together in groups of from four to ten adults, live under one roof (generally in some western or midwestern part of the country), work co-operatively together, and engage in a round-robin type of sex relationships. That is to say, few sexual orgies of any kind take place, but the males and females in the group keep pairing off, from day to day, with different partners, so that each group member regularly copulates with all the other members of the opposite sex.

As far as I can tell from communications from my correspondents, these group marriages last from about several months to a few years and then seem to break up for one reason or another, particularly for nonsexual reasons. Thus, some of the members of the co-operative will not work steadily at the jobs they are supposed to perform, or they exhibit personality traits that are highly distasteful to some of the other group members. Hence a breakup will occur.

In addition to my personal knowledge of American group marriages, there are reliable literature reports of a good many such arrangements during the last decade:

1. The Kerista movement was started several years ago, and reports on its activities have regularly appeared in its newspaper, *The Kerista Tribe*, in *The Modern Utopian*, and in various other publications. For a while its leaders, Jud Presmont and Dau, tried to get an active group started on Roatan Island, British Honduras, but were harassed by immigration regulations and lack of proper medical facilities; "the number of people who said they were coming down was many and the number of people who came down with the right spirit and attitude was few" (Presmont 1967, 1: 11–12). Kerista is very openly devoted to group sex-love relations and has had active communities going, at various times, in New York City, Los Angeles, San Francisco, and elsewhere.

The history of Kerista has been one of continual trouble, with new members coming into the fold, staying for a while, and then leaving. As Presmont (1967, p. 12) notes,

One of the biggest problems in the utopian communal thing is strangers— constant strangers—most of whom are dilettantes and dabblers, who come into your life in a steady flow and haven't the slightest interest in what's happening except perhaps to meet a new girl or a new man who'll make a marriage prospect and who can be pulled out of the communal thing into the other society. Anyway, we're learning more about it every day.

2. The hippie movement began a few years ago, largely in the Haight-Ashbury section of San Francisco, and then spread in a big way to New York City's Lower East Side. The hippies are largely

interested in "turning on" to psychedelic experiences, especially through smoking marijuana and taking LSD, in dropping out of the establishment and living in unconventional ways, and in love and community spirit, at least as far as their fellow members are concerned (Mitchel 1968; Shorris 1967; Time Magazine 1967). One of the common hippie customs is to have several males and females share an apartment (or "pad"), undress and sleep in the same room (with eight or ten of them often sleeping on mattresses or other makeshift beds at the same time), and have group sex relations. Although the hippies who share the same bedroom may not stay together for very long (some for a day, some for weeks or months), there is no question that at times they maintain a form of group marriage and that all the females in the group sexually share the same males, and *vice versa*.

Communal marriage among the hippies, however, usually is quite limited. As Shorris (1967, p. 113) notes,

Sex in the hippie world belongs to the seniors; the freshmen just arrived from Connecticut and Minnesota find there are five boys to every girl and the girls want the drug peddlers or musicians or any boy who has established himself as the hippie version of the letter man. The best the freshman can hope for is occasional group sex in a crash pad, a homosexual experience, or a gang rape.

Paul Krassner (1967, 1: 19) also wonders whether the hippies are truly and liberally devoted to group sex as, on the surface, they sometimes seem to be:

It's possible that many hippies indulge in mysticism because they have enough of a puritan hangover that they can't accept pleasure on its own terms; they have to rationalize it with spirituality.

3. Various other reports of group marriage appear from time to time in the literature on the Sexual Freedom League, the Rene Guyon Society, the Sexual Emancipation Movement, and various other sexually liberal organizations. Thus, H. Wayne Gourley (1967, 1: 36) reports,

The Amity Community, which existed from 1959 to 1963, practiced it with impressive results. Little experimentation has been done to determine how much group marriage is optimal. The widest example of group marriage practiced today is found among the mate-swappers. Of course, this is a partial group marriage, but is quite successful.

From all these reports, it can be seen that group marriage unquestionably exists today in the United States and in other parts of the world. But it leads a somewhat checkered career, never seems to become exceptionally well established, and is largely practiced by unstable groups which have a hard time getting started and an even more difficult time remaining in existence. Is, then, group marriage a possible alternative for the conventional kind of monogamous—or rather, monogynous—marital relationship that now normally exists in Western civilization? Not in the strict sense of the term (if "alternative" is taken to mean a choice between two things), for it is highly unlikely that group marriage will ever fully replace monogamic mating or even that the majority of Westerners will voluntarily choose it instead of our present marital system.

This is not to say that monogamy does not have its distinct disadvantages, for, of course, it does. It leads to monotony, to restrictiveness, to possessiveness, to sexual starvation for many unmarried individuals, to the demise of romantic love, and to many other evils (Ellis 1962, 1965). Consequently, it has always tended to be seriously modified by virtually all peoples who have legally adopted it. Thus in present-day America, we ostensibly marry only one member of the other sex and stay married to him or her for the remainder of our lives. Actually, however, we have very frequent resort to divorce, adultery, premarital permissiveness, prostitution, promiscuous petting outside of marriage, and various other forms of nonmonogamous sex relations. So our "monogamy" is honored more often in theory than in practice.

Group marriage, on the other hand, at least when it is practiced by a relatively small number of people, also involves many serious difficulties and disadvantages and is therefore not likely to become exceptionally popular. Among its distinct shortcomings are these:

1. It is quite difficult to find a group of four or more adults of both sexes who can truly live harmoniously with each other. The usual utopian-minded adult who seeks out such group marriages today is very frequently a highly peculiar, often emotionally disturbed, and exceptionally freedom-loving individual. And group marriage, in many ways, is not suited to this type of person, because it involves restrictions, restraints, and the kind of self-discipline that he has great trouble in achieving.

2. Even perfectly well-adjusted individuals in our society seem to have difficulty living together successfully in the same household with several other people. Co-operative living of this sort usually involves the scheduling of shopping, cleaning, eating, television-view-

ing, music-listening, and many other activities at certain times and places which are not going to be particularly convenient to some members of the community-living group. It is often hard enough for two people who love each other to stay together for long periods of time under the same roof, since they are different persons and have all kinds of different domestic and other tastes and interests; consequently, many otherwise fairly good monogamic marriages founder. When from four to fifteen people, with even more widely varying preferences and goals, try to live together continually, many toes are bound to get trod upon and the fur is often likely to fly.

3. Selecting a suitable group of several other individuals with whom one would like to have a group marriage often proves to be well-nigh impossible. It should be remembered, in this connection, that many bright and charming people find it most troublesome to find even a single member of the other sex whom they can fully trust and with whom they would like to settle down to domestic bliss. When these same people go out to search for several others to "marry" simultaneously, and when the others must also be compatible, it can readily be seen that an enormous selectivity problem arises. Even a highly efficient computer which is fed suitable data on tens of thousands of individuals, and thereby is able to "know" their characteristics and their likes and dislikes regarding others, will be hard put to select marital groups of, say, four males and four females who can beautifully tolerate—not to mention love!—each other for a considerable period of time. Simple wife-swapping, as it is sometimes carried on today, where a heterosexual couple try to find another heterosexual couple with whom to swap mates, largely for sexual purposes, tends to run into selection troubles, simply because if John and Jane find Hal and Helen, who are both sexually attractive to them, they then have to find that Hal and Helen also find *them* attractive and are willing to swap mates. Because of this selectivity problem, many couples who are quite eager to engage in mate-swapping actually rarely get around to doing so. Imagine, then, how hard it would be for John and Jane, if they wanted to join a group marriage household, to find a suitable Hal and Helen, Matthew and Mary, Bob and Betty—all of whom would also have to be "sent" by each other!

4. If three or four couples do manage to set up a group marriage arrangement, sex and love problems are almost certain to arise among them. Thus, Jane may get so devoted to Harold that she wants to be alone with him or to have sex with him only. Or Bob may be perfectly potent with Helen and Mary but not with Jane and Betty. Or

Helen may be highly attractive to all the males, while the rest of the girls are not. Or Betty may be the least attractive of the females and may want to have sex relations with the males more than all the other girls do. Or Matthew, who may be the sexiest one of all the males and the one whose presence really induced most of the females to join the group, may get disenchanted with most of the females and may engage in adulterous affairs outside the group. Or Jane may become so jealous of the other girls, because she thinks they are prettier or more competent than she is, that she may play nasty tricks on them and disrupt the household. All kinds of sex, love, and jealousy problems such as these may easily arise in any sex commune.

5. In our own society, there appear to be fewer females than males at the present time who are interested in group marriage. In Kerista and in hippie groups this phenomenon has often been discovered and has led to the disruption of the groups. Kathleen Griebe (1967) reports that, in the utopian community that was established at Walden House a few years ago, difficulty arose over the subject of group marriage, which was favored by the founder of the community, H. Wayne Gourley, and consequently, Mr. Gourley had to resign from the organization and sell the house to the remaining members. Miss Griebe (1967, p. 2) notes that

group marriage was not defeated at Walden House by a "vote." The simple fact is that there has never been a female at Walden House who had any interest in group marriage. . . . The day when a group of members within Walden House finds itself personally inclined to experiment with group marriage, they will simply do so, without anybody's permission or vote or consensus. Everybody here minds his own business strictly in these matters. In the meantime the idea suffers, as I said, from the lack of a single female interested in making the experiment.

Along with these disadvantages of group marriage, there are, of course, various advantages, including the following:

1. It affords a considerable degree of sexual varietism. If four or more adults get together on a group-marriage basis, they all have sexual access to each other; if enough males and females are members of the marital group, two individuals may have intercourse with each other relatively infrequently, even though each of them is having frequent sex relations on the whole. This kind of varietism may well serve to keep the participants more sexually alive than they otherwise would be and to make steady marital relations unusually tolerable.

2. Group marriage widens and enhances love relationships for many individuals. Such people do not want to limit themselves to loving one member of the other sex at a given time but feel that they can intensely love at least several other people. In group marriage, they have the opportunity to relate to, and live with, two or more members of the other sex. If they can find suitable partners, they feel much more fulfilled than they otherwise would.

3. Family life can be increased and intensified by group marriage. Instead of having merely one wife and a few children, all of whom may have rather different interests than his own, a man may have several wives and a good many children, some of whom are more likely to share his own vital absorptions. He may also find it more gratifying, for a number of reasons, to share family life with a relatively large, rather than a relatively small, number of people and may discover that his desires for close kinship are only met in this unusual manner.

4. Group marriages almost always constitute themselves as some kind of a co-operative living arrangement; this has economic and social advantages for many individuals. Thus, a ménage consisting of, say, six adults and ten children can economically share expenses in a large house; can nicely collaborate on shopping, cooking, cleaning, baby-sitting, and other household tasks; can easily arrange for social contacts and outlets; can work together on their own estate; can own expensive equipment, such as a truck or tractor, that smaller families might not be able to afford; can maintain a good measure of economic security even if some of the adult members are temporarily out of work; and can have many other benefits that would not be easily available to a single couple and their children.

5. Group marriage tends to add an experiential quality to human existence that is likely to be absent or reduced in monogamic mating. Under monogamy (or for that matter, polygyny) a woman tends to marry at an early age and to have long-term relations with one man and a few children for the rest of her life. Her intense and deep encounters with other human beings, therefore, tend to be quite limited; by the time she dies, it may be questionable whether she has ever truly lived. If this same woman participates for a number of years in a group marriage, it is almost certain that she will have multifaceted sex, love, child-rearing, and other human relations that she would otherwise never have and that she will thereby know herself as a person much better and develop along several fulfilling lines that she easily could have failed to know. And the same thing

is true, though perhaps to a lesser degree, for the average male in our society, who today has only one or two monogymous marital experiences.

6. Those individuals who are primarily interested in gaining a sense of the brotherhood of man and in loving and living co-operatively with a fairly large segment of their surrounding population may partially achieve this goal by participating in a group marriage. In this kind of a situation, they can devote themselves to a larger segment of humanity, in a highly personalized way, than they ordinarily would be able to do, and they may find this quite satisfying.

For reasons such as these, it is likely that some individuals will always favor some kind of group marriage, especially in theory, and that some will even find it good in actuality. There seems to be no reason why such people should not be able to practice what they preach, since there is no evidence that they will thereby interfere with the rights of others who may want to engage in monogamic, polygamic, or various other types of marriage.

It seems very doubtful, however, that a great many people will rush into group marriages in the near future; it seems even more unlikely that this form of mating and family life will replace monogamy or polygamy on a world-wide or even a national scale. Group sexuality—where three or more adults get together in the same room or in different rooms for the purposes of mate-swapping, heterosexual orgies, bisexual orgies, and other forms of plurisexual combinations—has already increased significantly in the United States during the last decade and is likely to increase more, as men and women become liberated from puritanical notions of what sex should be. It is even possible that within the next fifty years or so most Americans will participate, at some time or other, in some kind of simultaneous sex relationships. But it is highly probable that they will do so on an intermittent or temporary basis rather than steadily in the course of group marriage.

Group marriage, then, is a logical alternative to monogamic and other forms of marriage for a select few. In practice, marriage tends to be monogynous (that is, a man and a woman living fairly permanently, though not necessarily forever, only with each other and their own children) all over the world, even when other forms of mating are legally allowed. The chances are that this practice will largely continue but that a sizable minority of individuals will devise interesting variations on this major theme or else live in thoroughly non-monogamic unions, including group marriage.

References

Avebury, Lord. 1912. *The Origin of Civilization and the Primitive Condition of Man*. London: Longmans Green.

Baber, R. E. 1939. *Marriage and the Family*. New York: McGraw-Hill.

Bloch, I. 1908. *The Sexual Life of Our Time*. New York and London: Rebman.

Ellis, A. 1962. *The American Sexual Tragedy*. New York: Lyle Stuart and Grove Press.

———. 1965a. *The Case for Sexual Liberty*. Tucson: Seymour Press.

———. 1965b. *Sex without Guilt*. New York: Lyle Stuart and Grove Press.

———. 1966a. *The Search for Sexual Enjoyment*. New York: Macfadden-Bartell.

———. 1966b. *Sex and the Single Man*. New York: Lyle Stuart and Dell Books.

———. 1966c. *If This Be Sexual Heresy* . . . New York: Lyle Stuart and Tower Publications.

Frazer, J. G. 1910. *Totemism and Exogamy*. London: Macmillan.

Gourley, H. W. 1967. A Utopian Answer: Walden House plus Group Marriage. *Mod. Utopian* 1, no. 1.

Griebe, K. 1967. Walden House Talks Back. *Mod. Utopian* 1, no. 2.

Krassner, P. 1967. Blow-up: Psychedelic Sexualis and the War Game. *Realist* 1, no. 75.

Mitchel, J. 1968. Galahad's Pad. *Avant Garde* 1, no. 1.

Noyes, J. H. 1870. *History of American Socialisms*. Philadelphia: Lippincott.

Presmont, J. 1967. Kerista Tribe. *Mod. Utopian* 1, no. 5.

Shorris, E. 1967. Love Is Dead. *N. Y. Times Mag.* October 29, 1967.

Sumner, W. G. 1927. *Science of Society*. ed. A. G. Keller. New Haven: Yale University Press. 4 vols.

Time Mag. 1967. The Hippies.

Todd, A. J. 1913. *The Primitive Family*. New York: Putnam.

Westermarck, E. 1925. *The History of Human Marriage*. New York: Macmillan.

part two

Preliminary Research:
Findings and Interpretations

Group Sex among the Mid-Americans

Gilbert D. Bartell

Our data were collected from a selected sample of midwestern and southwestern white suburban and exurban couples and single individuals engaged in what they call "swinging."[1] We contacted and interviewed approximately 350 informants during the two years of our research, using data from 280 interviewees who fit into the above category.

These informants defined the term "swinging" as having sexual relations (as a couple) with at least one other individual. Since more than a simple dyadic relationship existed (whether the sexual activity involved took place together or apart), the fact remained that more than two people had to enter into an agreement to have sexual experiences together. We therefore concluded that this must be considered group sex.

We were interested in the growth and development of the broad

Reprinted, by permission of the publisher, from *J. Sex Res.* 6, no. 2. Dr. Bartell was assisted throughout his research by his wife, Ann Bartell.

[1] In some academic circles sex research is not considered pertinent. I therefore would very much like to thank the President of Northern Illinois University, Rhoten Smith, my anthropological colleagues, Drs. Pierre Gravel and James Gunnerson, and colleagues from other departments including sociology for their cooperation, assistance, and particularly their genuine moral support. I wish, furthermore, to acknowledge the help and assistance of Carole Dick and Nancy Frank in the preparation of this article and thank them for their efforts.

spectrum of activities associated with organized swinging, but we wished to concentrate specifically upon those individuals belonging to some form of sodality or swinging organization. We attempted to ascertain to what extent American cultural patterns would be transferred to this relatively new phenomenon. Since white middle class, non-inner-city people constitute the majority in the United States and we assume they are the major actors within the cultural system, our sample was restricted to these informants.

Interviews lasted anywhere from two to eight hours. We eliminated individuals from the inner city, Blacks, and Latin couples to keep our sample restricted. We did not misrepresent ourselves but told our informants that we were anthropologists interested in knowing more about swinging. We did not use a tape recorder or questionnaires, as these people were frequently too frightened to even give their right names, let alone fill out questionnaires or have their conversations taped. We were also able to attend a large number of parties and large-scale group sexual activities.

Our basic method of interviewing was the anthropological one of participant observer. As a result of the etiquette and social mores of swinging (as we shall detail below), we were able to observe and only act as though we were willing to participate.

Evidently, the interest in swinging or wife swapping, mate swapping, or group sex came about as the result of an article in *Mr. Magazine* in 1956. Since then, it has received a great deal of attention from the semipornographic press. However, it has received practically no attention from the scientific community, although there are an estimated one to ten million people involved in mate exchange. We do not have any statistically reliable figures on how many people are involved in swinging, but a club in a midwestern city published a list with names and addresses of 3,500 couples in the metropolitan area and its suburbs who are actively engaged in mate exchange.

The impetus toward swinging usually comes from the male, but it is the contention of a number of sophisticated swingers that it is often promoted by the female, who lets the male take the aggressive role in suggesting that they become involved in swapping. Although we also have gathered a great deal of background material on the initial introduction of the partners to group sex activity, which includes the acquiring of magazines, self-photography, discussion, and extramarital activity, this aspect of the subject is beyond the scope of this paper.

Within the area of investigation, we found that primarily four methods were used in acquiring similarly minded partners for sexual exchange: most prevalent, an advertisement in one or more of the various magazine/tabloids catering to these specialized interests; second, an introduction to another couple at a bar, set up exclusively for this purpose or through one of the swingers' sodalities; third, personal reference from one couple to another; and fourth, personal recruitment, seduction, or proselytizing.

In the first method, an advertisement was placed in one of the sensational tabloids, such as the *National Informer*. This might have read, for example:

Athens, Georgia marrieds. Attractive, college, married, white, want to hear from other marrieds. She, 36, 5'7", 35-22-36, 135. He, 40, 6'2", 190. Photo and phone a must. Discretion. Box #.

or

Florida Marrieds. Attractive, refined, professional marrieds would like to hear from similar liberal minded marrieds. Complete discretion required, and assured. Can travel Southern states. Photo and phone please. Box #.

Alternatively, the couple may have responded to such an ad. This method was the least expensive and time consuming as the *National Informer* sold for twenty-five cents and was printed and distributed weekly. The couple had to pay for an ad or a fee plus postage for their letter to be forwarded to an advertiser. Exactly the same method was used if the couple selected one of the large slick magazines, such as *Swinger's Life* or *Kindred Spirits*. The major difference between tabloids and slick magazines was that the magazines offer membership in a sodality and cater exclusively to swingers. Examples of such ads would be:

Baltimore, D.C., 60 mile radius, luscious, upper thirties, attractives, seeking couples, females to 40 for exotic French Culture etc. She, 35-27-35, 5'6". He, husky, muscular, but gentle. Let's trade pictures and telephone and addresses.

or

New Orleans, young couple, 28 and 32. She, a luscious red head, 5'7", 36-26-38. He, 5'9", 175, well built. Enjoy all cultures. Attractive couples main interest, but will consider extremely attractive single girls and men. Photo required for reply.

Please note the difference in the tenor and construction of the magazine and tabloid advertisements, remembering that the magazine sold for three dollars per copy. Additionally, these magazines offered instruction on what kinds of letters to write to attract the greatest results. Initial contacts were made through letters with descriptions formulated in such a way as to stimulate interest in making a personal contact with the other couple. These almost universally included a nude or seminude photograph of the female and sometimes, but much less frequently, a photograph of the male. These photographs were considered very important. Physical dimensions, particularly of the female, usually somewhat overly abundant in the mammary zone, were frequently included. Ages were given and usually minimized. Third, the written answer usually stated that the couple were fun loving, vivacious, friendly, and extremely talented sexually. This would lead, it was hoped, to a telephone contact with the other couple and from there to a first meeting, which was, by agreement, social in nature, with no obligations to swing on the part of anyone. If successful, this first meeting led to an invitation to swing, either open or closed (see below), or to an invitation to a party. If unsuccessful, it may have led only to a referral to another couple or to some club.

The second method of meeting other couples, an introduction at a bar or sodality, could be the result of a reference from another couple. In a few cases, the club or bar advertised openly in either a swinging magazine or a tabloid. These units or sodalities broke down into three categories. The very common, but least prominent, was the large-scale semiannual party social, advertised in one of the national swingers' magazines. The magazine advertised where the social would be held and the cost for dinner, dance, and drinks. The organizer most commonly was some local couple who had agreed to do the actual work. Usually these meetings, or socials, were held at a motel. The swingers bar was one which was open on certain nights of the week only to couples, and it was known to everyone that all couples present were either active or interested in becoming swingers. The bars were run by either an individual who had an interest in promulgating swinging or an organizer who contracted with the bar owner offering a guarantee for the use of the bar for the particular night involved. Occasionally, some interested couple or couples instituted a club which charged a membership fee and rented a hall or bar one or two nights a month, at which times known swingers congregated. These clubs were frequently chartered, operating as social organizations much like ski clubs. Inducements were offered to the members for recruiting new members. The club might, for example, sponsor "Bring another couple night" and only charge half price for extrance. A number of clubs sought to go beyond the purely sexual by organizing hay rides, beach parties, and picnics. Several attempts have been made within our area to organize a group tour of swingers to the Caribbean and to Las Vegas. These efforts have not been successful. In general, swinging did not take place on the premises of these bars or clubs, but instead, the couples made their alliances or organized private parties and left the bar in groups.

A third method of meeting other compatible swingers was a simple reference from another couple. If a couple had made a few contacts by either one of the two methods mentioned above or sometimes by accident, they could be referred to a number of other couples. A knowledgeable couple who had been swinging for some time would recommend other known swingers to the new couple. This in turn, of course, could lead to other contacts without their ever having to write letters, join a club, or go to a bar.

The fourth method of contacting new swingers appeared with the least degree of frequency in our sample. Many swingers, either as a result of the zeal of the convert or personal stimulus, attemped to seduce (to convert) other couples to what they call the "swinging life." We have reports of this method occasionally occurring in nudist camps or between couples who have known each other on a social basis for some time. In a few cases, couples who had been bridge partners or dance partners had mutually consented to exchange.

The neophytes coming onto the swinging scene, as it is referred to, were faced with a number of dilemmas. They had to find out, with a certain degree of care, exactly what actions were appropriate to allow them to participate in this venture, which was somewhat surrounded by mystery. The various books and magazines purporting to open the door and guide the novice through the intricacies of swinging universally exaggerated its ecstasies. In fact, what swingers did was relatively prosaic. For example, they might respond to an ad with a letter. This letter would state their interests and include a picture. The purpose of the letter was to present themselves in such a manner as to elicit further response in the form of a telephone call. Then, usually using only first names, such as Joe and Ruth, they would arrange a meeting.

This first meeting we call the "mating dance" (taken directly from ethologists). The couples went through a patterned ritual behavior. In effect, what they were doing was testing each other. If one couple were "baby swingers" (a baby swinger being one who had never been involved in a swinging situation before), of necessity they had to permit themselves to be seduced. This role also allowed them to ask questions which the experienced couple were more than pleased to answer. In most cases, this was the role we took. It was also advantageous in that you had to learn the secret vocabulary of swinging to interview effectively. These people had a definite secret language, or at least they thought it was secret. Terms most often used were: "TV" (transvestite), "S & M" (sadomasochist), "A-C D-C" (homosexual and heterosexual), "bisexual" (enjoying both males and females and usually applied to women only), "ambisexual" (the correct term, and yet less frequently used for the preceding two terms), "gay" (homosexual or lesbian), "B & D" (bondage and discipline), "French culture" (cunnilingus and fellatio), "Roman culture" (orgies), "Greek culture" (anal intercourse).

This first meeting was the equivalent of the dating coffee date or coke date. General etiquette dictated that this first contact be without sexual involvement. If it was decided that the foursome wanted to get together, they would meet later at a motel or at the house of one of the couples.

Once the decision to swing has been made we arrive at a three-part typology of swinging behavior: one, open and closed swinging; two, open and closed large-scale parties; and three, three-way parties. As defined locally, "closed swinging" means that the two couples exchange partners and then go off separately to a private area to engage in what amounts to straight, uncomplicated sexual intercourse. Then, after an agreed upon time, all four return to the central meeting place. Sexual behavior under these circumstances is relatively ritualized. It almost always includes fellatio, cunnilingus, and coitus, with the male either dorsal or ventral. In the vast majority of cases, fellatio does not lead to orgasm. Every attempt is made by the male to bring the female to climax by cunnilingus. Climax by the male after prolonged delay occurs most frequently during coitus with the female supine.

In contrast, "open swinging" in a foursome means that the couples at some time during the evening, engage in sexual activity together, either in the same room, on the same bed, or as a four-way participatory activity. In 75% of our cases, this generally included the two females engaging in some form of cunnilingal activity, although in approximately 15% of the cases one of the female partners was passive. Less than 1% of the cases reported that any male homosexual activity took place. We have only two or three reports of males performing fellatio, and in six or seven cases, the male informant was passive, permitting another male to fellate him. We have no reports of anal intercourse taking place in a swinging scene. Sometimes references were made to this type of intercourse, but we have no verification.

Occasionally, a foursome of the open variety may result in everyone devoting their attention to one person, three-on-one in effect, and again most frequently, two males and one female devoting their attention to the female. The only other variety was the so-called daisy chain, which is alternately fellatio and then cunnilingus in a circle.

The second type of swinging was the party, which could be organized in several different ways and run as an open or closed party. Certain individuals were known in this area as organizers. These individuals devoted a great deal of their time to the organization and promulgation of swinging activities. They might organize nothing more than social events in which people met to make future contacts or they might organize a party at which sexual activity was to take place. These parties were frequently held in private homes. Couples were invited by the organizer, who might or might not be the owner of the home. Frequently, each couple invited were asked to bring another couple who were known to be swingers. Although not always true, there was an implication that no one was required to swing. At other parties, no swinging activity took place until after a certain time, such as 10:30. Any couple still there past 10:30 were expected to participate. In contrast to the swingers' self image, they were not nudists and they were still relatively inhibited, hesitating to initiate any positive action. Therefore, the organizer or the host or some less patient swingers might initiate a game, the object of which, obviously, was the removal of everyone's clothing.

Parties in suburbia are restricted or limited to couples only. In the area of our research, singles—male or female—were discriminated against. Blacks were universally excluded. If the party was closed, there were rules, very definitely established and generally reinforced by the organizer and other swingers. These rules might even include clothing restrictions, "baby dolls" for the women and swinger's shorts (abbreviated boxer type) for the men. Or there might be a regulation that only one couple occupy a bedroom at a time or that they stay only so long or that no one appear nude in the central gathering area. Most parties were "bring-your-own bottle" parties, although in a few cases the host supplied the liquor. Food was often prepared by the hostess but seldom consumed. Stag films were generally not shown. Music was low-key fox trot, not infrequently Glenn Miller, and lighting was definitely not psychedelic, (usually nothing more than a few red or blue light bulbs). Marijuana and speed were not permitted.

The same generalized format was true for the open party, but the difference was that the party was less structured. Nudity was permitted in any part of the house and couples were free to form large groups of up to ten or twelve people in large sexually participating masses. Voyeurism was open and not objected to by the majority of the participants. Parties generally began around 9:00 in the evening and frequently continued until 9:00 the following morning in contrast to closed parties, which generally terminated around 1 A.M. It was not infrequent that, as the party proceeded and the males become progressively more exhausted, the females continued to party without males. Open parties in suburban groups appeared infrequent and when they did appear, they were held by the younger swingers between the ages of twenty and thirty-five who had begun swinging in the last year and a half. Culturally, this younger group resembled the older closed group, except that they had never been under the influence of the organizers. They had no ideas what was considered appropriate party behavior, as did the older group. This younger group apparently either was more innovative or was learning from the now-frequent popular writings on swinging. Some of the older swingers who were then participating in open parties stated that when they began swinging they "didn't know there was any other way to do it." Although most couples stated an interest in the taking of Polaroid pictures during sexual exchanges, in practice this was very infrequent. Among other attitudes, this pointed up the extreme caution and fear with which the majority of our informants reacted to the possibility of their identities being revealed.

The third type of swinging was in a threesome, which can hardly be called a ménage à trois, which implies a prolonged triadic relationship. Analysis of advertisements in swingers' magazines indicated that the vast majority of swingers, whether potential or experienced, advertised for either a couple or a female. Although the majority of threesomes constituted a couple and an alternate single female, 30% of our informants indicated that they had participated as a threesome with an alternate single male. (Cross-checking of informants caused our own figures to be revised upward as high as 60%.) The males reported that they enjoyed the voyeur qualities of watching their partner engaging in sexual activity with another male. Most commonly, threesomes with two females included ambisexual behavior of mutual cunnilingus between the females. Although in the majority of our cases, the triad was of relatively short duration, twelve couples report triadic relationships of longer duration, ranging from a low of two or three weeks to a high of as long as ten years. In three of the cases, the second woman lived in the household on a more or less permanent basis. In two cases, the male was a boarder, and in one case, the male lived in the household for ten years, during seven of which he had been involved in a ménage à trois.

Few other variations of sexual activity were reported. We have, in our entire sample, only two reports of bondage and/or discipline. Transvestism has never been reported. We have observed one case of bestiality. Obviously, from the preceding, homosexual males were not welcome. In a few cases, three to be exact, we have reports of a lesbian participating at a large party. Although she was not discriminated against, it should be noted that to accuse a woman of being "straight-gay" was considered pejorative. Clothes fetishists were uncommon. Bizarre costume was not considered proper, and clothing was decidedly not "mod" but very middle class.

The Informants

Ninety-five percent were white. We included Latin Americans in this category. Of our Latin Americans, ten individuals in all, each swung with a white partner. The predominant ethnic division was German. In fact, of all foreign-born informants, Germans constituted the single largest group, comprising twelve couples in our sample. We had only five black couples, none of whom lived in the suburbs. The ages of our informants ranged from eighteen to the midforties for the women, and from twenty-one to seventy for the males. The median age for women was twenty-eight to thirty-one. For males, it was twenty-nine to thirty-four. All couples, based on our knowledge of certain societal factors, tended to minimize their ages, except for the very young, twenty-one to thirty. In general, we believe the men gave younger ages when they were married to younger women. Age played an extremely important role in acceptance or rejection for swinging. Although informants almost universally verbalized that age was unimportant, in reality they tended to reject couples who were more than ten years older than themselves. Invitations to parties were generally along age lines also. With the emphasis on youth in our culture today, it was important to appear young, and our interviewees were reluctant to give exact ages.

Ninety percent of the women in our sample remained in the home as housewives. We have no exact figures as to how many worked previous to marriage. Of those who had been married only once, most had married between the ages of seventeen and twenty-one. Several were married as young as fifteen or seventeen. There were seventeen female teachers in our sample. Those who had advanced schooling, both males and females, had attended small colleges and junior colleges. About 25% of our males had some college. Forty percent to 50% of the men could be classified as salesmen of one sort or another. Our interviewees also included one doctor, one dentist, three university professors, three high-school teachers, and several owners of small service-oriented businesses. A number of swingers in this group were truck drivers, and some were employed in factory work. The largest professional group was lawyers. Earnings were extremely difficult to ascertain. We based our estimate on life-style, houses, and occupations. The range of annual income extended from six thousand dollars to a probable high of seventy-five thousand dollars.

Religion was seldom discussed. These people would not admit to atheism or agnosticism. They would say that they were Protestant, Catholic, or Jewish. The majority were Protestant, and the proportion of Jews was the same as in the general population. The proportion of Catholics was a little higher. The majority did not attend church regularly.

Universally, they were extremely cautious with regard to their children about phone calls and about visits from other swinging couples. The majority of couples would not swing if their children were in the house, and some made elaborate arrangements to have children visit friends or relatives on the nights when they were entertaining. All couples took precautions that their children did not find letters from other swinging couples, pictures, or swinging magazines. We found few instances when couples merely socialized, and brought their children together, although the children might be the same age and have the same interests. Only a few in our sample said that they would raise their children with the same degree of sexual libertarianism they themselves espoused or that they would give the girls the pill at a very early age.

In interviewing these respondents, we found that they had no outside activities or interests or hobbies. In contrast, the suburbanite is usually involved in community affairs, numerous sports, and fam- ily-centered activities. These people did nothing other than swing and watch television. About 10% were regular nudists and attended some nudist camps in the area during the summer. Their reading was restricted to newspapers, *occasional* news magazines and women's magazines, with the outstanding exception that 99% of the males read *Playboy*. Occasionally, a couple owned a power boat and spent a few week ends in the summertime boating. Yet, a striking con- tradiction is that fact that in their letters, they had listed their interests as travel, sports, movies, dancing, going out to dinner, theater, etc. In reality, they did none of these things. Therefore, all conversational topics were related to swinging, swingers, and television programs. Their backgrounds were usually rural or fringe area, not inner city.

As a result of the exclusion in the midwest of singles from the swinging scene, we found that approximately one-third of the swinging couples interviewed said they were married although they were not. To be included in parties and to avoid pressures and criticism from married couples, they introduced themselves as husband and wife. We were unable to compile exact statistics on the frequency or cause of divorce in the swinging scene. At least one partner and sometimes both had been married before. Frequently, they had children from a previous marriage. We have only hearsay evidence that couples have broken up because of swinging. However, we feel in general that the divorce rate was about that of any comparable group of people in the country. As we have not followed up any couples who have dropped out of swinging, these findings are susceptible to change.

Since much of the interviewing took place during the 1968 national presidential campaign, we had occasion to hear political views. Normally, politics was never discussed. There were many Republicans, and better than 60% of the respondents were Wallaceites (partially because of having changed from blue-collar to white-collar jobs). These people were anti-Negro. They were less antagonistic to Puerto Ricans and Mexicans. They were strongly antihippie, against the use of any and all drugs, and would not allow marijuana in their homes or people who used it if they had knowledge of it.

Because of overt statements in letters and advertisements, such as "whites only," and because blacks were seldom, if ever, invited to parties, it is safe to say that a strong anti-black prejudice existed. In conversation, antagonism, although veiled, was often expressed.

Informants reflected generalized white suburban attitudes, as outlined in almost any beginning sociology text. Their deviation existed mainly or primarily in the area of sex. And even this deviation had imposed upon it middle-class mores and attitudes. For example, some men had been paying prostitutes to pose as their swinging partners. In the few cases in which this occurred and became general knowledge, a large outcry from both males and females was heard. The same attitudes prevailed toward couples who were not married as toward singles, male or female. The reason was not so much the sanctity of marriage as the idea that the single individual or the prostitute had nothing to lose. They were absolutely terrified of involvement even though they thought of themselves as liberated sexually. If you swung with a couple only one time, you were obviously not very involved. It was taboo to call another man's wife or girlfriend afterward or to make dates on the side.

The consumption of alcohol, sometimes in large quantities, was perfectly permissible. Current fashions, such as miniskirts for women and bell-bottom trousers and beards for men, were seldom seen except among the youngest of the swingers.

Analysis

Obviously, because of the nature of a short article, we have been forced to be overly restrictive in a descriptive sense. We have only touched on the highlights and those points that would be considered pertinent to the vast majority of readers of this volume. With all due respect to our readers, we should like to give a brief sociopsychological analysis of our research.

As stated originally, we were particularly interested in swinging as a cultural phenomenon. We feel convinced that it reflects very much the culture of the individuals interviewed and observed. They represent white middle-class suburbia. They do not exhibit a high order of deviance. In fact, this is the single area of deviation from the norms of contemporary society, and there may be some question whether they really represent the acting out of an ideal image in our society rather than an attempt to be innovative. They represent an attempt to act out the cult of youth, the "in scene." They are, in their own minds, the avant garde, the leaders in a new sexual revolution. They see swinging as a "way of life." They refer, like the hippie, like the ghettoite, to the nonswinger as "straight." In contrast to their own conceptualization of themselves, the majority of swingers are very "straight" indeed. The mores, the fears, that plague our generation are evidenced as strongly in swingers as in any other sampling from suburbia. It has been said that our data reflect a mid-American bias; however, Nena and George O'Neill and Jay and Lynn Smith (personal communications) have indicated that the same phenomena can be found in suburbs of both the east and west coasts. What we find in these couples consistently is a boredom with marriage. Much of this problem stems from diffuse role expectations in the society. Americans have imposed upon themselves a number of possible roles, both ideal and real, which one may assume. We believe the action of the media to be crucial in the self-perception of ideological roles. Most of the male swingers want to see themselves as—and many groups actually call themselves—international "Jet Setters," the "Cosmopolitans," the "Travellers," the "Beautiful People"; instead, they have become a consequence of suburban life. They sit in silence and look at television. The woman who feels restricted to the household environment believes she should be out doing things, be a career woman, but she has her obligations. The man wants to be a swinger and to be in on the "scene" and know "where it's really at."

Within the psycho-socio-sexual context of contemporary American culture, we would like to present the positive and negative effects of swinging for the individuals involved. Please note that we have been unable to interview more than a few dropouts from swinging. Therefore, our information is based solely on those who are participants. Our interviews with people who have discontinued swinging, about six or seven couples, reflect what we shall call the negative aspects of swinging. But first, we should like to summarize what we believe to be the positive aspects of swinging. Among these, there is an increased sexual interest in the mate or partner. All of our respondents report that because of swinging they now have a better relationship, both socially and sexually. These people are replaying a mating game. They can relive their youth, and for many it is advantageous. They can get dressed up, go out together, and attempt a seduction. It is a form of togetherness that they never had before. There is the desire of each partner to reinforce in the other the idea that they are better sexually than any swinger they have encountered. There is a general increase in sexual excitation for both partners because of the anticipation of new types of sexual experiences and an increase in thought and discussion of actual sexual experiences. The woman receives a great deal of positive reinforcement if she is seen as the least bit desirable. She is actively committing men to her. A fifty-year-old man can "make it" with a twenty-two-year-old girl without any legal repercussions, and his wife will be equally "guilty." It must be a tremendous satisfaction. Women uniformly report that they have been able to shed sexual inhibitions. And our society certainly has an overabundance of sexual inhibitions, mainly because we impose different standards on different members of the society; the "Raquel Welches" of our world can perform in one fashion, but the good little housewife must perform in another. How does one adjust to this conflict between one's model and one's own activities? The female respondents state that one way to resolve this conflict is to swing.

The partners share an interest which can be explored, observed, and discussed between themselves and among their new "friends." Both partners can indulge in voyeurism at parties and thereby utilize the learning experience in their own relationship. Because most of these people have had few, if any, opportunities throughout their lives for actually observing or learning by observation how to act and respond to sexual stimuli, the swinging scene may be an experience which cannot be provided in any other way.

Swinging may be extremely exciting inasmuch as it carries certain elements of danger. Swingers may feel very avant garde in the breaking of cultural taboos or of legal codes. There is also a certain implied danger of the possibility of losing the love of one's partner; however, this is usually offset by the mutual reinforcement mentioned previously. There can be a great deal of sexual excitement provided by the stimulus of profane versus sacred love. Both partners can become conspirators in writing and hiding advertisements and letters and evidence of their new interest from children, relatives, "straight friends," and business colleagues. We feel that one of the greatest advantages in the relationship comes from the fact that the couple may spend more time together searching for new contacts and pursuing leads for parties, bars, and other compatible couples. They may plan weekend trips, vacations, etc. to other parts of the country to meet swingers. They feel that they have broadened their social horizon, and acquired new interests or hobbies as a by-product of their swinging contacts. Swingers seem to derive a great deal of satisfaction from merely meeting and gossiping with other swingers, which also gives them the role of proselytizing. For the first time in many years, because of the restrictions of early marriage, suburban environment, and the social and economic restraints of raising children, they may have the opportunity to dress up, make dinner dates, plan for parties, acquire a full social calendar, and be extremely busy with telephone conversations, letter writing, and picture taking. If they do prove to be a fairly "popular" couple and are in demand, they can feel that they are both beautiful or handsome and desirable. They see themselves and each other in a new light. They may feel that they are doing what the "in" people are doing and living up to their playboy image. Most swingers report unsatisfactory sexual relationships prior to swinging. As a result of the necessity of operating as a pair on the swinging scene, they may find that they actually have an increase in perception, awareness, and appreciation (sexual and otherwise) of each other.

One of the most important negative aspects, as we see it, is the inability to live up to one's own psychosexual myth and self-illusions. This is particularly disadvantageous in the case of the male. They read about sexual behavior in the outer world, and they realize they are not participating in this elaborate sexual life. Since the demise of many houses of prostitution, many early sexual contacts by males have become hit-and-miss propositions. Boys usually begin by masturbating; to masturbate, one must fantasize (Simon and Gagnon 1969). Most males have an elaborate fantasy world in their internalized sexual lives. One of the fantasies is that of having access to a bevy of females. He sees himself capable of satisfying any and all of them. He goes to a party, particularly a party of the younger group, and he has all these naked women running around in front of him. He experiences the anxiety of being incapable of performing up to his own expectations. This very anxiety may defeat him. In American society, the male is expected to be a tremendous performer sexually, and he must live up to his own publicity. This is extraordinarily difficult. He may find that he cannot maintain an erection, that he cannot perform. He finds himself envying younger men who are physically more attractive, and his anxiety and fears increase. For the woman, such self-doubts are less in evidence, although beyond a doubt all females upon initiation to the swinging scene go through a stage of comparison of their own physical appearance and sexual performance with those of the other females. Should the couple be both older and less attractive than the majority of swingers encountered, they may regard the whole swinging scene as a failure and withdraw immediately. For those who remain, other negative aspects include sexual jealousy. The male may find, and this is verbalized, after a number of parties in which his opportunity for satisfaction is limited and he sees the women around him engaging in homosexual activities and continuing to satisfy each other over and over again for the duration of the evening, that the "women have the best time," that the swinging scene is "unfair to men." We found that less than 25% of the men "turn on" regularly at large-scale open parties. In contrast to this, many men report that they "turn on" much more frequently at small-scale parties or in small groups of threesomes. This is the major deterrent to the swinging situation. If one keeps experiencing failure and continuously worries about this failure, one will keep failing. This is a complete feedback situation. In an attempt to "turn themselves on," the males push their women into having ambisexual relations with another girl. Most of them get the idea from either books or pornographic movies. Again, the male experiences disaster. Why? Sixty-five percent of the female respondents admit to enjoying their homosexual relationships with other females and liking them to the point that they would rather "turn on" to the female than to males.

For a couple who are relatively insecure with each other and with themselves, swinging may invoke a great deal of personal jealousy. The man who finds he is occasionally rejected or easily tired physically may resent his wife's responsiveness to other men. She, in turn, may feel that her partner is enjoying other women more or to a different degree than he enjoys her. These personal jealousies frequently erupt under the pressure of alcohol and the ensuing scene evolves into an event which makes all persons present uncomfortable, if not antagonistic, to the couple. This causes them to be excluded from future invitations and to be branded as troublemakers.

Another less common negativism in swinging is the "bad experience." A couple may encounter another couple who have sexual hang-ups, habits, or attitudes that are repulsive or objectionable to the initiating couple. If they encounter two or three consecutive "bad" couples, they may decide that it is not worth taking the risk of such exposure.

Some of our respondents report that, in the past, there have been incidences of venereal disease that were introduced into a swinging group by one couple, and for all concerned, this provoked a great deal of fear and embarrassment because of the necessity of seeking medical aid from sources that would not report them to the health authorities. Fear of disease is always present and discussed frequently.

For many swingers, a constant negative aspect of swinging is the perpetual hazard of discovery. To professional people and to those who work for state or national government or for very conservative business firms, there is a strong possibility of status diminution or loss of occupational position if they are discovered. All respondents consistently insist upon all possible discretion and some go so far as not to give out addresses, correct last names, and places of employment. The majority of swingers keep unlisted telephones. The upwardly mobile feel that their "life would be ruined" if the world knew they were swingers.

Although our findings are inconclusive on this last negative aspect, we feel it is important and may be the primary reason for the dropouts among the more sensitive intellectual group of people who enter swinging. These people seem to feel that swinging in general is much too mechanistic, that there is a loss of identity, absence of commitment, and a total noninvolvement that is the antithesis of sexual pleasure and satisfaction. Some explicitly say that the inconsistencies between the stated objectives and the actual performance are too great to overcome. Although a couple initially may report that they want new friends, interests, and activities in addition to pure sexual contact, in reality this is not so. As proof of this, we offer the fact that most couples will see another couple only once, and even on those occasions when they have relationships with the other couple, their social relationship is minimal even when their sexual relationship is maximal. In much the same light, their self-image of avant-garde/sexual "freedom-ists" suffers when one considers their worries vis-à-vis jealousy.

Since many people have asked us where we think swinging is lead-ing, we should like to make some comments on our personal attitudes toward the future of the swingers. We feel that the individuals in-terviewed in our sample are not really benefiting themselves because the ideals that led them into swinging have not been fully realized. They may very well be acting out and getting positive reinforcement, psychologically and physically, from their activities. However, their human relationships outside of the dyad are not good. Their activities with other couples reflect mechanical interaction rather than an intimacy of relationships. One cannot doubt that this reflects the impersonalization as well as the depersonalization of human relation-ships in our culture. One would suppose that the next generation will carry a duality of purpose rather than a single-minded interest in sexual performance. What we would like to see is a freedom of sexuality, but one more concerned with human relationships than with sexual relationships. We would also like to see human relationships become the primary goal of social interaction.

References

Simon, W., and Gagnon, J. 1969. Psycho-sexual Development. *Trans-action* 6 (March): 9–18.

Co-Marital Sex and the
Sexual Freedom Movement

James R. Smith and Lynn G. Smith

George and Nena O'Neill and Gilbert Bartell have described sub-cultural variations in group sexual activities in the New York City area and the Chicago suburbs, respectively.[1] Each employed a different means of investigative access—the O'Neills using informal channels and Bartell, at least initially, heavily relying on swingers' ads. Each used different criteria of sample selection. A most important distinction is that Bartell chose to study suburbanites, eliminating from their sample urban dwellers whom they found to be substantially different in their group sexual expression. We introduce to you a third variation, but one which bears a substantial similarity to the O'Neills' findings.

Our study was centered in the San Francisco Bay area, although we gained access initially through organized "sexual freedom" groups throughout California and in other areas of the country as well. Along with the more general differences in regional environments, we feel that the means of access and sample selection are important variables in accounting for and understanding the apparent differences in findings. When these variables are taken into account, the differences

Reprinted, by permission of the publisher, from *J. Sex Res.* 6, no. 2; this paper is a preliminary report of a larger study to be published under the title, "Consenting Adults: An Exploratory Study of the Sexual Freedom Movement" (in preparation).

[1] See *Editors' Note*, p. 213, for further comments on these studies.

seem to fall into rather clear subcultural variations evidencing two primary types of motivational patterns. The data we have gathered aid us in describing both types and there is no initial reason to believe the research to date is anything but compatible and, in fact, even mutually reinforcing.

In assessing the presentations, let us suggest two very common but useful analogies, that of the blind persons exploring the elephant and that of the iceberg. They are instructive in that they indicate serious limitations placed on any study designed at this point to analyze attempts to achieve sexual freedom.

A wide range of sociosexual phenomena, from public nudity on stages and in bars to private but accessible sex groups, are entering into that range of vision known as social science. As systematic observation and research pertaining to the sexual freedom movement become feasible, the temptation will be to substitute the fragments for the whole based on a kind of premature gestalt of what is being pieced together at a very slow pace. Our expectation is that we must for some time seek out the differences and dissimilarities before the similarities emerge, since we are focusing on what may be a general phenomenon of deviance which will manifest itself in a variety of styles and patterns of behavior. Our hope is that we may avoid the error which frequently has been made in analyzing other forms of sexual deviance, for example, homosexuality, where the overt behavior is lumped into one simplistic category and the diverse motivations and manifestations are treated as irrelevant variations.

If the initial successes of the sexual freedom movement are any indication and if the subcultures supporting it continue to expand, it is likely that more and more of this deviance will manifest itself in both publicly and scientifically observable ways. At this point we have a small handful of researchers from different disciplines and with different orientations still looking for the relevant questions, reliable generalizations being virtually impossible or at best suggestive.

Our efforts may be classified as an exploratory field study which relied on several information-gathering techniques. We began our study early in 1967 with discussions with leaders and organizers of several sexual freedom groups. These groups were organized for a number of purposes, but they were all flying the banner of sexual freedom and had in common a fundamental ideology. Most of the initial contact was with public or semipublic groups where access was relatively easy. A total of sixteen organized groups are represented in our data. The leaders were generally enthusiastic and cooperative, interested themselves in knowing more about their own membership as well as about other groups. Through contact with these groups and attendance at their social functions we were able to reach others in more private or esoteric settings, and we estimate we were in contact with fifteen to twenty such identifiable cliques.

We attended a wide variety of such parties through 1967 and 1968, in all a total of one hundred to one hundred twenty-five gatherings, sometimes making an appearance at as many as three per evening. In May 1967 we began sending out questionnaires through both the public organizations and the private groups. Approximately 1,700 questionnaires were distributed, with a return of 536, a 32% response rate. Thirty-three of these had to be eliminated because they did not meet the minimal criteria for inclusion in the study, which were (a) membership in a sexual freedom group and/or (b) attendance at a sexually liberal activity or gathering of some kind. In addition, we conducted informal interviews with approximately two hundred participants, usually at the parties, and with the group leaders. We also attended panel discussions, open houses, nude beaches, and other meeting places for persons seeking sexual contacts.

What we found was an emergent subculture complete with jargon, symbols, communication techniques, resources of various kinds, a relatively large population of participants and an even larger pool of recruits and prospective participants, with two distinct and recognizable motivation patterns. We found, in actuality, the "potential fifth deviant subculture" of "collective extramarital sex" which Gagnon and Simon referred to in an article on types of sexual deviance in 1968. This label, however, is inadequate and misleading for the purposes of general analysis, since the term "extramarital" is often inaccurate in this context. The justification for this, among other reasons, is that some respondents would answer no to questions pertaining to extramarital sexual experience but would answer yes to questions pertaining to mate sharing or co-marital relations.

Popularly the term which is fashionable in referring to this behavior is "swinging," but we wish to be equally clear that, though the jargon of swinging is likely to remain in vogue for some time, there are good reasons for avoiding it. It is dreadfully ambiguous, is often pernicious in its appellation, and is resisted as a label by many to whom it is presumed to apply. In all our discussions on the matter we have yet to see two persons agree on what the term "swinging" implies. To use it is roughly comparable to labeling homosexuals as "gay"; it is just as useful as a shorthand slang term and just as misleading as a theoretical one.

Instead we propose the phrase "co-marital sexual relations" to refer to what is at present the focal point of our discussion, noting that it refers only to married couples who are either actually involved together in establishing relationships beyond the marital dyad for sexual purposes or to couples in which there is both knowledge of and consent to such relationships regardless of whether the sexual activity includes both partners or is independent to some degree. This definition does not and is not intended to refer to larger groups of persons, or to unmarried persons, or to single persons. Nor does it refer to couples wherein the sexual activity is deceitful or lacks consent. For a complete and definitive analysis of group sexual activities and more generally of the sexual freedom movement as a whole, all of these variations would need explicit definition, but our main point here is simply to indicate the need for an adequate terminology and classification scheme that does justice to the richness and complexity of the behavior we are studying.

Reference should be made to a distinction between "recreational" and "utopian" motivation syndromes drawn by a young woman researcher at the University of California at Riverside (Symonds 1967). We feel that such a distinction, while useful, should be conceived as a distinction between "isolated" and "integrated" forms of deviance, wherein there is an option to treat co-marital sex and related activities either as a separate activity involving little or no emotional involvement or as a part of a total life style. This distinction has the advantage of being more clearly descriptive, though less colorful, and is potentially scalable as more data become available.

Generally speaking, our data and our observations indicate that this subculture, at least in California, is composed of relatively mobile, educated, affluent, mostly Caucasian, upper–middle class persons trying, sometimes desperately, to be free of taboos and restrictions upon their sexual lives. Because of existing social arrangements, they necessarily become deviant in the process. This places strains on them and sometimes exacts a cost they were not aware they would have to pay, but the ideal, as they see it, while it is surrounded with threats and uncertainties, is worth pursuing.

Three noteworthy questionnaire results were those dealing with education level, socioeconomic status, and religious affiliation. We have reason to believe our findings to be higher than the actual averages, but they do indicate a definite trend. Out of a sample of 503, over 80% of our respondents reported some college training; over 50% are college graduates; and 30% have attended graduate school or have some degree of professional training. Further, 18% of the sample had received higher degrees or certificates. We should also note that 12% of our sample were still students; but although the sexual freedom movement is college-bred, it is certainly not campus-bound, as some have contended.

If we employ the Hollingshead occupational scale, which does not include the students in the sample or the housewives, 72% of the respondents are in professional occupations. Hollingshead's two-factor index of social position indicates that the respondents are predominately middle class and above. Fifty percent of the respondents are in the top two social classes (out of five), and only 2% were in the lowest category. It is clear from this that we are witnessing this deviance primarily among a rather well-informed and socially stable group of persons, at least in the conventional sense of stability.

Religious affiliation was found to be quite low, with 56% of the respondents claiming no religious affiliation and 21% falling outside the conventional Protestant/Catholic/Jewish categories. This means that over three-fourths of our sample were religious deviates in some sense. The respondents, however, were not without religious upbringing, and the open-ended responses occasionally cited religious training as a factor in sexual problems and inhibitions.

With these more general figures as a background we can now turn to some of the directly relevant findings concerning sexual behavior. Ninety-two percent of our sample reported a history of premarital intercourse, a factor which we view as significant to their later sexual development and attempts to achieve sexual freedom. Ninety percent of the respondents who had attended parties had participated in nudity in the presence of others. Such nudity was condoned and expected, sometimes cajoled but never, to our knowledge, coerced. The personal response to group nudity was overwhelmingly favorable, and many persons reported it to be a significant growth experience in which they became aware of their own bodies in a new way.

Our figures on sexual activity at parties include the following. A total of 76% reported that they had witnessed or observed the sexual activities of others present. Sixty-four percent reported engaging in private heterosexual intercourse at parties, while 57% reported engaging in public heterosexual intercourse, and 52% reported engaging in some activity which they perceived as group sex. Roughly 25% reported engaging in either private or public homosexual relations at parties.

Many persons attend initially out of a kind of curiosity mixed with anxiety over what they will encounter and a desire to expand their sexual life. Our discussions with them lead us to believe that many of these initial fears turn out to be unfounded and are the result of ignorance and that those who continue to attend, while they may object to certain aspects of the social environment, are in fact fascinated by what is taking place and usually find groups of rather ordinary persons and not a gathering of freaks. The fact that in our culture the overwhelming part of sexual activity is kept both literally and metaphorically under the covers makes the fears and the fascination hardly surprising.

One interesting result is that for some women there is something of an about-face with regard to sexual values and sexual practices. A woman may initially resist such sexual activity and attend a few parties to satisfy an urge on the part of her husband only to find the effect upon her to be quite positive. Indeed, one of our more far-reaching conclusions is that women are better able to make the necessary adjustments to sexual freedom after the initial phases of involvement than are men, even though it is usually the case that the men instigate the initial involvement.

The issue of jealousy is a significant one in analyzing the impact of co-marital sex upon the depth and stability of the marriage as a whole. It seems that most of these persons feel some degree of jealousy upon entry into and initial involvement with this subculture but that those who maintain their involvement manage to modify and limit their jealousy feelings. It is especially interesting to us to consider *how* they do so.

A learning theory approach appears to be indicated, and stimulus differentiation seems to be an important factor. Though the full argument cannot be presented here, in summary it is this: *consensual* adultery is less likely to evoke a jealousy response to the extent that it differs from, or is perceived to differ from, *conventional* adultery. This is supported, among other factors, by the amount of emphasis which participants place on the differentiating features and by the recurrence of a jealousy response (though in a somewhat modified form) should an episode of conventional adultery occur.

Our readers are no strangers to myths regarding sexual behavior. While our study is only exploratory and certainly limited in its scope and applicability, we believe it provides clues to exploding a few myths, especially those concerning participation in the sexual freedom movement. There are many such myths, some of them propagated by popular press coverage, some of them the result of over-enthusiastic imaginations.

First, there is the myth that attendance at sex parties and related activities guarantees participation. This is simply not the case. Many persons are present on a simple look-and-see basis. Some never return.

In most cases participation is minimal during the initial parties. The women are often reticent, and the men often lack the graces that lead to acceptance and involvement. The assumption that any and everyone present at a sex party is automatically a potential sex partner is unsound and often leads to preemptory rejection on the part of the more experienced females.

The second myth is that participation in sex party activities is a priori evidence of a perverse, neurotic, and/or pathological disposition. We asked questions regarding psychiatric counseling and hospitalization on our questionnaire. The figures on counseling incidence were somewhat high, but the figures on hospitalization were distinctly low and included four of the nine male virgins in our sample. Forty percent of those answering the questionnaire reported at least some psychological or psychiatric counseling. We do not have information regarding the problem or the length, scope, and effect of this counseling, but it is significant that in most cases it occurred prior to any involvement with sex groups. In only one case did a respondent report that he had sought counseling as a result of participation in sexual activities of this sort.

This 40% figure is in and of itself easily misleading. A generally accepted statistic is that about one in four persons are subject to emotional disturbances sufficient to require professional help. Forty percent is of course well above this average. But it is at this point unknown and thus questionable whether the 40% would be higher than the incidence of counseling in an appropriately matched comparison group. A ready comparison which could be made within our sample was that between sex party attenders and nonattenders, and we found no difference on incidence of counseling experience.

Further, for those prophets of doom who claim that sexual permissiveness is the cause of every social ill from the downfall of Rome to the outbreak of World War II, there is the simple figure, which we have no reason to doubt at this point, that 60% of those responding to the questionnaire indicated no history of counseling or therapy whatever. This is certainly no absolute guarantee of mental health, but in the absence of contrary evidence there is no reason to assume that the desire for seemingly radical forms of sexual freedom causes mental illness or that only mentally ill individuals are attracted to these groups. In addition to these findings, we should like to quote—with full approval and a commitment to its relevance to the current topic—from Kinsey's report on the male to the effect that "most of the complications which are observable in sexual histories are the result of society's reactions when it obtains knowledge of an individual's behavior, or the individual's fear of how society would react if he were discovered" (Kinsey 1948, p. 202). This we believe to be as relevant to co-marital sex as to any other form of sexual deviance. Finally, while we cannot enter into the topic here, we might say that our research supports the thesis that the achievement of sexual freedom, when and where it is genuine, even if incomplete, can itself be psychologically beneficial and genuinely therapeutic in many respects.

The third myth we should like to illuminate is that regarding the necessity (and perhaps even the desirability) of sexual monogamy as a component in the viable marriage relationship. The relevant evidence comes from two sources. One has been available for nearly a generation in the form of the Kinsey studies pertaining to adultery, and the other consists of reports from couples who not only acknowledge and tolerate but actually encourage and promote sexual plurality within an otherwise conventional marriage setting. In a word, the myth is that sexual permissiveness and sexual plurality *inevitably* cause marital instability and divorce, a view that is just as misleading as the now antiquated belief that masturbation leads to insanity and debility. Both are cases of self-fulfilling prophesies.

Kinsey (1953) reported that 50% of the married males and 26% of the married females had engaged in adultery by the age of forty. This in and of itself is enough to puncture the myth of monogamy as a necessary component in marriage. Even as an unembodied ideal it has many shortcomings, but as an approximation to actual behavior it is surely misleading. Kinsey also noted that, even where there was knowledge of the extramarital activities, this did not automatically produce a deleterious effect and in some cases the partners had full knowledge and even approved of the behavior.

We have found that there are indeed a large number of couples who not only are capable of tolerating such relationships but actually promote them and make some effort to integrate them into their total social life, though with varying degrees of success. Our expectation is that the modal type of such behavior is neither through ads nor clubs nor sexual freedom organizations. It is quite likely that these are various surface manifestations of a much larger trend (though how large is difficult to say) and that most of the persons engaging in group, co-marital, or orgy behavior do so on a more personal, perhaps almost accidental, basis in the sociological sense. The fact that not all couples are married couples may provide insight into an initial phase of reorientation with regard to the place of sex in marriage as well as the place of marriage in social life. Forty-four percent of our sample were married, 32% were unmarried, and 25% were divorced, widowed, or separated.

Our data challenge a number of other dubious contentions, but we cannot deal with them all. There is one, however, that bears mention at this time, and it is the "key party" myth. Dr. Bartell encountered a high degree of structure and conformity among his sample, but we never came across a sex party structured in any approximation of that fashion. In fact, we were never even able to find an individual who had attended one until we met Dr. Bartell. Evidently they do occur, and we have unsubstantiated reports concerning them, but we suspect that the proliferation of the key-party concept has been supported for the most part as a result of fear and fantasy and that such behavior is manifest primarily in certain styles of restricted sociosexual interaction. Such predetermined structure, even though it has surface characteristics of spontaneity and anonymity, provides women with an excuse not to participate and is an extension of male insecurity in that such structured parties automatically provide the male with a partner, thereby eliminating the necessity of pursuit and the possibility of an eventual rejection. It also eliminates the responsibility for concrete moral decisions by acquiescence to the structured situation, but such acquiescence renders the label "sexual freedom" a possible misnomer.

If study of the sexual freedom movement provides an opportunity to explode such myths, it also makes possible a radical reassessment of the place of human sexuality in a civilized society. It is past time that we view the insistence on monogamous sexuality and the taboos and restrictions on a multiplicity of sexual relationships as requisites for a successful marriage as on a par with beliefs in a flat earth and a geocentric universe. The human species is multisexual and variably promiscuous, if not by "nature" then surely by inclination when the restrictions are removed. The question is then whether those restrictions (in the form of laws, codes, and customs) serve some higher norm which is independently justifiable. If it turns out that marriage and family relations are not only not destroyed but perhaps even improved by eliminating those restrictions, then we will have no justification for maintaining and supporting them in any form, especially when those most affected are asking for assistance in overcoming them and are turning to other sources of support when it is not forthcoming from the presumably qualified professionals.

We are hardly claiming that every person participating in or gravitating toward sexual freedom practices is a picture of sexual health or even that all those persons engaging in co-marital sex are sexually free. Many of them are badly confused; some are neurotic; some are exploiters; some are hypocrites. But without substantial evidence to the contrary, it is difficult for us to accept the various forms of resistance to what consenting adults do in private. Our view is that most of the problems they have in this area are not the consequences of predispositions toward deviance, perversion, or rebellion but rather the results of (1) a very confusing process of sexual socialization and (2) a variety of negative reactions (actual and potential) from their own social environment. The great problem is that the material and educational conditions for genuine sexual freedom, conceived as noncompulsive moral agency, are now at our disposal but that culturally and intellectually we may have never been more confused about how to achieve it.

The scope of sexual freedom cannot justifiably be restricted to a pseudo-enlightened kind of sex play within marriage. If we argue that sexual pleasure is a good, if we say that sexual play and sexual satisfaction are characteristics of the healthy individual and the healthy marriage, then we are going to be hard put to say that, once two (or more) persons have consented to engage in sexual relations, they may not be allowed or even encouraged to do so if they meet the conditions of responsible sexual agency. For consenting adults, at least, the sacred cow of the monogamous sexual relationship, and also the taboos of homosexuality, group sexual practices, nudity, and promiscuity, must be put to pasture. Our research indicates that the taboos have been broken by a significant number of persons and that they are likely to be challenged by an increasing number in the future.

These new practices and the norms which serve to justify them must, we believe, be viewed as historically significant. While there is a shift toward an increasing awareness and acceptance of co-marital sex, and also a number of other sexual deviations, it is not likely that group sex and co-marital sex will become universal. Our guess is that many couples will sample it and reject it and that even under optimal social conditions only some 15 to 25% of married couples would be attracted to it as a part of their marriage, however strange or incompatible such an arrangement may sound to the uninformed.

There was a time, after all, when we did not have trial by jury, due process, religious tolerance, private property, international law, representative government, or monogamy. These are various ways of solving problems of administration and organization in serving human welfare. And they are by no means universal or uniform today. The point is that at some time in human history these were instituted and became, if not standard practices, at least widespread ideals. The next steps in the struggle for human freedom, equality, and dignity may include abolition of the death penalty, a fixed minimum income, and the tolerance of sexual deviance.

There is no reason, therefore, to assume initially that co-marital sex and group sexual activity is a fad or passing fancy or even an act of rebellion or frustration on the part of a neurotic minority. It may well be the sane, considered, and totally healthy response of individuals in a certain sort of society who are able to participate in a certain sort of subculture, deviant only statistically and legally, and who are attempting to expand the range of sexual freedom, increase the depth of their sexual relationships, and pursue greater sexual pleasure and fulfillment. In the absence of clear contrary evidence which pins the causes of misery, unhappiness, mental illness, and social instability on the activity itself rather than on the responses to that activity by a legal system, medical facilities, educational and scientific institutions, and an insecure public, there is little justification for counseling these persons against it, except, that is, as a matter of defense against those institutionalized forces.

If further research produces evidence that an increase in sexual promiscuity and sexual license is symptomatic of the decline and breakdown of the traditional, officially monogamic family unit as the exclusive marital form, we must look for assistance to social policy and social philosophy. Rather than decrying and resisting the changes involved, it is imperative that we look for new ways to cope with them. We must court and experiment with novel types of family structures and family policies with new and hopefully expanded means of sexual fulfillment worthy of rational adult human beings. What we must do is make room in our society for a genuine plurality of social forms. The professionals in medicine, welfare, education, and social science must respond with a sympathetic, informed, or at least genuinely tolerant view in order to cope with this often ignored aspect of the struggle toward personal and social freedom. Our belief is that nothing less will do if we are not to have a literally sick and very confused and fragmented society, current sociopathic judgments notwithstanding, in less than a generation.

If we are not to continue in ignorance to limit and proscribe sexual activity without a sound knowledge of the effects of sexual freedom, we must have more research. We must not squander the opportunity which the existence of this subculture provides for an increased appreciation and understanding of human sexuality.

References

Gagnon, J. H., and Simon, W. 1968. Sexual Deviance in Contemporary America. *Ann. Amer. Acad. Pol. Soc. Sci.* 376: 106–22.

Kinsey, A. C., Pomeroy, W. B., and Martin, G. E. 1948. *Sexual Behavior in the Human Male.* Philadelphia: W. B. Saunders.

———, and Gebhard, P. H. 1953. *Sexual Behavior in the Human Female.* Philadelphia: W. B. Saunders.

Smith, J. R., and Smith, L. G. *Consenting Adults: An Exploratory Study of the Sexual Freedom Movement* (in preparation).

Symonds, C. 1967. Pilot Study of the Peripheral Behavior of Sexual Mate Swappers. Master's thesis, University of California, Riverside.

Editors' Note: We are referring to the Bartell study, "Group Sex among the Mid-Americans" (in this book, pp. 185–201), and to the study by George and Nena O'Neill, "Patterns in Group Sexual Activity" (*J. Sex Res. 6,* no. 2, pp. 101–12). The latter is a report of a study on marriage and sexual behavior centered in the greater New York City region in which "a total of 50 respondents were interviewed of which 38 were single and 12 were married." From a sample "comprised mainly of middle-class business and professional people spanning the occupational range from academia to the entertainment world" that included "beginners," "regulars," "dropouts," and persons claiming protracted involvement up to twenty years, the O'Neills conclude that

. . . some marrieds become involved in this type of activity because they need more sex than their spouse provides. Some, quite happy with their marital partners, nevertheless feel restricted by marital exclusivity and group sex provides a structured context in which to explore extramarital sex. Others, bored and restless with long-term sex with one mate, turn to group sex as a stimulant and sexual turn-on. Some are frankly and desperately trying to patch up a failing marriage. Most must struggle and come to grips with possessiveness and jealousy. Frequently a random exploration into group sex is enough to prove to a couple that what they have with each other is better than they thought. While for others, this activity presents conflict, doubt and, more often for females, a battle with guilt. . . . Our respondents stated that the openness and communication about their group sexual activity extends into other areas of their marriage and frequently forms a bond between them which was previously lacking in their relationship.

Communes, Group Marriage, and the Upper-Middle Class

James W. Ramey

Most current articles and discussions about communes and group marriage begin with the assumption that these phenomena are generally associated with youthful dropouts from society or religious fanatics. There would appear to be, however, a much more significant group, largely made up of upper-middle class, thoughtful, successful, and committed individuals, also involved in or exploring the possibility of setting up communes or group marriages. There are at least three reasons why this group is relatively unknown. First, sensational reporting sells newspapers, and dropouts in colorful clothing and unwashed beards tilling the soil are sensational. Second, most of us would prefer to think of such unusual life-styles as aberrant or deviate practices that would only be associated with inexperienced disaffected youth or religious "kooks." Finally, the people who set up communes or group marriages without dropping out of society take great care to remain unnoticed by their neighbors and associates.

In this report, spanning almost three years of activity among a sample of eighty couples, both husbands and wives were from the two top occupational classifications; that is, they were almost all in academic, professional, or managerial positions, if they were employed at all. These individuals believed that a commune or group marriage

Reprinted, by permission of the publisher, from *J. Marriage Fam.* November 1972.

might provide a framework in which they could do better as a group what they were already doing well as individuals. In order to function optimally within the present social and economic structure, they sought to organize family units on a more complex basis than the nuclear family structure could accommodate.

What is a commune? Structure and modus operandi among communes can differ to such a degree that the following working definition is suggested:

When individuals agree to make life commitments as members of one particular group rather than through many different groups, they *may* constitute a commune. The number of common commitments will vary from commune to commune, the critical number having been reached at the point at which the group sees itself as a commune rather than at some absolute number.

What, then, is a group marriage? The critical factor in group marriage is that each of the three or more participants considers himself to be married to at least two other members of the group. Actually, today we should say "pair-bonded" instead of married since some pair-bonded couples may not be legally married. The Constantines (1971) have coined the term "multilateral marriage" as a substitute for group marriage since, according to them, group marriage has traditionally involved two pairs and thus the term would not accommodate a triad group. I prefer to retain the more familiar term, which I believe is self-explanatory, whereas multilateral marriage is not.

This paper concerns both group marriage and "evolutionary" communes since the eighty couples in the study were curious about both forms. Although only eighteen of these couples had any previous experience with group marriage or communal living, they were all initially attracted to the group by advertisements in *Saturday Review*, *New York Review of Books*, and similar publications inviting couples interested in exploring the pros and cons of various forms of expanded family to meet with the group. The few couples who initiated this activity were open-minded as to the degree of complexity they were willing to consider, ranging from intimate friendship to group marriage, but they were not willing to accept everyone who answered their ads.

They devised a questionnaire as a preliminary screening device, and a request for a short essay indicating why the respondents wanted to join the group. The avowed purpose of this screening was to eliminate swingers and others whose interest was considered "not serious." Upon review of the questionnaire and essay, couples deemed tentatively acceptable were interviewed by telephone, and a decision was made either to suggest that they forget about this group or to invite them to an orientation session. In our three-year follow-up study,[1] we hope to interview the fifty-five couples who were not invited to join the group in addition to the eighty couples who "passed" to see if we can find any real differences between the "accepted" and "rejected."

We have reported elsewhere (Ramey 1972) the logarithmic increase in the degree of complexity in relationships as one moves from monogamous dyadic marriage through open marriage, intimate friendship, and communal living to group marriage. It should be recognized that the degree of intensity also increases as one moves up this scale in the complexity of marriage alternatives. "Intensity" might be called one of the primary characteristics of the subjects of this report. In addition to ability to deal with more complex relationships, there must be willingness to take on such a task.

In dyadic marriage the commitment is to the individual. Kanter (1968) calls this "cathectic commitment." I would call it "willingness to accept unlimited liability for." A commune is held together by a different kind of commitment, a group commitment rather than commitment to an individual. A group marriage combines these two types of commitment. In Kanter's terms, this would be the addition of cognitive and evaluative commitment to cathectic commitment.

The subjects of this study saw these differences in concrete terms. They were aware that dyadic marriage has become institutionalized in our society and internalized by each of us as we have grown up in such a way that the decisions facing a newly married couple are relatively minor ones (how many children?) within a well-defined formal structure. No such formal structure exists for intimate friendship, communes, or group marriage, however. The participants must evolve their own structure.

This group, then, expended considerable energies on working through cognitive commitment (was the group making sufficient progress to justify continuing to invest energy that could be directed elsewhere?) and evaluative commitment (were the perceived goals and aims of the group worthy of continued support?). These two types of commitment have long since been institutionalized for dyadic marriage.

It was not necessarily the intent of these eighty couples to form

---

[1] Throughout Dr. Ramey's research, he was assisted by his wife and colleague, Betty Ramey.—Eds.

communes or group marriages, although several did result from their activities. They seemed more intent on "hashing out" the actual ground rules and decision structure required for setting up alternatives to marriage at varying levels of complexity. Some couples were content to stop at the level of developing intimate friendships. Others were willing to take the additional step of adding propinquity to this relationship and forming some kind of commune, and a few found other couples with whom they were willing to take the final step of cathectic commitment, i.e., actually establishing multiple pair-bonds. Many couples found that they were either uncomfortable with the level of complexity required or "were still looking for the right people" with whom to become involved in some type of relationship more complex than dyadic marriage.

This paper indicates the kind of people involved in this activity, explicates the concerns that led them to become involved, and reports the kinds of problems they discussed and the various activities in which they engaged as a part of the exploration process. Several communes and group marriages have emerged from this group thus far, and it is expected that there will be others. This paper is based on the initial questionnaires, anecdotal information, correspondence files, and observation of group activities.

A few portions of the demographic data will be presented in comparative fashion, contrasting the eighteen couples who have actually lived or are living in communes or group marriages with the sixty-two couples who have expressed active interest in doing so, although it should be understood that the samples are so small that the numbers have no statistical significance. For the sake of brevity, the eighteen experienced couples will be called "doers" and the sixty-two inexperienced couples will be called "talkers."

Only six couples in the total sample live outside a major metropolitan area. The New York City, Boston, and Philadelphia metropolitan areas together account for 63% of the talkers and 79% of the doers. The age range in the two groups is indicated in table 1.

Most of these couples have at least one child, and the age ranges of the children in the two groups are comparable. Over two-thirds of each group have at least one child, and 50% have at least two, with comparable figures for three, four, and five, and insignificantly small numbers above five.

Standard Census Bureau occupational classification categories were collapsed together to arrive at the distribution shown in table 2. The national percentage distribution is included for comparison. An addi-

Table 1—Age of participants

| | Talkers | | Doers | |
Age Range	Male	Female	Male	Female
Youngest	21	21	24	23
First quartile	28	26	29	26
Median	33	28.5	33.5	28
Third quartile	42	38	38	37.5
Oldest	56	55	52	47
Mean	35.2	30.7	34.7	29.8
Standard deviation	8.66	6.48	3.89	3.87

Table 2—Percentages of occupational classifications of participants

| | Males | | | Females | | |
Classification	United States	Talkers	Doers	United States	Talkers	Doers
Professional, scientific, and kindred workers	11.9%	72.4%	81.3%	13.0%	44.1%	61.1%
Managers, officials, proprietors, etc.	13.2	19.0	18.7	4.4	6.8	22.2
Clerical, sales, and kindred workers	13.0	1.7	—	38.7	6.8	—
Craftsmen, foremen, and skilled workers	19.0	1.7	—	1.1	—	—
Operatives, service personnel, farmers, and laborers	42.9	—	—	42.8	—	—
Graduate students, retired, and housewives	—	5.2	—	—	42.3	16.7

tional category has been added to account for students, retired individuals, and housewives. The only statistically significant difference between the two groups shows up in this table, i.e., the percentage of housewives in the two groups is significant at the .05 level.

Academic level is consistent with occupational classification. About 90% of the men and 42% of the women have completed four or more years of college, and 22% of the men and 9% of the women hold a Ph.D.

The original impetus for this group came from several couples who were curious to see if there were others who shared their interest in complex marriage. They decided to run the aforementioned ad in *Saturday Review* and to list a phone for receiving calls from prospective members. The couple who agreed to answer the phone also accepted the responsibility for maintaining correspondence files and doing much of the secretarial work. At first the entire group screened prospects, but as soon as general criteria had been established, this task was turned over to a volunteer committee. The questionnaire used for initial screening is reproduced in table 3, with the composite answers of the

Table 3—Group-designed questionnaire for applicants[a]

	Talkers		Doers	
Item	Yes	No	Yes	No
1. We have formed close emotional ties with other families in the past.	69%	31%	83%	17%
2. We have formed close ties with other families that involved sexual intimacy.	47	53	72	28
3. Our ideal is to link up closely with other families, each retaining its own home and privacy but with much emotional sharing.	90	10	81	19
4. Our ideal is to form a commune.	43	57	53	47
5. Our ideal is to form a group marriage.	44	56	53	47
6. We've had experience in a commune or group marriage.	—	100	100	—
7. We have a professional background in the behavioral sciences.	50	50	67	33
8. We have participated in therapy, group therapy, sensitivity training, or encounter groups.	69	31	83	17
9. Children require firmness and consistency to guide them until they can determine their own attitudes.	71	29	81	19
10. Children should be given as much freedom as possible so long as they don't harm themselves or inconvenience others.	100	—	100	—
11. We take care that our children don't observe us in a sexual situation.	50	50	43	57
12. We would expect to be sexually free with any couple with whom we related really well.	76	24	88	12
13. We can enjoy sex with others without requiring an emotional involvement.	37	63	28	72

[a] Composite answers for the eighty couples in the study.

eighty couples. The original intent of these questions was to indicate the degree of "openness" in the marriages of applicants to the group. The answers to the questions numbered two and twelve suggest that this group was unusual along the sexual dimension as well as in other ways.

What concerns led these couples to spend as many as three nights a week in the various activities of this group? Predictably, certain problems were of greater concern for the women, others for the men, while a few seemed to be of equal concern for both. I have distilled the following basic issues from interviews, discussions, and anecdotal records and correspondence.

Wives seemed most concerned about (1) the sense of isolation that comes with raising children, (2) overdependence on the husband for adult contact, and (3) less than optimal development and use of their talents and training.

The problem of isolation occurs over a surprisingly wide age span. Many wives felt it even more severely because they waited until their late twenties to start families. Leaving budding careers made them feel even more isolated because of the children. These families tended to move more often than the general population. They seldom had a group of ready-made relatives and friends to rely on. Many who lived in the city were afraid to venture out at all unless absolutely necessary. Those who lived in the suburbs complained of a lack of any real community of interest with their neighbors, apart from the children, and even this was lacking unless the children were in the same age group.

Interwoven with this problem was the tendency toward overdependence on the husband for adult contact. Without support from kinship, friendship, and neighbor groups, husband and wife share isolation in the home, and, as Slater (1968) has stated, they must be lovers, friends, and mutual therapists. Because many of the couples moved every few years, they did not have time to develop many friendships. The husband satisfied his need for outside contact at the office, but the wife who was not employed outside the home faced a barren prospect indeed. It was not that she had no neighbors; she may have had many acquaintances among her neighbors, but one looks for one's friends among peers, and neighbors frequently seem not to provide peers from whom to choose friends.

Most of the women in this sample were college educated and were trained in a career specialty, but a substantial minority had not had the opportunity to develop a career that optimally utilized their training. Either they had dropped out of the job market while the children were small or they had been forced to make "willy-nilly" job changes when their husbands' careers moved their families to a new location. Others have been unable to make any use of their training and ability because their families were so large that their full-time presence in the home was required.

The men were particularly concerned about two problems that are probably universal among men in our society. They were seeking a means of freeing themselves from financial insecurity and the rat race. They also would have liked to achieve higher living standards.

The first of these concerns was often linked to the need for the wife to pursue her career goals. What does one do when a career opportunity for the husband necessitates a move to Oshkosh, Wisconsin, which would destroy the wife's career? Family financial security may be an overwhelming factor in the decision, if, for example, the husband's current job is being phased out. Will the family's financial resources permit them to remain in the area while he tries to match the Oshkosh offer locally? For many upper middle-class families the answer is, "Not for very long!" Aside from this kind of bind, most males must constantly evaluate and reevaluate the nature of "opportunity." Would it be fair to themselves and to their families to turn down an opportunity to move up the career ladder? Will their careers be blighted if the "opportunity" is turned down? How many pounds of flesh does one owe to Mammon (or to increasing family income) anyway?

The second concern for men was related to the first. Although they explored the idea cautiously, the notion of sharing at least some capital expenditures, perhaps a summer home, a houseboat, or hobby equipment, was an appealing partial solution to the problem of raising the family standard of living—one that men were as eager to explore as the problem of increasing financial security. Not only would it be economically sound, if done with the proper safeguards, it would even be ecologically desirable to conserve natural resources (this sounds "tongue-in-cheek" but has been a matter of serious discussion in the context of having to start somewhere, and so why not where it would be more personally rewarding). While initially concerned about stretching family resources, many of these men have come to realize that an enlarged family with multiple incomes and relatively reduced expenses would be very advantageous insofar as all family economic functions in our capitalistic society are concerned.

As long as the basic economic unit is a nuclear family that must survive on one or at the most two adult incomes, the family will have trouble just staying even with the ever-mounting cost of living. More and more families are approaching bankruptcy by just putting their children through college, now that the cost of a year of college is soaring as high as five thousand dollars, with no end to the mounting costs in sight. Setting aside money for investment seems far removed from the reality of trying to break even. The potential opportunities to share in the joys of capitalism are real enough—they abound at every turn—but without a stake they are unattainable. Conversations about pooling resources to buy big-ticket or luxury items almost invariably shift to consideration of the comparative advantages, within our societal structure, of a commune or group marriage. Setting up a "rainy-day" fund to weather a period of unemployment or a Clifford trust for educating the kids are possible solutions, but they pale in the wake of the tax and income-producing advantages of, for example, incorporating a group marriage or a small commune as a subchapter-S corporation or using the condominium approach in order to finance an apartment building.

Child-rearing and training were a major concern for both parents and nonparents among our sample. There was common concern for providing the growing child with a variety of adult relationships. Both the commune and group marriage seem to promise the kind of flexibility that would not only provide more adult models, but would provide a better male/female mix, since there would presumably be a greater degree of male presence in the home. There was also an expressed need to raise children among adults with compatible lifestyles so that the children would feel more secure with respect to differences in the life-style of their own family and their friends' families, especially after they reached school age. Many respondents were vitally interested in the training of the new generation, whether they had children of their own or not. They hoped to establish free schools or at least to explore the possibility of supplementary training.

A major concern of these couples was the freedom to include sexual intimacy among the joys of friendship when appropriate. Forty-one couples have formed ties with other families that included sexual intimacy and indicated that they would expect to be sexually free with any couple with whom they related really well. Although the other thirty-nine couples in the sample have not yet had such experience, only fourteen of them indicated that they would *not* expect to be sexually free with any couple with whom they related really well. One of three couples in the first group indicated that they also could enjoy casual sexual contacts. Only one of five couples in the second group indicated that they could enjoy such contacts.

This desire to be free to establish intimate friendships appeared to reflect both the need to broaden and deepen adult contact outside the dyadic marriage and the belief that such activity measurably strengthened the couple's own marriage. As noted above, there could be little doubt that the stress here is on person-to-person rather than genital-to-genital relationships. These individuals simply did not want to exclude the possibility of intimacy as a part of friendship where and when appropriate. They denied emphatically that intimate friendship was another term for swinging, and this distinction would seem to be substantiated by their responses with regard to casual sexual contacts. As I have noted elsewhere (Ramey 1972), there is a well-developed transitional pattern between swinging with minimal emotional involvement and "matured swinging groups," which Stoller (1970) calls "intimate family networks." I believe the term "intimate friendship" delineates this type of group or network in a more meaningful way, because it applies equally well to friendship with a single individual or couple and such friendships should not be excluded by terminology from our attempts to understand this kind of relationship, i.e., one in which the emphasis is on friendship rather than on intimacy.

The final major theme that brought these couples together was a shared concern for what is happening. In every age, there are a few individuals, often academic or professional people, at the growing edge of society, who question and examine new social issues before most people know they are issues, looking for new ways to maximize their potential, opportunities, and pleasure within current social structures. Many people seem to believe that youth has a corner on the market of challenging the accepted responses to problems of living and that the older generation simply follows where youth leads. History tells us otherwise. The couples in this sample were among the "life-style leaders" of today. By way of example, while social scientists are just now discussing seriously the possibilities inherent in consensual extramarital and comarital relationships, a preponderance of these eighty couples have already been involved in intimate friendships, some of them for over two decades, or since the "new generation" was in rompers!

How are these couples approaching the task of seriously considering group marriage or communal living? The array of interaction has covered a wide range of activities. Nearly every day at least one group was having a meeting, and on weekends there were usually several, such as regular Saturday afternoon children's activities, a music group, an ongoing encounter group, and orientation sessions for newcomers.

This latter activity was especially noteworthy because it set the tone for newcomer participation in other activities. Although there was no formal structure or organization among these couples (individuals simply initiated activities that interested them), several individuals volunteered to screen newcomers for the group. First the prospective couple sent in the questionnaire form on which the screening committee passed judgment. If the new family was found to be acceptable, they were invited to an orientation meeting, where the emphasis was on drawing out the newcomers, ascertaining their interests more specifically, and telling them about the various study groups, experimental groups, discussion groups, and other activities currently under way so that they might find their way into the various activities available to them. These initial sessions with newcomers were conducted at a level of candor seldom encountered in any but old established friendships. When asked about this, newcomers discussed both their anticipation, based on the screening they had survived, and the emphasis at the meeting on openness, feedback, acceptance of differences in perception and opinion, and willingness to dispense with the idea that any subject is taboo. This atmosphere of permissiveness and understanding in which feelings and attitudes could be freely and nonjudgmentally expressed and in which males and females tended to be treated as peers appeared to be characteristic of all the activities of these eighty couples.

Some of their activities involved only a few intensely interested people, while a few, such as family day outings, involved almost the entire group. A few activities were almost exclusively female, while a few attracted no females, but most tended to be couple projects. Some discussions or activities were short-lived, for example, putting together a complete listing of all families in the group, with addresses, phone numbers, and a one-hundred-word statement of their interests. The first time this was attempted it took six weeks or so, and two or three people were involved in the project. When it was attempted a second time, after the first listing was out of date, there wasn't enough interest among the group as a whole to get the project off the ground, even though several people were willing to do the work.

Some activities were longer term in nature. Study groups tackled a number of potential projects, for example, setting up a free school, converting a brownstone, running encounter groups, discussing the ins and outs of a subchapter-S corporation, setting up a baby-sitting co-op, building a boat, establishing food co-ops, setting up investment pools, buying condominiums and co-ops, building co-ops, discussing nonprofit corporation and foundation structure, establishing art and drama groups for the kids, and setting up a home-exchange program.

One of several experimental projects centered in a three-couple group marriage, which was the focus of a larger discussion group that provided a sounding board for the problems of the group marriage, which in turn was the guinea pig for the discussion group. This group met as often as the group marriage felt the need, and the discussion group survived the group marriage, which broke up after six months. The feedback was invaluable for all members of the group as well as for the six participants in the group marriage, who at this writing still maintain an intimate-friendship circle but do not feel ready to make a second attempt at establishing a group marriage.

While it was clearly understood by all members of the sample that their involvement in discussions and activities associated with determining just what their interest might be in group marriage and communes was not a commitment to actually undertake living in a commune or group marriage, it is nevertheless of interest to those investigating this area that three group marriages and several communes have developed as offshoots from this group of eighty families so far and others may reasonably be expected to develop.

Other experimental projects have included spending vacations, renting summer property, and living on weekends together. Another experimental activity was the partial exchange of predominantly male and female family roles between husband and wife or between several adults during periods of experimental living.

One of the important ongoing discussion themes was the working through of expectations that each couple brought to any consideration of communal living or group marriage, going through the give-and-take process of shaping the nature of the commitments involved, and determining the kinds of decision-making and ground rules that would be acceptable. This was a difficult but rewarding task, and one that inevitably gave rise to splinter groups as like-minded couples found each other.

A representative list of typical problem areas discussed will indicate the complexity of this undertaking. This list is not definitive, nor are the decision areas listed in order of importance, since rank order depended on who was involved in the discussion. Those primarily interested in group marriage had to consider many more personal issues dealing with the nature of marital interaction, in addition to the more general questions. Most groups were concerned about decision-making procedures, group goals, ground rules, prohibitions, intra- and extra-group sexual relationships, privacy, division of labor, role relationships, careers, relationships with outsiders, degree of visibility, legal jeopardy, dissolution of the group, personal responsibilities outside the group (such as parental support), geographic location, type of shelter, children, child-rearing practices, education of children, individual adult career education, taxes, the pooling of assets, income, legal structure, trial period, investment policy, sequential steps to establish a group, and prerequisites for membership.

One of the impressive aspects of this group was its lack of formal organization. In the beginning, a decision was apparently made to charge a three-dollar minimum application fee (a larger donation was acceptable) and to charge a three-dollar refreshment and finance fee to each couple attending any meeting of the group. This custom was observed very informally. Sometimes the host at a particular meeting would waive the fee, and at other times some couples might throw an extra twenty-dollar bill in the pot. In this manner, the group was able to finance an occasional newsletter, a membership register which involved a one-hundred-word description of each member family, frequent mailings of the calendar of coming meetings, and extensive correspondence with individuals, groups, organizations, and publishers interested in communes and group marriage.

The typical meeting would be hosted by a couple interested in a particular group activity or discussion topic, on a rotating basis, although some activities were always associated with a particular couple and place. The convention was to notify the host couple of their intent to attend at least forty-eight hours in advance. Several different couples acted as clearinghouses for certain activities. They could always be called for the dates, times, and locations of a particular activity. Except for family activities, there were few times when the entire group was involved in a specific meeting. Groups tended to limit themselves to a number small enough to involve all those who wished to become involved, generally about four to ten couples. Larger groups soon split up to achieve greater participation. Each group acted autonomously, and sometimes it was impossible to decide who was the leader of a given group. Some groups operated by consensus, others voted, and a few appeared simply to acquiesce to the decisions of one or two individuals within the group. Consensus was the most common means of reaching decisions when decisions were required. The second most frequent pattern was the delegation of this power to one couple who were trusted to understand the "sense" of the group and act accordingly.

One of the anomalies of the group was its inability to handle single-parent families or single adults. Since the avowed purpose of the group was to explore the possibilities for building complex family relationships with deliberately chosen members to "replace" the extended family (which few, if any, of these couples had actually experienced), one could reasonably expect that single-parent families and selected single adults would have been welcome. To the contrary, such individuals were systematically and almost invariably turned down by the screening committee. Occasionally, a single female or a female single-parent family was admitted to the group. No single males or male single-parent families were ever admitted. The reasons for the exceptions could not be ascertained satisfactorily, but the reason for the exclusions appeared to be fear of the "unsettling" influence of the single male.

In some cases, extensive correspondence and/or phone conversation with one of these applicants transpired before the decision was finally reached. Discussion with both the screening committee and the accepted singles failed to elicit the reasons why some were accepted and others were rejected. This remains an area in which the group has not reached consensus, and as long as a large minority feel that singles pose some sort of "take-over" or "free-loader" threat, the policy is unlikely to change.

The implementation of decisions by various activity groups within the total sample depended on both the level of interest and the ingenuity of the individuals involved. The same individuals could be observed behaving very differently as they moved from one group to another. One group, concerned about the personal qualities regarded as essential for self and others in a group marriage or commune, decided to take a poll. They circulated a questionnaire to all members who wished to participate (about forty couples), and the resulting profile is shown in figure 1.

The profile suggested value differences as well as differences in

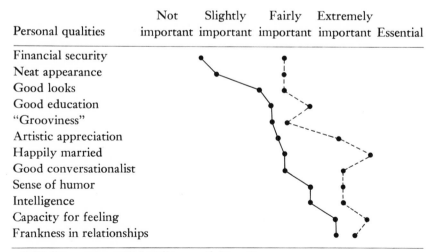

Personal qualities	Not important	Slightly important	Fairly important	Extremely important	Essential
Financial security					
Neat appearance					
Good looks					
Good education					
"Grooviness"					
Artistic appreciation					
Happily married					
Good conversationalist					
Sense of humor					
Intelligence					
Capacity for feeling					
Frankness in relationships					

Solid line = others; Dashed line = self. N = 40.

Figure 1—Group profile: Qualities valued in self and others

standards set for self and others. In the main, the highest values were placed on internal or "feeling" qualities rather than on such external factors as education or appearance. The fact that in every instance these couples set higher standards for self than for others was consistent with self-other reports in a number of other studies (Ramey 1958). There appears to be a consistent tendency to set "ideal" standards for self while appraising others in more realistic terms. One study, based on research of executive behavior in 1952, found that under stress, the individual was likely to revert to the type of behavior he predicted for others, even though under normal circumstances he made every effort to maintain his "ideal" pattern (Ramey 1958). We believe "other" to be an expression of minimum-role norms and expectations, whereas standards for "self" represent optimum behavior.

One other example of a group decision which led to action should suffice. A small splinter group consisting of three couples (two with small children and one with grown children) and a single female (with teenage children) were intensely interested in pooling resources and setting up a commune in an urban setting for the purpose of owning and operating a free school. As the nucleus of an action group, they took the initial step of renting a summer residence together so that they could actually share living quarters on an experimental basis. Next, they began a systematic survey of private schools in the metropolitan area that might be available for purchase, since they reasoned that it was more realistic and simpler to start with an existing school than to start with no usable facility. They located several schools that could be purchased for approximately $250,000 and began preparing budget projections and studies of the relationship of type of curriculum to expense, enrollment projections, and the like. They also began expanding the group on a carefully selective basis, taking into account the skills that would be needed as well as the simple desire of other couples to become involved. At each step of this process, the group acted as a committee of the whole with respect to major decisions but delegated many decision functions to individuals who had special competence in particular areas.

A major asset of the transactional process among these eighty couples was the fluidity of the group. The fact that the group was loose-knit led to an ebb and flow of interaction patterns that was definitely enhanced by input from the outside contacts of the member couples. Some were involved in various activities of the group for the entire three-year period. Some moved in and out depending on their interests and what was happening at a given time. Others were involved only long enough to find like-minded people with whom they then entered into a communal- or group-marriage arrangement at a distant location so that their further interaction became sporadic.

The proposed follow-up study should provide some interesting insights with respect to changes in attitude, interests, and life-style among those who sought more complex forms of interpersonal relationships than are possible within the confines of monogamous dyadic marriage.

References

Constantine, L., and Constantine, J. 1971. Multilateral Marriage: Alternate Family Structure in Practice. In *You and I Searching for Tomorrow*, ed. R. H. Rimmer. New York: New American Library.

Kanter, R. M. 1968. Commitment and Social Organization: A Study of Commitment Mechanisms in Utopian Communities. *Amer. Soc. Rev.* 33 (August): 499–517.

Ramey, J. W. 1958. The Relationship of Peer Group Rating to Certain Individual Perceptions of Personality. *J. Exper. Ed.* 27: 143–49.

———. 1972. Emerging Patterns of Behavior in Marriage: Deviations or Innovations? *J. Sex Res.* 8, no. 1, pp. 6–30.

Slater, P. E. 1968. Some Social Consequences of Temporary Systems. In *The Temporary Society*, ed. W. G. Bennis and P. E. Slater. New York: Harper and Row.

Stoller, F. H. 1970. The Intimate Network of Families as a New Structure. In *The Family in Search of a Future*, ed. H. Otto. New York: Appleton-Century-Crofts.

Sexual Liberality and Personality: A Pilot Study

Jon Twichell

It is obvious that the emotional loading of the subject of sexual behavior has increased in recent years. The publishing of the Masters and Johnson works; the proliferation of research on various related subjects; the emergence of sexual "how-to" books such as *The Sensuous Woman*, *The Sensuous Man*, Dr. David Reuben's notorious books, and others; the dramatically increased availability of erotic materials; and the vocalness of sexual minorities such as gay liberationist, woman's liberationists, and sexual freedom advocates—balanced by increased attacks on pornography and sex education—all serve to show that a great many people in our society consider sexual conduct and, more specifically, sexual liberality a crucial factor in the lives of all individuals, if not in the fabric of society itself. In short, the pursuit and proliferation of sexual liberality is a social issue of critical proportions affecting everyone regardless of sexual ideology and personal lifestyle.

Attempts have been made intermittently in recent years to sort out this emotional loading in order to arrive at some sensible and empiri-

The author would especially like to thank Herbert Naboisek, professor of psychology, San Francisco State College, for his encouragement and perceptive advice and Michael Davis for his invaluable computer skills and patience in the course of this study.

cally supported conclusions on sexual liberality. However, most researchers have been guilty, I feel, of carrying their morals to their work in one way or another. For instance, a study entitled "Sexual Promiscuity in the Pre-Marital Situation" leaves little suspense about what the researcher will find. On the other hand, the authors of marriage manuals and sexual how-to books extol the virtues of any and all sexual activity as being healthy and enhancing the psyche and body. Moreover, the recent, numerous studies on swinging couples (married couples engaging in sexual activities with others with their partner's consent) have suffered because many of the observers have also been participants and their enthusiasm has shown in their reports. And, many skeptics have argued, "So what if they studied 200 or even 500 people . . . they're *all* sick."

Much of my interest in this subject is based on sociopolitical factors. There are movements underway in most states to change many of the extreme antisexual laws on the books, and there are also countermovements against the spread and accessibility of erotic materials. Much energy is being expended, and there seems to be, as usual, more heat than light. The recent report of the President's Commission on Obscenity and Pornography (1970) presented and summarized a plethora of scientific research findings showing a lack of pathological effects from exposure to erotica, but the commission's conclusions have been virtually ignored or rejected by persons in positions of executive and legislative power. Even these studies, for the most part, carefully skirted the main issue and crux of much of the "problem" of sexually liberal behavior and values.

The question remains: Is sexual conduct, more specifically sexual liberality, indicative of basic personality traits, of a "sick" or "healthy" mind? Moralists have stated that sexual freedom is symptomatic of guilt, neurosis, psychosis, or mental illness and, conversely, that proliferate sexual activity is healthy, indicative of a self-actualized person, and indeed essential to psychic health. Attempts to track down a concrete answer from the present data and published studies of scientific research have been inconclusive and unsuccessful. From this search has grown another hypothesis: Sexual liberality per se is indicative of nothing in the psyche; such conduct does not correlate with any basic personality patterns and is simply a behavior, like many others, that is not a truly accurate indicator of mental aberration or even of a personality pattern. This article is a report of a preliminary study to determine the viability of this hypothesis and to demonstrate its relevance as the basis for a more comprehensive theory of sexual liberalism.

Literature Review

The scientific literature presently available on the subject of sexuality and personality is generally divisible into several areas: studies based on personal or social attitudes, with negative or neutral results; studies of sexual responsiveness and marital happiness, generally indicative of a positive relationship; and studies of sociopolitical factors and personality characteristics, generally inconclusive and largely limited to attitudinal rather than behavioral measures. Specific data on personality and sexual liberality, as both a set of attitudes *and* a complex of actual behaviors, especially based on standard measures such as the Minnesota Multiphasic Personality Inventory (MMPI), are sparse.

Some psychologists have argued that sexual liberality is related to personality problems. O. H. Mowrer (1967), for example, has claimed that "the control of sexuality is liberating in the long run" and further hypothesized (1960, 1961) that neurosis is the result of an individual's feeling guilty for having violated some moral precept. In a follow-up attempt to relate neurosis to sexual activity, Swenson conducted studies of men (1973) and women (1962) college students who sought psychotherapy, as compared with students who did not seek such counseling. The data for women showed somewhat more sexual activity in the group that sought help, while the control group of men showed more sexual activity than the counseling group.

Shope and Broderick (1967) conducted a study of female undergraduate volunteers, virgin versus nonvirgin, and found that virginity was positively related to self-predictions of marital happiness and sexual adjustment in marriage. He also found significant differences in the areas of prejudice and stability. No follow-up study was ever completed to determine the subsequent reliability of these predictions. Another study, also employing college students as subjects, by Stratton and Spitzen (1967), concluded that "individuals who feel it is acceptable for engaged persons to indulge in sexual intercourse have lower self-evaluation than those who do not." Reporting more neutral results based on a variety of scales, Wilson (1965) and Miller and Wilson (1968) found no significant correlation between sexual liberality and either avowed happiness or maladjustment.

All of the above studies have several common factors. They employed young college students, they generally relied on volunteered information, and they essentially dealt with moral and attitudinal questions. No follow-up studies were undertaken or probes made into the ramifications of actual practices versus reported attitudes. The generally negative results in relation to sexual attitudes are in decided contrast to the work that has been done on sexual responsiveness, in which a number of studies from Terman (1938) and Kinsey et al. (1948, 1953) to the present indicate a positive relationship between the physical enjoyment of sex and personal adjustment.

Shope (1967) reported that a comparison of nonvirgins who experienced orgasm and those who did not showed that the orgasmic group had more positive sexual attitudes, better overall relationships with males, and greater capacity for more intimate relationships. Relying upon Institute for Sex Research findings, Gebhard (1966) has stated that there is a strong positive relationship between female orgasm and marital happiness. Over thirty years ago, Terman (1938) reported in his study of psychological factors in marital happiness that the "passionate" group had a much higher mean happiness score than the "nonpassionate" group. The passionate group reported orgasmic response "usually or always" with twice the frequency of the nonpassionate group. Other evidences of higher sex drives and lower sexual inhibitions were also apparent. Burgess and Wallin (1953) state that 93% of men and 91% of women in their study reported that sexual intercourse had strengthened their engagement relationship. However, they also point out that this was a biased sample of persons who had had both premarital intercourse and lasting relationships.

Bell (1966) stated that premarital orgasm in women seems related to marital sexual satisfaction. Adams (1963) concluded from his studies of married female students and wives of male college students that there was a significant positive correlation between marital happiness and sexual adjustment and similarly between sexual adjustment and sexual responsiveness. Brown (1966), in an extensive discussion and review of the literature on female orgasm, presented data on both sides of the issue and concluded that lack of orgasm may be related to marital maladjustment. Other studies indicate that sexual activity may be related to general physical activity and that sexual contact and intercourse are more prevalent than in the past.

Kinsey, Pomeroy, and Martin (1948) found that males who mature early and engage early in masturbation and sexual relations also seem to be more alert, energetic, vivacious, spontaneous, physically active, socially extroverted, and/or aggressive individuals. Fisher and Osofsky (1967), in an investigation of the correlates of sexual responsiveness in women, reported that the greater a subject's self-described inclination to enjoy physical activities and the greater the use of large muscle groups, the higher her sexual responsiveness and orgasm scores. They also indicated a positive correlation of the sexual indexes and interest in food and oral satisfaction and a general responsiveness to activities that produce bodily satisfaction.

As for generally increased sexual activity, Zetterberg (1969) reported that a national random survey of the Swedish population showed 98% of the married population had intercourse before marriage. However, his survey also suggested that promiscuity, in the form of more than one partner concurrently, was not considered acceptable. For example, a very high proportion expressed disapproval of extramarital relations (93%) In general, an attitude of loyalty to one's primary partner, regardless of marital status, prevailed.

In surveying recent premarital intercourse studies in the United States, Davis (1970) concluded that sexual liberality is becoming more of an established fact, with participants exhibiting both a high rate of admission of awareness of sexual urges and a significant increase (an approximate doubling from the Kinsey figures) in sexual experience prior to first marriage. While these data generally indicate an increase in admitted sexual activities and the possibility of a positive correlation between sexual experience and marital happiness, they do not clearly provide an answer to whether sexual liberality, as expressed in *conscious* behavior and *overt* action, is related directly to personality type or structure. However, studies of purported relationships between personality characteristics and social class do provide some revealing results.

Reiss (1965) has stated, in contrast to Mowrer, that guilt feelings do not generally inhibit sexual behavior. The studies of Kinsey et al. (1953) also stand in contrast to Mowrer's findings. Kinsey found that 77% of married women surveyed did not regret engaging in premarital intercourse and that those who did regret it the most had the least experience. Reiss (1968) has also stated that increased premarital sexuality is not usually the result of a breakdown of normative standards but is rather the result of a particular and different type of organization of the social system.

Teevan (1968) has concluded that irreligiosity and political liberalism are positively correlated with sexual permissiveness. Bartell (1970), in apparent contrast, reported that a considerable number of the swinging couples he interviewed in the Chicago area had generally conservative attitudes. Bartell also observed that the chief characteristic which the 204 couples he studied shared was their inherent normality. However, other studies of swinging couples by the O'Neills (1970) and the Smiths (1970) tend to confirm the liberalism thesis.

Maslow (1942) and DeMartino (1963a) have suggested that sexual responsiveness is related to both dominance and self-image; people who have high self-esteem are more likely to achieve sexual fulfillment. Gilmartin (1964) has concluded that sexually liberal attitudes, values, and behavior tend to be associated with high scores on the California Personality Inventory scales of capacity for status, sociability, self-acceptance, and flexibility.

A number of studies reported by the President's Commission on Obscenity and Pornography touch on personality characteristics and sexual behavior. Many of these studies (1970, p. 285) tended to confirm the thesis that sexual offenders may be distinguished by their repressive childhood sexual experiences more than any other single factor. The commission also reported a survey of over 3,400 psychiatrists and clinical psychologists that indicated that over 80% had never encountered cases in which exposure to pornography had caused antisocial behavior.

These results seem to indicate that even very liberal sexual behavior is not related to antisocial behavior. However, attempts to relate directly certain personality aberrations and individual neuroses to specific overt sexual activities have been few and inconclusive. For instance, studies of the relationship of MMPI results and other basic personality tests to sexual attitudes and general conduct are sparse. Marsh, Hilliard, and Liechti (1955) reported the development of an MMPI scale for sexual deviance. Yamahiro and Griffith (1960) later found that this scale did not discriminate among sex offenders, hospitalized psychotics, and the wider category of neurotic personalities. A more recent study by B. Hartman (1967), comparing sexual deviates and sociopaths on a variety of MMPI scales, showed no significant difference between the scores. A detailed study of psychological changes in sexual psychopaths by Cutter (1959) also did not reveal any significant results. Thorne (1966) has reported the development of a Sex Inventory for the purpose of "investigation of sex delinquency," with items much like some MMPI items. However, recent investigations of the usefulness of the inventory have been contradictory (Cowden and Pacht 1969; Galbraith et al. 1968).

Several attempts have been made to use the MMPI for investigating sexual attitudes in nonhospitalized people. Neubeck and Schletzer (1962) suggested that married couples with a high psychopathic deviance (Pd) score might tend to become involved sexually with others, but no follow-up study was attempted to see if this actually was true. In a study entitled "Voyeurism and Exhibitionism," Blank and Roth (1966) administered MMPI's to a group of nudists and to the inevitable control group of students. When the MMPI scores revealed no significant abnormalities, an energetic search for deviant symptoms was undertaken by means of item analysis, leading the authors to conclude finally that nudists have greater personality deviations than the control group composed of undergraduate volunteer subjects.

Two additional recent studies have reached conclusions supportive of this hypothesis. Investigating the psychological correlates of sexual responsiveness in women, Fisher and Osofsky (1967) reported no significant correlations between responsiveness and the K and L scales of the MMPI. Further, an extensive study of two hundred nudists by Hartman, Fithian, and Johnson (1970), which investigated the hypothesis that a group labeled "socially and sexually deviant" will exhibit no significant abnormalities and which employed the MMPI, arrived at results described by an MMPI expert in terms which ranged from a "self-assured group of active . . . people" to "utterly normal."

To sum up this mass of sometimes contradictory, generally attitudinal, and mostly inconclusive data would be at best a very subjective task. There does not seem to be any clearly logical and dominant conclusion. Perhaps one of the most general statements in this area is also one of the most specific: Kirkendall and Libby (1962) have observed that a sexual relationship is an interpersonal relationship, and as such it is subject to the same principles and interactions as other relationships. While this attempt to assign a not-so-potent role to sex flies in the face of our increasing preoccupation with sex in America at this time, it is still perhaps a valid attempt to arrive at some realistic conclusions about sexual behavior without the usual emotional biases.

The Study

The hypothesis that there is no relationship between behaviorally expressed sexual liberality, on the one hand, and personality variables (in particular, mental disorder), on the other, was explored in a pilot study of an allegedly extreme sexual group, the Sexual Freedom League (SFL), and its members. Membership in this group is indicative of a definite commitment to believing in and engaging in sexual behavior that is socially and legally outside presently acceptable bounds. The SFL gives regular parties where all manner of sexual activity between consenting adults is encouraged, and it also sponsors discussion groups, encounter groups, and other activities designed to promote sexual freedom. Bisexuality and extramarital, premarital, and group sex are frequently encountered ideals among group members.

A pilot study of this group could be expected to yield certain positive indications, and a random sample of the overall population could be studied for confirmation and refinement. The presumed extremity of the group's views, however, might result in more extreme scores than a researcher would find in a random sample of people who consider themselves sexually liberal. In fact, several experts in the field hypothesized that I would obtain more extreme scores for the SFL group than would be found in the general population.

In order to investigate a variety of factors, I decided to utilize the MMPI as a basic and authoritative personality test. An abbreviated form of the Rokeach E Form Dogmatism scale, consisting of twenty items, was used, in addition to the entire Authoritarianism, Intolerance, and Time-Perspective scales, to test open- and closed-mindedness. A Semantic Differential exploration of the word "sex" was also included to obtain a more precise emotional evaluation of the word and its connotations. A basic questionnaire was used both to obtain demographic data and to explore the following areas: (1) emotional relationships, (2) overt sexual behavior patterns, (3) sexual identity, in particular, bisexuality, (4) attitudes toward the importance of sex, (5) enjoyment of physical activity and food (hypothesized as important in other studies), (6) motivation for joining the Sexual Freedom League, and (7) expressed satisfaction with present life situations. To standardize and quantify data, all items excepting the MMPI were offered on a five-point scale, ranging from strongly positive to strongly negative. Recruitment was from a population involved in a variety of party groups, encounter groups, and discussion groups organized by and for Sexual Freedom League members. The sample numbered forty-one, with an almost equal division in the number of male (N=22) and female (N=19) subjects, and with a similar break in those under thirty (N=19) and thirty and over (N=22).

Although I am generally against using college students as controls, a class at San Francisco State College was available to me, and 100% participation was secured (N=31). Use of the class gave both groups a comparable educational base, since the SFL group showed a very high educational level, and a similar geographical and political base. The null hypothesis was that the MMPI scores for the SFL sample would fall within the bounds defined as normal, that the dogmatism and semantic differential tests would show no essential differences, and that the basic questionnaire would show no great differences between the two groups. My hypotheses were that the MMPI scores would be normal, the dogmatism scale would show a more open attitude among SFL members, the semantic differential would show a more positive attitude toward sex among SFL members, and the basic questionnaire would show no differences that were not attributable to age and experience differences (the controls were all under age thirty).

In developing these hypotheses, a number of experts in the San

Francisco area were consulted, all of whom had had experience with the MMPI and sexually extreme individuals or groups, including one of the original developers of the test. There was general agreement that my hypothesis of normality would be proven false, and one professor who had had some experience with the SFL even drew a sample profile based on his prediction of abnormal scores. The developer of the MMPI felt that sexually liberal people in general would show up normal, but he felt the SFL group would show abnormal scores. In general, there was consensus among the half-dozen consultants that the results would show abnormally high scores on the Pd, Mf, Ma, and F scales.[1] Also mentioned was the hypothesis that sexually liberal people are attempting to compensate for poor emotional relationships with their parents and with other people.

Results

The Sexual Freedom League group showed a basically normal MMPI profile. The only scale out of the generally accepted normal range of 30–70 T-scores was the Mf scale for men. Elevated scores on this scale, moreover, are usually not interpreted to mean pathology but rather are considered indicative of a broad range of interests, generally higher IQ, and wide aesthetic interests. The two profiles (male and female SFL members) are very similar (including a strong "feminine" score on the Mf scale), indicating a possible common factor for both sexes. The scores for females were all within the T-score range of 45–60, showing slightly less elevation than the scores for males. This contradicts the commonly held stereotype of the sexually promiscuous female as psychologically disturbed and subject to severe emotional problems.

Comparison of these group profiles with other available group profiles serves to strengthen the hypothesis that sexual liberality is not a definable pattern on the MMPI. Lanyon's handbook of group MMPI profiles (1968) shows no similarity of pattern between the SFL group and sex offenders or heterosexual or homosexual prisoners. The greatest likeness is to patterns of Australian actors and actresses and to heterosexual and/or homosexual college graduates. The pattern of both the hetero- and homosexual graduates in the latter study was largely undifferentiated, with both resembling the SFL pattern. It would be logical

[1] Pd, psychopathic deviate; Mf, masculinity-femininity; Ma, hypomania; and F, validity.

to assume that, since the SFL group had a high educational level, the SFL pattern was simply indicative of a college education, if it is indicative of anything at all. Comparison of the MMPI profiles reported by Hartman, Fithian, and Johnson (1970) again shows a general similarity in patterning, with the nudist profiles exhibiting more flattened scores as a result of a substantially larger sample size. In sum, the SFL subjects could well be described as normal, active, and intelligent people. This is consistent with the observations of Smith and Smith (1970) and Bartell (1971), each of whom studied larger samples of sexually liberal persons with less scrutiny than the MMPI provides.

In analyzing the rest of the data, one must keep in mind that the experimental group drawn from the Sexual Freedom League cannot be viewed as representative of sexually liberal people in general. Rather, their response patterns must be viewed as indicative of, but probably more extreme than, the total liberal population. Therefore, analysis of the rest of the quantitative data is confined to simple observation of differences between the control and experimental groups and use of the t-ratio, two-tailed test, with a significance level of 0.01.

The Semantic Differential showed little difference between the two groups, confirming the null hypothesis. Both the SFL and control groups showed a strongly favorable attitude toward sex. The first nine items on the fifteen-item scale were from Osgood's original fifty bipolar scales, with the remaining six developed to explore specific items such as the double standard and individual emotional attitudes toward the value of sex. The main item of difference between the groups was the SFL view of sex as slightly more humorous (mean 2.88), while the control groups of students saw sex as slightly more serious (mean 3.45). The difference was not statistically significant. It may be said, in sum, that both groups regard sex favorably, as a valuable experience.

The abridged Rokeach Dogmatism scale also revealed few differences between the groups. Scoring of the twenty items ranged from slightly positive on some to generally unfavorable on others, with few significant differences. The most discriminating item of the scale was "a group which tolerates too much difference of opinion among its own members cannot exist for long." This item, the only one of the twenty items on which the difference was statistically significant, received a generally neutral mean score of 3.19 from the control group and a generally unfavorable mean score of 4.03 from the SFL group. Generally, this test scale showed both groups as taking neutral to generally unfavorable stands on dogmatic issues and revealed few differences between or extremism within the SFL and control groups. Again, the null hypothesis, indicating no essential difference between the two groups, was upheld.

The basic questionnaire, on the other hand, showed a variety of interesting items. In addition to the even division of age and sex in the SFL group, this group showed itself as an interesting social microcosm in other ways. For instance, 42% of the SFL subjects were married and living with their spouse, 37% were living alone, and 21% were unmarried but cohabiting. The control group was 75% single, with the remaining 25%, divided between married persons and those living with someone. While members of the control group had no children, half of the SFL members had at least one child.

Politically, two-thirds of the SFL subjects described themselves as liberal, with the remainder divided between radical and moderate; the control group was equally divided between liberal and moderate. Economically, both groups saw themselves as either middle class or "student." Educationally, the SFL group confirmed findings of other studies by showing a very high educational level: 93% had attended college (which may also be a product of using a sample from the San Francisco area), and 25% had attended graduate school. The questions on enjoyment of eating and general physical activity drew favorable responses from both groups. Questions dealing with the role of sex revealed no statistically significant differences. Both groups felt it was predominantly a way to enhance a loving relationship and that sexual activity should be generally free and based on personal choice. There was a significant disagreement, not unexpected, over the importance of sex. Most of the control group felt it was only one of many important things, while the SFL group accorded it generally greater priority.

There were also basic and statistically significant differences in the areas of oral sex and bisexuality. Approximately 93% of the SFL subjects practice oral sex to orgasm on an occasional to regular basis, and 100% give it ratings of "depends on the situation" to "highly recommend" for both themselves and others. Half of the control group reported occasional oral sex, but about 25% had never experienced it. The latter group's enjoyment and recommendation of oral sex fell more in the "depends on the situation" category. While approximately 30% of the SFL group reported bisexual or homosexual contacts on an occasional to regular basis, only 3% of the control group reported such contacts. Both groups generally felt that such contacts depended on the situation and did not express strong statements for or against same sex contacts, although the SFL recommendations were more favorable than those of the control group. The control group was negative on personal enjoyment of such contacts, while the SFL subjects were more neutral. The main item of interest, rather than significant differences in experience, was the nonevaluative attitudes of both groups toward sexual conduct, including homosexuality.

Analyzing the emotional data for the two groups is more complex. When questioned about their present life situation, both groups expressed general satisfaction. No difference was evident between the two groups. On the question of what the emotional relationship to one's sex partner should be, one-half of the SFL group answered "casual warmth and affection," with another third indicating "strong love." In the control group, these percentages were reversed. Again, the interesting fact was not the statistically significant differences in the answers, but both groups' extreme lack of interest in the "marriage only" category.

In evaluating emotional relationships with friends, both groups showed positive scores, in the area of "generally warm and close," with the control group having a slightly more positive score than the SFL. On the other hand, in describing emotional relationships with parents, the control group had a significantly more positive mean score than the SFL group: the SFL respondents described their parental relationships in neutral terms (mean score 2.90) of sometimes warm and sometimes distant; the control group described their parental relationships as generally close and warm (mean score 2.03). This finding is subject to several interpretations. It may be seen as lending credence to the theory that overt sexual liberality is related to an insecure relationship with parents. On the other hand, it could mean that the SFL group, half of whom were over thirty, developed a more realistic view of their parental relations as they grew older. Another alternative hypothesis is that Dr. Spock did indeed have a strong effect on child-raising, that the SFL parents were indeed more distant and unemotional by choice, and that the SFL scores accurately mirror real life. We might conclude from this that the SFL group could be characterized as more realistically in touch with their emotional relationships and needs and that their interest in greater sexual activity is part of greater self-knowledge.

In giving the reasons why they had joined the SFL, over half stated they wanted more warm sexual relationships with other people, as opposed to the satisfaction of simply sexual urges or an intellectual interest in sexual freedom. As to what they want from the league, the majority indicated intense group or one-to-one sexual and emotional experiences, as opposed to casual relationships. No one indicated a preference for increased sexual activity only.

It would be logical to assume, tentatively and on the basis of the preliminary data, that sexual activity is perceived in this group as part of human relationships in general, rather than as an isolated act. Because of the intelligence level of the group, the MMPI-supported lack of psychosis, and the generally positive level of avowed satisfaction with their life situations, it is also logical to conclude that this sexual activity is not compulsive but rather is an expression of a desire for physical and emotional communication.

Some Tentative Conclusions

Even if one considers that this is a pilot study, with all its attendant faults and virtues, several conclusions can be reached, which signal directions for further investigation and analysis.

First, solid quantitative data, in the form of MMPI profiles, indicate that sexual liberality cannot be characterized as symptomatic of psychosis, neurosis, or abnormality.

This supports the thesis that sexual liberality per se is not likely to generate mental illness nor is it the product of perverted, ill people. One can then proffer the hypothesis that people engaging in premarital, co-marital, or extramarital sex, group sex, oral sex, or even homosexuality or bisexuality are simply normal.

Second, the attitudes toward sex, as evidenced by the Semantic Differential and basic questionnaire, of both the SFL subjects and the control group of college students are positive and warm. This seems to be an excellent sign for the future, with sex perhaps being assigned a happier and more useful role in human relations. The attitudes of both groups toward such previously socially distasteful subjects as homosexuality are provisional and nonevaluative; even if one's own inclination is not in that direction, there is a manifest level of tolerance and a reluctance to judge others negatively for their acts. One should bear in mind, though, that both groups evidenced an attitude of general open-mindedness that may be a regional rather than a national sentiment.

Finally, the emotional attitudes and relationships of sexually liberal people require further investigation. These may be the product of (1) emotional deprivation from their parents, (2) emotional realism in correctly gauging what their relationships really were and are, or (3) emotional self-actualization by being in closer touch with and desiring to expand their emotional contacts. All three may well be present in partial form. The correlation with avowed favorable feelings toward their present life situation, interest in both emotional and sexual relationships through the Sexual Freedom League (despite the fact the SFL members characterized only casual interest as a sufficient reason for a sexual relationship), and emotional relations with friends, seems to indicate that SFL members wish to integrate sexual contacts into their overall emotional and social lives.

Sexual freedom and liberality may well be a healthy and positive reaction to the alienation that is so prevalent in modern society rather than the jaded and depersonalizing wife swapping it is thought to be in some quarters. While a study of SFL members does not allow the application of authoritative generalizations to all sexually liberal people, the indications from this preliminary work warrant further study and analysis.

References

Adams, C. R. 1963. An Informal Preliminary Report of Some Factors Relating to Sexual Responsiveness in Certain College Wives. In *Sexual Behavior and Personality Characteristics*, ed. M. F. DeMartino. New York: Citadel Press.

Bartell, G. D. 1970. Group Sex among the Mid-Americans. *J. Sex Res.* 6, no. 2, pp. 113–30. [In this book, pp. 185–201.]

———. 1971. *Group Sex*. New York: Peter H. Wyden.

Bell, R. R. 1966. *Premarital Sex in a Changing Society*. Englewood Cliffs: Prentice-Hall.

Blank, L., and Roth, C. 1966. Voyeurism and Exhibitionism. *Proceedings of the 1966 American Psychological Association.*

Brecher, E. M. 1969. *The Sex Researchers*. Boston: Little, Brown.

Brecher, R., and Brecher, E. M. 1966. *An Analysis of Human Sexual Response*. New York: New American Library.

Brown, D. G. 1966. Female Orgasm and Sexual Inadequacy. In *An Analysis of Human Sexual Response*, ed. R. Brecher and E. M. Brecher. New York: New American Library.

Burgess, E. W., and Wallin, P. 1953. *Engagement and Marriage*. New York: Lippincott.

Butcher, J. N. 1969. *MMPI: Research Developments and Clinical Applications*. New York: McGraw-Hill.

Cowden, J. E., and Pacht, A. R. 1969. The Sex Inventory as a Classification Instrument for Sex Offenders. *J. Clin. Psychol.* 25, no. 1, pp. 53–57.

Cutter, F. 1959. Psychological Changes in Sexual Psychopaths. *Psychol. Newsletter* 10: 322–29.

Davis, K. E. 1970. Sex on the Campus: Is There a Revolution? *Med. Aspects Human Sex.*, Winter.

DeMartino, M. F. 1963a. Dominance-Feeling, Security-Insecurity, and Sexuality in Women. In *Sexual Behavior and Personality Characteristics*, ed. M. F. DeMartino. New York: Citadel Press.

————. 1963b. *Sexual Behavior and Personality Characteristics*. New York: Citadel Press.

Fisher, S., and Osofsky, H. 1967. Sexual Responsiveness in Women. *Arch. Gen. Psychiat.* 17: 214–26.

Galbraith, G. G., Kaplan, B. E., Higgins, J. D., and Tuton, K. 1968. Subscale Intercorrelations of the Sex Inventory: Males and Females. *J. Clin. Psychol.* 24, no. 4, pp. 451–53.

Gebhard, P. 1966. The Sexual Renaissance. *J. Soc. Iss.* 22, no. 2, pp. 88–95.

Gilmartin, B. G. 1964. Relationship of Traits Measured by the California Personality Inventory to Premarital Sexual Standards and Behaviors. Master's thesis, University of Utah.

Hartman, B. 1967. Comparison of Selected MMPI Profiles of Sexual Deviates with Sociopaths without Sexual Deviation. *Psychol. Repts.* 20: 234.

Hartman, W. E., Fithian, M., and Johnson, D. 1970. *Nudist Society*. New York: Crown.

Kinsey, A. C., Pomeroy, W. B., and Martin, C. E. 1948. *Sexual Behavior in the Human Male*. Philadelphia: W. B. Saunders.

————, and Gebhard, P. H. 1953. *Sexual Behavior in the Human Female*. Philadelphia: W. B. Saunders.

Kirkendall, L. A., and Libby, R. W. 1962. Interpersonal Relationships— Crux of the Sexual Renaissance. *J. Soc. Iss.* 22: 45–59.

Lanyon, R. I. 1968. *A Handbook of MMPI Group Profiles*. Minneapolis: University of Minnesota Press.

Lipkin, M., and Carns, D. E. 1971. Poll of Mental Health Professions. *University of Chicago, Division of the Biological Sciences, and the Pritzker School of Medicine Reports.* 20 (Winter).

Marsh, J. T., Hilliard, J., and Liechti, R. 1955. A Sexual Deviation Scale for the MMPI. *J. Consult. Psychol.* 19: 55–59.

Maslow, A. H. 1942. Self Esteem (Dominance-Feeling) and Sexuality in Women. *J. Soc. Psychol.* 16: 259–94.

Miller, H., and Wilson, W. R. 1968. Relation of Sexual Behaviors, Values, and Conflicts to Avowed Happiness and Personal Adjustment. *Psychol. Repts.* 23: 1075–86.

Mowrer, O. H. 1960. *Learning Theory and the Symbolic Process*. New York: Wiley.

————. 1961. *The Crisis in Psychiatry and Religion*. New York: Van Nostrand.

————. 1967. A Revolution in Integrity. *Voices*. 3, no. 1, pp. 26–33.

Neubeck, G., and Schletzer, V. 1962. A Study of Extra-Marital Relationships. *Marriage Fam. Liv.* 24: 279–81.

O'Neill, G. C., and O'Neill, N. 1970. Patterns in Group Sexual Activity. *J. Sex. Res.* 6, no. 2, pp. 101–12.

President's Commission on Obscenity and Pornography. 1970. *The Report of the Commission on Obscenity and Pornography*. New York: Bantam.

Reiss, I. L. 1965. Social Class and Premarital Sexual Permissiveness: A Re-examination. *Amer. Soc. Rev.* 30: 747–56.

———. 1967. *The Social Context of Premarital Sexual Permissiveness.* New York: Holt, Rinehart, & Winston.

———. 1968. America's Sex Standards, How and Why They are Changing. *Trans-Action.* 5: 26–32.

Rokeach, M. 1960. *The Open and Closed Mind.* New York: Basic Books.

Shope, D. F. 1967. A Comparison of Selected College Females on Sexual Responsiveness and Non-Responsiveness. *Diss. Abstracts.* 27: 3734–35.

Shope, D. F., and Broderick, C. B. 1967. Level of Sexual Experience and Predicted Adjustment in Marriage. *J. Marriage Fam.* 29: 424–27.

Smith, J. R., and Smith, L. G. 1970. Co-Marital Sex and the Sexual Freedom Movement. *J. Sex Res.* 6, no. 2, pp. 131–42. [In this book, pp. 202–13.]

Snider, J. G., and Osgood, C. E. 1969. *Semantic Differential Technique.* Chicago: Aldine.

Stratton, J. R., and Spitzen, S. P. 1967. Sexual Permissiveness and Self-Evaluation: A Question of Substance and a Question of Method. *J. Marriage Fam.* 29: 434–46.

Swensen, C. H., Jr. 1962. Sexual Behavior and Psychopathology: A Test of Mowrer's Hypothesis. *J. Clin. Psychol.* 18: 406–9.

———. 1973. Sexual Behavior and Psychopathology: A Study of College Men. *J. Clin. Psychol.* 19: 403–4.

Teevan, J. J., Jr. 1968. Changing Reference Groups and Premarital Sexual Behavior. Ph.D. diss. Indiana University.

Terman, L. M. 1938. *Psychological Factors in Marital Happiness.* New York: McGraw-Hill.

Thorne, F. C. 1966. The Sex Inventory. *J. Clin. Psychol.* 22: 367–74.

Wilson, W. R. 1965. Relation of Sexual Behaviors, Values, and Conflicts to Avowed Happiness. *Psychol. Repts.* 17: 371–78.

Yamahiro, R. S., and Griffith, R. M. 1960. Validity of Two Indices of Sexual Deviancy. *J. Clin. Psychol.* 16: 20–24.

Zetterberg, H. L. 1969. *On Sexual Life in Sweden.* As cited in "The New Contraceptive Society," *Look*, February 4.

An Exploratory Study of Spouse Swapping

Charles A. Varni

This paper reports on my exploratory attempt to provide, through firsthand experience, both a descriptive and analytic account of a type of interaction known as swinging. The term "swinging," as it is utilized in this paper, refers to married couples exchanging spouses for the expressed purpose of sexual interaction, most usually intercourse. The acquisition of firsthand knowledge of the swinging world—as it is experienced and defined by its members in ongoing social contexts—is facilitated by the utilization of a form and degree of participant observation.[1] The methodology of participant observation is grounded in the theoretical perspectives of symbolic interactionism and phenomenology.

[1] As a participant observer, I did not observe persons swinging (i.e., actually engaged in sexual activity), but rather observed their reports of the behavioral acts and subjective meanings of swinging. In this paper, I am primarily reporting on swingers' reports of what they do and feel rather than on the existential interactive situation (that is, here and now, I and thou) which existed in our face-to-face meetings.

Reprinted by permission of the publisher, Sage Publications, Inc., from *Pacific Soc. Rev.* 15, no. 4; Richard H. Ogles, Bernard C. Kirby, and Lois B. DeFleur made helpful comments on earlier drafts of this paper. Jane L. Varni was an invaluable fellow researcher.

Research Methods

In order to gain entrance into the world of swinging, my wife and I presented ourselves as a couple favorably disposed to the idea of swinging, who wanted to meet with swingers to get a better idea of what it was all about. To make contact with swingers (that is, to generate a population), I placed advertisements in a local "underground" newspaper, which is one method used by swingers to meet one another. The first ad read, "Young sociologist and wife desire to learn about swinging. Ph. 282——," and the second, "Couple, attractive, 26 and 25, who have not yet swung, desire to meet swinging couple. P.O. Box ——." There was little difference in the type or amount of response (minus phone calls from nonswingers) to the two advertisements. We met face to face with sixteen swinging married couples, usually in their homes. All were white and lower-middle to upper-middle class. Their ages ranged from nineteen to sixty with the majority being less than thirty-three years old. Length of marriage ranged from three months to thirty years, with the mode falling between two and six years. Although the frequency varied, almost all couples reported swinging no more than twice a month on the average. All but three of the couples had children, and all lived in the San Diego metropolitan area. I did not divulge my researcher role to any of the couples.

The problem of insuring validity is realized most fully in the contact between researcher and subject, by which method data are gathered. In this study, the contact consisted of face-to-face interaction with swinging couples, in which my wife and I presented ourselves as novice swingers who were anxious to learn more about swinging, though not necessarily experientially. Knowledge of the form and content of these interactive situations is indispensable when judging the validity of the method. Rather than deal with the unexplicated, taken-for-granted assumptions underlying most interactive situations between persons from the same culture, I will list the most relevant aspects.

First, there was an assumed mutual interest in swinging. I assumed this of the responding couple simply because they responded to the advertisement, and the swinging couple assumed it of me because I had placed it. Couples further assumed my interest to be personal; that is, my wife and I represented potential swinging partners. Second, there was an assumed dichotomy of knowledge about swinging in which my wife and I were the receivers of information and the other couple were the givers. This "student-teacher" relationship characterized all the interactive situations. Third, I strove to effect a feeling of mutual trust, in which the couple would feel comfortable being open and honest about their feelings and attitudes. To facilitate this mutual trust, I utilized two complementary methods. First, I felt that I was open and honest about my own feelings and attitudes, which, besides providing a role model when necessary, helped create the impression that I was a person who could be trusted. Second, I was generally accepting and nonjudgmental of the person's actions, beliefs, and attitudes. My role was that of the interested and understanding listener. I had no "hidden" questionnaire and tried to facilitate the couple expressing their thoughts on those aspects of swinging they felt to be most important or relevant. The recording of data took place immediately upon leaving a meeting. My wife and I dictated everything we could recall that was said or expressed. I later transcribed, organized, and added to these recordings.

With regard to the degree of participant observation, neither my wife nor I engaged in any sexual interaction with any of the couples we met. We maintained our roles as novice swingers throughout the study. I cannot, therefore, characterize my relationship with the swingers as intimate. However, given the limits of my researcher/swinger role and the interactive situation, I feel a sufficient amount of intimacy was attained. Time spent with each couple averaged about three hours.

Findings

There are two essential conditions which together define what it is to be a swinger. First, the married individuals engage in extramarital sex with full knowledge and consent of one another. There is no ignorance, lying, or cheating involved. Second, the couple engages in extramarital sex together—both temporally and, in degrees, spatially. The fact that they do it together is emphasized by all swingers and constitutes a necessary condition of swinging. Because swingers engage in extramarital sex with the full knowledge of their spouses and because they do it together, they do not think of themselves as adulterers. In contrast, they see themselves as having transcended the perceived pettiness, hypocrisy, immaturity, and dishonesty of adulterous affairs engaged in by the majority of married couples. This definition of what it is to be a swinger, while providing legitimation and reinforcement to a swinging life-style, at the same time disavows any deviant label and, with some success, turns the deviant label around and applies it to those non-swinging marrieds who engage in extramarital sex.

Becoming a Swinger

Although each individual uniquely experienced his or her learning of the swinger role, there are aspects of the experience common to most swingers. To call this learning experience a "process" implies a "from-to" form of change; that is, the person moves *from* a thing which he "gives up" *to* a thing which he "takes on." The "things" are social realities. A social reality consists of a collection of social meanings. A social meaning can be characterized as the (usually moral) attribute(s) persons impute or intend to an object (that is, a physical, behavioral, or symbolic "thing") in their social world. It is evident that social meanings are infused with both normative ("ought to") and ontological ("the way things are") judgments. This moral aspect of social meanings functions as a mechanism of social control since behavior which departs from that prescribed by the social meanings may be thought of as immoral and, therefore, deviant. It follows that in "giving up" any social reality, an individual must "deal with" the moral (i.e., social control) aspects of the social reality he is moving away from. Becoming a swinger involves a change in the social meanings of sexual behavior and swingers must "deal with" the "old" social meanings of sex, which is a problem for both men and women.

The meaning of sex which swingers moved away from was that commonly held by many persons in our culture—namely, the double standard. The double standard of sexual behavior means that sex without love and extramarital sex are wrong for a woman while sex without love and, to a lesser degree, extramarital sex are all right for a man. The swingers I met had generally subscribed to this meaning of sexual behavior. For example, eleven of the sixteen women reported being virgins when they met their husbands, and most stated they had had "puritanical" attitudes toward sex. The men reported having some sexual experience prior to marriage, and a few reported extramarital experiences.

The problem for the man in dealing with the proscriptions against swinging was that of accepting the idea of sexual freedom (within the confines of a swinging relationship) for the wife. The usual response of men who want sex outside marriage is to engage in extramarital sex, not in swinging. Why do men reject the double standard and accept the idea of swinging? There are two typical reasons which are given by two different types of men. The first type I call the *user*. This type uses his wife to gain entrance into swinging; he does not appear to be very concerned with her feelings or desires; he has little ego involvement with her, and his rejection of the double standard is on "Machiavellian" grounds. The second type I call the *encourager*. This type rejects the double standard on more idealistic grounds, mainly egalitarianism. He feels swinging will be a positive experience for both him and his wife. The togetherness and open and honest expression of sexuality he perceives as part of swinging appeal to him. I characterized five men as users and eleven as encouragers.

The man, in all but one case, initially brought up the idea of swinging, which was invariably met with a negative reaction by the wife. The most typical reaction of the woman was that something was wrong with her or the marriage, coupled with a strong sense of revulsion for the whole idea. At this point, the husband began a "convincing [or coercing] process" which usually sought to allay the wife's fears.

The main problem for women in dealing with the proscriptions against swinging was their confounding of sex and love. Most women had great difficulty in separating the two, believing it was nearly impossible to have one without the other. Coupled with this problem was the fear that perhaps their husbands no longer cared for them and that their desire to swing marked the beginning of the end. Few women allowed themselves to entertain positive thoughts about swinging, although a few reported curiosity at what it would be like to be with another man. Despite the husbands' convincing process, every woman approached her first swinging experience with varying degrees of anxiety, apprehension, and misgiving. The men were also anxious and apprehensive, but less so than the women. With the exception of two, every woman stated she agreed to try swinging once to please her husband.

The main effect of the first swinging experience was to greatly reduce the level of anxiety, especially the woman's, and thus provide a climate in which the experience could be evaluated in a more "objective" light. If anything, the experience was anticlimatic in relation to the woman's expectations. The typical response was that it was not such a big deal after all. Many women made guardedly positive remarks such as, "Well, it wasn't as bad as I thought it would be," or "I might try it again."

The factors which appeared to be important in a woman's becoming favorably disposed to swinging are (1) her perception of her marriage relationship and (2) her own subjective experience. If she feels that the relationship has not been damaged, she is relieved, and if it looks as if the relationship may have been improved, she is pleased. If her subjective experience was not negative, she is relieved, and if at all positive, she is pleased. Most women appear to attach more importance to the first factor, especially in the early stages of becoming a swinger. Later, when assured that the relationship is not threatened, her subjective experiences take on greater priority. The same two factors determine the man's response, but the importance attached to either factor is more favorable. For some men (the users), their own subjective experience may be more important than any possible effects on the relationship, and for others (the encouragers), just the opposite may be true. However, all men have a vested interest in their wives' obtaining a positive experience, since their continued swinging is dependent on her participation.

The new meaning which sex assumes for many persons after their first swinging experience may be accounted for by a "meaning void." Novice swingers who approach the swinging situation with definite expectations (even if they are unspecified) and have these expectations radically unfulfilled will be thrust into a situation which is existentially experienced as being meaningless or having ambiguous meaning. New meanings are "created" to fill this void. These meanings are developed by the individual as he interprets his experience with relation to earlier expectations and to those meanings which are supplied by other swinging members.

If nothing traumatic happens in the first swinging experience, the couple is likely to try it again. The second encounter (other things being equal) is usually more enjoyable, since the couple has a more realistic expectation of what will take place and, with lower levels of anxiety, is more able to relax and enjoy themselves. This second experience, if it proves to be nonthreatening—and especially if it is enjoyable —is usually the clincher in that it validates the nonuniqueness of the first experience.

If a couple decides that they will not continue swinging, swingers report, it is almost always because of unmanageable jealousy on the part of either the husband or the wife, sometimes both. Swingers agreed that the prerequisites for successful swinging were that (1) the couple have a viable relationship based on love; (2) each person have no serious hangups; and (3) there be no jealousy.

Forms of Swinging

On the basis of group-size preference, swingers can be divided into two groups, those who prefer to swing with only one couple at a time (whom I call one-couple swingers) and those who prefer to swing in party situations involving three or more couples (whom I call party swingers). Of the couples I met, seven were strictly one-couple swing-ers and never attended parties. The other nine couples were party swingers, although they also swung in one-couple situations.

A sensitizing typology of party swingers based on stability of membership in the swinging group yields (1) the very stable group which is characterized as close-knit, cohesive, with little membership turnover; (2) the fairly stable group which is a relatively large amalga-mation of swingers who are known to one another, are loosely orga-nized (sometimes in cliques), and have a somewhat fluid membership; and (3) the unstable group which consists of couples who come to-gether only for one night.

The fairly stable group was, by far, the most commonly encoun-tered. The amalgamation of anywhere from ten to thirty couples who make up the group is loosely organized, with members being directly or indirectly known to each other. When a couple has a party, they will invite from this "pool" a number of couples. Also invited may be some "new" (not necessarily novice) couples acquainted with the host or a guest. Thus, a party may consist of couples who are well ac-quainted, somewhat acquainted, and not acquainted at all.

The party situation itself resembles any other weekend evening social gathering in a private home, with couples either sitting in one room or freely circulating. Most persons have drinks, and the conver-sation revolves around common areas of discourse such as jobs, chil-dren, what the individuals have been doing since they last saw each other, and generally superficial topics. The host will many times help facilitate the transition from social to sexual behavior by calling atten-tion to the fact that it is time to get started or by dimming the lights. Other transition devices, known as "ice-breakers," are sometimes used, such as sexually oriented parlor games or erotic movies. The role of the ice-breaker is often crucial, and a few swingers reported they had sat around for hours at parties where everyone was afraid to make the first move.

The selection process whereby individuals make their temporary alliances is similar to that of a large group of people making dates with one another. As is common in our culture, the man is usually the overt aggressor in the partner-selection process. It is his responsibility to make first contact. The woman is not passive in this dating game, and through the use of eye contact, smiles, and other conversations of ges-ture, she communicates her availability or attraction. The man's invita-tion to swing is usually preceded by some light, "get to know one another" conversation. The man's invitation to swing is significant in that he has presented himself to the woman and now asks her judgment of him as someone she would like to have intercourse with. Even though swingers have greatly "normalized" sexual behavior, this invitation to sex is still more significant and involves substantially more aspects of the man's self than does an invitation to coffee. To be rejected as a sexual partner could be damaging to a person's self-concept or, in the least, could result in hurt feelings. Swingers seek to minimize these risks in the following manner: When a woman rejects an invitation, the rejection is made in such a way that no negative valuation of the man is evident. The woman usually places the cause of rejection on herself by utilizing excuses such as "I don't really feel like it right now," "I'm a little tired at the moment," or "I just finished with another man." Taken at face value, the meaning of the rejection is that the man approached at the wrong moment and might be successful at another time, but in actuality, it constitutes a rejection of him as sexual partner. The meaning of the rejection is shared by the individuals and is verified by the fact that rarely will a man make a second attempt to swing with the woman unless she has given him obvious reason to ask again.

The general acceptance of the giving and receiving of rejection among swingers is facilitated by two commonly held norms. First, no one should do anything he does not want to. This norm supports the woman in her rejection of the man. Second, no one should be coerced to do anything he does not want to. This norm exerts pressure on the man who may be so inclined. Also, acceptance of rejection by the man is made easier because (1) his sense of self is not overtly threatened by the form of the rejection, and (2) he can always find a woman who will swing with him.

The spatial distribution of sexual behavior varies with the needs of those at the party. Sometimes behavior will be highly visible, with all couples in the same room, and other times each couple will go to a private room and shut the door. Many times, especially at parties attended by social nudists, everyone may remain nude, although sexual behavior is not necessarily visible.

Party swingers perceived certain advantages to this type of swinging. First, at a party, there were a relatively large number of potential partners to choose from, a distinct advantage over one-couple situations. Second, sociability and the chance to meet different types of persons was emphasized by party swingers. Third, two couples said they enjoyed the greater impersonality afforded by the party situation, as they had previously experienced trouble and uncomfortableness in extricating themselves from one-couple situations in which they did not want to swing and felt this was easier to do in the party situation. Fourth, sexual stimulation and enjoyment, for both men and women, was felt to be another advantage. Both sexes reported multiple orgasms. Some women cited their advantage over men of being able to continue intercourse while men had to wait for another erection. Similarly, half the women said they greatly enjoyed the feeling of being desired and wanted by a number of men.

The other basic form of swinging is the one-couple type. One-couple swingers do not attend parties, and this fact distinguishes them from swingers who swing in both party and one-couple situations. One-couple swingers usually seek an interpersonal rapport with their swinging partners and, either through experience or intuition, have come to the conclusion that a party situation is not conducive to fulfilling this desire. The party is seen as an impersonal experience. One-couple swingers want more of a friendship-type relationship with their swinging partners. They want to engage in nonswinging social and recreational activities with them.

One-couple swingers differ on the spatial distribution of their sexual behavior; three couples preferred to be in the same room, three preferred to be in separate rooms, and one had no preference. Same-room swingers like the feeling of doing it together and enjoy watching one another. Different-room swingers emphasized the individuality of the experience and were against same-room swinging. When these two types met, the same room swingers deferred to the wishes of different room swingers.

Methods of Meeting and Selection Factors

There are three methods used by swingers to make contact with one another. A common one is advertising in a local newspaper, usually of the underground variety. The ads are worded similarly to the ones I placed and are accompanied by a post-office box number. In responding to an ad, swingers will usually give a brief description of themselves, any special sexual desires, and their phone numbers, or they may ask the originating couple to respond in a like manner. In either case, a phone call is usually placed. The first meeting between two swinging couples is almost always defined as being strictly social in nature, and there is no expectation to swing on the part of either couple. The role of the purely social meeting is to allow the couples to meet face to face so that they may evaluate one another as potential swinging partners.

There are many reasons, some being more universalistic than others, why couples reject one another as swinging partners. This rejection may take place any time during the meeting process described above. For example, most swingers will not cross racial lines. They will usually not swing with unmarried couples, reportedly from fear of contracting venereal disease. Interpersonal compatability, in various degrees, is desired by many swingers and, if it is felt to be lacking, will be cause for rejection. Also, differentials in age are important to "younger" swingers who will not usually swing with those defined as "too old," although the converse was not true for "older" swingers. All persons considered unclean about their bodies, and all "weirdos" will be rejected.

The closest thing to a universalistic factor of acceptance among swingers is physical attractiveness. An attractive couple, on their appearance alone, would be accepted as swinging partners by most couples. However, an unattractive couple would not experience universal rejection, for unattractiveness is much more particularistic in nature—one man's weed being another man's flower. Attractiveness constitutes a sufficient but not necessary condition of acceptance among swingers.

It appears that the selection factors which operate in swinging to bring people together and drive them apart are little, if any, different from those operating in the larger culture. Some swingers are highly selective, swinging with as few as one of every ten couples they meet; others, with less stringent requirements, swing with perhaps as many as eight of ten couples they meet.

A second method used by swingers to meet one another is personal referral. A couple may feel that their swinging partners would like another couple they know and thus ask permission to give the other couple their partners' number so that a meeting can be arranged. These "matchmaker"-arranged meetings will usually not have the strictly social expectation, since there is an assumption that the couples will be compatible.

A third method consists of direct contact between swingers. This contact rarely takes place in everyday life but rather in known spots where swingers congregate, called "swing clubs," or at parties. The swing club appears to function for swingers in many of the same ways gay bars do for homosexuals. It provides a place to socialize and meet with other swingers. Very importantly, it provides a mode of entrance for would-be swingers.

Effects of Swinging

The most often reported effect of swinging (by eight couples) was an increased feeling of warmth, closeness, and love between the husband and wife. This feeling was most intense when they returned to each others' arms after swinging with another couple(s). It was as if the swinging experience was proof and validation of their love. They could ignore one of the traditional and (supposedly) essential boundary determining criteria of marriage—that of sexual fidelity—and find greater strength, security, and trust in their relationship. Another reported positive effect was a more fully developed knowledge and competence in sexual technique. Three couples reported a more enriched and active social life as a benefit of swinging. A number of couples felt that swinging had facilitated their becoming more open and honest with one another in all areas of their relationship. Four women reported not being completely happy with swinging. Two of the women had originally agreed to swing on the condition that their husbands no longer "sneak around" behind their backs. These women felt more in control and less threatened by the swinging situation. The other two said they had never really enjoyed swinging but continued in order to please their husbands.

Swingers engage in a wide variety of sexual behavior, most of it heterosexual, some of it homosexual. Heterosexual behavior consists mainly of varied positions of vaginal intercourse and oral-genital sex. Many swingers were introduced to the varied forms of sexual activity in swinging, especially those of an oral-genital nature. Homosexual behavior, consisting mainly of cunnilingus between two women, is not uncommon. Three of the women had had homosexual experiences in swinging situations. Homosexuality involving men is rare.

Becoming a swinger is most always accompanied by a change in the meaning of sex. First of all, the meaning of what is appropriate sexual behavior, in what situation and with whom, is changed. It is more broadly defined to accommodate a wider range and choice of behavior. For example, the woman who, in the presence of her husband, engaged in mutual oral-genital sex with a relative stranger whom she does not love appears to have imbued sexual behavior with a different meaning. The meaning of the idea of exclusivity of sex between the marriage partners as symbolizing devotion, trust, security, or love for one another has been transformed to just the opposite; that is, non-exclusivity comes to symbolize many of these same things. The meaning of sexual behavior as a thing in itself is also transformed from one of relative nonacceptance to one of relative acceptance. Sexual behavior loses its mystery, secretive, "something-done-in-the-dark" aspect, and takes on more the character of a taken-for-granted, normal activity.

Typology of Swingers

The term swinging encompasses a wide range of behavior. The following typology was developed with the idea of sensitizing persons to the varied forms of behavior included within this range. Its sole function is to communicate a "feeling" and appreciation for the world of swingers. Although presented in a crudely continuous fashion, it in no way purports to be ideal, pure, or exhaustive.

The major criterion around which the typology is organized is the degree of emotional involvement a swinger desires with his or her partner(s). Generally speaking, movement along the continuum from "hard-core" to "communal" involves going from unstable to very stable group or couple affiliation, from user to encourager husbands, and from having nonswinging to swinging friends. Also, the meaning of sexual behavior (and thus, by definition, of swinging) differs among the types. It should be pointed out that this is a typology of individuals, not of couples (although at times I treat it as if it were). While it is usually the case that both members of the dyad come to have the "same" desires with regard to swinging relationships, it is not always so.

Hard-core swingers are ones who want no emotional involvement with their partners and, with little selectivity, swing with as many couples as possible. They are felt to be cold, unfeeling, and deviant by other types of swingers. Often, the woman is coerced into swinging. Hard-core swingers participate in unstable party and one-couple situations.

Egotistical swingers seek little emotional involvement with their partners and are usually fairly selective. They want purely sexual/ sensual experiences and seek to gratify their own sexual needs and desires, which may involve feeling attractive, virile, sexy, and desired by other persons. Swinging is viewed as a separate and distinct part of their lives, and they have very few, if any, social relationships, much less friendships, with their swinging partners. They enjoy both party and one-couple situations. The husband uses his wife, and she may never become a devoted swinger.

Recreational swingers emphasize the social aspects associated with swinging. They are members of fairly stable groups, enjoy both party and one-couple situations, and engage in nonswinging activities with one another. Swinging is viewed as an entertaining, social, "get-your-kicks" hedonistic activity in which significant emotional involvement with the partner is neither needed nor desired. Recreational swingers have both swinging and nonswinging friends. Wives are both partially used and encouraged by their husbands and usually become dedicated swingers.

Interpersonal swingers desire and emphasize close emotional relationships with their partners. They are seeking intimate and viable friendships with couples with whom they can share themselves emotionally (which includes sex) in an open and honest manner. Sex comes to mean a complete and fulfilling relationship and life experience. Usually, the husband has encouraged his wife, and they both see swinging as having a more or less "natural" congruence with their total life style. They are likely to be quite selective in whom they swing with, prefer one-couple situations almost exclusively, and many of their friends will be swingers.

Communal swingers are very similar to interpersonal, except that they advocate some form of group marriage, an idea rejected by almost all other swingers.

Of the thirty-two swingers I met, none were hard-core, five were egotistical, eleven were recreational, eleven were interpersonal, one was communal, and four could not be categorized.

Concluding Remarks

For me, the study of swinging—as a thing in itself—is both interesting and worthwhile. It is hoped that this somewhat ethnographic account of a "new" social phenomenon will provide unfamiliar persons with at least a provisional understanding, both behavioral and motivational, of swinging.

It is also my belief that swinging is an important (that is, strategic) instance of a much broader and historically recurrent class of social behavior—the eternal struggle between forces of change and stability, between the individual and society, and between persons and social structure. In other words, swinging is an instance of social change and exhibits important features of this phenomenon, especially with regard to power differentials in the ability to redefine social reality. Certainly, for most persons, the process of becoming a swinger involves a somewhat agonizing redefinition of social reality. Swingers are examples of persons "breaking through" the traditional, taken for granted way of doing things and creating what for them are new ways of being.

Our understanding of this process of social change, both as sociologists and as human beings, would appear to be most important in providing impetus to our achievement of a basic humanistic goal, that of broadening the range of viable alternatives in American society. The further study of swinging and like phenomena will help provide this understanding.

Dropouts from Swinging: The Marriage Counselor as Informant

Duane Denfeld

Introduction

The literature on swinging, or mate swapping (an agreement between husband and wife to have sexual relations with other people usually at the same time) has portrayed this behavior as supportive of the marriage. Bartell (1971) reports that swinging appears to contribute positively to the marital adjustment of a substantial number of his three hundred fifty Chicago-area respondents. The Smiths (1970) came to a similar conclusion in their study of over five hundred California swingers. A review of all the serious literature on swinging noted that every study done thus far had found positive contributions in swinging (Denfeld and Gordon 1970).

Another research finding of swinging is the conservative, traditional, middle-class background of swingers. Swingers tend to be conservative and very "straight"; they do not fit the stereotypical image of the deviant. Swingers tend to be normal, conventional, and respectable citizens of the community. Although swingers as young as eighteen and as old as seventy have been discovered, the most common age range is twenty-five to thirty-five. Swingers are not a rebellious youth who have substituted a new value system but rather people who grew up in the 1940s and 1950s; they were exposed to the values of the time, which included the importance of sexual fidelity and guilt following sexual infidelity. However, in spite of these values, swingers report little difficulty overcoming or replacing values concerned with marital fidelity.

These two findings surprise many social scientists. It amazes many people that the consensual exchange of partners can be accomplished without guilt and without threatening the marriage. Swingers respond that they have discovered more honest and genuine values. Swingers, it is reported, have adopted rules and developed strategies that insure the protection of their marriages and that, in addition, serve to give new life and variety to their marital relationship. For example, swingers view the sexual relationship of the marriage as one of love and emotion; the consensual extramarital relationship is physical. To insure paternity, swingers drop out of swinging if the wife desires to get pregnant to assure that the husband is the child's father. Jealousy is avoided by giving the marriage paramount loyalty and by avoiding emotional attachments with others.

Among swinging couples there is an attempt to replace the old sexual values by new ones. They recognize that most couples violate the rule of marital fidelity, which results in lying and cheating. Swingers argue that lying and cheating, as opposed to actual sexual contact, are the damaging aspects of extramarital sex. They contend that if these aspects are removed, nonemotional extramarital sex can be beneficial to the marriage because it can provide excitement and variety without threatening the marital relationship.

Even the best-planned social systems are often likely to work out differently than foreseen, and frequently, failure is the end product. However, the failures in swinging, or swinging dropouts, have not found their way into our research because of the research designs. Studies of swinging have involved "snowball" samples which are limited to active swingers; the unsuccessful have dropped out. There has not been a study of swingers using a probability sample which would include past, present, and future swingers. For this reason, this study was an attempt to locate swinging dropouts and learn about their problems and reasons for dropping out.

Method

Questionnaires were mailed to 2,147 marriage counselors. They were asked to discuss the histories of clients who had dropped out of swinging. All the marriage counselors whose names were listed in the directories of the American Association of Marriage and Family Counselors and the California Association of Marriage and Family Counselors were sent questionnaires.

Of the total 2,147 questionnaires mailed, 966 (45% were returned. A response this small does not allow us to generalize to all counselors in these two associations. It is possible, however, to use the results to gain insight into the problems that caused swingers to drop out. It must also be pointed out that the counselors' interpretation may influence the delineation of problems.

Telephone follow-up calls were made to fifty nonrespondents. These calls were to determine if the answers of the nonrespondents were different than the respondents. Based upon these telephone calls it can be assumed that the returned questionnaires are representative of all counselors' experiences.

Findings

Table 1 indicates that 49%, or 473, of the marriage counselors had counseled at least one swinging dropout couple. However, the actual percentage of counselors who have counseled at least one dropout couple is 55% when the retired, inactive, or specialized counselors are excluded. Specialized counselors are those without an opportunity to counsel swinging dropouts (for example, a counselor in California who dealt primarily with disturbed children).

A total of 1,175 swinging dropout couples were seen by the counselors. The median number of dropout couples treated by the counselors was 2.5. This study did not produce any evidence which would indicate why one counselor and not another had treated swinging dropouts. It was not uncommon for counselors to report, "In my 22 years of practice I have never treated a swinging couple." There were counselors in cities as large as San Francisco or Los Angeles who had never counseled a couple who reported swinging activities, while some

Table 1—Marriage counselors and counseling of dropouts

Marriage Counseling Experience	No. Marriage Counselors
Never counseled a dropout couple	368
Had counseled at least one dropout couple	473
Retired, inactive, or in specialized practice	125
	966

counselors in smaller cities had counseled dropouts. The only variable that seemed related to a counselor seeing a dropout couple was whether the counselor was engaged in pastoral counseling. Pastoral counselors had rarely treated exswingers, and they believed it was because exswingers were fearful of censure or criticism on religious grounds.

In view of the fact that all the dropout couples reported problems it is possible to infer that the rules and strategies of swinging do not work for all couples. The findings reported here allow us to delineate the problems that were encountered. To do so does not refute the notion that the "family that swings together clings together." The problems that some couples experience may have serious consequences in terms of marital relations and psychological adjustment. One can only make guesses as to the possible number of swinging dropouts. Clearly, the 966 counselors who returned questionnaires represent a small part of the total counseling practices; there are perhaps fifty to seventy-five times as many more counselors when one includes mental-health offices, psychiatrists, and general practitioners. All that can be said is that there may be as many as 75,000 dropouts in counseling (and many more not in counseling situation who might, will, or should be) out of an estimated swinging population of 714,000 (based upon an estimated swinging rate of 1.7% of the married couples in the total married population [Spanier and Cole 1972]).

The problems or reasons for dropping out are listed in order of frequency in table 2. The problems are not surprising; they are just what one might expect. Additional reasons cited included pregnancy, vene-

Table 2—Problems or reasons for dropping out of swinging

Problems	Number of Couples	Percentage
Jealousy	109	23%
Guilt	68	14
Threatening marriage	68	14
Development of emotional attachment with other partners	53	11
Boredom and loss of interest	49	11
Disappointment	33	7
Divorce or separation	29	7
Wife's inability to "take it"	29	7
Fear of discovery: community/children	15	3
Impotence of husband	14	3
	467	100%

real disease, feelings of being excluded, and difficulty in finding suitable couples. Jealousy and guilt were the most common problems. They were ranked by the counselors as the major reason for couples dropping out. A typical description was that "the husband (or wife) could not handle the jealousy rising out of his (or her) mate having sex with another person." Husbands reported more jealousy than wives. A number of husbands became quite concerned about their wives' popularity, their sexual performance (for example, endurance capabilities), or that their wives were having more fun than they were. When wives reported jealousy it was more likely related to fear of losing their mate. These findings suggest the influence of the double standard; the emphasis for the husband is on his pleasure and satisfaction as compared to his wife's pleasure and satisfaction, whereas the emphasis for the wife is on the maintenance of the marital unit.

Jealousy and guilt may also be part of the third most-cited problem, which is the threat to the marital bond. The problems listed are not without some overlap (i.e., boredom and disappointment may be two definitions of the same problem). Dropout couples report that swinging weakened rather than strengthened the marriage. Swinging can lead to other marital problems; fighting and hostilities became more frequent after swinging.

Some swingers attempt to protect against the development of emotional attachment by swinging only once with another couple and also by avoiding expressions of personal feelings such as "I care for you." In spite of these efforts, swinging couples have become emotionally attached to people with whom they swing. The emotional attachment to swinging partners in a number of cases led to divorce and sometimes to new marriages. For example, a counselor reported that "wife A and husband B got divorced and married eath other; the four thus felt they could no longer share sex mutually. Husband A resisted the divorce, but later he and wife B married each other. The husbands couldn't handle it any longer." In some cases, the new emotional attachment in the swinging relationship lasted a short period or led the swinger(s) to a marriage counselor. Lying and cheating, another violation of swinging rules, was also uncovered—clandestine meetings in violation of swingers' rules were reported. When these meetings were discovered, conflict or separation resulted. Swinging for these couples did not destroy the interest in extramarital affairs or the possibility of development of emotional attachment.

The next two reasons (boredom and loss of interest and disappointment) cited for dropping out can be described as a gap between fantasy and reality. Swinging for many couples was boring; it did not always provide the excitement that the couple had fantasized. For some other couples, swinging did not offer the anticipated benefits; for these couples, swinging was a disappointment. Complaints included: "did not live up to expectations as to improved relationships with spouse; did not meet emotional needs or social needs; strong dislike for other participating person." Other swinging dropouts said it became boring and uninteresting. The main reason cited for the gap between fantasy and reality was the absence of seduction and emotion necessitated by a swinging relationship.

The next two problems (divorce or separation and wife's inability to "take it") are similar in that very frequently one partner was more troubled or upset than the other partner. The wife was most likely the one to respond that she could not take it or threatened divorce. These findings question some additional beliefs concerning swinging. The first is that swinging emphasizes sexual equality (Denfeld and Gordon 1970) and that swinging greatly benefits the wives. Henshel (1973) has questioned the finding that swinging favors the "wives as much as, and in certain respects, more than their husbands." Henshel discovered in her Canadian swinging group that husbands initiated swinging activities 58.7% of the time. Wives were the initiators in only 12% of the cases. In the other cases, the decision was mutual. If wives are hesitant to swing and have less interest, we can expect more women to initiate the dropping out. Some investigators have argued, however, that women, once they "get their feet wet," enjoy swinging more than men. The findings here do not support that view; dropping out was initiated by the wives 54% of the time, by the husbands 34%, and mutually 12%.

The marriage counselors suggested that wives were considerably more troubled by swinging than husbands. Wives expressed such feelings as disgust or repulsion. Husbands were more likely to initiate dropping out not for reasons of distaste but rather that they were bothered by their wives' popularity or sexuality. Wives were forced into swinging as a promise or commitment to the marriage. Husbands were described as "children with new toys." One counselor reported a common finding among the counselors which is: "In all my cases (3) the men initiated the swinging and the women forced the termination."

The enthusiasm of the men was not matched by a similar feeling among the women. Swinging was a way for these men to have sexual variety, and they needed their wives to accomplish it. In such cases, the double standard and exploitation of women was very much a part of the arrangement. Wives were forced into swinging for their husbands' benefit. Swinging also demonstrated male dominance in terms of male impotence resulting from their contact with "aggressive women" and an inability to accomplish sexual intercourse.

Another problem experienced by swingers was the fear of discovery by the community or their children. Some counselors reported instances of swinging couples dropping out to satisfy neighbors who had discovered their swinging activities. The white-collar or professional backgrounds of swingers make discovery a threat to their business and social reputation. A number of counselors reported that couples dropped out because their children were beginning to question their activities. This was particularly true for couples with teenaged children. In cases where the children had discovered the swinging activity, family functioning was seriously disturbed. Because the parents had kept their swinging activities a secret from their children, discovery came as a shock to the children.

One hundred seventy couples, or 40% of the cases in which information was available, reported improvement in marital relationship. A number of these couples discovered the improved marital relationships to be temporary.

Current Swingers

Counselors were also asked to discuss clients who are presently engaged in swinging. Of the 620 counselors who responded to this question, 192 were counseling couples who were presently swinging. A comparison of the problems experienced by current swingers and dropouts was undertaken. The two lists were very similar, with jealousy, guilt, and threat to marriage the prime problems in both lists. The major difference between the two lists was the greater presence of "fears" in the current swingers' list of problems. Active swingers report fears of discovery by children and the community, of venereal disease, and of rejection. It, of course, is not surprising that current swingers should be more fearful of discovery than exswingers. Swinging dropouts would have already been discovered or had avoided detection and would not report these as fears. Fear of discovery appears to exceed the real danger, although a number of dropouts have been discovered by the community.

Since they were taking part in counseling, it is not surprising that contemporary swingers in this study reported problems. It is also important to note that all but twenty-five of the active swingers linked their problems to swinging. Difficulties with swinging brought many of the active swingers to the marriage counselor.

Conclusion

The findings of this study do not allow us to reject the optimistic view of swinging. They do, however, raise some questions about the degree of positive outcomes and also document some of the problems associated with the consensual exchange of marriage partners. The problems of swinging have received little attention because successful swingers were more likely to be included in the various studies. Another possible explanation for the very positive portrayal of swinging may be that many swinging researchers are in fact "swinging" researchers who, wittingly or unwittingly, play the role of advocate with a sometimes missionary zeal. The delineation of problems may add some balance to our understanding of swinging.

It is clear from the marriage counselors' reports that many couples left swinging psychologically damaged. Knowing this should give pause to the recommendation or implication that swinging will help a couple's marriage. The positive image presented may have actually encouraged couples to engage in swinging, and some of these couples may not be capable of coping with the emotional strains encountered in the course of involvement. Swinging is not always a safe way to revitalize a marriage. Many couples may be inadequately prepared for the consensual exchange of partners. And while others may participate in swinging with few, if any, major problems or serious conflicts, the findings presented here suggest the need for a critically balanced approach to the assessment of the viability of the swinging experience.

References

Bartell, G. D. 1971. *Group Sex.* New York: Peter H. Wyden.

Denfeld, D., and Gordon, M. 1970. The Sociology of Mate Swapping: Or the Family that Swings Together Clings Together. *J. Sex Res.* 6, no. 2, pp. 85–100. [In this book, pp. 68–83.]

Henshel, A-M. 1973. Swinging: A Study of Decision Making in Marriage. *Amer. J. Soc.* 78: 885–91.

Smith, J. R., and Smith, L. G. 1970. Co-Marital Sex and the Sexual Freedom Movement. *J. Sex Res.* 6, no. 2, pp. 131–42. [In this book, pp. 202–13.]

Spanier, G. B., and Cole, C. L. 1972. Mate Swapping: Participation, Knowledge, and Values in a Midwestern Community. Paper presented at the annual meeting of the Midwest Sociological Society, Kansas City, Mo.

Sexual Aspects of Multilateral Relations

Larry L. Constantine and Joan M. Constantine

Sex is not marriage. No responsible professional concerned with this field would fail to recognize this inequality. Yet there is a tendency, we have found, even for professionals to approach deviant social phenomena that may only *include* a sexual element as if they were entirely sexual in nature. In the area of our research—contemporary marriages involving three or more partners in the conjugal unit—the exaggeration of the sexual dimension is readily understandable. Communal child-rearing, cooperative economic structure, and joint residence are more or less acceptable, at least separately. And deep personal affection shared by several individuals may even be lauded. But if one combines these elements with open sexual expression of that affection, moral sensibilities, even among scientists and supporting professionals, are likely to be offended.

We have found multilateral marriage to be an exceptionally complex phenomenon. To the rich fabric of practical, sexual, psychological, and social threads that run through all marriages must be added the em-

Reprinted, by permission of the publisher, from *J. Sex Res.* 7, no. 3; we are most grateful for the extended assistance, encouragement, and critical feedback of Dr. Louis J. Gerstman, our consultant on measurements and statistics. Without his confidence in us and the concept that research competence is not measured by credentials, our use of psychometrics—indeed, the study itself—would, quite literally, not have been possible. For his assistance, he should, however, in no way be held responsible for our shortcomings in either design or analysis.

broidery of complexity that grows from the intense interaction and involvement of not just two marital partners but three, four, five, or more. Though our focus is on the sexual aspects of this matrix, the sexual pattern cannot be truly understood without regard to its larger context. For it is essential to recognize that this context is a marital one, and that we are dealing with sex in that framework, however exceptional multilateral marriage may be in our culture. Therefore, recognizing that to discuss the entire marital relationship is beyond the scope of this endeavor, we caution the reader to keep things in perspective.

Multilateral Marriage

We define a multilateral marriage operationally as a group in which each member considers himself married or committed in an essentially equivalent manner to at least two other members of the group. Some three-person relationships are multilateral marriages, though they are not group marriages according to the traditional definition.

The evidence is that the present experimentation is a discrete new phenomenon dating from the midsixties and the popularization of certain novels by Robert Rimmer (*Harrad Experiment*, *Yale Marratt*) and Robert Heinlein (*Stranger in a Strange Land*, *The Moon is a Harsh Mistress*). While interest and speculation are great, the Multilateral Relations Study Project started by us in 1969 is the only full-scale investigation at this time. Judging from our experience in trying to locate functioning groups, actual attempts at multilateral marriage are exceeded many fold by interest in it. (For example, more than five thousand respondents in a *Psychology Today* survey (Athanasiou, Shaver, and Tavris 1970) were interested in or were in favor of group marriage.) Following over two hundred distinct leads from organizations, family service professionals, and publicity in above- and underground press, we verified only thirty-one multilateral marriages. To these must be added eight earlier attempts of which we have some informal knowledge and a total of about fifty claimed by other professionals and journalists (but not verified by us). No reasonable estimate of the total number is possible at this point, but it is clearly still a comparatively rare phenomenon, though the indications are that both interest and attempts are increasing.

The Multilateral Relations Study Project is an ongoing independent research effort attempting to develop systematic, in-depth insight into the realities of contemporary multiperson alternatives in marriage and family structure. Information sharing, counseling for nonconventional families, and coordination of professional networks for research and counseling are among the nonresearch functions of the Study Project.

Our research has an evolving, open-ended design involving a variety of data-gathering techniques focusing on almost every aspect of multilateral marriage. Tapes of semistructured individual interviews and prolonged observation of family interaction are augmented by several questionnaires, standard psychometric instruments, and special-purpose techniques. In some cases continuing correspondence and even personal diaries supplement these data.

Sixteen groups comprising sixty-four adult members and thirty-one children have participated in the study; one of them has withdrawn. The remainder continue to cooperate with the project, although eleven groups have dissolved since entering the study, three of them before more than nominal contact had been made. The modal size is four adults usually formed of two prior dyadic couples. Triads are next most common. The largest conjugal group ever located by us consists of six adults.

This analysis will focus specifically on sexual aspects as represented in certain early returns. The role of sex as a motivational factor, in group sexual activities, jealousy, sleeping arrangements, other sexual problems, and sex role differentiation will each be discussed separately after a sociological and theoretical framework is provided.

Basic Characteristics. The sample for purposes of this analysis is a subset of respondents consisting of all those individuals who by December 1, 1970, had completed individual questionnaires and Edwards Personal Preference Schedules (EPPS). This sample consists of twenty respondents from six dissolved groups and ten respondents from three extant groups. Multilateral marriage is not, as many have guessed, a distinctly young person's phenomenon. The median age of these respondents was thirty-one years at the time of formation of the multilateral marriage, and the range was from twenty-three to fifty-nine years of age. The majority were married at the time of entry, entering as couples. The average duration for the prior marriage was seven years. Five were in a second marriage. Of the seven not married at formation of the multilateral marriage, three had been married previously and were divorced.

As one indicator of socioeconomic status, median individual income for employed individuals was six thousand dollars per annum. Median total group income was fifteen thousand dollars per annum, but this ranged from nine thousand to three hundred forty thousand dollars. Among these respondents, one had a medical degree, three had master's degrees, six had bachelor's degrees, and only three had no college education. Eleven are currently pursuing undergraduate degrees.

The questionnaire, known as the "Individual Summary," was given to each member to complete independently and to return to us. It covered basic background data, reasons for participation, problems experienced, varieties of sexual experience, preferences among other members (sexual and other), and relationships with outsiders.

Framework for Inference. Of particular interest to us are the possibility of distinguishing functional from dysfunctional factors—that is, the factors contributing to worthwhile participation in alternate marital forms—and eventually, the development of aids for counseling those already in or those considering alternative life-styles. We deliberately wish to avoid the connotations of "success" and "failure." In our framework, the success of any marriage is ultimately measured in terms of the extent to which the marriage contributes to the happiness and self-realization of family members. In no form of marriage is longevity a meaningful indicator of success. While longevity and dissolution may be usefully related to other observed factors in other contexts, we attach no secondary meaning to the two terms. Thus, we will simply refer to dissolved and extant groups to identify those groups that had or had not dissolved by the cutoff date of December 15, 1970. "Enduring groups" are simply those which at dissolution or the cutoff date had lasted two or more years. "Early responses" refers to returns completed before the first anniversary of a group, "late responses" to those after the first anniversary. (Dichotomizing responses on each of these three dimensions yields different pictures of the interplay of elements of the relationship.) We will also relate the questionnaire results to the ages of respondents, divided into those younger than the median and those equal to or older than the median. It is this multidimensional framework in which our attempts to draw inferences will be cast.

Contrasts: Swinging and Communes

Multilateral marriage is often confused with two of the more publicized forms of contemporary deviance in marital living arrangements, (1) swinging or social mate swapping and (2) communes and the communal-living movement.

The sharpest contrasts are with the ideology and life-style of the swinger. Numerous investigators, among them Bell and Silvan (1970),

Denfeld and Gordon (1970), and Symonds (1968), have stated that swingers are conventional and conforming in nearly every aspect of their life-style except the pattern of co-marital sexual involvement. The sexual element is highly compartmentalized, and the remainder of the marriage is perhaps even overconventionalized in compensation (Denfeld and Gordon 1970). The prevailing ethos is one in which sexual involvement is isolated and limited to a physical experience. Interpersonal involvement outside the dyadic marriage is subject to severe limitations. It should be noted, however, that not all swingers eschew interpersonal relations for purely sexual activities; the "utopian" or ideological swingers (Symonds 1970) constitute a minority seeking stable close relationships.

As a rule, our respondents were liberal in much more than their marital and sexual ethic. Functionally, group marriage appeared to represent much more of a total life-style commitment than an isolated departure. From the participants' perspective, the important elements were the close relationship with their partners, the expanded family, and the growth through interpersonal interaction; it was not specifically or predominantly a sexual experience. Interestingly, half reported having had swinging or mate-swapping experience. Interviews revealed that nearly all had sought contacts with people having similar interests in establishing close, stable relationships and that they had been disappointed by the swingers' emphasis on gymnastics. This suggests that the utopian swingers or "communal" and "interpersonal" swingers (Varni 1970) are a population from which multilateral marriages might emerge. Most respondents concluded, however, that swinging was not a productive way to work toward a multilateral marriage relationship. (Fourteen of the fifteen who indicated they had swinging experience were in groups that have since dissolved. This cannot be given statistical significance, however, since swinging almost always occurs among couples.)

Multilateral marriage may be also contrasted with communes and communal living. Operationally, multilateral marriages differ from communal arrangements in that the former are somewhat more stable and longer-lived than the latter. The characteristics of communes are high turnover and a continual flux of participants. Multilateral marriages follow a pattern similar to conventional dyadic marriage. They are formed by several people who continue the relationship for some time. If and when the group dissolves, the relationship dissolves completely (although prior dyads generally remain together); there is no turnover of people. Moreover, there is no ambiguity in distinguishing members of the conjugal unit from guests, neighbors, community members, or relatives. In communes, it is often difficult even for participants to separate members from various classes of nonmembers. There are other differences, all of which stem from distinct and disparate basic structures for communes and multilateral marriages (Constantine and Constantine 1971b).

The Theoretical Context

From the outset we have been interested in the motivation for formation of a group marriage. The most common question we are asked is: Why would anyone want to be in a multilateral relationship? In a broad sociological sense, the progressive nuclearization and increasing isolation of the contemporary family, the growing interest in self-realization, and the greater opportunity for the individual to define alternative life-styles are certainly factors. The problems and limitations of the conventional monogynous marriage have already been widely discussed in this context (Constantine and Constantine 1972; Mazur 1970; Roy and Roy 1970).

The same question may also be construed as an inquiry into more general sexual and marital proclivities. We feel there is only small risk of being incorrect in asserting that both men and women would prefer sexual intercourse with a number of partners. Not only is polygamy the norm in more than twice as many cultures as monogamy (Nimkoff 1965), but exceptions to fidelity are the rule in most monogamous cultures. Reported differences in polysexual propensities between men and women are explained more than adequately by actual differences in opportunity and socialization. In a *non*volunteer suburban population, Johnson (1970) found that just over two-thirds of the men and 56% of the women had a high potential for extramarital involvement, if they were given the opportunity.

There is also reason to believe that human beings are intrinsically ambisexual, that in the absence of cultural counterpressures, most healthy individuals would manifest sexual activities with both sexes, although showing heterosexual preferences. There is considerable ethological and anthropological support for this position (See, for example, Davenport 1966; Moore 1969).

The psychoanalytic position that interest in group sexual activities or in situations with a potential for group sex (such as multilateral marriage) is purely an indication of repressed or latent homosexuality is certainly too narrow if homosexuality is taken to mean a *preference* for sexual activities exclusively or primarily with the same sex. Only one respondent was found to be significantly homosexual in orientation, and he was decidedly ambisexual. Ambisexual activities within group sexual contexts were common but not predominant.

Sex as Motivation

While the public may tend to see multilateral marriage solely in terms of sex, there is a tendency, at certain levels of disclosure, for the participants to deemphasize the significance of sexual motives. The "public" level is that level of motivation disclosed in comparatively casual contacts with outsiders, for example, in position statements written by members for consumption by nonmembers. At this public level, the emphasis is on elements of "community," benefits to the children, and potential for personal growth facilitation. The marked deemphasis of sex is probably a reasonable protective mechanism (See Stein 1970), considering the general disapproval of open multiperson sexual involvement as an integral part of a family structure. The disparity between the public-level disclosures of motivation and what became accessible to us as researchers and confidants suggested a multilevel structure of motivation for entry into multilateral marriage. At the private level, personal-growth opportunities emerged as most important. While sexual interest is acknowledged at the private level, it could hardly be said to be emphasized. Certainly, there is a sense of motivation beyond what an individual may verbalize or otherwise report. Access to such "deep" levels may be difficult for all but a spouse, counselor, or analyst. We chose to approach this deeper level by inquiring into the relationship between personality structure and involvement in multilateral marriage.

The questionnaire we used was designed to reach the "private" level of motivation. In the individual questionnaires completed independently by respondents, four of a list of forty-seven possible reasons for participation were specifically sexual. This list included both "deficit" and "being" motivations (Maslow 1962) and items pertaining to personal and familial interests, which were compiled from interviews and fictional justifications and revised through several rounds of experimental use. Respondents were asked to indicate which were their reasons and which were their strong reasons and unrealized expectations. They were also asked to add any missing reasons not listed in the questionnaire: in practice, the list has proved to be comprehensive.

We believe that those groups formed *predominantly* because of sexual interests are less likely to survive than those formed primarily because of interpersonal involvement for which participants sought sexual expression. Table 1 shows the responses of those who participated in multilateral marriage for the four specifically sexual motivations. The vast majority of respondents gave "variety of sexual partners" as among their (possibly many) reasons. Specific forms of sexual activities were comparatively unimportant as reasons for desiring a multilateral marriage. If our hypothesis is correct, there would be more responses indicating "variety of partners" as a strong reason and fewer responses indicating "sexual expression of an existing relationship" as a strong reason among respondents in groups that eventually dissolved. Both these differences were found to be significant (p <.01). The difference for *total* responses (reason or strong reason) on the former was not significant, while it was for the latter (p <.05). What is clearly suggested is that interest in a variety of sexual partners provides motivation for participation in a multilateral marriage in both extant and dissolved groups. However, our results also suggest that if this is a primary (strong) reason, caution is in order. The same significant difference on "variety" was found between enduring groups and those of less than two years duration. No other differences by age, duration, or time of response were significant.

"Deeper Level" Motivations

The Edwards Personal Preference Schedule, or EPPS (Edwards 1959), is one of the standard instruments used in the study. In keeping with the overriding intent of the study, this instrument was used in the context of a creative-learning experience based on the "interpersonal perception schema" of Drewery (1969). In our adaptation (Constantine and Constantine 1971a), respondents reported their perceptions of their own and each other's needs after completing the EPPS. Our ultimate aim was to derive insights into the relationship between group functioning and both the structure of those perceptions and the perceived satisfaction of needs.

The EPPS develops ipsative measures of fifteen normal personality needs. A consistent pattern of needs among participants might provide one answer to the question of deeper-level motivation. It might suggest that satisfaction of these needs could motivate participation. Our early contact, and especially the discovery of the de-emphasis of sexual aspects at the public level, suggested to us that the role of sex was basic to the personality structure of participants but was protected by adaptive behavior in contact with outsiders.

Table 1—Responses to questionnaire items on specifically sexual motivations for group participation

Reason for Participation	No. Indicating Reason				No. Indicating Strong Reason				No. Indicating Expectation Not Satisfied			
	In Extant Groups (N = 10)		In Dissolved Groups (N = 20)		In Extant Groups (N = 10)		In Dissolved Groups (N = 20)		In Extant Groups (N = 10)		In Dissolved Groups (N = 20)	
	No.	%	No.	%	No.	%	No.	%	No.	%	No.	%
Variety of sexual partners	9	90	11	55	0	0	5[a]	25	1	10	0	0
Sexual expression of existing relationship	3	30	4	20	4	40	0[b]	0	0	0	0	0
Group sex	2	20	8	40	3	30	0	0	1	10	1	5
Bisexual opportunity	2	20	0	0	0	0	0	0	0	0	0	0

[a] Fisher test, exact probability .00549.
[b] Fisher test, exact probability .00766.

Our hypothesis was that sexual interest or high sexual drive *is* a motivating factor for participation in a multilateral marriage—specifically, the desire or need for multiple sexual partners. In terms of the EPPS scales, patricipants should appear significantly above average on the manifest needs for sex (*het*) and for change (*chg*).[1] Even if this combination were to be found, we felt it would be insufficient to account for participation in a life-style as socially extreme as multilateral marriage. This also requires a low level of submission to cultural norms. Thus, a significantly low score on the EPPS need for deference (*def*) was predicted. (*Deference* is the need for dependence, to defer, to follow orders [and others], to conform, and to be conventional.) The all-pervading nature of a commitment to group marriage makes it considerably more "deviant" from prevailing norms than alternative methods of satisfying the needs for sex and change. Extramarital affairs are almost a cultural norm; swinging is an isolated deviance in a swinger's life.

Edwards's general adult normative groups (Edwards 1959) were used as the second sample in two-sample tests, in order to avoid the impression that the observed normative distribution represented the *actual* general population distribution. The nonparametric Kolmogorov-Smirnov test was used in a one-tailed test of the null hypothesis to determine whether or not the two distributions were the same against the hypotheses that our sample was stochastically larger on *chg* and *het* and smaller on *def*.

The differences for *deference* and *heterosexuality* were found in the stated direction and were highly significant in both males and females, as shown in table 2. The distribution for *change*, although having the expected characteristics, was not sufficiently different to reject the null hypotheses for either males or females alone. For the combined sample, however, the difference was significant (p <.01). Evidence for the meaningfulness of the combination was found in the low intercorrelations normally found among these scales: —.09 between *het* and *chg*, .09 between *chg* and *def*, and —.28 between *het* and *def* (Edwards 1959).

It is also interesting to note the difference in the scores for males and females on *heterosexuality*. This suggests that, *compared with other members of the same sex* in the general population, females who choose multilateral marriage have higher sexual needs than their male counter-

---

[1] *Heterosexuality* is the need for the opposite sex, for sexual activities, and for doing things involving sex; *change* is the need for change, variety, and novelty and the need to experiment, to try new things, and to experience change in routine (adapted from Edwards [1959] and Kilgo [1969]).

Table 2—Respondents' scores on selected Edwards Personal Preference Schedule Scales

	Manifest Need	Median[a]	Semi-inter-quartile Ranges[a]	D	Probability[b]
Males ($N^1 = 14$, $N_2 = 4031$)[c]	deference	15	4–25	.514	<.001
	change	76	18–87	.30	(<.10) not significant
	hetero-sexuality	85.5	76–93	.557	<.001
Females ($N^1 = 15$, $N_2 = 4932$)[c]	deference	9	5–27	.533	<.001
	change	76	37–87	.267	(<.15) not significant
	hetero-sexuality	94	89–96	.80	<<.001
All respondents ($N^1 = 29$, $N_2 = 8963$)[c]	change	76	30–87	.283	<.01

[a] Expressed as percentiles of general adult norms (Edwards 1959), separate norms for males and females.

[b] One tail, two-sample Kolmogorov-Smirnov test, χ^2 approximation for large samples (Siegal 1956).

[c] Second sample in each case is "General Adult Group" (Edwards 1959) for appropriate sex or combined groups.

parts. (By the median test for this difference, p <.10, $\chi^2 = 2.82$.) Since the prevailing norms reflect the obverse in the general population, it is clear that females among respondents are more nearly equal in need for sex to the males than are their counterparts in the normative group.

It is our conjecture that those in the vanguard of any form of social deviance or innovation which requires exceptional motivation to enter and persist will show considerable homogeneity of personality-need structure in terms of the needs relevant to participation.

Group Sex

Group sex was reported by only one of six respondents as one of the motivating factors in multilateral involvement. Nevertheless, the potential for group sexual activities may be considered characteristic of the multilateral marriage, and this is almost the only context where this might occur in a deep relational framework. We define group sex somewhat more narrowly than other writers (Bartell 1970; O'Neill and O'Neill 1970) as three or more individuals actively interacting in mutual, overt sexual activities. We have specifically been interested in whether one of our hypotheses could be proved—that is, that group sexual involvement *within* the group acts as a cohesive or integrative element, much as sexual interaction in a dyadic marriage *can* be important in cohesion.

During the earliest phases of our study, group sex was a relatively rare phenomenon. Recently, we have noticed a trend toward more group sex as groups endure and a similar trend toward the formation of more new groups to engage in group sex. In other words, the character of group marriage, at least in terms of group sexual activity, may be changing, although the nature of our early efforts has not allowed us to support this quantitatively.

We did *not* find that group sex within the group was reported more often in extant groups than in dissolved ones. It *was* reported later in a group's history as opposed to earlier. In enduring groups, internal group sex was reported more often than in nonenduring ones. We also found greater total variety of group sexual experience reported among respondents of extant groups and of enduring groups than in dissolved and nonenduring groups (1.8 different types per respondent reported in extant groups versus 1.35 in the dissolved, and 2.6 per respondent in the enduring groups versus 1.0 per respondent in the nonenduring groups). This was probably not explainable strictly as a function of time, as we found 1.58 different types per respondent in the late-response groups versus 1.36 per respondent in the early-response groups, a much smaller difference. These results are summarized in table 3. It was not possible to test these data statistically in this form, as individual experiences in group sex are clearly not independent.

Although most respondents considered group sex as positive and acceptable, and in some cases, even described it as a peak experience (Maslow 1962), there appeared to be some definite problems. For example, many reported that four-person sex tended to become two side-by-side couples rather than an integrated experience with the group "becoming one." The men tended to become competitive and tense, which was manifested in such ways as becoming temporarily impotent or trying to outperform each other. In three-person sex, it appeared easier for the females to form same-sex bonds and to relate sexually in the group context; for the men it was much more difficult, probably because of strong cultural conditioning against almost any nonviolent, physical expression of warmth between men.

Table 3—Group sexual experience among respondents to questionnaires

Type of Experience	Totals of all Groups (N = 30)		Extant Groups (N = 10)		Dissolved Groups (N = 20)		Enduring Groups (N = 11)		Nonenduring Groups (N = 19)		Late-response Groups (N = 19)		Early-response Groups (N = 11)	
	No.	%	No.	%	No.	%	No.	%	No.	%	No.	%	No.	%
Group sexual experience in this group	13	43.3	6	60	7	35	9	81.7	4	21.1	9	47.4	4	36.3
One-male/two-females	13	43.3	3	30	10	50	6	54.5	7	36.8	7	36.8	6	54.5
One-female/two-males	10	33.3	6	60	4	20	7	63.5	3	15.8	8	42.2	2	18.3
Two couples	14	47.0	7	70	7	35	9	81.7	5	26.3	10	52.6	4	36.3
Other group sex	8	26.6	2	20	6	30	4	36.3	4	21.1	5	26.3	3	27.2
Mean number different experiences checked per respondent	1.5		1.8		1.35		2.6		1		1.58		1.36	

The predominance of male-female-female triads (table 3) over male-male-female triads was consistent with our other sources of information for the same groups and with most studies of swinging (Bartell 1970; O'Neill and O'Neill 1970).

Jealousy

When discussing the sexual aspects of multilateral marriage, inevitably the subject of jealousy arises. Eighty percent of respondents considered jealousy a problem. We have learned a great deal from our respondents about jealousy and have developed the basis for a conceptualization radically different from the generally accepted view (Constantine 1971). We have come to see jealousy not as an emotion but rather as behavior, an expression of a great variety of intrapsychic experiences. For example, a person may be experiencing a real or imagined fear of loss of another person, or he may be experiencing a loss of status; he may desire to control or to possess another person and be experiencing the frustration of this desire; or he may simply be feeling left out. Possibly, he is not able to spend enough time with someone. Jealousy (or more correctly, jealous behavior) is, of course, not strictly a sex problem, although it is often brought out by sex. In any case, it is a complex subject.

We have found that jealous behavior is a significantly smaller problem among enduring groups, as shown in table 4. This could reflect causality in either direction or it could be a function of another variable. But over half of the early-response groups listed jealousy as a major problem, and *none* of the late-response groups did, a significant difference (p $<$.01). Thus, it appears that groups did learn with time to cope with jealousy or even to overcome it. Jealousy was also a function of age: all respondents under age thirty-one listed jealousy as a problem, but only nine of fifteen over thirty-one years old did. This was highly significant (p $<$.001) and suggested that in this context non-jealousy and maturity may be related, a suggestion later supported by interviews and prolonged interaction with groups.

Sleeping Arrangements

Aside from the option of group sex, which has not been the major mode of sexual interaction in most groups, many people asked us about sleeping arrangements: where, when, how often, and with whom. Bedroom

Table 4—Responses to questionnaire items relating to jealousy

Response	Totals of all Groups (N=30)		Extant Groups (N=10)		Dissolved Groups (N=20)		Enduring Groups (N=11)		Nonenduring Groups (N=19)		Late-response Groups (N=19)		Early-response Groups (N=11)		Young Groups (N=15)		Older Groups (N=15)	
	No.	%	No.	%	No.	%	No.	%	No.	%	No.	%	No.	%	No.	%	No.	%
A problem	18	60	6	60	12	60	7	64.6	11	57.9	13	68.4	5	45.4	10	66.7	8	53.4
A major problem	6	20	2	20	4	20	0	0	6[a]	31.6	0	0	6[a]	54.5	5	33.3	1[b]	6.7
Problem has been solved	6	20	2	20	4	20	2	18.2	5	26.3	5	26.3	1	9.1	4	26.7	2	13.3

[a] Fisher test, exact probability .00506.
[b] Fisher test, exact probability .000766.

setups varied, from each person having his own bed and his own room to all persons in one bed (in the case of some triads). Since the mode was four people (two men and two women), the most common setup was one bedroom and one bed per two people. Of course, space was a factor; there may only have been three bedrooms for six adults, for example. And, of course, it was much easier for three to fit in a bed than five or six.

As for "with whom and when," there were two major classes of approach. The first was "free choice," that is, everyone was free to choose whomever he desired each night. Many groups preferred this method because of the potential for freedom and spontaneity, but some also found it difficult to be truly free and spontaneous in expressing choices. The discussion, attempts to deduce what everyone wants, and decision-making, can become quite involved and may lead to use of the second method: "rotation."

Rotation was a method whereby with one initial decision, the group decided who would sleep with whom and for what period of time. Thus, there was less opportunity to show favoritism, and the schedule usually did not allow for exceptions. The period may be important (that is, how long one person sleeps with another before everyone switches partners). The optimal period seemed to be roughly three days to a week; longer or shorter periods were perceived as leading to integration problems. Frequent switching worked against building a sense of unity with a particular partner while longer periods left other dyads out of touch too long to maintain a deep sense of intimacy with each other. Although rotation did seem to be easier from a purely practical point of view, it had certain disadvantages and therefore was sometimes used only as an interim solution. It has been suggested that the rotation method results in everyone being in equal sexual demand. In practice, this was not so. Sleeping with someone did not necessarily mean having sexual relations with them, and people do have preferences. As groups learned the necessary skills for the special decision-making, they might switch over to using free choice. The special decision-making process included learning to present one's unbiased, unprocessed preference first, being able to substitute a processed preference later (that is, a decision taking into account all the variables, including other individuals' preferences, etc.), and then making the final decisions as a group. Without the presentation of each person's real unbiased wishes, the sleeping decisions would have been based on everyone's guesses about the wishes of everyone else, and possibly no one would have ended up happy.

It is interesting to note that "sleeping with" was *not* a euphemism for intercourse among most groups, but it implied considerably more.

Both the sexual act *and* the joint sleeping have been mentioned separately as promoting a sense of intimacy. Moreover, sleeping together was often a major factor in the opportunity for private intimate conversation as a dyad. Thus, the sleeping arrangements may have been central in the integration of dyads and the cohesion of the group. What was optimal, even for specific groups, is not clear yet, although the tendency was to use rotation to overcome certain problems and then later to abandon it for free choice.

Sixteen respondents checked sleeping arrangements as a problem on our questionnaire (table 5); three of the sixteen indicated that the problem had been resolved. Fifteen checked choice of sex partner (resolved in four of these cases) as a problem. Most interesting of all is the finding that only six of a possible twenty-six listed their spouse as their preferred sex partner; all of these six individuals were in groups that have since dissolved. This finding may indicate that sexual preference has a negative role in holding the group together.

Cohesion

Among the remaining twenty were eight who refused to answer regarding preferences because they said they did and should prefer everyone equally. In interviews with these individuals, we found that they really did have preferences but were trying to live up to an ideal of equal love, trust, and sexual attraction. On close examination, we found this attempt contributed to group problems. Broader experience suggested that evaluating and comparing in specific dimensions were normal and intrinsically human. Thus, there will always be a disparity between performance and an ideal of perfect equality. We found that an open acknowledgment that preferences exist but are not essential issues was more functional in the multilateral-marriage context. Many of the individuals (seventeen) had intimate relations with others outside their group. (The only two groups who had a fidelity ethic were among the total of five still extant; this was neither statistically nor functionally significant.)

Beltz (1969) has proposed a fundamental learning theory model in which deterioration of the conjugal unit can be predicted in marriages with altered contracts that eliminate fidelity. Essentially, the easiest route to need satisfaction is exterior involvement rather than internal problem-solving. Eventually, all problem-solving in dyads may deteriorate as the "lesson" is applied recursively. We extend this model by noting that specific mechanisms may prevent deterioration. Any specific mechanism which limits the modality of alternate-need satisfaction

Table 5—Specifically sexual problems among respondents to questionnaire

Type of Problem	Totals of all Groups (N=30)		Extant Groups (N=10)		Dissolved Groups (N=20)		Enduring Groups (N=11)		Nonenduring Groups (N=19)		Late-response Groups (N=19)		Early-response Groups (N=11)		Young Groups (N=15)		Older Groups (N=15)	
	No.	%	No.	%	No.	%	No.	%	No.	%	No.	%	No.	%	No.	%	No.	%
Sexual compatibility	13	43.4	5	50	8	40	4	36.4	9	47.4	7	36.9	6	54.5	6	40	7	46.7
Sleeping arrangements	8	26.7	3	30	5	25	2	18.2	6	31.6	4	21.1	4	36.4	4	26.7	4	26.7
Choice of sex partners	16	53.4	5	50	11	55	2	18.2	14	73.6	6	31.6	10	90.9	7	46.7	9	60.0
Sex	16	53.4	6	60	10	50	7	63.5	9	47.4	9	47.4	7	63.5	6	40.0	10	66.7
Number of different problems checked per respondent	1.75		1.90		1.70		1.36		2.00		1.38		2.46		1.53		2.00	

or gives a preference to internal problem-solving is sufficient. The fidelity ethic in a monogamous marriage serves as such a mechanism to keep the husband and wife solving problems in their relationship. Compartmentalization of sex as an isolated modality is another such mechanism. This is one way to interpret conventionality in the dyadic marriage and restriction of nonsexual contact among swingers (Denfeld and Gordon 1970). Since many group marriages do not have a fidelity ethic, they need other mechanisms to keep them together and to solve problems. Two such mechanisms are commitment to the group as a whole and primary bonds, that is, a dyadic bond within the group (usually the legal spouse) that holds precedence in critical issues or problems.

We have found some support for the view that a previously established dyadic relationship that is not only sound but has a clear-cut precedence over other relationships is a prerequisite for "successful" participation in a multilateral marriage. Such a relationship would constitute a truly *primary* bond. By all indications, some form of primary bond with a spouse existed for nearly every couple among respondents. The apparent anomaly that all individuals who preferred their spouse as their sexual partner were in dissolved groups can be easily explained if our assertion is correct. If the primary affective bond *and* the sexual preference are both with the prior spouse, what is left to tie participants into the group?

Sexual Problems

Table 5 reports the responses on problems reported by respondents as specifically sexual. Reported sexual problems varied with the longevity of the group, diminishing with time. It seems to follow either that groups that endure solved their problems or that groups that solved their problems endure. But dissolved and extant groups reported about the same number of problems! Moreover, substantially more problems (2.45 per respondent) were reported for those answering the questionnaire early as compared with those answering the questionnaire after being in a group more than a year (1.37 per respondent). This clearly suggested that sexual problems diminish as a function of group experience. Again, age of the respondents was a factor. Those over thirty-one reported somewhat more sex problems than those younger than thirty-one.

Some specific sexual problems have come up in interviews and prolonged interaction which should be mentioned briefly. In one case, homosexuality was a possible contributing factor in the dissolution of a group. One man had been predominantly homosexual for a brief period and continued to be bisexual. The other male member of the group felt very uncomfortable in relating sexually with another male. After one mutual homosexual experience during the absence of both wives, the relationship between the two men disintegrated, resulting in considerable tension and friction. There were other known problems of long standing in this group, and it is impossible to attach relative significance to this one factor. Four men and four women indicated on questionnaires that they had had homosexual experiences, although none was with members of their groups. The structure of the questionnaire reflected the attitude as seen by respondents in separating homosexual from bisexual involvement in a group sexual context.

We know of eight women who had not previously experienced orgasm (five respondents and three others involved in multilateral relations) who reported experiencing their first orgasm while involved in a multilateral experience. We merely report this, noting that almost any strong novel stimulus may serve the same function (Clark 1970), and we do not advocate multilateral relations as a solution to this or any other problem, marital or sexual.

There was one instance of prolonged secondary impotence with a spouse which began and was resolved during the multilateral marriage. Lastly, there were two instances of dyspareunia with a possible psychological cause. One was a brief problem, which predated the multilateral involvement and cleared up immediately and permanently during the first intercourse with someone other than the spouse. The other continues to be a problem. In view of the number of dyads involved and the time span covered by our data-gathering, the number of problems seen as distinctly sexual did not appear to be greater than in the general population.

Roles and Sex Differences

Sex differences are often postulated with regard to multilateral marriage. Questions are often asked about male dominance and sex role differences in terms of who runs the house, who takes care of the kids, and who does the "dirty work." Interestingly, we found no significant differences between men and women in number of reported sex problems, sexual experience, or reasons for involvement.

First, we have no indications that men are dragging their protesting wives into group marriages. The initiation of involvement and the enthusiasm were equally distributed. At least at the level accessible to us, this distinguishes group marriage from swinging, where male initiative is noted widely. As for household duties and careers, there appeared to be substantially less sex-role differentiation than in the average nuclear family. Men took care of the children and did some of the cooking and dishwashing; women had more involvement in careers, education, outside activities, and decision-making. The groups espoused an equalitarian ethic and substantially achieved it in decision-making and participation in family policy formulation.

Competition among members of the same sex is often predicted in groups. A novel solution emerged in most groups as individuals became leaders in distinct functional areas. In one group, for example, one woman kept the books and exercised monetary leadership over her group; another person was acknowledged as public spokesman and correspondent; someone else was generally the organizer of care for the children; still another held the role of wise-man—"guru." One consistent disappointment involved the residual work no one wanted to do. This usually fell upon the least assertive person or the one with the highest need for order. In our culture, both are more likely to be women than men. In general, our respondents felt that, with the larger numbers in a group marriage, there was more freedom in choice of roles and tasks.

Conclusions

A pattern is suggested in which sex plays an important role in motivating attempts at multilateral marriages. Participants as a rule de-emphasized the sexual aspects publicly but demonstrated their awareness of them privately. They also revealed a pattern of normal needs suggestive of a need for sexual variety. On the other hand, while sex may be a strong motivation, meaningful interpersonal relationships are probably needed to hold a group together.

As groups endured, problems seen as specifically sexual diminished, as did jealousy problems. At the same time, group sexual involvement became more common, a factor which we feel was both an indicator and facilitator of intimacy. In general, we found that the groups learned to cope with the problems of a multilateral marriage through maturation and a variety of adaptive mechanisms, such as special frameworks for decision-making.

Many questions remain not only unanswered but unasked. The circumstances which initiated the current study have led us to concentrate quantitatively on only a limited number of factors; we are now in the process of pursuing others. Among sexual factors are satisfaction with sex life in the prior dyad and in the group and the effect of the group experience on frequency of sexual intercourse. Ongoing access to respondents enables us to follow up on questions uncovered in our unstructured study and to fill in gaps as a result of early limitations. We are particularly interested in the effects on dyads and will soon be able to add objective measures of prior marital adjustment and postgroup adjustment to our clinical observations.

We are convinced that real knowledge of innovations in marital patterns will, in the long run, have a profound impact not only on the alternatives in our society but on conventional marriages as well. This study will, we hope, add an increment to that knowledge.

References

Athanasiou, R., Shaver, P., and Tavris, C. 1970. Sex. *Psychol. Today.* 4, no. 2, pp. 37–52.

Bartell, G. D. 1970. Group Sex among the Mid-Americans. *J. Sex Res.* 6, no. 2, pp. 113–30. [In this book, pp.185–201.]

Bell, R. R., and Silvan, L. 1970. Swinging: The Sexual Exchange of Marriage Partners. Paper presented at the meeting of the Society for the Study of Social Problems, Washington, D.C.

Beltz, S. E. 1969. Five Year Effects of Altered Marital Contracts. In *Extramarital Relations*, ed. G. Neubeck. Englewood Cliffs: Prentice-Hall.

Clark, L. 1970. Is There a Difference between a Clitoral and a Vaginal Orgasm? *J. Sex Res.* 6, no. 1, pp. 25–28.

Constantine, Larry L. 1971. Personal Growth in Multiperson Marriages. *Rad. Ther.* 2, no. 1, pp. 18–20.

Constantine, L. L., and Constantine, J. M. 1971a. Counseling Implications of Comarital and Multilateral Relations. Unpublished paper.

————. 1971b. Group and Multilateral Marriage: Definitional Notes, Glossary, and Annotated Bibliography. *Fam. Process* 10 (June 1971): 157–76.

————. 1971c. Multilateral Marriage: Alternate Family Structure in Practice. In *You and I Searching for Tomorrow*, ed. R. H. Rimmer. New York: New American Library.

————. 1972. Multilateral Marriage. In *The Nuclear Family in Crisis: The Search for an Alternative*, ed. M. Gordon. New York: Harper and Row.

Davenport, W. 1966. Sexual Patterns in a Southwest Pacific Society. In *An Analysis of Human Sexual Response*, ed. R. Brecher and E. Brecher. New York: Signet Books.

Denfeld, D., and Gordon, M. 1970. The Sociology of Mate Swapping: Or, the Family that Swings Together Clings Together. *J. Sex Res.* 6, no. 2, pp. 85–100. [In this book, pp. 68–83.]

Drewery, J. 1969. An Interpersonal Perception Technique. *Br. J. Med. Psychol.* 42: 171–81.

Edwards, A. L. 1959. *Edwards Personal Preference Schedule (Manual).* New York: Psychological Corporation.

Johnson, R. E. 1970. Extramarital Sexual Intercourse: A Methodological Note. *J. Marriage Fam.* 32, no. 2.

Kilgo, R. D. 1969. The Use of the Edwards Personal Preference Schedule in Pre-Marital Counseling. Paper presented at the annual meeting of the National Council on Family Relations, Washington, D.C.

Maslow, A. H. 1962. *Toward a Psychology of Being.* Princeton, N.J.: D. Van Nostrand Company.

Mazur, R. 1970. Beyond Morality: Toward the Humanization of the Sexes. Paper presented at the annual meeting of the National Council on Family Relations, Chicago.

Moore, J. E. 1969. Problematic Sexual Behavior. In *The Individual, Sex, and Society*, ed. C. Broderick and J. Bernard. Baltimore: The Johns Hopkins Press.

Nimkoff, M. F., ed. 1965. *Comparative Family Systems.* Boston: Houghton Mifflin.

O'Neill, G. C., and O'Neill, N. 1970. Patterns in Group Sexual Activity. *J. Sex Res.* 6, no. 2, pp. 101–12.

Roy, R., and Roy, D. 1970. Monogamy: Where We Stand Today. *Humanist*, March/April.

Siegal, S. 1956. *Nonparametric Statistics: For the Behavioral Sciences.* New York: McGraw-Hill.

Stein, R. 1970. Not Just an Ordinary Family. *San Francisco Chronicle*, August 28, 1970.

Symonds, C. 1968. Pilot Study of the Peripheral Behavior of Sexual Mate Swappers. Master's thesis, University of California, Riverside.

———. 1970. The Utopian Aspects of Sexual Mate Swapping. Paper presented at the annual meeting of the Society for the Study of Social Problems, Washington, D.C.

Varni, C. A. 1970. An Exploratory Study of Spouse Swapping. Master's thesis, San Diego State College. [In this book, pp. 246–59.]

Sexual Deviance and Social Networks: A Study of Social, Family, and Marital Interaction Patterns among Co-marital Sex Participants

Brian G. Gilmartin

Few variables are of greater significance to the study of social control than that of sexuality. Human beings are all born with pretty nearly the same sexual potentialities, and yet the variability in sexual behavior and custom from one part of the world to another is very great indeed. Even throughout our own country, the variations in erotic practices surprise many. A heterogeneity of sexual customs and values pervades all major segments of American society, including that of the so-called white, middle-class, Anglo-Saxon Protestants. In this segment, one major school of values continues to be strongly championed by people in positions of power and authority, but the extent of variation even here is remarkable.

This research is part of a larger study on co-marital sexual behavior prepared as a Ph.D. dissertation for the department of sociology at the University of Iowa. Additional papers and a monograph are planned which will explore in much greater depth the plethora of findings obtained. The monograph will be published under the title, "The social context of comarital sexual behavior." This research was supported, in part, by National Science Foundation Grant No. GS-3047. I am very grateful for the funds provided by this grant and for the suggestions and helpful encouragement of Professor Hallowell Pope, of the University of Iowa, and Professor Ira L. Reiss, of the University of Minnesota. In addition, I should like to thank Keith and Iris Bancroft of the Topanga Canyon based Elysium Institute, and Tom Kilfoyle, the manager of Club "101," for their time, suggestions, and intellectually stimulating conversation.

This paper is concerned with the behavior of white middle- and upper middle-class Americans—a segment of our population that might be expected to be especially nonadventurous as far as nonconformist erotic practices are concerned. It is this part of society that receives the most education, achieves the best jobs, and is characterized by the greatest self-discipline, particularly in terms of the ability to defer gratification. And it is within this very population that people are especially likely to be socialized to view deviant sexuality as incompatible with self-discipline, a good education, and success in general. Of course, not everyone in this segment of the population internalizes this message, and virtually thousands every year literally disprove its empirical validity by earning fine educations and jobs while at the same time leading sexually unconventional lives.

Perhaps the most interesting and theoretically meaningful of these "respectable," albeit sexually deviant, adventurous individuals is the legally married middle-class swinger. The major objective of this paper will be to explore the personal and social characteristics of people who call themselves "swingers."

Sociologists, in particular, have often viewed themselves as the practitioners of a "myth debunking science," and if swinging could be shown to coexist with such things as a happy, stable marriage, a productive and disciplined involvement in the business or professional world, and reasonable mental health and happiness, it would be an important discovery. Murdock (1949) and other anthropologists have already shown that a stable family system can exist for many generations under a wide variety of different structural forms. Perhaps within even a highly pluralistic society such as the United States, there is more than one answer to the problem of how family systems can be structured to function smoothly, and perhaps swingers have come up with some viable alternatives. Empirical data already obtained by Bartell (1971), the Smiths (1970), the Galants (1966b), and others strongly suggest that this may be the case.

For purposes of this paper "swinging" will be defined as that form of extramarital sexual behavior which involves legally married spouses together sharing coitus and other forms of erotic behavior with other legally married couples in a social context defined by all participants as a form of recreational-convivial play. Social scientists often refer to swinging as "co-marital sexual behavior" or "mate sharing." As these three terms will be used interchangeably throughout the paper, the reader should understand that they all refer to the same phenomenon.

Description of the Study

A total of one hundred swinging middle-class couples were involved in the study. All of the couples were legally married, and all were living in what may be considered suburban residential areas. Specifically, 70% of the couples were from the San Fernando Valley suburbs of Los Angeles, and the remaining 30% were from the East Bay suburbs of the San Francisco region. The names of 80% of the swinging couples were obtained through the cooperation of sexual freedom groups in both the Los Angeles and San Francisco areas, while the remaining 20% were obtained through the help of swinging couples who do not belong to any clubs. Some of the organized groups whose help was employed cater exclusively to the needs of married swinging couples, while others do not. However, a major "raison d'être" of both kinds of organizations was that of facilitating the efforts of married swingers to meet compatible couples.

Unlike most of the previous research conducted on comarital sexual behavior, this study employed a control group. Because of both financial and temporal limitations it was not possible to pursue a rigorous matched-pair design. Nevertheless, it was feasible to obtain a group of one hundred legally married couples who were very similar to the swinging couples in age, neighborhood of residence, annual income, level of education, and number of children. Inasmuch as these factors are crucial determinants of life-style, it was felt that the control group, despite its methodological shortcomings, would provide an interesting and useful contrast with the experimental or swinging couples. It was further felt that such a comparison would reveal theoretically meaningful differences which at the very least could be considered *suggestive*.

In general, the swinging couples were more cooperative than the control group, since most of the swingers who were approached indicated a willingness to cooperate, as compared with only 40% of the nonswinging suburbanites. While each of the one hundred swinging couples was paid ten dollars in return for the time and data they provided (the control couples were each paid five dollars), it was felt that something more than money motivated their compliance. Many swingers seem to enjoy talking about themselves and their life-styles, particularly when they know that the interviewer is able, both emotionally and intellectually, to accept them. It is also probable that the more a swinger discusses his sexual ideology, the more thoroughly and firmly he internalizes it, and the more confident he personally comes to feel about it. This is not to suggest, however, that these people are at all ambivalent about their ideology or behavior.

Each couple in both the swinging and the control groups was asked to complete a detailed questionnaire that dealt with a variety of topics concerning married life, children, child-rearing attitudes, political and social attitudes, sexual behavior before and after marriage, courtship attitudes and personal experiences, early family history, psychological adjustment, and other items. Each respondent took between sixty and ninety minutes to answer all of the questions, and care was taken to insure that each person completed his or her form independently. Only the questionnaire data were obtained from the controls. The swinging couples were also interviewed together at some length.

Results and Discussion

The upper middle-class American suburbanite experiences certain kinds of daily stresses which are common to people in his social position. And these stresses can be and indeed are adapted to in a wide variety of ways. A crucial question for the understanding of deviance is: What leads some people to pursue rather conventional ways of releasing tension while other people of very similar attitudes pursue some highly nonconformist behaviors? In a highly pluralistic society such as the United States, people usually can choose from a wide variety of alternatives. Generally speaking, the greater the variety of alternatives, the greater is the likelihood that a person will find an effective alternative which serves to promote optimal adjustment (see especially Cuber 1965). But concurrently there is also a greater possibility that a person will find some mode of adjustment which a large majority of persons define, rightly or wrongly, as highly deviant and undesirable. These "definitions" by the dominant majority may be prejudiced and may be the result of a certain mindless gut reaction that was conditioned and internalized in early childhood. These "definitions" are themselves influential as a means of social control.

Psychologists continue to stress temperament and personality as primary determinants of the way a person will select for adapting to his life situation. Eysenck (1971), for example, argues that the extroverted person is likely to be more naturally adventurous and less introspective than most people. Such a person is thus more likely to find some socially unpopular responses, particularly regarding sex. Nevertheless, Eysenck's findings are inconsistent at best and scarcely can be considered convincing evidence.

Without discounting the importance of inborn temperamental proclivities, sociologists have found it far more useful to focus upon environmental variables as determinants of the ways in which a person will cope with the situations confronting him. Indeed, even personality (in contradistinction to temperament) is believed to be heavily determined by the social context in which an individual spent his formative years. It is the group of functionaries within this social context that condition personality, mold the mind, and construct individual social reality.

The functionaries referred to are those of the so-called "social-control" institutions, the most powerful of which is the family. Some of the analyses of the conditions promoting social change have suggested that the more "functionally autonomous" a part of the system is, the more it is likely to press for and accept social change (especially when such change is consonant with its own autonomy). Functionally inter-dependent system parts, on the other hand (i.e., those which need to depend to a greater or lesser extent upon other subsystems for emotional stability or even survival), will be significantly less likely to undergo change even though, like all system parts, they are likely to press for a somewhat greater degree of functional autonomy.

If one considers humans as system parts, it must be stressed that emotional and psychic dependency upon others can be extremely strong long after physical dependency has terminated. Emotional dependency is a powerful learned response pattern, and it is likely to be particularly strong and protracted in especially gratifying and mutually rewarding relationships. In simplest terms, the most powerful social control is that which is basically unperceived by the individual. Such control is an unintended by-product of a long history of friendly, convivial conversations with family group members. It is therefore likely that individuals who enjoyed friendly, cordial relations with their families as a child and adolescent will behave as adults in accordance with values that are in reasonable harmony with those which permeated the household. One's internalized norms will in large measure be a carbon copy of those of his family. Inasmuch as most American families espouse relatively conventional values vis-à-vis their children, swingers are very likely to have developed from early in life a far greater degree of intellectual and emotional autonomy with regard to their parents than nonswingers of the same social class. It must be realized, of course, that the *emotional* commitment to norms is invariably far greater than the *cognitive* commitment when the individual's relations vis-à-vis the family members were always good. It is this very emotional commitment which instills a trained incapacity for even considering the possibility that some of the internalized norms may be intellectually unsound. The norms thus remain an integral part of social reality and as such determine at least in part all social perceptions.

As a rule, we would expect that the more deviant a behavior is, as defined by the majority of persons, the more tenuous the ties of those who regularly engage in that behavior are likely to be to their kin. Correlatively, the more deviant the behavior the greater the personal autonomy the perpetrators of that behavior must have had from such agents of social control as the family and conventional religion. A form of behavior widely viewed in a society as only mildly deviant would not require so great a degree of personal autonomy. Moralists quite commonly think of deviance *itself* causing consequences viewed as undesirable (e.g., guilt or strained, nongratifying family relationships). I am suggesting that strained family relationships are themselves a very important antecedent of any behavior if and only if that behavior is defined by most people in a particular society as deviant. If the behavior is defined as deviant in society A but not in society B, then citizens of society A who enjoy that form of deviance can be expected to be relatively alienated from their parents while those in society B who behave in exactly the same manner will not be so alienated. For example, in the United States dropping out of high school at age sixteen is defined as highly deviant behavior; in England, on the other hand, it is quite typical for respectable middle-class people to leave school at that age. Cervantes (1965) has shown that even within the lower classes nondropouts in the United States are far less likely to have experienced emotionally unrewarding relationships with their parents than the dropouts. In England, on the other hand, dropping out of high school does not appear to be in any sense associated with tenuous or unsatisfying family relationships (see Young and Willmott 1957). On the basis of these theoretical considerations, the following hypotheses were derived:

H_1: Relations with parents during the formative years were significantly less happy and emotionally gratifying for the swingers than they were for controls.
H_2: Swingers interact with relatives and kin (other than spouse and children) significantly less frequently than do controls.
H_3: Swingers view relatives and kin as being of significantly less importance to their personal lives than do controls.

The data obtained provided strong support for each of the above propositions. As can be seen in table 1, the controls were significantly more likely than the swingers to remember their adolescent years as

Table 1—Degree of remembered personal happiness during adolescent years

Degree of Happiness	Husbands		Wives	
	Swingers	Controls	Swingers	Controls
Happy	33	55	39	56
Fairly happy	42	25	38	25
Unhappy	25	20	23	19

Throughout, in the presentation of data, the frequency and percentages in each cell are equivalent.

$\chi^2 = 10.3690$, $df = 2$ $\chi^2 = 6.1058$, $df = 2$
$p < .01$ $p < .05$
gamma $= -.30$ gamma $= -.24$

happy. Moreover, the childhood years were also significantly more likely to have been remembered by the controls as happy and rewarding.

Further analysis of the data suggested several reasons why the parents of swingers were not very effective in influencing their children or inspiring their children to love them very deeply. As revealed in tables 2, 3, and 4, swingers are significantly less likely than the controls to remember their parents respecting them or inspiring very much genuine parent-child communication. A widely accepted proposition in sociology is that mutually gratifying social interaction (communication) is a prerequisite for any kind of social control or influence. Most parents strongly desire to influence their children in a manner which they believe will be constructive. Yet in their well-meaning hyperconscientiousness some become overbearing and excessively threatening. It is in this manner that parents sometimes unintentionally create an invisible

Table 2—Responses to question, "At the age of seventeen, how satisfied were you with the amount of freedom and autonomy your parents permitted you?"

Degree of Satisfaction	Husbands		Wives	
	Swingers	Controls	Swingers	Controls
Satisfied	48	69	42	66
Mildly satisfied	22	16	24	18
Dissatisfied	30	15	34	16

$\chi^2 = 9.7166$, $df = 2$ $\chi^2 = 12.6706$, $df = 2$
$p < .01$ $p < .01$
gamma $= -.38$ gamma $= -.42$

Table 3—Responses to statement, "My parents always respected me, I always felt free to discuss my problems with them"

	Husbands		Wives	
Response	Swingers	Controls	Swingers	Controls
True	40	68	42	65
False	60	32	58	35

$\chi^2 = 15.7310, df = 1$ $\chi^2 = 10.6321, df = 1$
p < .001   p < .01
gamma = −.52   gamma = −.44

Table 4—Responses to question, "How frequently did you enjoy informal conversations with either of your parents about any topic?"

	Husbands		Wives	
Response	Swingers	Controls	Swingers	Controls
Frequently	23	36	32	48
Moderately frequently	24	22	27	26
Infrequently	53	42	41	26

$\chi^2 = 4.2250, df = 2$ $\chi^2 = 6.5770, df = 2$
(not significant)   p < .05
gamma = −.23   gamma = −.29

wall between themselves and their children. Specifically, social distance within the family social system becomes an unintended, unrecognized by-product of their approach to their children. Without communication there can be little social control and probably even less true internalization of parental norms. Paradoxically, the more ardently parents endeavor to control their children, the less they are likely to succeed. The most powerful social control is unfelt and occurs as an integral (albeit invisible) part of mutually gratifying, convivial conversation and social interaction.

The data in this study strongly suggest that the swingers were reared in accordance with either an authoritarian or a laissez-faire kind of regime far more often than the controls. At first glance, authoritarianism and laissez-faireism appear to be highly disparate practices. However different these two approaches may be, they do share some significant points in common. For example, both the parents who engage in laissez-faire and authoritarian practices tend to be extremely insensitive to the child as an individual with a unique set of needs. These parents tend to manifest this insensitivity in quite different ways, of course, but the basic effect seems to be very much the same. The authoritarian parent views the child as a personal possession and has an inflexible set of preconceived notions of what he would like the child to become. Such parents also have an inflexible set of behavior standards, which they arbitrarily impose and enforce. Intrafamily communication is, by the very nature of this approach, impossible because collaborative decision-making between parent and child is so very rare in authoritarian families.

In contrast, the laissez-faire parent tends to be basically disinterested in children. The seeming "freedom" which the children of such parents experience (and they usually do not experience it as freedom) is basically an unintended by-product of the parents' lack of interest and involvement in the child's world. Such parents never developed any real interest or competence in dealing with children.

When parents are uninterested and uninvolved in their children, and hence remain largely aloof, they are manifesting basically the same insensitivity as the authoritarian parent, and the consequences, as demonstrated by a variety of studies, seem to be surprisingly similar. Kandel and Lesser (1969), for example, show that in both Denmark and the United States children reared in accordance with a laissez-faire regime feel that their parents accorded them *less* freedom than do children reared in an egalitarian-democratic type of atmosphere. Paradoxical though this finding may appear, many other researchers have also found this to be the case. Teen-age runaways, for example, have been found to come almost entirely from authoritarian or laissez-faire families. My research revealed a very similar pattern. Few swingers have pleasant memories of their families of orientation or remember them as being notably democratic or egalitarian.

If one considers the relatively strained relations which swingers had with their parents throughout childhood and adolescence, it should not seem surprising that their informal visitation with them now is comparatively minimal. Similarly, it is not surprising that swingers tend to perceive relatives as being of significantly less importance than friends. Tables 5 through 8 summarize the data, all of which provide firm support for the second and third hypotheses.

As can be seen in Table 5, swingers interact significantly less often with their relatives and kin than do members of the control group. And it is interesting to note that the findings reveal a higher level of statistical significance for wives than they do for husbands. It is quite likely that this is due to the fact that women require a greater degree of func-

Table 5—Extent of informal visitation among relatives and kin (other than spouse and children)

Extent of Visitation	Husbands		Wives	
	Swingers	Controls	Swingers	Controls
Once per week or more	7	13	10	23
A few times per month	10	24	11	23
About once per month	18	20	9	14
About once every two or three months	18	8	18	15
Less often	47	35	52	25

$\chi^2 = 13.2722, df = 4$ $\chi^2 = 20.1838, df = 4$
p < .02   p < .001
gamma = −.30   gamma = −.44

Table 6—Responses to question, "Considering friends as compared to relatives who do not live with you, which would you say are most important to you?"

Degree of Importance	Husbands		Wives	
	Swingers	Controls	Swingers	Controls
Relatives more important	18	51	35	70
Equal importance	3	7	6	4
Friends more important	79	42	59	26

$\chi^2 = 28.6966, df = 2$ $\chi^2 = 24.8785, df = 2$
p < .001   p < .001
gamma = −.65   gamma = −.60

tional autonomy to engage in something as highly deviant as co-marital sexuality. As stated earlier, the more deviant a given behavior is the greater the degree of functional autonomy the participants in that form of deviance will require vis-à-vis their family and kin (who are the de-facto agents of socialization and indoctrination). It thus follows that if a certain behavior is generally regarded as more deviant for females than for males, or as more deviant for sixteen year olds than for twenty-one year olds, then (assuming that the level of deviant involvement remains constant) the female participants will have significantly less close family and kinship ties than will the male participants. Similarly, the sixteen-year-old participants would be expected to have more tenuous kin ties than the twenty-one-year-old participants.

Table 7—Extent of subjective importance of relatives to swinging and to control respondents

Relatives Are:	Husbands		Wives	
	Swingers	Controls	Swingers	Controls
One of the most important aspects of my life	1	4	4	10
Generally important in my overall scheme of things	15	32	17	38
Somewhat important in my overall scheme of things	38	36	52	40
Unimportant in my overall scheme of things	46	28	27	12

$\chi^2 = 12.3814, df = 3$ \
p < .01 \
gamma = −.38

$\chi^2 = 38.5096, df = 3$ \
p < .001 \
gamma = −.46

Table 8—Percent of respondents who have at least some major relatives (other than spouse and children) living within an hour's driving distance

Relatives within an Hour's Driving Distance	Husbands		Wives	
	Swingers	Controls	Swingers	Controls
Yes	39	51	42	50
No	61	49	58	50

$\chi^2 = 2.9090, df = 1$ \
not significant \
gamma = −.61

$\chi^2 = 1.2882, df = 1$ \
not significant \
gamma = −.16

Of course, statistically deviant persons always can be expected to arise in any pluralistic society. Specifically, there will always be mothers and fathers who sincerely believe in the moral validity and righteousness of a "freer" normative approach to life than that which is sanctioned by the dominant majority. One might also expect that swingers are significantly more likely than nonswingers of the same social class to socialize their own children in accordance with a liberal philosophy, particularly with reference to sex. When the parents themselves uphold as acceptable certain behaviors which most adults of the same society define as morally objectionable, it should be possible for the young people who engage in those behaviors to remain emotionally close to their families and to experience no guilt reactions in connection with those behaviors.

But for the majority of people who come from more or less conventional backgrounds, psychological differentiation from the parents would seem to be a precondition for deviant behavior. The greater the degree of emotional dependence on the parents for love and approval, the weaker the proclivity to think differently from these authority figures. More generally, as any behavior gradually becomes more widely accepted in a society the actual participation in that behavior will become decreasingly associated with strained or functionally autonomous ties with the extended family.

As can be seen in Table 8, swingers were found to be less likely than the controls to have some major relatives living within an hour's driving distance—a point which is of considerable significance for social control as some (albeit a minority) of swingers worry about inopportune surprise visits. Yet the findings on physical proximity did not quite attain statistical significance. In essence, it would appear that sheer physical proximity is of far less significance for social control than is the mindless, unquestioning internalization of parental norms which was inspired by a history of mutually gratifying parent-child relations. Even when one considers only couples whose relatives are living within the same metropolitan area, the swingers interact with kin considerably less than do the controls. Indeed, for the wives the finding was somewhat stronger even than in the zero-order case (see table 5). Of interest too is the fact that 38.0% of the swinging wives with relatives in the immediate area see their kin less than once per month compared to 25.6% of the swinging husbands. If it is true that women are more closely tied to their family of orientation than men are in our society, then this is an especially impressive and revealing finding. For even a strongly independent husband is likely to fail in his efforts to become a part of the swinging movement unless his wife is willing to think and to develop values in a highly independent, autonomous manner regardless of the nature of her ties to her kin.

The data of this study also indicate that swingers tend to be significantly less attached to virtually all of the conventional agencies of social control than nonswingers. The family is for most people the most powerful of all social-control forces, and it is the one that is emphasized here. But it is also interesting to compare the outlook of swingers and controls with respect to religious institutions. Almost two-thirds of the swingers compared to one-quarter of the controls agreed with the statement, "Religion is one of the greatest sources of hate, intolerance, and oppression that the world has ever known." The controls were far more concerned about getting their children to practice religion than they were about practicing it themselves; the swingers did not reveal this inconsistency. This finding, along with many similar ones which are beyond the scope of this paper, shows the swingers to be far less committed than the controls to the majority of conventional American ideology and to virtually all social-control structures.

Parenthetically, like all persons who are for the most part alienated from conventional religious structures, swingers seem to have tolerant attitudes toward "underdogs" and deprived and oppressed peoples. In essence, the present study provides further documentation for what is now considered by most sociologists to be a basic social fact: Conventionally religious people tend to be significantly less tolerant and humanistic in their outlook than unconventional people. These findings would further seem to support some of the key results of Freedman and Doob (1968) who studied artificially contrived deviance under laboratory conditions. They found that deviants of all kinds—including those who were poles apart in the nature of their deviance—tended to stick together and to side with each other against the "conformists." Conformists, on the other hand, tended to view all deviants in a rather callous, biased, noncompassionate manner.

These findings, by the way, coincide quite well with earlier reports on the behavior of American social nudists. Both Weiberg (1966) and Ilfeld and Lauer (1964) point out that nudists interact significantly less with parents and other close relatives than do non-nudists of the same social class. They also point out, however, that nudists interact significantly less with friends as well, thus rendering them significantly more isolated than the majority of people in the general population. In fact, the greater the amount of time American nudists were involved in their own movement, the more socially isolated they were. As Phillips (1967) has convincingly documented, lack of involvement with people is the single most powerful determinant of unhappiness and of psychological instability. Because of this finding, swingers were compared to controls with respect to how frequently they interacted with their friends.

The results indicated that the deviance of swingers appears to have a markedly different effect on their nonfamilial social lives than the deviance of nudists. Swingers were found to interact significantly more frequently with their friends than the controls living in the same neighborhoods did with theirs. Moreover, this was found to be true for both husbands and wives. For example, 74% of the male swingers as compared to 33% of the controls indicated that they visited with their friends at least once or more per week. The analogous figures for the females were 74% of the swingers as opposed to only 46% of the controls. A more thorough analysis of the data revealed that the number of months or years spent in swinging had no effect on the amount of social involvement with friends. The length of time involved in swinging did have a mildly negative effect upon frequency of interaction with relatives and kin, but this relationship was very small. It would appear that a person's decision to commit himself to swinging initially —and hence to label himself as a swinger—serves as a far more powerful predictor of frequency of visitation with kin than does actual amount of time spent within the swinging movement.

Some investigators (see especially Galant and Galant 1966b) have suggested that swinging sodalities have themselves become for many mate sharers a quasi-kin group providing much of the in-group intimacy conventional people find through close interaction with relatives. Of course, as Bartell (1971) and others have documented, some swingers prefer not to develop any close friendship ties with other swingers, and some even prefer the impersonal anonymity that group-sex encounters with total strangers provide. While the present sample of swingers included both kinds, I felt that most of the couples interviewed felt a strong bond with mate sharers everywhere. Indeed, some even maintain lists of recommended swinging couples in various parts of the country, and when these couples travel they feel quite free to contact the recommended couples. Very often swinging families will go on weekend or vacation trips together. Although arrangements are made so that the sexual activity of the adults almost never takes place around the children, as a result of these and other shared activities, the closeness of the friendship bond found among some of these couples tends to be strikingly similar to that which is found among relatives in more conventional social groupings.

Some of the couples who go on brief vacation trips together do not even know each other personally at the inception of such trips. One Los Angeles couple told me of a business trip to Atlanta. Even though this couple took their children, they still contacted a recommended mate-sharing couple whom they had never met before. This couple also had children, and they put the visiting couple up at their home for four nights during which time, among other things, they engaged in a number of family-type recreations. While most contemporary American swingers evidently do not permit themselves to become quite so intimately involved on a social level, it seems likely that for an increasing proportion of couples involved in co-marital sex the "swingers' network" is becoming a functional equivalent for the modified extended family. Also, the greater the number of years a couple has been involved in co-marital sex, the greater the likelihood that they will be actively involved in "family" visiting within such a network.

Let us now consider informal social interaction among neighbors, i.e., people who reside within the same immediate neighborhood. Neighbors can be thought of as people who live either next door or within easy walking distance. Up until World War II, neighbors constituted the large bulk of the average man or woman's friends. In contemporary suburbia, however, it is possible to reside within a neighborhood for more than a decade and not really get to know anyone unless, of course, one happens to have a child in the local elementary school.

There are numerous reasons why neighbors are no longer the main source of friends for most people. Few people are any longer constrained by necessity to cultivate friends exclusively within small isolated communities. Today speedy, efficient transportation is easily available to most people, thus making it possible to choose friends from all over a metropolitan area. And in most metropolitan areas there is a plethora of subgroups and special interest groups (of which sexual mate sharing is clearly one) in which a person can become involved and from which he can draw his friends. In the small rural town, people had to depend upon relatives and neighbors unless they were veritable hermits. Today, most people enjoy far wider possibilities (if they have the social skills necessary for taking advantage of them) for making friends. Then too, the typical suburban community today is commonly thought of as a "bedroom community"; one's job is quite likely to be located outside one's habitat. It follows that the greater the percentage of time one spends outside a community, the less interaction one is likely to have within that community.

Even today, the more traditional a community is, the more important neighbors are to each other. Contemporary suburban communities can hardly be considered "traditional" in any literal sense of the word, and clearly, swingers are at least a few steps less traditional than the typical suburban resident. As expected (given the cosmopolitan image they have of themselves), swingers interact significantly less with neighbors than do the controls. Sixty-two percent of the swinging wives saw their neighbors less than once every three months, compared with only 36% of the control wives. However, 62% of the swinging wives were employed at the time of the study, compared with only 33% of the control wives, which would keep the former out of their neighborhoods a good deal more than the latter.

Perhaps a key reason for this pattern of relative alienation from those living in the immediate neighborhood is that swingers tend to perceive neighbors as a potential threat. A substantial proportion of the swingers interviewed for this study told me that they frequently worried about the possibility of unplanned visits by relatives. Friendly relationships with people in the same immediate neighborhood could intensify this concern. The sight of numerous automobiles parked in front of a swinger's house might make befriended neighbors feel slighted, or they might walk over and ring the doorbell uninvited. Some of the sensational press on mate sharing suggests that swingers often seduce neighbors and strangers whom they might meet. Neither this nor any other scholarly study known to this researcher suggests that this actually happens.

In sum, this study emphasizes that swingers are not in any sense socially isolated even though their emotional ties to the more conventional agencies of social control tend to be weak in comparison with what is typical among the middle class in American society. According to Goode (1963), 79% of housewives interviewed in a Detroit-area study indicated that relatives were of greater personal importance to them than friends, while only 17% thought that the importance of friends surpassed that of relatives. Yet, as can be seen in table 6, while 70% of the suburban California control wives similarly thought relatives were more important to them than friends, only 35% of the swinging wives expressed this priority. Indeed, 79% of the swinging husbands and 59% of the swinging wives viewed their friends as being of greater personal importance to them than their relatives. (The meaning of "friends" here, of course, is any kind of friend, not just fellow swingers.) These basic differences in values are highlighted even more lucidly in table 7, where it is shown that swingers are a great deal more likely than controls to feel that relatives are unimportant in the overall scheme of things. These findings further support the view that the visitation patterns of swingers actually are a reflection of their values and social ideology.

Assuming that the results of this study reflect actual behavior patterns and that subjective personal happiness is strongly influenced by frequent active informal involvement with others, the following propositions follow:

H_4: The extent of subjective personal happiness is no different among swingers than it is among controls.
H_5: Personal "anomie" is no greater among swingers than it is among controls.

H_6: The extent of subjective marital happiness is no different among swingers than it is among controls.

H_7: Swingers are no more likely than controls to suffer from feelings of boredom in their personal lives.

H_8: Swingers are no more likely than controls to consume alcoholic beverages excessively.

H_9: Swingers are no more likely than controls to have experienced any form of psychotherapy.

The popular press over the past two years has had a good deal to say regarding each of these hypotheses. A recent article edited by Bell (1971) in the short-lived publication *Sexual Behavior* can be viewed as typical. Certain psychiatrists, lawyers, and theologians known to support the status quo on most matters were chosen to give their opinions on the phenomenon of swinging, and almost all asserted with a high degree of confidence that it is associated with personal and social pathology. Seldom did these writers endeavor to provide any empirical support for their views other than their own personal interpretation of interviews they might have had with people whom they counseled.

A widely accepted proposition in sociology is that social reality for all human beings is constructed throughout the long process of socialization, including normative indoctrination. In American society, "sinfulness" and "pathology" are typically seen as an intrinsic part of any "far-out" form of social deviance. It is this kind of perspective which generates a trained incapacity for raising the kinds of questions that would shed an explanatory light on swinging, its antecedents, and its consequences.

It is very doubtful if swinging, or any other form of nonconformist deviance, is intrinsically pathological. When seemingly strange behaviors are viewed in their social and cultural context, an underlying harmony can ordinarily be seen between the behaviors and the pattern of internalized norms. Disharmony, pathology, and negative consequences can ordinarily be seen as by-products of behavior that is not fully accepted by the people who engage in it. With a phenomenon like swinging in a society like the United States, it is inevitable that some of the practitioners (especially the comparative neophytes to co-marital sex) will not fully believe in the moral validity of their actions. But that all or even most participants will not accept what they do as morally acceptable seems highly unlikely.

This study uncovered a great deal of data bearing on the overall "adjustment" of swingers, only the most representative of which will be presented here. With respect to the fourth hypothesis, no meaningful difference could be found between the swingers and the controls on the variable of subjective personal happiness. This was true for both the wives and the husbands (see table 9). This finding is not surprising, especially when compared to those concerning degree of involvement with people. Of course, there is the possibility that the swingers might have been misrepresenting their general feelings of happiness and contentment. It is difficult to determine, however, why they might have had any more reason for wanting to "fake good" than the controls. Moreover, it would seem unlikely that people who consciously feel unhappy would be motivated to deny it on a written questionnaire completed privately.

In addition to active involvement with people, there are several other variables that have previously been found to relate closely to feelings of subjective happiness. For a man, degree of satisfaction with his employment is very important, and for both sexes, overall marital satisfaction is of the utmost importance. In fact, America's high divorce and remarriage rates undoubtedly reflect, in part, the widespread tendency to view emotionally gratifying conjugal relationships as the most important factor for personal well-being and contentment.

As can be seen in tables 10 and 11, there is no indication that swinging husbands are any less satisfied with their careers or occupations than the control husbands. Approximately 30% of each group claimed that they derive a "very great deal" of personal satisfaction out of their work, and 78% and 79% of the swinging and control husbands, respectively, claimed that if they were twenty years old and had the chance to start all over again they would choose roughly the same kind of work. This relatively high occupational satisfaction is consistent with what has commonly been found by sociologists for white-collar groups. And since none of the men in either sample had been unemployed dur-

Table 9—Extent of subjective personal happiness among swingers and controls

	Husbands		Wives	
Degree of Happiness	Swingers	Controls	Swingers	Controls
Very happy	28	30	41	42
Happy	49	43	39	37
Fairly happy	20	23	17	18
Unhappy	3	4	3	3

$\chi^2 = .8126, df = 3$ $\chi^2 = .0932, df = 3$
not significant   not significant
gamma $= .02$ gamma $= -.00$

Table 10—Responses to question, "If you were twenty years old and had the chance to start all over again, would you select an occupation at least roughly similar to the one which you are now in?"

Response	Swingers	Controls
Yes	78	79
No	22	21

$\chi^2 = .0296, df = 1$
not significant
gamma $= -.03$

Table 11—Degree of personal satisfaction derived from occupation

	Husbands	
Degree of Satisfaction	Swingers	Controls
A very great deal	29	31
A considerable amount	32	42
A fair amount	21	16
A slight amount	13	9
Dissatisfied	5	2

$\chi^2 = 4.1066, df = 4$
not significant
gamma $= -.14$

ing the preceding two years, the fairly widespread notion that swinging men are unstable and undisciplined seems unlikely.

The findings regarding overall subjective marital happiness again show no statistically significant difference between the swingers and the controls for either the husbands or the wives. But this time, as table 12 indicates, the swinging couples actually seem to be somewhat happier together than the controls. Again, a tendency on the part of the swingers to "fake good" could be suspected, but the strength and consistency of a number of other related findings suggest that this is not likely. For example, 57% of the swinging husbands answered "emphatically yes" to the question, "Does your spouse seem to have an easy capacity for occasionally saying 'I love you' to you?", compared with only 31% of the control husbands. The swingers were also much more

Table 12—Extent of subjective marital happiness among swingers and controls

	Husbands		Wives	
Degree of Happiness	Swingers	Controls	Swingers	Controls
Very happy	56	43	58	49
Happy	29	33	23	31
Fairly happy	13	20	15	18
Unhappy	2	4	4	2

$\chi^2 = 4.1164$, $df = 3$ $\chi^2 = 2.8816$, $df = 3$
not significant   not significant
gamma $= .24$ gamma $= .12$

likely than the controls to be well satisfied with the amount of affection their spouses spontaneously display toward them.

The basic theoretical significance of these findings cannot be ignored. In recent years, several studies have shown quite clearly that spontaneous, positive, expressive socioemotional interaction between husbands and wives is strongly related to subjective overall marital satisfaction (Levinger 1964; Pineo 1961; and Rainwater 1966). Indeed, these studies strongly suggest that for the United States at least, there are few variables (if any) of greater predictive significance for marital success than those relating to spontaneous displays of affection and mutually gratifying socioemotional interaction between spouses. Moreover, Goode has stated (1971) that the American marriage institution has specialized in the expressive area, and thus unusually heavy demands tend to be placed upon it for effectively satisfying the psychological needs of its members.

Rainwater (1966) showed that couples whose roles are "joint" tend to view themselves as happily married more than those whose roles are more or less "segregated." Simply stated, this means that given the nature of American values toward marriage, the more couples do together at home and in their recreational patterns, the happier they are likely to be together. The general theory here is consistent with Homans's (1950) well-researched proposition concerning the "mode of standardization," which states that the more two people (or two groups) interact with each other, the more these two people (or groups) will come to like or love each other, and the more they will come to share values, interests, hopes, desires, dreams, and aspirations. Swinging, of course, is a joint type of recreation. Unique among the various patterns of adultery, swinging actually requires that the couple participate in this form of behavior *as a couple*. Hence, there is a possibility that couples who swing actually engage in a good deal more joint activity than do most other couples of similar class background. Although my data on this point are inconclusive, they do provide some support for this assertion.

While only some couples swing as members of an organized social club, those who do are very often required as a prerequisite for membership to convince the leaders that they are happily married. A major southern California club which runs at least two parties per week in its own painstakingly adapted mansion requires that all prospective couples be interviewed by two separate evaluating officers before membership is granted; in this particular club only about two out of every five applicants are permitted to join.

An unhappily married couple at a swinging party is commonly regarded as constituting somewhat of a threat to the other couples. Like the single man, an unhappily married person does not have much, if anything, to lose. He or she may have an unconscious need to "fall in love" in a deeply emotional sense with someone else's spouse, which could lead to formidable embarrassment and difficulty. Such persons may also be more prone to jealousy. If one partner wants to maintain the marriage more than the other, he or she is likely to enjoy considerably less bargaining power with respect to his/her spouse than the spouse is likely to enjoy. Such persons are likely to feel quite nervous about this, but more commonly, both members of the couple are likely to be viewed by club managers as inadequately "happy-go-lucky" and carefree.

Besides the screening, which tends to weed out unhappy couples, there is also the swinging ideology, which undoubtedly has a unique effect on selection, recruitment, and subsequent participation in co-marital activities. One of the most common themes pervading the discussions of swinging leaders is that co-marital sex embellishes and enriches marriages in all areas, and especially in the erotic sector. At the same time, these leaders characteristically insist that swinging is not a viable therapy for poor marriages, but the very consistent message is that it can, and almost always does, make good marriages even better.

According to the principle of the self-fulfilling prophecy, when one defines things or ideas as real, these things or ideas tend to become real in their consequences. Clearly, it follows from this principle that couples who possess the requisite characteristics, and who do not become alienated from mate sharing by a few bad experiences, are highly likely to see their marriages (and especially their sexual lives together as a couple) as becoming even better, because this is what they have been led to expect. Also, the longer a couple has been exposed to swinging, the greater the exposure to the ideology they are likely to have experienced. Everything else being equal, frequency of exposure to the ideology should be related directly to thoroughness of mental and emotional internalization of that ideology, hence, to the construction of an important new social reality for the persons involved.

The jointness of swingers' recreation patterns has implications for the seventh hypothesis as well. One of the most frequently observed criticisms of swinging is that its practitioners use it to "escape from boredom" rather than to face up to their "personal problems" in a direct and "mature" manner. The intimation in all moralistic journalism on this subject is that a person could not conceivably practice mate sharing without being immature and without having serious psychological problems, whether or not he "consciously" recognizes them. This study uncovered quite a bit of data regarding feelings of boredom in the lives of swingers. The most representative of these data are summarized in tables 13 and 14. Of special interest is the fact that the swingers seem to be slightly less bored with their situation than the controls. Indeed, on the basis of these findings one might well wonder why swingers are so often accused by "square" society (as well as by some psychiatrists) of wanton escapism. Further indication that swinging husbands and wives probably do not have any greater need than most people to escape from their families can be seen in findings dealing with familial commensalism. Most of the couples in both groups were found to eat the majority of their evening meals together. In fact, the swinging wives were somewhat more likely than the control wives to have the companionship of their husbands at dinner at least five nights per week (85% versus 76%).

Table 13—Responses to question, "Do you often find yourself with too few interesting or meaningful things to do?"

	Husbands		Wives	
Response	Swingers	Controls	Swingers	Controls
Yes	13	18	15	17
Uncertain	2	11	1	1
No	85	71	84	82

$\chi^2 = 8.2936, df = 2$ $\chi^2 = .1490, df = 2$
p < .02   not significant
gamma = −.35   gamma = −.07

Table 14—Responses to question, "In general, would you say that your life is busy enough?"

Response	Husbands		Wives	
	Swingers	Controls	Swingers	Controls
Emphatically yes	45	42	47	51
Mostly yes	47	43	41	43
Uncertain	4	6	7	2
No	4	9	5	4

$\chi^2 = 2.6042, df = 3$
not significant
gamma = .11

$\chi^2 = 3.0998, df = 3$
not significant
gamma = −.11

One of the most commonly observed indices of adjustment and self-discipline is the ability of a person or group to remain sober under stress. Alcohol has long been a major social problem in America, and people who develop an undisciplined dependency on it or who otherwise drink excessively are typically viewed as highly objectionable deviants. The available literature on swinging is unfortunately very ambiguous when it comes to the matter of alcohol. Bartell (1971) points out how social drinking was an integral feature of the mate-sharing activities that he observed, but he presented no data as to the actual amount of alcohol consumed or of the relative consumption of swingers to nonswingers of the same class.

The Galants (1966b) point out how the undisciplined use of alcohol runs counter to the ideology of co-marital sex and how those who have difficulty controlling their intake of alcohol swiftly become blackballed in the swinging community. The owner-manager of Club "101" in Los Angeles made it quite clear that any undisciplined consumption of alcohol is very much against swingers' etiquette even though social drinking is almost always involved in swinging festivities. There are some swingers, however, who will not drink at all prior to actual swinging; moreover, many mate sharers are very careful to eat very lightly prior to an erotic event, since food and alcohol are believed by some to have a deleterious effect on sexual performance. Even though the data of this study cannot be considered definitive, the results strongly suggest that at the very least swingers are no more likely than nonswingers of the same social class to be undisciplined or "problem" drinkers. Even if one grants the possibility of some exaggeration by the respondents, it seems significant that only 19% of the control husbands said that they average "one or none" alcoholic beverages at a typical social gathering compared with 37% of the swinging husbands. The analogous data for the wives were 31% for the controls and 48% for the swingers. In short, the present study suggests that swingers drink less, not more, than most people.

The respondents were also asked whether or not they ever have any difficulty refusing further drinks once they feel that they have had enough. Again, even though this kind of question may invite distortion, the data strongly suggest that swingers have as much self-control in this regard as nonswingers. Moreover, even if there was some unconscious or semiconscious response distortion, there does not appear to be any reason to believe that the swingers were any more guilty of distortion than the controls.

Swingers are often alleged to rate high on personal anomie. Socially isolated people are especially likely to suffer from feelings of normlessness and deregulation. And as McClosky and Schaar have found (1965) in what is probably the most thorough and penetrating empirical study to date on the subject, persons with a high degree of anomie are significantly more likely than those who have a low degree to be characterized by high guilt, low self-confidence, high contempt for weakness and intolerance of human frailty, high alienation, low overall satisfaction with life, strong feelings of political futility, low sense of social responsibility, high status frustration, high pessimism, and high personal hostility and paranoia. In this study, the nine-item McClosky and Schaar (1965) anomie scale was used to measure the dependent variable. The findings, as summarized in table 15, are indeed rather surprising. First, the findings for all four groups tended to suggest relatively low levels of anomie. If everything else was equal, this would be expected for well-educated, middle- to upper-middle class suburbanites. Beyond this,

Table 15—Extent of personal anomie[a]

Score	Husbands		Wives	
	Swingers	Controls	Swingers	Controls
High (score 6–9)	9	10	13	20
Medium (score 3–5)	30	49	31	41
Low (score 0–2)	61	41	56	39

[a] Anomie was measured by the nine-item McClosky and Schaar scale (1965).

$\chi^2 = 8.5438$, $df = 2$
$p < .02$
gamma $= -.31$

$\chi^2 = 5.9158$, $df = 2$
$p < .06$ (not significant)
gamma $= -.28$

it should be noted that the control husbands scored significantly *higher* on anomie than did the swinging husbands (p <.02), and the control wives similarly appeared demonstrably more anomic than the swinging wives (p <.06). The control wives had the highest degree of the four groups, a fact which may reflect the overprotected, socially isolated, lethargic state of an untold proportion of unemployed American house-wives. Only 39% of the control wives obtained a low anomie score compared to 56% of the swinging wives. Among the husbands, 61% of the swingers scored "low" versus 41% of the controls.

The level of anomie can be interpreted as a general index of personal adjustment to one's life and interpersonal integration. Another common but crude index of adjustment is that of whether or not a person has ever experienced any kind of psychotherapeutic help for personal prob-lems. In fact, some researchers in this area have focused exclusively on respondents who have been consulting with psychiatric professionals. Recently, Schofield (1965) was able to show that homosexuals in psychotherapy are not representative of homosexuals in the general population, that the large majority of homosexuals never seek psycho-therapeutic aid, and that those who do tend to be considerably less well adjusted and happy than those who do not. Table 16 summarizes the findings as to the prevalence of psychotherapeutic experience among participants in co-marital sex.

As can be observed, the data fail to support the ninth hypothesis, a fact of considerable surprise given the favorable responses of the swingers on the other questions dealing with personal adjustment. In-deed, if the swingers had a greater tendency than the controls to "fake good" on the adjustment questions, one might well wonder why they failed to follow through on this item. Among the husbands the data show that virtually twice as many swingers as controls had experienced at least some psychotherapy in their lifetime (36% versus 18%).

Table 16—History of psychological counseling

History	Husbands		Wives	
	Swingers	Controls	Swingers	Controls
Yes	36	18	35	24
No	64	82	65	76

$\chi^2 = 8.2192, df = 1$
p < .01
gamma = .44

$\chi^2 = 2.9090, df = 1$
not significant
gamma = .26

Among the wives, it was 35% of the swingers compared with 24% of the controls. Of course, despite these differences, it also should be noted that almost two-thirds of the swinging husbands and wives had never experienced any psychotherapy.

While post-facto explanations of unexpected findings are usually somewhat risky, it appears likely that the much greater incidence of psychotherapy among the swingers may simply have been a by-product of the greater effort they expended during later adolescence and early adulthood to "find themselves," i.e., to establish a firm personal identity and an acceptable morality. The swingers do appear to be as happy as the controls, if not even happier. But as I have already documented, the data also show that the childhood and adolescence of the swingers was less happy and serene than that of the controls. As virtually none of the swingers was undergoing psychotherapeutic treatment at the time of the study, it would certainly appear likely that their adjustment problems were primarily a past experience.

It therefore seems probable that swingers do tend to be significantly less stable and less serene than most people during their adolescent and early adulthood period but that after they have developed their coping and adaptive behavior for dealing with life problems, they enjoy a degree of personal happiness and adjustment which at the very least seems to be no different than that which other people of the same social-class level enjoy. This pattern of development also has implications for the question of marital stability among swingers. As a group the swingers had been married for almost as many years as the controls. But while only 15% of the control husbands had ever been divorced, 49% of the swinging husbands had had that experience. The analogous figures for the wives were 14% and 34%.

The belief that mate sharing *causes* divorce and marital and family disorganization is widely held by moralists and by psychiatrists who have an awareness of co-marital sex. Yet, despite the above-mentioned findings, this study has furnished strong evidence suggestive of an alternate interpretation. Specifically, *none* of the divorces occurred *after* a man or woman had become active with either a present or a former spouse in co-marital sexual behavior. (This, of course, is not to suggest that other, more conventional forms of extramarital relationships were not common among the antecedents of the divorces.) In short, this study indicates that, among swinging husbands and wives, divorce antedates the initial mutual involvement in mate sharing; it does not postdate it.

The swinging husbands generally contracted their first marriage at an unusually early age. They tended to first marry women to whom they had felt immensely physically attracted after very short court-ships, well before any adequately comprehensive knowledge and appre-ciation of the values and personal attributes of each other could be realized at a rational, intellectual level. The research of numerous so-ciologists has shown that during the early months of a relationship, "love" tends to serve as a smoke screen blinding the lovers to many of each other's most essential personal attributes. This blinding smoke screen—combined with the weak social control of the family and the strong psychological tendency toward autonomy of preswinging males —all function as powerful forces pressing toward early marriage. In American society, marriage is quite often seen by adolescents as con-stituting a key indicator of adult status. And the status of independent, fully autonomous adults is one that the swinging males were likely to have craved unusually early in their youth—too early even to have given any serious consideration to the nonconformist compromise of cohabitation without marriage. (On the other hand, many of these same people did practice "living together" prior to their *second* marriage when they were in their midtwenties.)

A quite common outcome of these early marriages was that men gradually began to find their partners "too conventional" for them. In fact, several of the swinging wives made similar points with regard to their first husbands. Usually within one to three years of the marriage, the clash of developing values between the preswingers and their first spouses gave rise to conflict, alienation, and unhealable cleavages. After divorce (and very often before), the preswinger began to socialize with politically liberal and/or socially unconventional groups of young peo-ple. "Swinging-singles" groups and sexual-freedom organizations in particular tended to be frequented on a fairly regular basis. In fact, a sizeable proportion of the swinging couples in this study (those who had experienced only one marriage and those who had been divorced) claimed that they actually met their present spouse at "swinging-singles" gatherings. In short, swinging for many of these couples actually pre-ceded marriage. This seems to explain why the swinging couples were as happy, and in some respects even happier with each other than the controls even though they, as a group, were far more likely to have experienced at least one divorce in their lifetime. It would appear that when swingers choose their second spouse they tend to be quite careful about selecting someone whose major life values, outlook on life, rec-reational interests, and personal perspective are reasonably similar to their own. Virtually all family sociologists agreed that a reasonable homogeneity of major values and interests between a husband and wife is a major precondition of marital success and happiness. Of course, only a longitudinal study could determine the duration of marriage and rate of divorce among couples with co-marital experience.

It is surprising how many otherwise highly sophisticated scholars and laymen cannot understand how a couple could "swing" and still remain happily married. It seems that the answer lies basically in this matter of relative congruence of value systems between husband and wife. If both a husband and a wife share essentially the same pattern of expectations about their marital relationship, it is difficult to see how their relationship could falter. This idea of value congruence between spouses coincides with the assertion that a person's internalized norms ("social reality") promote the "self-fulfilling prophecy." Behaviors such as co-marital sex, premarital sex, or marijuana use cannot themselves create conflict and disharmony among people. These behaviors cannot cause a relationship between a man and a woman to deteriorate, nor can they promote a diminution of positive self-regard or self-esteem. What can and does make an immense amount of difference is (1) what the actor himself thinks and feels about the behavior he has been engaging in—a matter determined by what the individual has been socially conditioned to think and feel, which in turn is a function of the type of social context in which the individual has developed; and (2) the degree of congruence between the internalized norms (regarding the behavior in question) of the actor and his or her primary companion. For example, a wife who has been led to define extramarital sex in any form as incompatible with a happy and emotionally satisfying marriage is very likely to have a highly unsatisfying marriage, if her husband should fail to conceal adequately an extramarital "fling" he might have had. She will remain happily married, on the other hand, so long as her husband either remains "faithful" or successfully conceals his flings. When the husband in such a case asserts that he loves his wife, he may be quite sincere, but since the internalized norms of the wife are very different from his own interpretations of his adulterous behavior, the situation will quite commonly give rise to a "self-fulfilling prophecy" and hence to a deteriorating relationship.

Of course, people change over time, and this change often occurs at a different rate in each spouse (a fact that can, of course, lead to difficulties), but there is no evidence suggesting that swingers are likely to encounter greater difficulty than the controls on differential rates of personal change. Indeed, the fact that they tend to do more together as a couple than the controls would suggest that they would be somewhat less likely than most couples to develop in divergent directions. Certainly, Homans's "mode of standardization" principle, if accurate, would suggest that such a prediction should eventually prove reliable.

Finally, it is interesting to observe that extramarital sex of the conventional, nonswinging variety is not an especially uncommon phenomenon among the middle-class population. For example, among the controls in the present study, 31% of the husbands and 8% of the wives claimed that they had engaged in extramarital sex at some time in their present marriages. What may be of a considerably greater surprise to most readers, however, is the fact that the large majority of both husbands and wives in these relationships viewed their marriages as being either "happy" or "very happy." While space limitations prohibit a detailed presentation of these findings in this report, it is interesting to point out that deception was involved in almost all of the control-group marriages involving extramarital sex. Specifically, the control husbands gave every indication that they sincerely loved their wives and that they were happily married. They saw deception as indispensable lest their mutually gratifying relationship with their wives be placed in serious jeopardy because their wives "wouldn't understand." A careful cross-checking of the marital-happiness ratings of the spouses in these marriages revealed a high level of agreement between each spouse. In other words, if a wife rated her marriage as "happy," her husband, in almost every case, similarly rated it as "happy" or as "very happy."

Summary and Conclusions

The major objective of this paper has been to provide an overview of the most important social and personal characteristics that differentiate swingers from nonswingers. The term "swinging" as used in this paper denotes "mate sharing" (co-marital sexual behavior) among legally married couples.

As a group, swingers were found to have experienced significantly less satisfying ties with their parents and kin than had the controls. Compared with the latter they interact as adults less frequently with their relatives and are less influenced by them. The most powerful social control is that which is unperceived as such and which occurs in the course of everyday friendly, mutually gratifying, convivial conversation with people in the companionship of whom one can relax and let down one's guard. Since swingers' relations with parents throughout adolescence tended to be strained, the parents failed to inspire the relatively uncritical acceptance and internalization of traditional norms and values which normally occurs in families.

Even though swingers were less happy as adolescents than the controls, they were sufficiently competent socially to be respected by their peers. Swingers learned early to depend far more heavily on peers than on parents for emotional support and recognition, a dependency which as adults continued to distinguish them from their nonswinging neighbors. Despite more serious adjustment and personal identity-seeking problems during later adolescence and early adulthood, swinging husbands and wives tended to emerge into maturity with at least as high a level of personal happiness as the controls. Indeed, besides being as happy with their personal and marital situations as the controls, the swingers were also found to be no more likely to suffer from feelings of boredom, occupational dissatisfaction, or social isolation. In fact, on most of the indices, gender was found to be a more powerful determinant of feelings of personal boredom, alienation, and isolation than was status as a swinger. For example, wives were found to suffer from stronger feelings of personal anomie than were husbands. But there was no indication in the data that swinging wives tend to be any more anomic than control wives. In fact, the swinging husbands were found to be significantly less anomic than their nonswinging neighbors. It is quite likely that one of the key reasons for the significantly lower anomie scores for the swinging wives is that they were far more likely than their counterparts in the control group to be working full time outside the home.

Inasmuch as swingers likely had a stormier youth than the controls they were significantly more likely during that period of their lives to have experienced psychotherapy. They were also more likely during that period to have married quite early and to have divorced relatively soon afterward. However, upon finding a spouse with values similar to their own, they seemed to arrive at a level of adjustment somewhat superior even to that of the controls. In fact, at the time of the study, fewer of the swingers than of the controls were seeing a psychiatrist or clinical psychologist.

Finally, there is the very practical consideration of the effect that swinging has upon the conjugal relationship and upon family life. Bartell (1971) suggested that swinging is likely to be very good for some couples and very bad for others. I believe that it should now be possible to predict with a high degree of accuracy which couples swinging would be bad for and which ones it would be good for. To begin with, it was concluded that swinging cannot per se precipitate negative consequences for any couple or person. The consequences of swinging depend on the social and cultural context within which it occurs. If the internalized norms and values of a person are either in harmony or in potential harmony with the ideology of swinging, then that person could not himself be "turned off" by the idea of this form of nonconformity. If the spouse of that person shares largely the same outlook on life as he does, and if their relationship together is a good one, then it is highly unlikely that any active involvement of both in mate-sharing activities would serve to undermine the quality of their marital union. But husbands and wives who are not especially happy with each other, and/or whose normative perceptions of social reality (especially as they relate to mate sharing) tend to be markedly disparate, would be well advised to avoid this form of nonconformist recreation, as it would be quite likely to precipitate a deterioration of the relationship and undermine self-esteem.

References

Bartell, G. D. 1970. Group Sex among the Mid-Americans. *J. Sex Res.* 6, no. 2, pp. 113–30. [In this book, pp. 185–201.]

———. 1971. *Group Sex: A Scientist's Eyewitness Report on the American Way of Swinging.* New York: Peter H. Wyden.

Bell, R. R., and Silvan, L. 1971. Swinging: The Sexual Exchange of Marriage Partners. *Sex. Behavior* 1 (May): 70–79.

Brecher, E. M. 1969. *The Sex Researchers.* Boston: Little, Brown.

Cervantes, L. F. 1965. *The Dropout: Causes and Cures.* Ann Arbor: University of Michigan Press.

Christensen, H. T., and Gregg, C. F. 1970. Changing Sex Norms in America and Scandinavia. *J. Marriage Fam.* 32 (November): 616–27.

Cuber, J. F., and Harroff, P. B. 1965. *The Significant Americans.* New York: Appleton-Century.

DeMartino, M. F. 1963. Dominance-Feeling, Security-Insecurity, and Sexuality in Women. In *Sexual Behavior and Personality Characteristics,* ed. M. F. DeMartino. New York: Citadel.

———. 1969. *The New Female Sexuality.* New York: Julian.

Eysenck, H. J. 1971. Introverts, Extroverts and Sex. *Psychol. Today* 4 (January): 14–19.

Flacks, R. 1967. The Liberated Generation: An Exploration of the Roots of Student Protest. *J. Soc. Issues* 23 (July): 52–75.

Freedman, J. L., and Doob, A. N. 1968. *Deviancy: The Psychology of Being Different.* New York: Academic.

Freud, S. 1927. *The Future of an Illusion.* Garden City, New York: Anchor Books.

———. 1929. *Civilization and Its Discontents.* New York: Norton.

Galant, M., and Galant, K. 1966a. *The Lesbian in Group Love.* Cleveland: Century Books.

———. 1966b. *Sex Rebels.* San Diego: Publisher's Export Company.

———. 1967a. *Mate Swapping Syndrome.* Los Angeles: Triumph Fact Books.

————. 1967b. *The Swinging Bisexuals*. Cleveland: Century Books.

————. 1967c. *Wife Swapping in Business*. Cleveland: Century Books.

————. 1967d. *Wife Swapping: The People*. San Diego: Publisher's Export Company.

Gilmartin, B. G. 1964. Relationship of Traits Measured by the California Psychological Inventory to Premarital Sexual Standards and Behaviors. Master's thesis, University of Utah.

Glock, C. Y., and Stark, R. 1970. Sounds of Silence. *Psychol. Today* 3 (April): 38–43.

Goode, W. J. 1963. *World Revolution and Family Patterns*. New York: Free Press of Glencoe.

————. 1971. Introduction. *The Contemporary American Family*, ed. W. J. Goode. Chicago: Quadrangle Books.

Hirschi, T. 1969. *Causes of Delinquency*. Berkeley: University of California Press.

Homans, G. C. 1950. *The Human Group*. New York: Harcourt, Brace and World.

Ilfeld, F., Jr., and Lauer, R. 1964. *Social Nudism in America*. New Haven: College and University Press.

Kandel, D., and Lesser, G. S. 1969. Parent-Adolescent Relationships and Adolescent Independence in the United States and Denmark. *J. Marriage Fam.* 31 (May): 348–58.

Kinsey, A. C., Pomeroy, W. B., and Martin, C. E. 1948. *Sexual Behavior in the Human Male*. Philadelphia: W. B. Saunders.

————, and Gebhard, P. H. 1953. *Sexual Behavior in the Human Female*. Philadelphia: W. B. Saunders.

Levinger, G. 1964. Task and Social Behavior in Marriage. *Sociometry* 27 (December): 433–48.

Martin, R. M., and Marcuse, F. L. 1957. Characteristics of Volunteers and Nonvolunteers for Hypnosis. *J. Clin. Exper. Hypnosis* 5 (October): 176–79.

Maslow, A. H. 1942. Self-Esteem (Dominance-Feeling) and Sexuality in Women. *J. Soc. Psychol.* 16 (September): 259–94.

————, and Sakoda, J. M. 1955. Volunteer-Error in the Kinsey Study. In *Sexual Behavior in American Society*, ed. J. Himelhoch and S. F. Fava. New York: Norton.

McClosky, H., and Schaar, J. H. 1965. Psychological Dimensions of Anomie. *Amer. Soc. Rev.* 30 (February): 14–40.

Moskin, J. R. 1969. The New Contraceptive Society. *Look* 33 (February 4): 50–53.

Murdock, G. P. 1949. *Social Structure*. New York: Macmillan.

O'Neill, G. C., and O'Neill, N. 1970. Patterns in Group Sexual Activity. *J. Sex Res.* 6, no. 2, pp. 101–12.

Phillips, D. L. 1967. Mental Health Status, Social Participation, and Happiness. *Journal of Health and Social Behavior* 8 (December): 285–91.

Pineo, P. C. 1961. Disenchantment in the Later Years of Marriage. *J. Marriage Fam.* 23 (February): 3–11.

Rainwater, L. 1966. Some Aspects of Lower Class Sexual Behavior. *J. Soc. Issues* 22 (April): 96–108.

Reiss, I. L. 1965. Social Class and Premarital Sexual Permissiveness: A Re-Examination. *Amer. Soc. Rev.* 30 (October): 747–56.

———. 1967. *The Social Context of Premarital Sexual Permissiveness.* New York: Holt, Rinehart and Winston.

Schofield, M. 1965. *Sociological Aspects of Homosexuality.* Boston: Little, Brown.

Silberman, C. E. 1970. *Crisis in the Classroom.* New York: Random House.

Smith, J. R., and Smith, L. G. 1970. Co-Marital Sex and the Sexual Freedom Movement. *J. Sex Res.* 6, no. 2, pp. 131–42. [In this book, pp. 202–13.]

Symonds, C. 1968. Pilot Study of the Peripheral Behavior of Sexual Mate Swappers. Master's thesis, University of California, Riverside.

———. 1971. Sexual Mate Swapping and the Swingers. *Marriage Counseling Quarterly* 6 (Spring): 1–12.

Warren, J. T. 1966. *Age of the Wife Swappers.* New York: Lancer Books.

Weinberg, M. S. 1966. Becoming a Nudist. *Psychiatry: J. Study Interpersonal Processes* 29 (February): 21–33.

Wilson, T. J. B., and Meyers, E. 1965. *Wife Swapping: A Complete 8 Year Survey of Morals in North America.* New York: Volitant Press.

Young, M., and Willmott, P. 1957. *Family and Kinship in East London.* Baltimore: Penguin-Pelican Books.

Contributors

GILBERT D. BARTELL, Ph.D., is associate professor of anthropology at Northern Illinois University. His publications and interests are in culture and personality, systems analysis, culture change and theory, and primitive art and religion. He is the author of *Group Sex: A Scientist's Eyewitness Report on the American Way of Swinging* (1971).

JESSIE BERNARD, Ph.D., is a family sociologist and an independent writer and research scholar. She is professor emeritus of sociology of The Pennsylvania State University and the author of several books, including *The Sex Game* (1968) and *The Future of Marriage* (1972).

ALEX COMFORT, Ph.D., heads the Aging Research Institute at University College in London and is an associate fellow of The Center for the Study of Democratic Institutions in Santa Barbara. He is the author of several books, including *Sex in Society* (1936), and the editor of the current bestseller, *The Joy of Sex* (1972).

JOAN M. CONSTANTINE is coordinator of the Center for Family Change and a family therapist in private practice in Acton, Massachusetts. She and her husband, Larry, are the authors of *Group Marriage* (1973), which is based on their three years of research into contemporary multilateral marriages.

LARRY L. CONSTANTINE is a faculty member of The Tufts University School of Medicine. He also teaches and supervises family therapy trainees at the Center for Training in Family Therapy at Boston State Hospital.

DUANE DENFELD, Ph.D., is assistant professor of sociology at The University of Connecticut and author of *Streetwise Criminology* (1974).

ALBERT ELLIS, Ph.D., is a clinical psychologist and director of the Institute for Advanced Study in Psychotherapy in New York City. He is the author of over thirty-five books on psychology and sex, including *The American Sexual Tragedy*, *The Art and Science of Love*, and *Reason and Emotion in Psychotherapy*.

BRIAN GILMARTIN is completing his Ph.D. at The University of Iowa. His area of study is contemporary sexuality and marital interaction.

MICHAEL GORDON, Ph.D., is associate professor of sociology at The University of Connecticut. He is the author of several books on the family and sexual behavior in American society and has recently edited *The American Family in Social-Historical Perspective* (1974).

GEORGE C. O'NEILL, Ph.D., is associate professor of anthropology at The City College of New York and the New School for Social Research. Currently a member of the executive committee of the Society for the Scientific Study of Sex, he has participated in several anthropological expeditions and is the author of numerous articles. He is co-author with his wife, Nena, of the recent bestseller *Open Marriage: A New Lifestyle for Couples* (1972).

NENA O'NEIL is currently pursuing a Ph.D. in anthropology at The City College of New York. She has participated in ethnological and archeological field research in Puerto Rico, Mexico, and the Caribbean and has served as research consultant for several educational programs. She is senior author of *Open Marriage: A New Lifestyle for Couples* (1972).

JAMES W. RAMEY, Ed.D., is the founder and director of the Center for the Study of Innovative Life Styles and is currently a consultant to Mount Sinai Medical School in the department of community medicine. He has been a professor in the graduate school of Drexel University, associate dean of the Pratt Institute, and executive director of the Institute for the Advancement of Medical Communication. He is the author of over fifty books, monographs, and papers.

JAMES R. SMITH is currently a Ph.D. candidate in political science at the University of California, Berkeley. He received his M.A. in philosophy in 1964 and his M.A. in political science in 1966 from the University of Hawaii. Director of The Self-Actualization Laboratory, he is currently preparing, with his wife Lynn, a manuscript entitled "Consenting Adults," a report and interpretation of a six-year study of the sexual freedom movement.

LYNN G. SMITH, Ph.D., is currently an intern in clinical psychology at the University of California, Berkeley. She received her M.A. in social psychology from the University of California, Berkeley, in 1969 and her Ph.D. in 1973. Formerly a research assistant for the Institute for Sex Research and a lecturer in sociology at Sonoma State College, she has recently received training in sex therapy at the University of California School of Medicine and will be coordinating research and couples' therapy programs for The Self-Actualization Laboratory.

JON TWICHELL is currently a doctoral student in political science at The University of California, Berkeley, and a part-time instructor at San Francisco State College.

CHARLES A. VARNI, Ph.D., is currently a lecturer in sociology at California State University at Chico. His current research interests revolve around the study of face-to-face interaction, sex roles, and human liberation.

MARY LINDENSTEIN WALSHOK, Ph.D., was assistant professor of sociology at California State College at Fullerton for three years and is currently director of the women's program at the University of California at San Diego. Previously a research fellow at the Institute for Sex Research in Bloomington, Indiana, her interests lie in women's roles, deviant behavior, research methods, and youth and adult socialization.

Name Index

Adams, C. R., 233
Alpert, H., 72
Athanasiou, R., 85, 86, 98, 269
Avebury, Lord, 171

Babchuck, N., 106
Baber, R. E., 173
Bartell, G. D., 13n, 14n, 76, 78, 81, 85, 86, 110, 117, 119, 120, 167, 185–201, 202, 234, 239, 260, 279, 281, 292, 304, 313, 320
Bates, A. P., 106
Beach, F. A., 32n
Becker, H., 69
Beigel, H., 100, 103
Bell, R. R., 86, 114, 233, 271, 307
Beltz, S. E., 284
Benedict, R., 63
Bernard, J., 138–58
Bird, C., 106
Blank, L., 235
Bloch, I., 171
Bott, E., 106, 108
Bowman, C. C., 97
Brecher, E. M., 79, 80, 81, 110, 115, 117

Breedlove, J., 76, 78, 80, 85, 115, 116, 119, 159
Breedlove, W., 76, 78, 80 85 115, 116, 119, 159
Broderick, C. B., 232
Brown, D. G., 233
Brown, H. G., 144
Buber, M., 114
Burgess, E. W., 233

Calhoun, A. W., 69
Campbell, A. A., 74
Campbell, J., 18n
Carden, M. L., 123
Cervantes, L. F., 296
Christensen, H. T., 97, 98
Clark, L., 287
Cogswell, B. E., 9n, 36n
Cohen, A., 68, 71, 75
Cole, C. L., 263
Collier, J., 20, 124
Comfort, A., 24n, 25n, 27, 29, 49–55, 97
Constantine, J., 128, 130, 131, 215, 268–90

Note: Name and Subject Indexes were prepared by Margie Kahn.

Subject Index

This book was composed in Janson text and Delphin display type by The Maryland Linotype Composition Co., Inc., from a design by Beverly Baum. It was printed on 60-lb. Warren 1854 paper and bound in Columbia Bayside Chambray cloth by The Maple Press Company.